T0301442

Strategy for Sustainability Transitions

Strategy for Sustainability Transitions

Governance, Community and Environment

Kristof Van Assche

University of Alberta, Canada

Raoul Beunen

Open University, the Netherlands

Monica Gruezmacher

University of Alberta, Canada

 Edward **Elgar**
PUBLISHING

Cheltenham, UK • Northampton, MA, USA

Cover image: Marije Louwsma.

Published by
Edward Elgar Publishing Limited
The Lypiatts
15 Lansdown Road
Cheltenham
Glos GL50 2JA
UK

Edward Elgar Publishing, Inc.
William Pratt House
9 Dewey Court
Northampton
Massachusetts 01060
USA

A catalogue record for this book
is available from the British Library

Library of Congress Control Number: 2024930491

This book is available electronically in the **Elgar**online
Geography, Planning and Tourism subject collection
http://dx.doi.org/10.4337/9781035324002

ISBN 978 1 0353 2399 9 (cased)
ISBN 978 1 0353 2400 2 (eBook)

Printed and bound in Great Britain by
TJ Books Limited, Padstow, Cornwall

'*Sustainability transitions and transformations are indeed political strug-gles. The Agenda 2030 is a political, not a technical agenda. Reducing it to implementation means that the conflicts of interest between different actor groups and governance levels, the trade-offs between different sustainability concerns and the power differences that are real and generally prioritize the existing rather than the to be achieved are not addressed. Transitional change brings about winners and losers. It is a struggle between private sector, civil society, policy-making and academia, with politics being its moderator. The presented volume gives insights into this non-linear search process and reflects on it conceptually, methodologically and based on empirical examples from across the world. Worth reading by anyone inter-ested in societal change processes for sustainable futures.*'
Anna-Katharina Hornidge, German Institute of Development and
Sustainability (IDOS)

'*Kristof Van Assche, Raoul Beunen and Monica Gruezmacher's book starts with a quote by Machiavelli. Therefore it might be appropriate to close it with another, no less fitting, Machiavelli quote: "It must be considered that there is nothing more difficult to carry out, nor more doubtful of success, nor more dangerous to handle, than to initiate a new order of things."* Strategy for Sustainability Transitions *is a courageous book that might help readers to rethink the order of things and start exploring new possible orders.*'
Martin Kornberger, Vienna University of Economics and Business, Austria,
Stockholm School of Economics, Sweden and University of New South
Wales, Australia

Contents

Figures

It is not unknown to me how many men have had, and still have, the opinion that the affairs of the world are in such way governed by fortune and by God that men with their wisdom cannot direct them and that no one can even help them; and because of this they would have us believe that it is not necessary to labour much in affairs, but to let chance govern them. This opinion has been more credited in our times because of the great changes in affairs which have been seen, and may still be seen, every day, beyond all human conjecture. Sometimes pondering over this, I am in some degree inclined to their opinion. Nevertheless, not to extinguish our free will, I hold it to be true that Fortune is the arbiter of one-half of our actions, but that she still leaves us to direct the other half, or perhaps a little less. I compare her to one of those raging rivers, which when in flood overflows the plains, sweeping away trees and buildings, bearing away the soil from place to place; everything flies before it, all yield to its violence, without being able in any way to withstand it; and yet, though its nature be such, it does not follow therefore that men, when the weather becomes fair, shall not make provision, both with defences and barriers, in such a manner that, rising again, the waters may pass away by canal, and their force be neither so unrestrained nor so dangerous. So it happens with fortune, who shows her power where valour has not prepared to resist her, and thither she turns her forces where she knows that barriers and defences have not been raised to constrain her.

(Niccolo Machiavelli (1513), The Prince, chapter XXV)

1. Introduction: transitions, Grand Challenges and big promises

CHALLENGES GRAND AND EVERYWHERE

Few observers of 21st-century earth would be inclined to say that all is well. Climate change, biodiversity decline, pollution, food security, poverty and inequality are some of the crucial challenges society is facing. These issues and their social and environmental impact manifest themselves in myriad manners across the globe, while communities at national, regional and local levels are dealing with a host of other social and environmental problems. Many of these issues are acknowledged in the Sustainable Development Goals, a comprehensive framework for addressing global challenges and promoting sustainable development in its economic, social and environmental dimensions (Glass & Newig, 2019; Grin et al., 2010; Sachs et al., 2019). Others have pointed to the different planetary boundaries that represent the limits within which humanity can safely operate to ensure the long-term sustainability of the Earth's ecosystems and the well-being of all living beings (Gerten et al., 2020; O'Neill et al., 2018; Steffen et al., 2015). These planetary boundaries encompass various interconnected and interdependent aspects of our environment, including climate change, biodiversity loss, land use change, freshwater use, ocean acidification, chemical pollution and atmospheric aerosol loading. Crossing these boundaries not only threatens the stability and functioning of ecosystems, but also poses significant risks to human well-being and the sustainability of our societies. The concept of planetary boundaries has therefore also been linked to social and economic systems, as for example in the model of the doughnut economics (Raworth, 2017).

What some scholars optimistically call Grand Challenges pile up, and new conflicts do not help. These challenges are characterized by their magnitude, urgency and the need for innovative and collaborative solutions. They encompass a wide range of areas, including environmental sustainability, public health, poverty eradication, social inequality, technological advancements, and more. The Grand Challenges are not isolated issues, but are interconnected and interdependent, requiring integrated approaches and coordinated efforts from governments, businesses, civil society and academia to address them effectively. Positive signs do emerge from academia, where disciplines such as management studies, relatively new to the green table, pick up the Grand Challenge, and where inter- and trans-disciplinary initiatives mushroom (Bergmann et al., 2021; Coenen et al., 2015; Ferraro et al., 2015; George et al., 2016; Huntjens & Kemp, 2022; Jahn et al., 2022).

Awareness that transitioning from current unsustainable practices to new governance systems and social structures is urgently needed is finally growing, and growing rapidly (Grin et al., 2010; Herrfahrdt-Pähle et al., 2020; Kemp & Loorbach, 2006; Köhler et al., 2019; Patterson et al., 2015). Transitions are not only crucial for safeguarding the Earth's ecosystems, but also for promoting social equity, economic prosperity and human well-being. Thinking about transitions involves rethinking how we use resources, make decisions, and collaborate across sectors and scales. This awareness is reflected in an ever-growing body of literature that focuses on sustainability transitions and the shifts in governance systems necessary to enable sustainable and equitable management of resources, protection of ecosystems and mitigation of environmental risks. Such transitions go beyond traditional approaches to environmental management. They require integrated, holistic and transformative approaches that take into account the interconnectedness of social, economic and environmental systems (Feola et al., 2021; Herrfahrdt-Pähle et al., 2020).

The literature on transitions encompasses a range of approaches that seek to address the limitations of existing governance systems and foster positive change (Köhler et al., 2019; Loorbach et al., 2017). It involves rethinking the way decisions are made, power is distributed and resources are managed, with the ultimate goal of achieving better outcomes for society as a whole. The common call for a transition, for enhanced resilience, for transformational governance is reflected in a growing repertoire of terms used to refer to the needed fundamental and structural changes in society and its governance. Within the literature terms like transition, transformation, transformative governance co-exist (Hölscher et al., 2018). Different terms are partly used for rhetorical reasons, to highlight novelty, or to emphasize differences from more traditional domains such as public policy and administration or environmental planning and management that have dealt with similar issues for decades.

Whereas the term transitions is used for many different types of social or technological changes, the label transformative governance more specifically focuses on the need to change governance systems and to highlight governance processes through which transitions can be initiated, stimulated or realized (Chaffin et al., 2016; Visseren-Hamakers et al., 2021). Transformative governance involves reimagining and reconfiguring existing governance structures, its institutions, and it practices to align with the principles of sustainability, equity and inclusivity. Although perspectives, focus, approaches and used frameworks do certainly differ, several recurring themes can be discerned, such as participation (Glass & Newig, 2019; Huttunen et al., 2022; Seyfang & Smith, 2007), social learning (Gerlak et al., 2018; Newig et al., 2019; Van Assche, Beunen, et al., 2022), adaptation (Armitage, 2010; Cleaver & Whaley, 2018; Folke et al., 2005; Voß & Bornemann, 2011), policy integration (Atkinson & Klausen, 2011; Candel & Biesbroek, 2016; Jordan & Lenschow, 2010; Tosun & Leininger, 2017), and just transitions (Bennett et al., 2019; Bouzarovski, 2022; Burch et al., 2019; Wang & Lo, 2021).

We are not so much interested in the different labels as such. In this book we will mostly stick to the terminology of transition as it does indicate the need to move from one state of society to a different one, where we can recognize a more sustainable version of the social-ecological system. A rich literature has developed under the label, and a variety of others, similarly recognizing a need for structural change in society and a new relation with the natural environment, can be found under different topical and disciplinary labels. Many disciplines, including geography, sociology, political science, ecology, public policy and administration and others have contributed to the thinking on transitions, and inter-disciplinary domains for the study of transitions, innovation, transformation and resilience have opened up.

Within this broad perspective on transitions, the link with strategy is easily made. In the course of this book we will elaborate on the difficulties and dilemmas of strategy in governance and show that there are always choices to be made, that societies are always faced with dilemmas, and that each decision will generate winners and losers, backlash, counter-reactions, feedback loops and trade-offs. How strategies and transitions will play out is largely unpredictable and can certainly not be prescribed in a general way. It all depends on the particularities of the context.

WHY SIMPLE SOLUTIONS ARE NOT LIKELY TO WORK

Experiences all over the world, at all levels of governance, show that the much-needed transitions do not come about easily, are progressing very slowly, or even fail. Environmentally motivated changes in governance are not necessarily putting societies on a more sustainable and just path, and environmental arguments can trigger backlash or be deployed by actors minimally interested in sustainability goals. Just as rich as the literature on sustainability transitions is the literature on policy failure, democratic deficits, corruption, state capture, land and water grabbing, and the obstacles and barriers for sustainable development. All these phenomena are part of governance and society and require attention if one wants to understand transitions.

At the outset of our book, a long effort to delineate what strategy for transition could be, we can already distinguish several reasons why it is particularly challenging.

1. Steering in governance is challenging and bounded by a series of factors and mechanisms that are difficult to observe and understand, let alone control.
2. Steering is complicated because there are no perfect models for governance. What works, what can be coordinated and how depends on history, culture, material environment, ideology, familiarity with certain policy tools and other factors identified in later chapters.
3. Steering towards sustainability is furthermore complicated because of the ambiguity of the concept of sustainability and the various ideas, ideals and ideologies that all bring forward their own version. Although it might sometimes be clear what needs to be done under the label of sustainability (e.g., reduce greenhouse gas emissions) that clarity might be deceptive and certainly not shared by everyone in governance and the wider community.
4. Steering towards sustainability is likely to face opposition. For many sustainability issues it has become clear that profound changes (in governance, but also in production and consumption) are required and hence every step towards sustainability implies shifts for current practices, vested interests and existing power relations. Such changes will face resistance. Opponents – and they come in many guises – deploy a range of strategies to prevent change or steer things into a different direction.
5. The interplay between steering attempts, between strategizing pro and contra sustainability, and the effects of strategy are interdependent with an ever-changing social-material environment. This interdependence entails a multiplicity of only partly observed feedback loops. Strategies and policies can create opposition then deployed by populist parties that become more powerful and reinforce opposition against sustainability strategies. Or, inaction leads to disasters which put sustainability higher on the agenda, yet the urgent calls for radical action create blind spots, undermine checks and balances, exclude valuable expert advice, throw up obstacles for policy integration.

We will therefore argue that strategizing for transitions requires first and foremost a thorough understanding of governance systems and their functioning, and a recognition of the possibilities and limits these governance systems pose for steering, strategy and transition. For these reasons this book will firmly embed strategy and transition in a theory of governance. It will give due attention to the dilemmas, diverse and contingent pathways and the trade-offs that come with every choice of transition goal and every transition strategy.

Meanwhile, we find reasons for optimism in the same complexity of governance and its couplings to social and ecological systems. Governance can create new understandings of the environment, of possible futures, and it can find new tools to re-align community and environment.

Governance, policy, strategy, transition and sustainability are covered by a web of literatures. All these have their own tradition and set of concepts and theoretical approaches. We respect these traditions and have used them selectively in this book, without relying on one of them exclusively. Evolutionary Governance Theory (EGT), the basis for our perspective on change and coordinated change in governance and through governance, tends to be cautious with normativity and prescription (Beunen et al., 2015; Van Assche et al., 2014). EGT is not a theory of transition, but a theory of governance. The theory has evolved over the years to become more sensitive to the embeddings in social-ecological systems, to the problems associated with societal steering and with ambitious collective strategy. This book is a development and application of EGT, enriched with other notions, to the question of strategy for transition. This is the reason why most of the book is not about transition as such, but about governance, about bringing about change in governance, about coordinated change, and the implications for strategy and transition. We need, in other words, to present and explain the rather elaborate architecture of EGT, to clearly articulate its meaning for strategy and transition.

This book does not present an overview or a synthesis of all the literatures on transitions and governance. It engages with a variety of authors and ideas, some recognizable as 'transition' related, others less so. Systems theory, especially in the version of Niklas Luhmann, post-structuralism, notably in the style of Michel Foucault, psychoanalysis, but also institutional economics, critical management studies, and the less normative versions of public policy, administration and spatial planning were formative. They are sometimes present in the background, sometimes more explicitly, and some of the ideas derived from them have been integrated already in our earlier work on Evolutionary Governance Theory (EGT).

GOVERNANCE AS A CENTRAL CONCEPT

Hence, we can present the book as a theory of governance, with major implications for the understanding of sustainability, strategy, transition and strategy for sustainability transition. This will be immediately apparent to the reader, who will find a series of chapters on governance, its capacity for stability and change, and the way it can relate to social and ecological environments. While such an approach might ask a bit more patience from the reader, and while it clearly differs from other transition perspectives which prefer to plunge straight into the heart of the matter, we believe the payoff of building a governance theory first is substantial. Rather than developing an idea of transition, and adding the social and ecological environments later, or rather than constructing an idea of social-ecological systems, and then contemplating what governance might be, we believe it is worthwhile to start with governance, as the taking of collectively binding decisions in a community, and then see what transition might look like in terms of ever-evolving governance systems.

Governance for us is politics in the broadest sense, yet recognizing that formal political and administrative actors do have different responsibilities from other actors (Bell & Hindmoor, 2009; Pierre & Peters, 2000). Ignoring the need for institutional capacity, and for strong administration to create, stabilize and diversify this capacity, will undermine the potential for transition or transformation. Governance was always there, always involved formal and informal institutions, and always existed as multi-level systems, where what is possible and allowed at one level hinges crucially on what happened in the prior interaction between levels. The rigid pyramid of 'government,' sometimes invoked by older governance literature as a contrast in the past, never really existed. It only existed in the self-descriptions of certain regimes and polities, not in their realities of governance, in their practical statecraft, or in their always shifting patterns of participation and representation. Indeed, participation as even an imagined pyramid could take on many shapes, in a process that involved many beyond those appointed to represent the people or the leader.

Evolutionary Governance Theory (EGT) enables the unpacking of the complexities of governance systems by recognizing its influential elements and interactions and acknowledging the importance of past elements and interactions in shaping present governance arrangements and enabling (or disabling) future opportunities. Its main concepts and most recent elaborations will be navigated in the next few chapters. Co-evolution is the key concept, as actors and institutions, formal and informal institutions, power and knowledge are analysed as mutually molding each other over time. They define, enable and constrain what the other entities can do, and how they can combine. Actors can be individuals, groups and organizations, but the process of governance exerts pressure towards organization, as this enables the reproduction and further differentiation of governance, the widening of its net, the increase of its capacity to coordinate.

As EGT, in dialogue with social-ecological systems thinking, and ideas in political ecology, anthropology and geography, broadened its perspective to conceptualize more precisely the double embedding of governance in community and community in the social-ecological system, the question of sustainability moved to the foreground. The question of steering had to be asked, since the co-evolutionary processes in governance generate path and other dependencies (see later), structural rigidities and limits to steering and, hence, strategy. This book integrates both these recent developments of EGT, its rethinking of strategy in and through governance (Van Assche et al., 2020), its new understanding of social-ecological relations and observations (Duineveld et al., 2017; Van Assche, Duineveld, et al., 2022), into a perspective on strategy for transitions. The EGT perspective on governance can only be made useful for the understanding of transition if the limits and potential for steering are clearly delineated, if the nature of collective strategy, aiming to steer, can be understood, and if the couplings between governance systems and their layered environments can be illuminated to the extent that an understanding of the effects of strategy and steering can come within reach.

Strategy, in the account presented here, is not a matter of winning or beating competitors. Nor is it an activity restricted to the highest rungs of leadership, while it cannot be relegated to lower levels of administration or technical consultants either. Strategy is not a technical exercise, nor the product of a visionary individual. Strategy, as we will detail it later, is both an institution and a narrative, and it is a special kind of institution, one which coordinates or integrates others. Strategy for transition must go through governance, as it intends to bind the community not to a decision pertaining to one place, topic or policy domain, but to a drastically revived future and, likely, a redefined identity.

The potential for a strategy might slowly emerge, might slowly become visible or imaginable within a community or its governance system. Or, even more fundamentally, a decision might only look important in hindsight; its relevance for a way forward might not be observed at first. What looks like an asset for a viable and more sustainable future might not appear as such first. The asset might be less visible to those in governance, wedded to old stories, old identities, and broken or unsustainable economies. Furthermore, within a community, there might be little trust in even the possibility to plan, to steer the community in a more sustainable direction. In such cases, the potential of collective action is not seen and not used.

Societal transitions imply fundamental and deliberate changes in the narratives that shape collective decisions. Steering change effectively requires an understanding of these narratives, the way they have influenced rules, roles and power dynamics in the governance system. A plan forward, a strategy for a different future will need to coordinate new narratives with old and new actors and institutions. A strategy for sustainable transitions will need to present a rearrangement of elements in governance, rendered cohesive by a new narrative accepted or at least tolerated by the community at large. In other words, regardless of the form transition strategy takes, it will need to be embraced within governance and community for it to be translated into actions.

We pay close attention to the variety of knowledge that is present, can be present and should be present in governance, in order to optimize the potential for seeing and organizing more sustainable paths of development. No form of expert knowledge, no version of local knowledge and no utopian narrative should dominate decision-making on sustainable futures. Expert knowledge can lead a community astray, as each perspective is limited by itself, often blind to its own assumptions. The way forms of expertise are integrated into policy can itself be a problem, as combinations are more than additions. They introduce hierarchies, intensities of analysis and expertise which vary per place, time and topic, a feature of governance we will designate as shards. Similarly, local knowledges are diverse and their integration with expert knowledge cannot be streamlined objectively into a process leading to optimal sustainability policies, or a perfect transition pathway.

LAYOUT OF THE BOOK

The early chapters first introduce the basics of EGT, elaborating upon its understanding of actors and institutions, formal and informal. Governance is presented as structured in substantive domains, which reflect a structure of topics and a history of competition; the domains are not always spatially delineated or segmented and are not always tied to one level or entity of government. We dwell on the idea of the arena, where, depending on perspective and situation, an actor can function as an arena. Governance paths form over time and reflect a unique set of couplings between elements within governance, and a unique co-evolution with the embedding social-ecological system. In the governance path, a particular set of capacities and constraints for change emerges, a distinct potential for understanding and organizing alternative futures. In the governance path, the community is not only reflected, but also constituted; governance makes it a political community, even where formal politics is far beyond the horizon.

Subsequent chapters, more inspired by post-structuralist perspectives on policy, politics and administration, bring us to the realm of discourse, in governance and in the community. In Foucauldian fashion, we emphasize the patterns of exclusion and inclusion that governance can produce and reproduce, by means of institutions, and by means of forms of knowledge that reflect realities, select realities and ignore others. Governance and its epistemic apparatus, its tools to define problems, methods, solutions, to assess realities and results, is equipped to exclude, and to naturalize what is per definition contingent. Power, then, is the power to impose rules and the power to create realities, physical or discursive. We discuss narratives as nested in governance, and discourses as existing in configurations, a patterning and coupling which contributes to the power of naturalization in governance. However, such mechanisms of stabilization never exclude sources of instability, and sometimes resuscitate them. Indeed, governance, especially in democratic settings, feeds off difference, and invites and creates difference, while diversity in perspectives, memories and interests contributes to environmental adaptation.

The nexus between thinking and organizing is a running theme in the book, one which we owe to organization theorists such as Barbara Czarniawska and management scholars such as Mats Alvesson, David Seidl and Martin Kornberger. Patterns in thinking and patterns in organizing can stabilize themselves and each other and function as path dependencies in governance. As governance is about more than one organization, one interest, one interpretation of the world, managing complexity and diversity is a taller order than in one organization, yet governance is *also* a process of organizing, governance is only possible because of specialized organizations, and many of the mechanisms analysed in organization and management studies pertaining to the thinking/organizing nexus are empirically observable in governance. They do appear in more elaborate patterns of contestation, coagulation, transformation and creation. Indeed, creation, as governance, both in its more collaborative and its more conflict-ridden modes, is not only a game of participation and representation of people, places, ideas and interests already in existence, but also a site of production of ideas, narratives, of objects and subjects. As decisions need to be taken, as the rewards of participating in governance are always there, and as decisions need to be based on something in the world of ideas but lead to something in the world of organization, thinking and organizing exert continuous pressure on each other in evolving governance.

Chapter 7 further analyses the dependencies that form in governance paths, the rigidities that stem from ideas, institutions, forms of organization, which keep themselves in place, on account of inherent stabilization mechanisms, or their place in configurations with other governance elements, i.e. through couplings. Thinking and organizing have different modes of transformation, patterns of stability and change, yet the nexus of thinking and organizing in governance triggers stabilization through establishment of power relations, through positioning of institutions referring to each other and slowing transformation, and through naturalization. Governance invites difference and competition, as what can be rewarded in politics and while climbing the ladder in organizations requires difference (from other actors, ideas, futures) and as, per definition, not everything and everyone can have the same weight in and access to decisions. Master narratives and master signifiers regulate where change is valued, and where not, yet change is a driver of differentiation and an asset in competition within governance and in currying favor or finding traction in the community. Small differences can be magnified to define a position, present a narrative as different, or construct a new narrative. Narrative and more generally discursive dynamics enter governance from many sides, and the motives for discursive creation and transformation are so numerous that the counterforce of institutional stabilization cannot be missed.

Following EGT, we discuss path dependencies, recognized in institutional economics and political theory, interdependencies, best known from systems theory, and material dependencies, as seen in anthropology, but with a sharp focus on the effects in governance of tight couplings with material environments. Unique to EGT is the recognition of goal dependencies, effects in governance which describe the effects in governance of visions of the future, as circulating narrative and as codified institutions (plans, policies, visions, strategies). Goal dependencies can vary widely, can contradict each other, and can certainly undermine the intention of a policy or strategy. They can produce effects in the community that deviate significantly from the reality effects intended by a strategy, which makes *leadership* an art of managing goal dependencies and their alignment with intended reality effects.

The interplay between the dependencies, as rigidities in the governance path, is, in most cases, not to be understood as an addition or accretion of rigidities, into an ossified structure. It is precisely the interplay of rigidities that offers openings for change, although a mode of change which is not easy to steer or even predict. In Chapter 8 we distinguish other sources of change in governance, ranging from mere repetition of interactions, to learning, shock and conflict, and the patterning of roles. We distinguish several forms of learning in governance, their limited susceptibility to steering, their distributed character in space and time, and their amenability to use, abuse, synergy and mutual erosion. Deliberate non-thinking plays an important role in organizations and governance systems, dark learning sees knowledge of governance itself used for factional gain, but reflexive learning and dialectical learning, or creating new ideas through deliberation and discussion, can help to observe and manage the problems with dark learning and non-learning. Roles are entities that enable the reproduction and diversification of governance, including the enhancement of its learning ability. We analyse them as couplings between thinking and organizing, power and knowledge that are further both stability and instability, driven by inherent tensions between aspired, ascribed and practiced roles.

After the analysis of change in governance, we focus on the construction and functioning of temporality. Organizations, narratives, actors and institutions are marked by or construct their own temporalities, and the same applies to systems in the environment of governance. Governance for the long term, for sustainability transitions, hence, requires careful coupling of different temporalities in order to make them manageable and transforming some of them. We deploy the phenomenological ideal that people (and groups) construct their past, present and future at the same time, and this specifically human temporality is key to the understanding of governance strategy, as such strategy will have to reinterpret the past in order to reinvent the future, while grounded in the realities of the present, and its cognitive and organizational limitations. What can be remembered in governance, its selectivity in remembering and forgetting, enters through the actors, their embeddings in society, hence through social memory, but also through institutional and organizational memory. This brings us to the very practical sides of memory infrastructures in governance and community, which can make the past opaque, rigid or, on the contrary, diverse, open to reflection and debate, and visible. The functioning of memory will affect how futures can be imagined, and which one, while the overall structure of governance, its arenas, learning sites and mechanisms, will set additional parameters.

Chapter 10 brings together strands of thought developed in the previous chapters in a full presentation of strategy. It asks a question central to the quest for transition: what strategy in governance can mean, given the dependencies, sources of change, discursive dynamics, mnemonic mechanisms, and always specific forms and uses of futures discussed earlier. Strategy, as we mentioned, is presented as narrative and as an institution intended to coordinate others. As the task of strategy in governance, and more so of transition strategy, is daunting, many attempts end up gathering dust on a shelf, as a dead institution. Parallel, not integrated visions of the future persist, but so do competing or overlapping strategies. If a strategy does not work, it is, in our view, not a strategy; strategizing is a process and if the process does not occur, the paper symbolizing and summarizing the strategy cannot be called strategy.

Chapter 11, subsequently, allows us to articulate what a transition can look like, in the light of our theory of governance and strategy in coupled social-ecological systems. We discuss transitions already under way when the strategists wake up, transitions initiated through a process of collective strategy, and we distinguish transitions focused on a limited goal from broader reinvention ideals, while acknowledging that several transitions might be going on at the same time. Drawing on the notions proposed in previous chapters, we argue that transitions have to chart their own course, that not only the path, but also the nature of the transition, will be unique for each case, and that dilemmas will be faced. Each institutional design, each pattern of organizing, and each configuration of knowing, remembering and predicting comes with strengths and weaknesses, with adaptations and non-adaptations. A chosen transition path is imbued with institutional and adaptive capacities that cannot be qualified as more or less, but as a qualitative range of possible modes of coordination and adaptation. Choosing one institutional design is, usually unwittingly, choosing blind spots, accepting defective adaptations and fostering problematic exclusions where transition goals outweigh other considerations or where no interest is perceived. Not choosing is not possible, combining opposite sides of the dilemma is not functional. Strategy for transition is by nature characterized by paradox.

One of the dilemmas discussed in Chapter 11 deserves special mention here, as it appears elsewhere for its diverse implications: flexibility versus rigidity. If thinking and organizing aim to stay the course, if the goal of transition is believed to be known, if the path is considered a certainty, and if support is high, leadership might show themselves strong by enforcing rigidity, through incentive structures, adoption of laws, reorganization of administration, pushing hard towards policy integration and knowledge integration around the strategy and its all-important goal. This can, of course, deliver great results, but at some costs, including opportunity costs, transaction costs and adaptivity costs, which are great and hard to observe.

Other, even less visible, costs can be involved, which brings us to the next chapter, on resistance, backlash and counterstrategy. Attempts at structural change such as transition strategies will almost certainly face opposition. In fact, most sustainability transitions are a painful slog, demonstrating many pitfalls. Moreover, strategy tends to trigger counterstrategy, often with success. If people do not like it, get fed up or start to hate a transition strategy, if it alienates segments of the population, if political entrepreneurs create new divisions building on widespread dissatisfaction, not only can strategists and strategy get in trouble, but the community or society as a whole can suffer. If backlash corrodes the relation with the community to such a degree that no future strategy will be trusted, the costs are enormous. Hidden exclusions, marginalization, trauma, forgetting, resentment and conflict can come to haunt the strategist and the community later. Hence our argument that processes of strategizing for transition should entail an unearthing and re-politization of issues that were routinized, delegated or forgotten. This requires an investment in reflexive and dialectical learning, and possibly a phase of transitional governance, particularly in times when the governance capacity to discern a sustainable future and a realistic path is not there yet.

Right before a set of succinct conclusions, which do not aim to summarize but rather to highlight key insights, we reserve space for a discussion, rather in depth, of good governance. Why this belated interest in a seemingly outdated concept, slightly disconnected from the main line of reasoning? For several reasons. As pointed out before, transition strategies are likely associated with governance reform, before, during and after the articulation of the strategy. In order to understand better what governance reform should aim at beyond sustainability goals, and which qualities of governance it has to preserve during and after strategizing, one cannot avoid the question of what good governance ought to be. Governance ought to have certain qualities that enable it to discern sustainability problems and organize transition strategies, while the strategy itself cannot jeopardize other essential aspects of good governance.

Different understandings of democracy, of politics, rule of law, the balance between participation and representation, offer different ideas of good governance, and those ideas have been subject to political and academic fashions. What can be articulated, however, as a criterion is that corruption, as undermining of the public interest, cannot be tolerated, and we stick to our generic definition of well-functioning governance (used in earlier chapters) as a state of formal/informal institutional configurations which deliver the (public) goods, enable predictable self-transformation and maintain differentiation, valuable to manage complexity and generate institutional capacity. We add to this starting point the capacity to strategize for sustainability transitions, the tools to maintain diverse perspectives and redundancies, and the willingness to cultivate reflexivity in conjunction with other learning modes.

Transition strategies are on the edge of what is possible, in cognitive and organizational terms. They balance on the edge of what is governable and on the cusp of what is legitimate. People will have to be pushed, and pain will be inflicted; values, feelings and identity narratives will be scrutinized and questioned. Power relations will be reconfigured, and so will discursive coalitions. Nevertheless, while the risks are great, so are the rewards. The risk of *not* doing anything, of *not* coordinating action, of *not* thinking about what a sustainable future and a change of course could mean here and now, is immeasurably greater.

REFERENCES

Armitage, D. R. (2010). *Adaptive capacity and environmental governance*. Springer.

Atkinson, R. & Klausen, J. E. (2011). Understanding sustainability policy: Governance, knowledge and the search for integration. *Journal of Environmental Policy & Planning, 13*(3), 231–251. https://doi.org/10.1080/1523908X.2011.578403

Bell, S. & Hindmoor, A. (2009). *Rethinking governance: The centrality of the state in modern society*. Cambridge University Press.

Bennett, N. J., Blythe, J., Cisneros-Montemayor, A. M., Singh, G. G. & Sumaila, U. R. (2019). Just transformations to sustainability. *Sustainability, 11*(14), article 14. https://doi.org/10.3390/su11143881

Bergmann, M., Schäpke, N., Marg, O., Stelzer, F., Lang, D. J., Bossert, M., Gantert, M., Häußler, E., Marquardt, E., Piontek, F. M., Potthast, T., Rhodius, R., Rudolph, M., Ruddat, M., Seebacher, A. & Sußmann, N. (2021). Transdisciplinary sustainability research in real-world labs: Success factors and methods for change. *Sustainability Science, 16*(2), 541–564. https://doi.org/10.1007/s11625-020-00886-8

Beunen, R., Van Assche, K. & Duineveld, M. (2015). *Evolutionary governance theory: Theory and applications*. Springer.

Bouzarovski, S. (2022). Just transitions: A political ecology critique. *Antipode, 54*(4), 1003–1020. https://doi.org/10.1111/anti.12823

Burch, S., Gupta, A., Inoue, C. Y. A., Kalfagianni, A., Persson, Å., Gerlak, A. K., Ishii, A., Patterson, J., Pickering, J., Scobie, M., Van der Heijden, J., Vervoort, J., Adler, C., Bloomfield, M., Djalante, R., Dryzek, J., Galaz, V., Gordon, C., Harmon, R., ... Zondervan, R. (2019). New directions in earth system governance research. *Earth System Governance, 1*, 100006. https://doi.org/10.1016/j.esg.2019.100006

Candel, J. J. & Biesbroek, R. (2016). Toward a processual understanding of policy integration. *Policy Sciences*, *49*(3), 211–231.

Chaffin, B. C., Garmestani, A. S., Gunderson, L. H., Benson, M. H., Angeler, D. G., Arnold, C. A. (Tony), Cosens, B., Craig, R. K., Ruhl, J. B. & Allen, C. R. (2016). Transformative environmental governance. *Annual Review of Environment and Resources*, *41*(1), 399–423. https://doi.org/10.1146/annurev-environ-110615-085817

Cleaver, F. & Whaley, L. (2018). Understanding process, power, and meaning in adaptive governance. *Ecology and Society*, *23*(2).

Coenen, L., Hansen, T. & Rekers, J. V. (2015). Innovation policy for grand challenges. An economic geography perspective. *Geography Compass*, *9*(9), 483–496. https://doi.org/10.1111/gec3.12231

Duineveld, M., Van Assche, K. & Beunen, R. (2017). Re-conceptualising political landscapes after the material turn: A typology of material events. *Landscape Research*, *42*(4), 375–384.

Feola, G., Vincent, O. & Moore, D. (2021). (Un)making in sustainability transformation beyond capitalism. *Global Environmental Change*, *69*, 102290. https://doi.org/10.1016/j.gloenvcha.2021.102290

Ferraro, F., Etzion, D. & Gehman, J. (2015). Tackling grand challenges pragmatically: Robust action revisited. *Organization Studies*, *36*(3), 363–390. https://doi.org/10.1177/0170840614563742

Folke, C., Hahn, T., Olsson, P. & Norberg, J. (2005). Adaptive governance of social-ecological systems. *Annual Review of Environment and Resources*, *30*, 441–473.

George, G., Howard-Grenville, J., Joshi, A. & Tihanyi, L. (2016). Understanding and tackling societal grand challenges through management research. *Academy of Management Journal*, *59*(6), 1880–1895. https://doi.org/10.5465/amj.2016.4007

Gerlak, A. K., Heikkila, T., Smolinski, S. L., Huitema, D. & Armitage, D. (2018). Learning our way out of environmental policy problems: A review of the scholarship. *Policy Sciences*, *51*(3), 335–371.

Gerten, D., Heck, V., Jägermeyr, J., Bodirsky, B. L., Fetzer, I., Jalava, M., Kummu, M., Lucht, W., Rockström, J., Schaphoff, S. & Schellnhuber, H. J. (2020). Feeding ten billion people is possible within four terrestrial planetary boundaries. *Nature Sustainability*, *3*(3), article 3. https://doi.org/10.1038/s41893-019-0465-1

Glass, L.-M. & Newig, J. (2019). Governance for achieving the Sustainable Development Goals: How important are participation, policy coherence, reflexivity, adaptation and democratic institutions? *Earth System Governance*, *2*, 100031.

Grin, J., Rotmans, J. & Schot, J. (2010). *Transitions to sustainable development: New directions in the study of long-term transformative change.* Routledge.

Herrfahrdt-Pähle, E., Schlüter, M., Olsson, P., Folke, C., Gelcich, S. & Pahl-Wostl, C. (2020). Sustainability transformations: Socio-political shocks as opportunities for governance transitions. *Global Environmental Change*, *63*, 102097.

Hölscher, K., Wittmayer, J. M. & Loorbach, D. (2018). Transition versus transformation: What's the difference? *Environmental Innovation and Societal Transitions*, *27*, 1–3. https://doi.org/10.1016/j.eist.2017.10.007

Huntjens, P. & Kemp, R. (2022). The importance of a natural social contract and co-evolutionary governance for sustainability transitions. *Sustainability*, *14*(5), article 5. https://doi.org/10.3390/su14052976

Huttunen, S., Ojanen, M., Ott, A. & Saarikoski, H. (2022). What about citizens? A literature review of citizen engagement in sustainability transitions research. *Energy Research & Social Science, 91*, 102714. https://doi.org/10.1016/j.erss.2022.102714

Jahn, S., Newig, J., Lang, D. J., Kahle, J. & Bergmann, M. (2022). Demarcating transdisciplinary research in sustainability science: Five clusters of research modes based on evidence from 59 research projects. *Sustainable Development, 30*(2), 343–357. https://doi.org/10.1002/sd.2278

Jordan, A. & Lenschow, A. (2010). Environmental policy integration: A state of the art review. *Environmental Policy and Governance, 20*(3), 147–158.

Kemp, R. & Loorbach, D. (2006). Transition management: A reflexive governance approach. In J.-P. Voß, D. Bauknecht & R. Kemp (eds.), *Reflexive governance for sustainable development* (pp. 103–130). Edward Elgar.

Köhler, J., Geels, F. W., Kern, F., Markard, J., Onsongo, E., Wieczorek, A., Alkemade, F., Avelino, F., Bergek, A., Boons, F., Fünfschilling, L., Hess, D., Holtz, G., Hyysalo, S., Jenkins, K., Kivimaa, P., Martiskainen, M., McMeekin, A., Mühlemeier, M. S., … Wells, P. (2019). An agenda for sustainability transitions research: State of the art and future directions. *Environmental Innovation and Societal Transitions, 31*, 1–32. https://doi.org/10.1016/j.eist.2019.01.004

Loorbach, D., Frantzeskaki, N. & Avelino, F. (2017). Sustainability transitions research: Transforming science and practice for societal change. *Annual Review of Environment and Resources, 42*(1), 599–626. https:// doi .org/ 10 .1146/ annurev -environ-102014-021340

Newig, J., Jager, N. W., Kochskämper, E. & Challies, E. (2019). Learning in participatory environmental governance – its antecedents and effects. Findings from a case survey meta-analysis. *Journal of Environmental Policy & Planning, 21*(3), 213–227.

O'Neill, D. W., Fanning, A. L., Lamb, W. F. & Steinberger, J. K. (2018). A good life for all within planetary boundaries. *Nature Sustainability, 1*(2), article 2. https://doi .org/10.1038/s41893-018-0021-4

Patterson, J., Schulz, K., Vervoort, J., Adler, C., Hurlbert, M., van der Hel, S., Schmidt, A., Barau, A., Obani, P. & Sethi, M. (2015). Transformations towards sustainability. Emerging approaches, critical reflections and a research agenda. *Earth System Governance Working Paper, 34*.

Pierre, J. & Peters, B. G. (2000). *Governance, politics, and the state*. Macmillan.

Raworth, K. (2017). *Doughnut economics: Seven ways to think like a 21st-century economist*. Chelsea Green Publishing.

Sachs, J. D., Schmidt-Traub, G., Mazzucato, M., Messner, D., Nakicenovic, N. & Rockström, J. (2019). Six transformations to achieve the Sustainable Development Goals. *Nature Sustainability, 2*(9), article 9. https:// doi .org/ 10 .1038/ s41893 -019 -0352-9

Seyfang, G. & Smith, A. (2007). Grassroots innovations for sustainable development: Towards a new research and policy agenda. *Environmental Politics, 16*(4), 584–603. https://doi.org/10.1080/09644010701419121

Steffen, W., Richardson, K., Rockström, J., Cornell, S. E., Fetzer, I., Bennett, E. M., Biggs, R., Carpenter, S. R., de Vries, W., de Wit, C. A., Folke, C., Gerten, D., Heinke, J., Mace, G. M., Persson, L. M., Ramanathan, V., Reyers, B., & Sörlin, S. (2015). Planetary boundaries: Guiding human development on a changing planet. *Science, 347*(6223), 1259855. https://doi.org/10.1126/science.1259855

Tosun, J. & Leininger, J. (2017). Governing the interlinkages between the Sustainable Development Goals: Approaches to attain policy integration. *Global Challenges, 1*(9), 1700036. https://doi.org/10.1002/gch2.201700036

Van Assche, K., Beunen, R. & Duineveld, M. (2014). *Evolutionary governance theory: An introduction*. Springer.

Van Assche, K., Beunen, R., Gruezmacher, M. & Duineveld, M. (2020). Rethinking strategy in environmental governance. *Journal of Environmental Policy & Planning*, 1–14.

Van Assche, K., Beunen, R., Verweij, S., Evans, J. & Gruezmacher, M. (2022). Policy learning and adaptation in governance; a co-evolutionary perspective. *Administration & Society*, *54*(7), 1226–1254. https://doi.org/10.1177/00953997211059165

Van Assche, K., Duineveld, M., Beunen, R., Valentinov, V. & Gruezmacher, M. (2022). Material dependencies: Hidden underpinnings of sustainability transitions. *Journal of Environmental Policy & Planning*, *24*(3), 281–296. https://doi.org/10.1080/1523908X.2022.2049715

Visseren-Hamakers, I. J., Razzaque, J., McElwee, P., Turnhout, E., Kelemen, E., Rusch, G. M., Fernández-Llamazares, Á., Chan, I., Lim, M., Islar, M., Gautam, A. P., Williams, M., Mungatana, E., Karim, M. S., Muradian, R., Gerber, L. R., Lui, G., Liu, J., Spangenberg, J. H. & Zaleski, D. (2021). Transformative governance of biodiversity: Insights for sustainable development. *Current Opinion in Environmental Sustainability*, *53*, 20–28. https://doi.org/10.1016/j.cosust.2021.06.002

Voß, J.-P. & Bornemann, B. (2011). The politics of reflexive governance: challenges for designing adaptive management and transition management. *Ecology and Society*, *16*, 9.

Wang, X. & Lo, K. (2021). Just transition: A conceptual review. *Energy Research & Social Science*, *82*, 102291. https://doi.org/10.1016/j.erss.2021.102291

2. Basic concepts for transition mapping: governance and its actors

GOVERNANCE

Governance is a concept that is defined and understood in various ways, generally focusing on the system of decision-making in an organization or society and the various elements and processes in that system. The literature on governance took off in the 1990s with key publications elaborating on how the concept of governance relates to older strands of literature that focused on government, the state and public administration (Bevir, 2004; Pierre & Peters, 2000a; Rhodes, 1997; Stoker, 1998). Within the context of environment and sustainability, the concept of governance has brought more attention to the various roles of non-state actors in decision-making (Bowles et al., 2008; Bulkeley, 2005; Castells, 1996; Partelow et al., 2020), the diversity of tools for coordination and steering that are used (Jordan et al., 2005), and processes of decentralization and globalization (Biermann et al., 2017; Farazmand & Pinkowski, 2006; Fukuyama, 2014; Held, 1999; Young, 1997). The literature on governance has also come with a warning about normative assumptions and has explained that governance should not be seen as an alternative to government and that the key role of governmental organizations in governance systems should not be overlooked or even ignored (Bell & Hindmoor, 2009).

Governance has always been there. It is neither a new phenomenon nor a new model for organizing decision-making. Governance is not necessarily tied to democratic politics and polities, to one scale of decision-making, nor to situations where governmental actors move to the background. Governance is the taking of collectively binding decisions, and that collective can be quite different things, whereby different forms of decision-making co-exist and are changing all the time. Some of the literature on governance spoke of a move from 'government' to 'governance,' and presumed that, in many countries, a period of supposedly failed central steering by higher-level governmental actors was and should be followed by a period of more inclusive, maybe bottom-up, decision-making, with a greater role of non-governmental actors. 'Government' was supposed be a style of steering associated with modernist states, often welfare states, where central governments knew what was best for people in local communities, and decided on the direction of development, and the provision of services. This phase of central steering in our view never existed, even in the regimes where such steering was at the core of their ideology, as in the USSR. This does not mean that the ambitions were not there, or the belief that such steering was desirable and even possible. It simply means that actual practices are always more diverse than assumed in those simplified understandings of governance.

What historians, anthropologists, geographers and others knew for a long time, and what Michel Foucault had politely pointed out in years of archival investigations, is that the reality of decision-making was always more complex. States formed over the centuries and the western idea of the nation state only became reality in the 17th century. These ideas of the state received a technocratic boost in the 18th century, when enlightenment ideas gave birth to modernist statecraft, to ideals and practices of central steering aided by science and complex administrations, aiming not only at maintenance of state power, but also at common goods which could be defined easily by referring to shared values, cultural identity and science. At the same time, the center of central steering was always dependent on the periphery, the top on the bottom, and of course, the middle. Power, as observed by Foucault and the other disciplines mentioned above, has always been exerted in all directions. Top-down systems rely on low-level bureaucrats who tend to have their own opinion, and the top or the center tends to be embedded in governance structures which allow certain decisions and certain policies to emerge, not others. Power triggers counter-power in unique and creative patterns; Foucault spoke of gymnastics (Foucault, 1979).

Governance thus takes on many different forms, as what can be decided upon, the community to which the decision applies, and the force which comes to and implements the decision, are always unique. Certainly, states learn from each other, cities, kingdoms, abbots and popes learn from each other, and conditions will favor certain forms of organization and tools of coordination. Similarities thus emerge between polities, and between styles of governance. The philosophy, technology, trade relations and statecraft of the early modern period in Europe did favor processes of consolidation and centralization, which we now label as the birth of the nation state, and the birth of 'government.' Yet, each nation state did function differently, related in different manners to its neighbors, to local and regional governance, to its peripheries, and its internal diversity, and it organized the connection between politics, law and administration in different ways. Meanwhile, the formal and informal influence of local traditions that differed from the new state ideology espoused by the center would assert itself in patterns of ebb and flood, and in waves as unique in their patterning as the real surf. We will come to refine our narrative of governance configurations and evolutions in the course of this book, but we have to stake out our position here, a position which understands the transition of 'government' to 'governance' to be a myth.

Such positioning does not say much, yet, about the nature of governance. Given the diversity, the unique character of governance everywhere, the unique scaling of governance in different areas, the unique relations between levels of governance, and given our already signaled distrust of simple explanatory models and grand concepts, how do we establish regularities, find commonalities, discern mechanisms in this diversity, which could tell us something about the possibilities and limits of steering towards sustainability transitions? We intend to use not just this chapter but the whole book as a place to answer such questions.

More elementary questions do arise, however. What is the collective bound by the decision? It can be a collective associated with an administrative or political territory, yet also a religious group living in different countries, a group worried about one topic, a population similar only in its being subjected to regulation of one sort. The territory can be aligned with natural boundaries, as with a watershed, yet it can also be entirely artificial, resulting from the materiality of an artificial landscape, such as a polder or irrigated landscape. We speak in this book of a 'community,' yet this is not the community of romantic theory. We do not necessarily assume there is always a group with a shared identity, a common culture, a desire to govern itself, and a form of governance recognized or not recognized in the nation state it happens to exist in. Such situations are real, and the romantic theory was inspired in part by the fragmented ethnic landscapes and multi-cultural empires of the era, but for our governance theory, they are neither the norm, nor the natural situation.

Our perspective applies to any community that is associated with a set of collectively binding decisions. A history of decision-making can lead to the formation of governance structures, which will be discussed at length in the following chapters, but which cannot be reduced to the structures of government. Governance is not possible solely based on formal institutions and state organizations; it never was and never will be. Nevertheless, ignoring the often important and always unique role of different sets of governmental organizations in governance, their importance for stability, capacity, and legitimacy in governance, would undermine the explanatory power of the theory from the start.

Participation in governance rests on a combination of direct participation and representation. Who actually participates, and who is really influential, is not immediately visible, and, again, is not readily legible in the formal structures of political and administrative organization. Who participates and with which effects becomes visible from observation of the practice of governance. Actors, moreover, as well as whole configurations of governance, can be formally sanctioned, or willed into being by leaders, by higher levels of government, *or not.* Actors can pre-exist their participation in formal governance, or they can be a product of governance, its pattern of inclusion and exclusions, the attractiveness or repulsiveness of its actions for the population. To speak of actors, however, they need to have an influence on governance, on the process of collective decision-making. This means that an individual, group or organization can become an actor formally or informally, visibly or invisibly, and occupying a role in structures of participation and representation, or not. Yet there needs to be an understanding with the actor that there is a collectively binding decision and a collective at stake; hence, most likely, an idea of what is a better or worse future for the community, depending on the nature of the decision taken. The fact that a decision-situation is envisioned conjures up a future and a community at the same time, and it is likely to trigger a process of self-reflection and internal consolidation in actors (who are we, what do we represent?).

Governance configurations – that is, configurations of actors and the tools of coordination, which we call institutions – emerge over time, in unique conditions and unique histories, part of which is the history of governance itself (Acemoglu & Robinson, 2012; Greif, 2006; North, 2005; Seabright, 2010). This already intimates that the variety of forms already indicated includes a variety of 'good' forms. 'Good governance,' just as 'democracy,' as a broader category and an infrastructure of good governance, takes on many shapes, as different configurations emerge in diverse situations to which they are adapted. These contexts are not entirely visible, neither for insiders, nor for outside observers, so assessing why something works or not, why a system could be called good governance or not, is not an easy matter. It takes observation and reflection. This theme, too, we develop in later chapters, but we can see here already that good governance has to be more than a matter of conformity to criteria imposed by external actors or external observers.

Governance exists outside the realm of nation states, it exists in dictatorships, in authoritarian and hybrid regimes, in theocracies and in plutocracies, and it evolves even where such evolution is not supposed to exist. Part of such evolution is the gradual transformation of notions of 'good governance' in systems telling themselves they are perfect and timeless. Ancient Egypt codified stability in its politics, religion and art, yet the Pharaoh asserting that nothing had changed in 1,000 years might be ruling over a fragmented state, dealing with assertive merchant classes, immigrants, aggressive neighbors, shifts in religious hierarchies, a declining economy, new technologies requiring foreigners to explain them, and enabling the ruler to conquer territories that were never Egyptian before. And when he dies, there might be no pyramid anymore. Closer to the present, a European welfare state might have perceived itself as entirely democratic for decades, yet an imperceptible shift in the semantics of democracy might lead to a shifting perception of politics, its relation with administration and expertise, and to a populist backlash against a system now felt to be undemocratic.

The thinking on governance has brought forward new concepts and approaches that highlight certain aspects and dimensions of decision-making (Bell & Hindmoor, 2009; Pierre & Peters, 2000a; Rhodes, 1997). In a globalizing world, terms like multi-level governance, polycentric governance and meta-governance have, for example, become frames for analysis, as well as normative ideals on how things should be organized. In the context of sustainability increasing attention is paid to adaptive, reflexive and transformative governance. Each of these concepts will be elaborated on later in this book, but it is good to mention that these concepts refer to particular characteristics of governance systems that could facilitate learning, adaptation and a shift towards more sustainable forms of organizing and using natural resources, ecosystems and the environment more in general, as well as towards ideas on how and why this shift should be organized. The concepts thus have a clear normative dimension, although, as we will see later on, learning, adaptation and transformation do not necessarily mean that societies or social-ecological systems indeed become more just or sustainable.

GOVERNANCE DOMAINS

Not all areas of action, types of action and topics of decision-making are regulated. That is, not everything in life is governed. There might be groups of people and groups of topics which over time become associated in governance and we can speak then of the crystallization of *governance domains.* Governance domains can thus be defined as domains of decision-making, where a group of people, which can be called a community, takes decisions on a certain range of topics. Those domains can be formalized, in ministries, departments, councils, with political or administrative emphasis, yet this is not always the case. There can be domains where non-state organizations, such as the church are influential and the recognized site of decision-making, and there might be areas where no formal organization seems present or relevant, even though there is a form of coordination in the community. We discuss informal institutions later, yet we can already mention here that the acceptance of such informal domains of governance does not open the door to chaos. It is not because no written rules exist, and there is no official arena to take decisions and make new decision rules, that there is no governance. Governance can emerge more spontaneously, and it can form around imposed rules, yet there is always *selectivity* in the formation of domains, its association with groups, and the linkage between topics in the domains. In some cases, there might be informal rules, no clear arena, but a domain; in other cases, there might be an arena, yet an openness with regards to the domain.

Within a recognized governance domain, governance topics can slowly crystallize over time or they can pre-exist in public discourse, possibly creating their own domain, before becoming subsumed in larger domains. Climate governance is a clear example of such a domain that emerged in the past decades, out of increased knowledge about the impact of human activities on the climate and the growing awareness that addressing climate change requires coordinated action at all levels, and particularly at the global level (Andonova et al., 2009; Jordan et al., 2015). Various governance domains can, furthermore, co-exist, partly overlap, and be part of more general domains. In some communities, there are only individual domains articulated for governance, without them coalescing into overall governance structures. Elsewhere, the idea and the practice of comprehensive governance developed. Comprehensive governance then means the idea of a system of systems, a network of arenas where collectively binding decisions on many topics can be taken.

This does not necessarily require a central authority, yet one can point to a rather remarkable development, observed by Niklas Luhmann, Max Weber and others, that a process of *differentiation* took place over centuries, whereby new forms of organization emerged which then could coordinate action in more and more specialized domains (Luhmann, 1990, 1995; Weber, 1895). From a central authority in ancient times, where religious, legal and political authority could be combined in one person, to a maze-like bureaucracy and a separation of church and state, and an autonomy of legislative, judicial and executive branches of government (Graeber & Wengrow, 2021). Rather remarkably, this line of evolution gave rise to a seeming counter-current, where more and more comprehensive policies were envisioned, starting in the 18th century, by a more and more ambitious and less self-serving state. Here we find the birth of what James Scott calls the high modernist state (Scott, 1998).

The relative independence of governance domains, and their arenas (see below) can thus exist in very different polities and is neither a more primitive nor a more advanced state of affairs. Both in early societies and in more recent forms of governance, such as the European Union (EU), one can recognize such relative autonomy, while tight couplings of domains, arenas and a high level of steering ambitions can be found in ancient and modern times. The presence of a governance system that envisions the regulation of the community does not always come with steering ambitions, and it does not always imply that there is a vision for the future, let alone a strategy to move towards a desirable future. Overall governance for us means that there is a semantics of unity, a story of a community embedded in the wider community, which makes it possible to envision a better form of organization, a better moral, economic, military status for that community, and the possibility and need to articulate policies for more than one topic (Koch et al., 2021; Van Assche et al., 2023).

As soon as the idea of community enters, ideas of a better community emerge, and as soon as there is a power which is or aspires to be in charge, this becomes more realistic. One can speak of a cognitive openness for new topics and domains, where there is overall governance, and the potential for coordinating them towards more integrated goals.

The relations between power, governance and community require more scrutiny, for certain, and we will develop our perspective on these relations in later chapters. We can point here to the diversity of pathways and contingent relations, where sometimes a central authority imposes an idea of community, which then becomes performativity, meaning that it comes alive, with people identifying with the community, maybe over generations, and even asking for a return, through new rules and regulations, new conquests, to the 'real' community they belong to. One can think of the Roman Empire, which was borne out of a republic, conquered all its neighbors, later including more and more faraway lands, centralized power, and inspired a desire to identify with it not only in newly conquered peoples, who had clear paths to citizenship, but even with neighboring peoples, to the extent that after the collapse of the western Roman Empire, many Germanic tribes ruling the land preferred to identify as Roman. In other cases, a history of trade ties and mutually beneficial co-existence in multi-level forms of governance, in a community with more autonomous governance domains, is later reinterpreted as a history of oppression and brutal conquest. Yet elsewhere, the conquest was indeed brutal, remembered as such, and as soon as central authority started to wane, regions reasserted old identities and moved towards self-governance.

The diversity of pathways in the relation between community, governance domains and arenas shows itself also in the diversity of visions that can be found. Sometimes, partial visions can be found in one governance domain, and not in others. Strategies might exist, for the development of one area, or the improvement of one policy domain, yet not for other areas and domains (Chandler, 2000). Furthermore, coordination between domains is more or less likely depending on the historical development of the community, of the co-existence of groups, ideas, conquerors and conquered, similar and different peoples. Proud and independent cities might have clear aspirations and strategies towards self-improvement, or maybe more autonomy from a higher authority, yet villages in the same region might rely more on that central authority to protect themselves from those urban aspirations. Similarly, water governance might develop at local level, leading to a perceived need for coordination and the formation of regional structures and policies for water governance, but this does not imply that there is a universal logic which makes this the starting point of an integration into larger polities and a coupling to other governance domains (Arato & Luhmann, 1994; Sand, 2008).

How governance domains crystallize, therefore, is unique for each community. The same is true for how these governance domains relate to each other, integrate or not, associate with identities or not, and develop visions for the future or not. Even if the name for a governance domain is the same in several communities or polities, this does not mean that there will be a strong similarity with regards to the topics covered, the relations with other domains, or the tools of coordination. Planning is a good example here. The domain of planning exists in many countries, but what planning actually means, how it is organized, and to what extent it does make a difference in the governance system and wider society, largely differs (Bishwapriya, 2012; Gunder et al., 2017). The unicity of governance domains is further underlined by the fact that not only actors compete, but also governance domains. Central topics in one domain can become so important that the domain absorbs other domains or serves as their site of coordination.

Governance domains have hierarchies, which can be imported from somewhere else or produced in the domain itself. Hierarchies can be visible in the hierarchy of topics internally, in the importance of certain actors, arenas, institutions (Donnison et al., 2021; Taub, 2022; Wildavsky, 2005). Learning and copying takes place, and similarities in values and economies do exist between communities, so similarities and congruences between communities, in their structuring of domains, do occur. Material conditions can be similar, and this, too, can contribute to a production of similarity, to similar domains being defined in different communities. Domains, therefore, are first and foremost existing in the domain of semantics, of discourse, yet they are not merely conceptual structures linking topics of governance and community. They are action-oriented as well as community-oriented, meaning that they only make sense if understood as ideas which can help guide a community in decision-making, which then guides its self-organization. For that to work, for discourse and collective action to be linked, to materialize in the life of the community, other things such as ideas, places and rules are needed, and these will be elucidated in the following sections.

GOVERNANCE DIMENSIONS

The term governance dimension refers to a particular aspect or sets of aspects that can be distinguished in a governance system. Well-known examples include the political, economic, legal or policy dimension, but also forms of democracy, the types of knowledge or the way of organizing can be seen as governance dimensions. In a given polity, with certain domains and topics of governance, governance *dimensions* emerge over time. These dimensions, as the domains, are not universal nor necessarily structured in a certain manner. They are contingent. They evolve in paths that create their own reality and

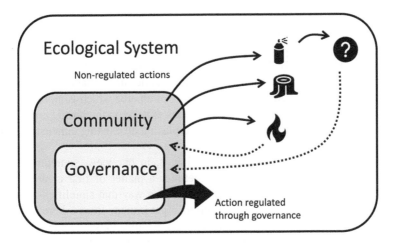

Figure 2.1   Community, environment and governance[1]

context of adaptation, and in each case they could have been different. The dimensions are based on distinctions that are made within the community, and which slowly take on meaning as organizing principles (Gruezmacher & Van Assche, 2014; Van Assche et al., 2013). The distinctions made can differ, and the choice of a side of the distinction will differ. Two sides of the distinction can be unfolded as the ends of a scale, or they can remain closer to a distinction, as sides of an opposition. The scaling and distinguishing creates a set of options for governance in a community (Brans, 2012).

This process of making distinctions is linked to the structure of the domains and their topics (Seidl & Becker, 2006). It hinges on the dominant values, identifications and activities in the community, and on its set of *necessities*: what do we *need* to decide on, given our environment and livelihoods. Domains and topics create dimensions, while dimensions engender or favor domains or topics. It is a dialectic process that is part of a larger set of processes making the world understandable and *governable* for the community itself (Ghani & Lockhart, 2009; Jentoft, 2007). Once again, relevant differences in pathways in the formation of governance dimensions can be found in different

---

[1]   A community organizes itself through collectively binding decisions, through governance. These decisions affect the environment, the ecological system. When actions bypass governance, they are more difficult to coordinate; oversight is not possible. Environmental effects become harder to observe, to assess, to mitigate. Tracing environmental consequences of human actions, diagnosing environmental quality, and understanding the relation between social and ecological systems are rendered almost impossible.

relations between authority and subjects, between histories of oppression and self-organization, between communities, existing as discursively bound groups, organizing themselves, and polities which stem from an imposition of power, with possible but not necessary implications for the formation of new identities (Held, 1996). The kind of group, in other words, that serves as the starting point for the formation of governance dimensions, makes a difference. If an existing polity takes over another one, or an area which is more loosely or locally organized, governance dimensions existing in the hostile polity can be imposed, although likely not entirely replacing all existing dimensions and associated institutions (Woods, 2004).

Making the world governable therefore is, in our view, sometimes first a matter of imposition of power, sometimes a matter of first creating distinctions, making the world understandable in a way that simplifies drawing conclusions with regards to its preferred organization. Even where a polity imposes its dimensions of governance on people, these people must be convinced somehow that this makes sense if the polity intends to be sustainable and not to be mired in endless civil unrest. In other words, a connection must exist, or be made persuasive, between the distinctions of the ruling authority and the distinctions made by the governed. More elementarily, those intending to govern cannot escape the need to make distinctions, as the basis for their governing. This need to make distinctions matters in terms of understanding (what are we supposed to do and why, why are decisions taken at all on this topic?), but also in terms of selectivity and functionality (one cannot organize a polity to decide on anything in any possible relation between topics).

In order for the world to become governable, it has to be first of all understandable (Luhmann, 1990). This understanding has to be shared between those who govern and those who are governed (which could be the same people). For the need to take decisions on certain things to look like natural and logical for a community, at least the basics of a worldview needs to be shared, but also the acceptance of a decision authority, and the need to select domains and topics where decisions could make sense. We can add that a history of decision-making, and observable effects of those decisions, sets the community on a path of governance evolution, since observing a result can persuade members of the community that it is possible to take a decision, with an effect, and an effect which affects something we define as important. If any step in this chain is missing, governability will be reduced.

Given what was said above, it comes as no surprise that in a certain polity older and newer dimensions of governance co-exist, just as older and new domains and topics co-exist, and older and newer arenas, actors and institutions. An old dimension, in for example many western countries, is the dimension *religious-worldly*, which organizes which collectively binding decisions can be taken by religious actors, what counts as religious, and which religious topics ought to come on the political agenda in what manner. And conversely, which decisions are taken by worldly leaders, even if it concerns not so worldly topics? This, again, hinges on understandings of the world, of the position of the transcendent in society, in daily life, its perceived relation to authority and to the present. Another old dimension, less relevant in many places, is the one based on the distinction *civic-aristocratic*, a dimension which was however central to the organization of politics in the world of Machiavelli and Renaissance Italy (Martines, 1983). For Machiavelli, the power of the lords in his landscape of city-states was not entirely broken yet, and some of the lords had moved into business, while some business people (most notably the Medicis) found it worthwhile to pursue noble titles (Machiavelli, 1996). Since in contemporary Europe the power of the nobility has largely vanished, not only have the positions on this axis shifted, but the dimension itself has lost relevance as a structuring tool for governance and therefore also for understanding governance. That said, the term elites is increasingly coined to create and grasp new distinctions between groups in society and governance, to account for their different roles and influence on governance, politics or the economy, and for their different perspectives on sustainability transitions (Schmid et al., 2021).

Central steering-network steering is a dimension that acquires relevance in many polities, old and new, while the distinction *formal-informal* governance is always there, though not always openly admitted (Helmke & Levitsky, 2004; Klijn, 2008; Ledeneva, 2006; Van Assche et al., 2014b). A more recent dimension is that of *national vs. local* governance, as the nation states are relatively recent creations (Ersoy et al., 2010; Foucault, 2007; Gellner, 1983). Another dimension that is relatively recent is that of *local vs. expert governance*, as the role of experts is also relatively recent, while the reduction of what people know to 'local' knowledge is part of the same reshuffling of power and knowledge (Fischer, 2000; Scott, 1998; Turner, 2013).

Not all polities are democratic, of course, and the dimension *autocratic-democratic* became relevant when the option to organize things along democratic lines (still open to many forms of organization) became recognized more widely as a real option, and not only as a historical (possibly Greek) exception (Gay, 1954). Once the two sides of the distinction, or the two polarities on the axis, are perceived as real, in terms of thinking and organizing, then the dimension becomes real, and choices for observers and participants alike can be structured along the line of that dimension. It is possible that a dimension first exists in theory, then in practice, while the other direction can be just as real, with practice inspiring theory to make distinctions which could possibly be picked up again in practice later.

Each community thus organizes itself along the lines of several distinctions at once, and marks itself, or can be marked by others, in terms of positions on the resulting axes (Gruezmacher & Van Assche, 2014). The characterization of the governance configuration can vary between insiders and outsiders, or even between different groups of insiders. Each governance configuration is unique in terms of its combination of dimensions, and its positions on each dimension. The set of dimensions can mark the *what* and *how* of a governance configuration, a set of particular links to topics, tools and actors. A further reason for the unique character of the set of dimensions and positions is the fact that the emergence of one dimension can have effect for the stability, emergence or slow vanishing of another one, and that, more in detail, the positions (sometimes choices) on one dimension can affect positions on others. An authoritarian regime is unlikely to rest on principles of localism and give central place to local knowledge. Maybe counter-intuitively, such authoritarianism can still rely on network steering, an indication that in the assessment of couplings between dimensions, between positions, one needs to be cautious with assumptions.

ACTORS

We have encountered the idea of 'actors' already and we can now develop it more easily. We speak of actors if there is agency and intention. If there is no basic unity that can be recognized in a group or organization, no possibility to articulate a common point of view or desire, then it is difficult to participate in governance as an actor (Bartolini, 2000; Devas, 2014). There could still be participation, but then as a shifting collection of actors, or short-term participants. If there is such basic unity, it becomes more likely that the actor becomes recognized as such in governance and in the community, and that a role can be defined and stabilized. One can also speak of a basic unity of voice, which needs to be recognized internally (if the actor is a group or organization) and externally. There needs to be some cohesion of the meanings bestowed upon self and world. It is not possible to define a priori how strong the unity of voice, intention and meaning must be in order to speak of an actor, and more particularly about an actor which can actually act and play a role in the functioning of governance. One can only deduce a posteriori that the unity was apparently sufficient to enable functioning in the unique environment of a particular governance configuration.

Individuals, groups and organizations can play the role of actor in governance, with individuals often representing organizations or groups in governance arenas and with groups often organizing in order to participate in governance, or organizations finding new groups to associate with, in order to magnify their importance in governance (Van Assche et al., 2014a). The precise relation between individual, group and organization can be hard to pin down, and can shift. It must be deduced from empirical observation, and since there might be reasons to obscure the nature of the relation, such observation and deduction can be difficult. Similarly, agency and unity of voice need to be observed, and cannot be deduced from the formal structure of governance and its organizations. It is entirely possible that one group organized itself, acquired a recognized role in governance, after which it became subjected to the will of authoritarian individuals representing the group. It is also rather common that a role is defined, but not played, and that presence is no guarantee for participation. Actors can be dead in terms of their role in governance but can be there: *zombie actors*. They can be invisible but can be there: *shadow actors* (Cribb, 2009; Mazzuca & Robinson, 2009).

We know that actors are not always visible and that they cannot be assumed to exist. Mapping actors is not an easy task. Even more difficult is answering the question: Who should be an actor? Referring to 'stakeholders' is simply shifting the question, as it is not clear who is and should be a stakeholder. Answering the question is providing an assessment of the quality of governance, of current patterns of inclusion and exclusion, and such assessment cannot be presumed to exist and be agreed upon (in the community). One should, therefore, as participant and as observer, approach this question with caution, and cultivate self-reflection: What are our own assumptions here? Do we start from a perceived injustice? An unfair form of participation? A problematic relation between participation and representation? A creeping form of authoritarianism? Or do we start our advocacy for formation or inclusion of new actors from the idea that new activities, ideals, values, identities require a new map of actors representing a new choir of voices?

As communities never cease to change, governance configurations are always in transformation: new actors come, old ones go, some merge, others transform or play new roles. Actors can exist – as a group or organization, as an individual – and enter governance, or they can *emerge*, outside or inside of governance (Beunen et al., 2015; Van Assche et al., 2014a). Businesses organize themselves in associations through which they try to influence decision-making processes, and they can initiate and fund think tanks, non-governmental organizations or research foundations that become part of a governance system. Citizens worried about the environment can do the same. Such newly created organizations can be small, focusing on local issues, or develop into important actors in the national or international arena. A perspective, a voice associated with a group or individual, can form and enter governance, or the activities in governance can lead to the emergence of a group, or a perspective, or a voice. Voice can create group and vice versa, as a discourse can come into existence, without attaching itself to a group, or belonging to a pre-existing group, while later producing a group of people identifying with it. An organization can be at the table for a long time without being an actor, at some point finally becoming one. The becoming of an actor, having influence on collective decision-making, can itself take different paths and forms, but an absence of participation is more easily observed. We can say at this point that the voicing of arguments, aspirations, ideas is participation and marks the presence of an actor, even when those arguments are rejected in the final decision, as it is not the decision but the process of decision-making we consider to be the essence of governance. We can also add a meta-level of participation that can function as condition of participation, or, more simply, we can say that awareness of desired participation and influence is a precondition for speaking of an 'actor' (Ansell & Torfing, 2021; Jessop, 2002). There needs to be awareness of the game one is part of, even if the knowledge of the rules is imperfect, and even if one is usually on the losing side.

Actors emerge and do something, their role in governance can evolve. There might be a formally defined role, but this can differ from the actual role and from the aspired role. These differences can trigger action and strategy in the direction of that aspired role, or towards formal recognition of a role already played. Roles are a matter of practice, and of discourse. As practice and discourse never fully coincide, this gives rise to tensions that can be creative and productive, or negative. A strong actor identity which differs from the formal role can create conflict or change, while shifting professional identities in an organization can bring in different forms of expertise, changing perspectives, problem definitions, and a strong desire to redefine a role. Which then can lead to a transformation in governance, as other roles might have to shift, as other actors might have to respond, as institutions might be reinterpreted, rendered obsolete, or invented.

Perfect agreement on the map of actors might not exist, as some might have reasons to hide, or to overemphasize their role. It can be unclear whether an actor is actually more an arena than an actor: Is the chamber of commerce an actor? We can say with more certainty that referring to formal roles, responsibilities and procedures (all defining actors and their inclusion) is not the final answer regarding actual participation and agency. What actors actually do rarely coincides with the role they are supposed to play, while the role they would like to play tends to differ from the role they can actually play in the current configuration. Furthermore, individuals can play several roles at once, as their identities are complex and because of their layered identifications, and as governance systems and communities are complex. A person can be mayor and former head of the chamber of commerce, as well as chief of the local fishing association and protector of one particular natural area, which happens to be a favorite fishing spot. Individuals thus relate to 'actors' in complex manners, often rife with tensions and contradictions, and they can be unaware themselves which actor they represent at any given moment. Often, it is fairer to speak of complex interests and identities that partly associate with actors, partly with voices not represented in governance, and in part with purely individual interests.

Groups and Identities

If complexity and lack of cohesion marks the individual, it certainly marks groups. It also marks the relation between individual and group, between groups and organizations, and between organizations and governance. Governance makes groups and groups make governance, as we know. Not all groups in the community organize themselves, not all groups participate in governance, can participate, and should participate. Groups can be active in governance through participation or representation, or through both lines of power and via various links between individual and polity. They can prefer to exert influence visibly or invisibly, directly or indirectly, and foster broader appeal (to enhance governance roles) or not.

Groups, if organized, can have internal governance structures, or not. These structures can in turn rely on a combination of participation and representation. If groups have long histories of differentiation or mergers, if they represent coalitions of pre-existing groups or actors, this interplay of internal politics and external politics can be complex, so internal competition can affect what happens in governance and the community. If actors dominate a polity for a long time, a process of differentiation often takes place, so new sub-groups or organizations can associate with existing identities, interests or groups in the community, and an indirect form of representation and competition can take shape. One-party states can still have mechanisms of representation and competition with certain parts of the party, and of administration connecting to groups in society (merchants, farmers, fishermen, industrialists, teachers, Catholics, etc.).

Groups can be weakly or strongly defined, and the group identity can be important or not to the members, or to the community at large. The group can be associated with a livelihood, an ethnicity, a business interest, an ideology, but also with a hobby, or with one domain of policy. Groups do have an identity, some form of cohesion or self-similarity, otherwise they would not be groups (Barth, 1998). That group identity might not be tightly coupled to personal identity at first, but such coupling can become relevant later, while political relevance might also emerge only after a long period of time. In Rome, horse-racing was popular since the early days of the republic, but only in the Byzantine Empire, in the later history of the eastern Roman Empire, did the different teams and their colors acquire a political significance and start to function as factions, without ever losing a connection to the races. Races thus became politicized, and politics could not ignore the races. Those Byzantine hooligans could decide on the fate of emperors, while crafty emperors knew how to manipulate the factions and the races.

Group identities can evolve and they evolve in their importance for individuals. Some identities might become more central to individuals, because of changes in communities, in life. Religious, cultural, gender and ethnic categories can acquire a new importance for individuals at some point, driven by personal experiences, broader trends and events, and emerging narratives and forms of organization (de Vries & Aalvanger, 2015; Eriksen, 2010). New identifications can inspire new aspirations for participation or representation in governance, as members of the associated group. Such a process can trigger processes of organization, creation of new actors, or increased prominence of existing ones. Some European countries saw the formation of political parties for the elderly and the ageing, while the cruelty of the industrial food system led to counter-discourses, mobilization and the creation of parties revolving around animal welfare.

If identities are reduced to a schematic understanding of the world, to few and simple categories, and politics becomes structured along the lines of such identities, governance tends to be reduced to *identity politics.* This, we argue, might look like a solution to real problems at the moment, but in the longer run it makes governance less adaptive, hardens boundaries of identities and factions, and aggravates processes of polarization (Friedmann, 1992; Yashar, 2007). Conflict, in such circumstances, can start to look as the only way out, and either getting rid of the other faction or somehow convincing that their identity should be transformed starts to appear as rational (Eriksen, 2001).

Narratives of place, of past and future can be mobilized in such conflicts, and in identity politics more generally, but one needs to observe rather clinically that group identities commonly form themselves by means of narratives of place, history and future (Hinchman & Hinchman, 1997). They can associate more closely with certain topics and domains of particular importance for them. The stories about place, past and future can be produced by groups, and they can pre-exist the groups, or exist in parallel with the discursive dynamics of the group for a long time. If the group embraces a version of the future and the past, this past or future is likely to be transformed in the process, to connect better to values and ideologies espoused, to features of discursive identity cherished, to goals already defined (Bollens, 1998; Somer, 2001).

This brings us to a point we cherish, and which was already adumbrated in several guises: that identities can pre-exist stories of the place, the future, or *a particular strategy hopefully producing a future,* but they can also be a product of those. Different relations are possible as are different temporal orders. An identity can produce a history, while a history can produce an identity. Central for the theme of this book, a community strategy can represent an improved future for a community and its constituent groups and identities, yet it can also produce histories, place meanings and identities, while it can reshuffle the map of actors in governance.

Organizations as Actors

In complex societies, actors tend to take the form of organizations (Luhmann, 2018). Groups are more likely to participate if they take on the form of organizations, or if organizations are formed which can be represented in governance processes. Organizations have membership rules, procedures for decision-making, an identity which guides those decisions towards a particular purpose, and the potential to develop internal hierarchies and differentiations, where particular functions such as accounting, quality control but also strategy formulation can find a home.

Organizations can be for profit, not for profit and governmental. This last type must be mentioned, as it is often forgotten that 'the government' or 'the state' is a web of actors, not a single actor, and that those actors almost always have the form of an organization. Not all state organizations, however, are actors, and one needs to be cautious with overstretching the concept of governance to include all state organizations routinely as actors. While the early proponents and theorists of governance persuasively argued that many administrative organizations were not merely implementing decisions taken in the political sphere but actively shaped the agenda and influenced decision-making, just as non-governmental actors had an influence inside and outside the formal procedures of participation and representation, some governmental organizations are indeed simply registering, checking or implementing decisions taken elsewhere (Bevir, 2010; Pierre & Peters, 2000b). Other state organizations can be de facto marginal in the process of governance, and others might lack voice and cohesion.

State organizations can become actors over time, as they develop a stronger identity and voice, and become used to a particular form of governance where they can carve out a niche. Stability helps here, especially when politics is volatile, when higher-level leadership is politicized and volatile, when the organization itself is stable, under stable leadership (Boin & Lodge, 2016). Another source of agency can be the presence or development of a form of expertise appreciated in governance or expertly sold as important to decision-makers. Over time, governmental organizations can expand their role in governance in this way, increase their autonomy, entrench themselves in procedures, divert flows of resources and influence the articulation of policies in which they themselves play an important role. Such a process is not unavoidable, not always undesirable (in terms of common goods) and not always intended by governmental organizations. What is clear, however, is that referring to the formal role of an organization does not say much about its actual or desired role.

Behind the agency of state organizations can be an evolving role or aspired role in terms of a common good envisioned clearly by the organization, but there can be other reasons. These include the prominence of professional identities, the reinforcement of the organizational identity in intra-state competition, or the creation of linkages with external actors in the private sector, the world of NGOs, or academia. The state actor can establish links with external groups, which then do not have to rely on the form of organization, but remain relatively loosely organized, as a group, trusting in their connections with the state actor as an informal way of representation. Again, we encounter a complex interplay between organizations and groups, and between governmental and other actors. To this complex interplay we can add the importance of individuals, which can be the product of organizations, but which can also use organizations as vehicles for their own ambitions.

Governance can function as a goal for groups, driving their organization. More precisely, the promise or aspiration of participation in governance can trigger processes of (self-) organization, as future influence over collective decision-making can be a powerful attractor. One can recognize Aristotle's *final cause*, as a future state which drives current developments, as an attractor (Trott, 2013). In other cases, identity narratives can drive organization towards participation, and this can be recognized as Aristotle's *formal cause*, while elsewhere the driver of organization is a perceived need to do something (*material cause* in Aristotelean terms).

Organizations can be established quickly, through self-organization in groups, or by smaller groups deciding to start an organization, and they can be established by authorities deciding to do so, for example, to perform an administrative, educational or scientific function. Organizations can be deliberately designed to try something, to make an experiment possible, in the market, but also in administration, and as a non-governmental, non-profit organization (Van Assche, Valentinov, et al., 2021). Governance can become more flexible and adaptive through such experiments, and this flexibility is further aided by the potential to limit their existence in time, to define their time horizon (how they look forward), their membership rules and resources, and their goal and scope of ambitions.

Of course, such initial design does not always survive the growing ambitions and diverging ideas of an organization once established, but this is not necessarily a problem. If limited autonomy, ambition and lifespan are deemed important for those founding the organization, these founders are likely governmental actors with enough authority to make these limitations binding. Project organizations, working groups and inter-departmental task forces or regional visioning teams are examples where the limited scope can be enforced, while specialized implementation organizations can, if prestigious or powerful enough, sometimes succeed in redefining themselves and surviving beyond the death of their original task. Similarly, loose collaborations of organizations can develop their own identity which can override the identity of the participating organizations, if they fill a governance gap, associate with strong identities or aspirations in the community, or if they collectively control flows of resources which would otherwise be inaccessible or scattered (Czarniawska, 1997).

New organizations can be established if a new domain of governance emerges, or if a new problem, a new goal, a new location to be governed, a new threat or enemy to be dealt with, or a new ambition which requires higher levels of coordination or integration becomes visible (Levy & Roseman, 2001). A new emerging identity can trigger the formation of new organizations, before a new arena is formed and before new actors appear. Truly in the spirit of experimental governance, a new organization can pursue a new but risky solution for a governance problem. Larger companies can start or spin off an organization, or can simply buy up another one, to try something, while larger non-profit organizations can support the development of other non-profits, as well as for-profit organizations, to pursue their aspirations. Most relevant for us are governmental organizations, which can create new ministries and departments, but also the less permanent forms of organization which can enable experimentalist forms of governance.

A new organization can serve to bring actors together and it can bridge divides (as in housing or development corporations). It can represent a governmental or community agenda that is new or that was not fully pursued in the existing governance configuration (Armitage, 2008; Valentinov et al., 2019). Organizations can be designed to pursue common goods while remaining at arms length from governmental actors, for example to increase flexibility and adaptivity. Organizations themselves can thus be more or less adaptive, while organizations can be seen as tools to make governance as a whole more adaptive (Will et al., 2018). A counterforce can be the afore-mentioned possibility that new organizational identities form, which could spur new group identities and interest groups, which can undermine the initial ambition to increase flexibility in governance. It is not always easy to assess how different a new organization will be from the ones participating in it, or establishing it, as the ties might be less visible and numerous. Cultural and professional identities and hierarchies might survive, as might ideologies dominant in the area, or in the network of governmental actors deciding to innovate.

Relations Between Individuals, Groups and Organizations

Both individuals and collective actors matter in governance. Without individuals with skills, organizations would have less influence in governance. Without individuals, no organizations would form. Conversely, a representative of an organization can redefine or reinterpret the identity and goals of the organization, and the expected form of participation in governance. Self-interest can overtake the interest of the collective or the organization. Individuals might identify with organizations but can never be subsumed by them. Individuals, just like organizations, shape themselves by means of external narratives, part of which is provided by organizations (Luhmann, 2018; Seidl & Becker, 2006). This shaping, however, takes place in patterns not entirely transparent to the individual, let alone to the organization trying to instrumentalize the individual. If such an individual then, on behalf of the organization, takes a seat in the governance of a larger whole, promising a larger influence, the programming of the individual, the strict definition of the way the representation of the organization in governance is supposed to take place, becomes hard indeed.

'Leadership' is supposed to inspire identification with the organization, and guidance in complex landscapes of competition, innovation and regulation. The notion of leadership is often attributed to individuals, but also organizations, such as companies or cities, can be seen as leaders (Young, 1991). Many fictions surround the idea of the leader or, more generally, the entrepreneur or manager (Alvesson & Kärreman, 2016). We return to this theme of mythologized leadership later. For now it is important to note that leadership can take many forms and that there will always be differences between roles, attributions and realities. An individual can be in a position to lead, but not lead. Or he or she can lead without a formal position in the organization or in governance. An organization can take on a clear unified voice and exercise leadership in governance, while internally leadership can be very diffuse. The voice can be there, with leadership functions, but it does not need to be associated with an individual, nor with a clear and simple pattern of responsibilities. The leadership function can appear situationally. Participation in governance might forge the voice, just for the moment or might make the only half-meaningful utterances of the representatives of the organization sound meaningful. Leadership can be attributed, and can become real as others take their cues from an assumed meaning and position. A unified voice and a leadership function can thus appear in complex patterns, which are not always easy to grasp. The identity of the organization can suddenly appear to be embodied in one person, just as the needs and aspirations of the common might suddenly be projected or recognized in the organization and its representative (Ashmos et al., 2000).

Meanwhile, individuals, groups, organizations, as potential actors in governance, can relate differently to ideology, narratives, forms of knowledge, or expertise because of their qualitatively different kinds of complexity, of internal organization, differentiation, identity formation, cohesion, leadership styles, histories and imagined futures or lack thereof (Van Assche et al., 2016; Van Assche, Duineveld, et al., 2021). These different positionalities and potentialities in relation to discourse, power and community create a formidable pallet of design and participation options in governance. This diversity greatly contributes to the evolutionary productivity, the adaptive capacity of governance, and to the creation of ever-larger areas of the world and ever-expanding lists of topics, domains of human activity which can become governable.

REFERENCES

Acemoglu, D. & Robinson, J. (2012). *Why nations fail. The origins of power, prosperity and poverty.* Crown Business.

Alvesson, M. & Kärreman, D. (2016). Intellectual failure and ideological success in organization studies: The case of transformational leadership. *Journal of Management Inquiry, 25*(2), 139–152.

Andonova, L. B., Betsill, M. M. & Bulkeley, H. (2009). Transnational climate governance. *Global Environmental Politics, 9*(2), 52–73. https://doi.org/10.1162/glep.2009.9.2.52

Ansell, C. & Torfing, J. (2021). *Public governance as co-creation: A strategy for revitalizing the public sector and rejuvenating democracy.* Cambridge Core; Cambridge University Press. https://doi.org/10.1017/9781108765381

Arato, A. & Luhmann, N. (1994). Civil society and political theory in the work of Luhmann and beyond. *New German Critique, 61*, 129–142. https://doi.org/10.2307/488624

Armitage, D. (2008). Governance and the commons in a multi-level world. *International Journal of the Commons, 2*(1), 7–32.

Ashmos, D. P., Duchon, D. & McDaniel, R. R. (2000). Organizational responses to complexity: The effect on organizational performance. *Journal of Organizational Change Management, 13*(6), 577–595.

Barth, F. (1998). *Ethnic groups and boundaries: The social organization of culture difference.* Waveland Press.

Bartolini, S. (2000). *The political mobilization of the European left, 1860–1980: The class cleavage.* Cambridge University Press.

Bell, S. & Hindmoor, A. (2009). *Rethinking governance: The centrality of the state in modern society.* Cambridge University Press.

Beunen, R., Van Assche, K. & Duineveld, M. (2015). *Evolutionary governance theory: Theory and applications.* Springer.

Bevir, M. (2004). Governance and interpretation: What are the implications of post-foundationalism? *Public Administration, 82*(3), 605–625.

Bevir, M. (2010). *Democratic governance.* Princeton University Press.

Biermann, F., Kanie, N. & Kim, R. E. (2017). Global governance by goal-setting: The novel approach of the UN Sustainable Development Goals. *Current Opinion in Environmental Sustainability, 26–27*, 26–31. https://doi.org/10.1016/j.cosust.2017.01.010

Bishwapriya, S. (2012). *Comparative planning cultures.* Routledge.

Boin, A. & Lodge, M. (2016). Designing Resilient institutions for transboundary crisis management: A time for public administration. *Public Administration, 94*(2), 289–298. https://doi.org/10.1111/padm.12264

Bollens, S. A. (1998). Urban policy in ethnically polarized societies. *International Political Science Review*, *19*(2), 187–215. https:// doi .org/ 10 .1177/ 019251298019002007

Bowles, S., Gintis, H. & Gustafsson, B. (2008). *Markets and democracy: Participation, accountability and efficiency*. Cambridge University Press.

Brans, M. (2012). Comparative public administration: From general theory to general frameworks. *The SAGE handbook of public administration*. London: SAGE Publications, pp. 511–532.

Bulkeley, H. (2005). Reconfiguring environmental governance: Towards a politics of scales and networks. *Political Geography*, *24*(8), 875–902. https://doi.org/10.1016/j.polgeo.2005.07.002

Castells, M. (1996). *The rise of the network society*. Blackwell.

Chandler, J. A. (2000). *Comparative public administration*. Psychology Press.

Cribb, R. (2009). Introduction: Parapolitics, shadow governance and criminal sovereignty. In *government of the shadows: Parapolitics and criminal sovereignty*. Pluto Press.

Czarniawska, B. (1997). *Narrating the organization. Dramas of institutional identity*. University of Chicago Press.

de Vries, J. & Aalvanger, A. (2015). Negotiating differences: The role of social identity in the emergence of institutions for local governance. In R. Beunen, K. Van Assche & M. Duineveld (eds.), *Evolutionary governance theory: Theory and applications* (pp. 291–304). Springer International Publishing. https://doi.org/10.1007/978-3-319 -12274-8_19

Devas, N. (2014). *Urban governance voice and poverty in the developing world*. Routledge.

Donnison, D., Chapman, V., Meacher, M., Sears, A. & Urwin, K. (2021). *Social policy and administration revisited: Studies in the development of social services at the local level*. Routledge.

Eriksen, T. H. (2001). Ethnic identity, national identity, and intergroup conflict. *Social Identity, Intergroup Conflict, and Conflict Reduction*, *3*, 42–68.

Eriksen, T. H. (2010). *Ethnicity and nationalism: Anthropological perspectives: Third edition*. Pluto Press.

Ersoy, A., Gȼrny, M. & Kechriotis, V. (2010). *Modernism: The creation of nation-states: Discourses of collective identity in Central and Southeast Europe 1770–1945: Texts and commentaries, volume III/1*. Central European University Press.

Farazmand, A. & Pinkowski, J. (2006). *Handbook of globalization, governance, and public administration*. CRC Press.

Fischer, F. (2000). *Citizens, experts and the environment. The politics of local knowledge*. Duke University Press.

Foucault, M. (1979). *Discipline and punish: The birth of the prison*. Penguin Books.

Foucault, M. (2007). *Security, territory, population: Lectures at the Collège de France, 1977–78*. Palgrave Macmillan.

Friedmann, J. (1992). The past in the future: History and the politics of identity. *American Anthropologist*, *94*(4), 837–859.

Fukuyama, F. (2014). *Political order and political decay: From the Industrial Revolution to the globalization of democracy*. Macmillan.

Gay, P. (1954). The Enlightenment in the history of political theory. *Political Science Quarterly*, *69*(3), 374–389. https://doi.org/10.2307/2145276

Gellner, E. (1983). *Nations and nationalism*. Cornell University Press.

Ghani, A. & Lockhart, C. (2009). *Fixing failed states: A framework for rebuilding a fractured world.* Oxford University Press.

Graeber, D. & Wengrow, D. (2021). *The dawn of everything: A new history of humanity.* Penguin UK.

Greif, A. (2006). *Institutions and the path to the modern economy: Lessons from medieval trade.* Cambridge University Press.

Gruezmacher, M. & Van Assche, K. (2014). The evolution of socio-ecological systems: Changing palm species management in the Colombian Amazon as an indicator of ecological and institutional change. *Journal of Environmental Planning and Management*, 1–22. https://doi.org/10.1080/09640568.2014.973480

Gunder, M., Madanipour, A. & Watson, V. (2017). *The Routledge handbook of planning theory.* Routledge.

Held, D. (1996). *Models of democracy* (2nd edn.). Polity.

Held, D. (1999). *Global transformations: Politics, economics and culture.* Stanford University Press.

Helmke, G. & Levitsky, S. (2004). Informal institutions and comparative politics: A research agenda. *Perspectives on Politics*, *2*(04), 725–740. https://doi.org/doi:10.1017/S1537592704040472

Hinchman, L. P. & Hinchman, S. (1997). *Memory, identity, community: The idea of narrative in the human sciences.* SUNY Press.

Jentoft, S. (2007). Limits of governability: Institutional implications for fisheries and coastal governance. *Marine Policy*, *31*(4), 360–370. https://doi.org/10.1016/j.marpol.2006.11.003

Jessop, B. (2002). Governance and meta-governance in the face of complexity: On the roles of requisite variety, reflexive observation, and romantic irony in participatory governance. In H. Heinelt, P. Getimis, G. Kafkalas, R. Smith & E. Swyngedouw (eds.), *Participatory governance in multi-level context: Concepts and experience* (pp. 33–58). VS Verlag für Sozialwissenschaften. https://doi.org/10.1007/978-3-663-11005-7_2

Jordan, A., Huitema, D., Hildén, M., Van Asselt, H., Rayner, T. J., Schoenefeld, J. J., Tosun, J., Forster, J. & Boasson, E. L. (2015). Emergence of polycentric climate governance and its future prospects. *Nature Climate Change*, *5*(11), 977–982.

Jordan, A., Wurzel, R. K. W. & Zito, A. (2005). The rise of 'new' policy instruments in comparative perspective: Has governance eclipsed government? *Political Studies*, *53*(3), 477–496.

Klijn, E.-H. (2008). Governance and governance networks in Europe. *Public Management Review*, *10*(4), 505–525. https://doi.org/10.1080/14719030802263954

Koch, L., Gorris, P. & Pahl-Wostl, C. (2021). Narratives, narrations and social structure in environmental governance. *Global Environmental Change*, *69*, 102317. https://doi.org/10.1016/j.gloenvcha.2021.102317

Ledeneva, A. (2006). *How Russia really works. The informal practices that shaped post-Soviet politics and business.* Cornell University Press.

Levy, C. & Roseman, M. (2001). *Three postwar eras in comparison: Western Europe 1918–1945–1989.* Springer.

Luhmann, N. (1990). *Political theory in the welfare state.* Mouton de Gruyter.

Luhmann, N. (1995). *Social systems.* Stanford University Press.

Luhmann, N. (2018). *Organization and decision.* Cambridge University Press.

Machiavelli, N. (1996). Il principe. In D. Wootton (ed.), *Modern political thought: Readings from Machiavelli to Nietzsche.* (pp. 6–57). Hackett.

Martines, L. (1983). *Power and imagination: City-states in Renaissance Italy* (1st edn.). Penguin.

Mazzuca, S. & Robinson, J. A. (2009). Political conflict and power sharing in the origins of modern Colombia. *Hispanic American Historical Review, 89*(2), 285–321. https://doi.org/10.1215/00182168-2008-085

North, D. C. (2005). *Understanding the process of economic change.* Princeton University Press.

Partelow, S., Schlüter, A., Armitage, D., Bavinck, M., Carlisle, K., Gruby, R. L., Hornidge, A.-K., Le Tissier, M., Pittman, J. B., Song, A. M., Sousa, L. P., Văidianu, N. & Van Assche, K. (2020). Environmental governance theories: A review and application to coastal systems. *Ecology and Society, 25*(4). https://doi.org/10.5751/ES-12067-250419

Pierre, J. & Peters, B. G. (2000a). *Governance, politics, and the state.* Macmillan.

Pierre, J. & Peters, B. G. (2000b). *Governance, politics, and the state.* Macmillan.

Rhodes, R. A. W. (1997). *Understanding governance. Policy networks, governance, reflexivity and accountability.* Open University Press.

Sand, I.-J. (2008). The interaction of society, politics and law: The legal and communicative theories of Habermas, Luhmann and Teubner. *Scandinavian Studies in Law, 53*, 45–75.

Schmid, N., Beaton, C., Kern, F., McCulloch, N., Sugathan, A. & Urpelainen, J. (2021). Elite vs. mass politics of sustainability transitions. *Environmental Innovation and Societal Transitions, 41*, 67–70. https://doi.org/10.1016/j.eist.2021.09.014

Scott, J. C. (1998). *Seeing like a state: How certain schemes to improve the human condition have failed.* Yale University Press.

Seabright, P. (2010). *The company of strangers: A natural history of economic life.* Princeton University Press.

Seidl, D. & Becker, K. H. (2006). Organizations as distinction generating and processing systems: Niklas Luhmann's contribution to organization studies. *Organization, 13*(1), 9–35. https://doi.org/10.1177/1350508406059635

Somer, M. (2001). Cascades of ethnic polarization: Lessons from Yugoslavia. *The ANNALS of the American Academy of Political and Social Science, 573*(1), 127–151. https://doi.org/10.1177/000271620157300107

Stoker, G. (1998). Governance as theory: Five propositions. *International Social Science Journal, 50*(155), 17–28.

Taub, R. P. (2022). *Bureaucrats under stress: Administrators and administration in an Indian state.* University of California Press.

Trott, A. M. (2013). *Aristotle on the nature of community.* Cambridge University Press.

Turner, S. P. (2013). *The politics of expertise.* Routledge.

Valentinov, V., Roth, S. & Will, M. G. (2019). Stakeholder theory: A Luhmannian perspective. *Administration & Society, 51*(5), 826–849. https://doi.org/10.1177/0095399718789076

Van Assche, K., Beunen, R. & Duineveld, M. (2014a). *Evolutionary governance theory: An introduction.* Springer.

Van Assche, K., Beunen, R. & Duineveld, M. (2014b). Formal/informal dialectics and the self-transformation of spatial planning systems: An exploration. *Administration & Society, 46*(6), 654–683. https://doi.org/10.1177/0095399712469194

Van Assche, K., Beunen, R. & Duineveld, M. (2016). Citizens, leaders and the common good in a world of necessity and scarcity: Machiavelli's lessons for community-based natural resource management. *Ethics, Policy & Environment, 19*(1), 19–36.

Van Assche, K., Duineveld, M., Gruezmacher, M. & Beunen, R. (2021). Steering as path creation: Leadership and the art of managing dependencies and reality effects. *Politics and Governance*, *9*(2), 369–380. https://doi.org/10.17645/pag.v9i2.4027

Van Assche, K., Gruezmacher, M., Lochner, M. & Perez-Sindin, X. (2023). *Resource communities: Past legacies and future pathways* (1st edn.). https://www.routledge.com/ Resource -Communities -Past -Legacies -and -Future -Pathways/ Assche -Gruezmacher-Marais-Sindin/p/book/9781032364728

Van Assche, K., Valentinov, V. & Verschraegen, G. (2021). Adaptive governance: Learning from what organizations do and managing the role they play. *Kybernetes*, *51*(5), 1738–1758. https://doi.org/10.1108/K-11-2020-0759

Van Assche, K., Van Biesebroeck, J. & Holm, J. (2013). Governing the ice. Ice fishing villages on Lake Mille Lacs and the creation of environmental governance institutions. *Journal of Environmental Planning and Management*, 1–24. https://doi.org/10.1080/09640568.2013.787054

Weber, M. (1895). *Der Nationalstaat und die Volkswirtschaftspolitik: Akademische Antrittsrede*. Freiburg.

Wildavsky, A. (2005). Administration without hierarchy? Bureaucracy without authority? In *Cultural Analysis*. Routledge.

Will, M. G., Roth, S. & Valentinov, V. (2018). From nonprofit diversity to organizational multifunctionality: A systems-theoretical proposal. *Administration & Society*, *50*(7), 1015–1036. https://doi.org/10.1177/0095399717728093

Woods, P. (2004). Democratic leadership: Drawing distinctions with distributed leadership. *International Journal of Leadership in Education*, *7*(1), 3–26. https://doi.org/10.1080/1360312032000154522

Yashar, D. J. (2007). Resistance and identity politics in an age of globalization. *The ANNALS of the American Academy of Political and Social Science*, *610*(1), 160–181. https://doi.org/10.1177/0002716206297960

Young, O. R. (1991). Political leadership and regime formation: On the development of institutions in international society. *International Organization*, 281–308.

Young, O. R. (1997). *Global governance: Drawing insights from the environmental experience*. The MIT Press.

3. Basic concepts for transition mapping: institutions

TYPES

Institution is a key concept in much of the literature on governance and related fields such as public policy, development studies and economics. The concept is defined and understood in many different ways that can be more or less specific. Douglass North defines institutions as 'the humanly devised constraints that structure political, economic, and social interaction' (North, 1991, p. 97). Elinor Ostrom refers to 'the prescriptions that humans use to organize all forms of repetitive and structured interactions including those within families, neighborhoods, markets, firms, sports leagues, churches, private associations, and governments at all scales' (Ostrom, 2005, p 3).

Institutions for us are tools of coordination. They function in governance, to coordinate actors, as well as actors and other institutions, and they play a role in the community, where they represent what is collectively binding, coordinate action in that direction, including enforcement (Eggertsson, 2005; North, 1990; Ostrom, 1990). Institutions we consider, following institutional economics, as the 'rules of the game,' but, in a move parallel to the one made by Douglass North in his later works, we expand this 'game' beyond economic transactions, to include potentially all social interactions (D. C. North, 1990, 2005). As we noticed when considering governance domains and governability, this is a potentiality, as in practice each community develops its own selectivity in what is governed and not, what is a matter of collectively binding decisions and what not.

Institutions are intended to organize society, the community, but in order to do so the subsystem of governance has to be organized itself. A form of coordination in governance is necessary to make the production and use of institutions predictable both in governance and in the community, where the institutions need to be implemented. Governance thus both uses and produces institutions, and it uses both old and new institutions, produced by the current and by previous configurations. This perspective on institutions includes both formal and informal institutions, varying between laws, policies or property rights, to sanctions, custom or codes of conduct (North, 1991; Ostrom, 2005;

Van Assche et al., 2014b), a distinction we will come back to later in this chapter.

We add one additional rather basic distinction, between decision and institution. A decision can be taken in governance, yet not all decisions translate into rules. A government can decide on the construction of a dam, a decision which is supposed to bind the collective, in the sense that, once taken, all actors in governance and all citizens are supposed to follow that course of action. The same government can also articulate a rule prohibiting the construction of dams, which would be an institution, yet in our view a simple one, comparable to the rules governing the interpretation of traffic lights. Institutions, even simple ones, in other words, require *interpretation* in order to be implementable, and to make an aspect of life governable (Griffiths, 2003). This point will prove important in later chapters.

We already encountered more complex forms of institutions, and distinguished *policies, plans and laws.* The level of complexity of institutions can differ and complex institutions can incorporate or coordinate the use of other institutions. Law can for example oblige the formulation of plans or monitoring schemes, or prescribe assessment procedures in which other laws need to be considered as well (Luhmann et al., 2004). Institutions, in governance, can thus form complex configurations in complex patterns of layering. A complex institution, such as a comprehensive plan or an ambitious energy transition policy, can require for its implementation and even articulation a set of other institutions that then require further layers of institutions to make them operable.

The difference between policies, laws and plans is a contingent one, meaning that these categories themselves emerged in histories which could have been different, and that their relative importance and conditions of use are also contingent. Indeed, some nations rely on laws where others would use policies and plans; some would use plans where others would use policies, and the scope and ambitions levels of plans deemed acceptable will also differ on the nature and evolution of a governance configuration.

Institutions and institutional configurations evolve (Greif, 2014; Ostrom, 2014; Thelen, 2004; Van Assche et al., 2014a) and institutions can be created, maintained and disrupted in many ways (Beunen & Patterson, 2016; Lawrence et al., 2009). In order to understand the roles, potential roles and potential transformation of one institution, the whole configuration or, if one prefers, network of institutions has to be considered. Each configuration of institutions over time develops its own *modes and rules of self-transformation,* whereby conscious rules are not the only guiding principles. In democracies, rules to change the rules are essential, core to the most general definition of democracy, but those rules are not enough to understand the actual self-transformation of the governance system (Albert & Hilkermeier, 2004). We can add that in democracies, *rules to correct rules* need to function in order for the system to function, akin to Machiavelli's procedures of complaint and accusation (McCormick, 2006).

A third type we can introduce here are the rules that uphold the others, not in a functional sense but in the sense of representing their legitimacy. Institutions can be upheld by others for different reasons, we now know: for implementation, codifying, detailing, for legitimacy, and towards transformation.

In most states, the triad of policies, plans and laws developed, and each type can be considered a specialization, enabling further differentiation, and enabling the different functions mentioned above. Laws are articulated with greater difficulty, and more slowly, than the others, yet their implementation and enforcement in many contexts is easier. Laws can legitimize other laws and other institutions, but also function as implementation devices for policies and plans (Rosenfeld, 2000). Plans tend to spatialize policies, and spatial plans can serve as tools to integrate other institutions, with reference to one spatial domain. Laws do not only render other institutions legitimate (with spatial planning requiring enabling legislation in most polities), or implementable (supporting harder rules guiding action), but they also, purposefully, slow down the self-transformation of the governance system, by imposing strict conditions for their articulation, and for allowable relations with other laws (respecting hierarchies of laws and courts, non-contradiction principles, due process ideas, etc.) (Cosens et al., 2017; Luhmann, 2004).

Institutions are contingent, and that means that they *emerge* in a process that can take different directions. As institutions rely on others for their functioning in governance, we can speak of *co-evolution* of institutions. This co-evolution leads to *path dependencies*, meaning that the production, implementation and combination of institutions in a governance system at moment B cannot be understood without reference to moment A, and that a proposed change for moment C has to take into account the existing set of institutions, their relations and principles of self-transformation.

Institutions emerge and evolve as a community evolves, focusing on different activities, changing its values, guiding distinctions and narratives, preferred modes of ordering society (Ellickson, 1991; Greif, 2006; North et al., 2009). Institutions emerge *as actors emerge*, each with goals and needs, often with conflicts, and this introduces a second aspect of co-evolution: actors and institutions co-evolve. They shape each other over time. Institutions emerge, as we know, when other institutions emerge, which require detailing, implementation, translation, coordination. The proliferation of institutions in a community leads to a need for *policy coordination and integration* (Van Assche et al., 2019, 2021). Otherwise, contradictions, lost opportunities and opportunities for abuse will occur.

Once a community, or at least the actors in its governance system, becomes fully familiarized with the potential of complex institutions to organize society, to structure collective action as well as individual action, the level of ambition may grow, and so will the interest in articulation binding *visions* for the community, beyond one topic or domain (Beck et al., 2021; Haahr & Walters, 2004; Van Assche et al., 2021). Such ambition and such visions generate a further need for policy integration, and one can observe here a process of imbricated positive feedback loops which is sometimes described as the natural tendency of bureaucracies to proliferate, but which in our view can better be understood as a self-reinforcing tendency in governance to deal with ever more topics and domains (Crozier, 2009; Luhmann, 2018). This tendency can be understood as a learning process, where new tools lead to new applications and to more tools. It can also be described as a trust-building process, where trust in governance to structure action and guide the community on more topics becomes acceptable. It can also be seen as a process involving logical and practical necessity, as the proliferation of institutions comes with side effects, with imperfections discovered during implementation and with the need to link to and respond to other institutions, actors and societal demands. Thus, a *configuration* of institutions emerges that starts to reproduce itself according to its own logic, whereby the growing complexity and multiplicity of institutions, a process of divergence, triggers a call and a need for convergence, for coordination of what was just fragmented (Caiden & Wildavsky, 1980; Greenwood et al., 1975).

The form such coordination and convergence can take hinges on the pattern of policy domains and topics, the divisions between governmental actors, their patterns of collaboration and competition, and their hierarchies and power relations. How policy coordination, and its more advanced form, policy integration, can work depends on the design of the whole governance system (Candel & Biesbroek, 2016; Stead & Meijers, 2009; Van Assche & Djanibekov, 2012). Each feature of the system (and we are not done with uncovering those features) can contribute to the difficulty or ease of policy integration. Features of the associated actors play a role, of the institutions and their relations with other institutions, of ideology, knowledge and expertise, which can be combined easily or not.

A policy domain can crystallize, and within that a theme, a series of connected topics, a set of actors, or a configuration of institutions. More complex institutions slowly form because coordinating actors, actions, institutions *first had to come into existence.* New specialized entities, tools, activities, can be relatively new, and the need for and options for their coordination can be unclear at first: Can we handle this with our current tools? Do we need to recombine, integrate them in a different manner? Or do we require new actors or new institutions to govern what is now requiring governance? The increasing complexity of a governance configuration, which can happen in lockstep with increasing complexity in society, thus produces a need for more and new governance tools and for continuing modification (Berkes et al., 2008; Chaffin & Gunderson, 2016; de Roo et al., 2012). An increasing need for policy coordination and integration is the result of new boundaries being introduced first, not only between new specialized departments, but also between forms of knowledge, between types of institutions. As the formation of boundaries and their entities occurs in contingent patterns, the options for integration, for crossing boundaries, are marked by contingency as well (Brans & Rossbach, 1997).

INSTITUTIONS AND STORIES

Institutions emerge out of specific understandings of the world and ideas about how that world should be organized. Conversely, these understandings and perspectives influence the interpretation and use of institutions. North, for example, clearly links the processes of institutional change to the ways humans interpret their environment, bringing more attention to the belief systems within communities (North, 2005). Elinor Ostrom also refers to these belief systems in order to understand how people make sense of institutions (Ostrom, 1990, 2005). Processes of interpretation and meaning making are thus clearly relevant to the understanding of institutions and institutional change. Complex institutions can work because they are linked to other institutions, and we can easily deduce that this complexity can also lead to obstruction, intentional reinterpretation, ignoring and forms of abuse. Yet complex institutions can also work because they can link to and integrate *knowledge*, including stories and forms of expertise. These links can help embedding institutions in the community and facilitate their implementation.

The links between institutions and knowledge can also make for myriad frictions and obstacles. The disputes about cattle ranging in California, explored by Robert C. Ellickson, can illustrate how opposing belief systems triggered different sets of institutions, different interpretations of existing rules, and via a series of conflicts an evolution of the configuration of institutions (Ellickson, 1991). In a similar way stories about a sustainability transition might drive proposals for the revision of current institutions or the introduction of new ones, which might trigger institutional change, but very likely also opposition via contrasting stories that emphasize the importance of current institutions and that aim to delay, disrupt or undermine the sustainability transitions. New perspectives on sustainability easily conflict with existing ones or with narratives that do not emphasize long-term perspectives on environmental quality, and the ways these perspectives have been embedded in formal and informal institutions. Institutional change is a process that is for a large part played out via stories and knowledge more in general and hence a link with learning is often made (Bettini et al., 2015; Czarniawska, 1998; Lawrence et al., 2009; Van Assche et al., 2013).

The links between institutions and knowledge means that institutions can look more attractive and can inspire more uses and users. A Green Deal, as for example promoted by the European Commission, is just as much a comprehensive story about societal change as it is a proposal for institutional change, while it is particularly the story that attracts most attention. Such a story can attract enthusiasm and support, but also competition, reinterpretation and resistance. More ambitious and comprehensive institutions can start to form their own micro-cosmos of knowledge, both in the analysis of the situation and in the solutions and interventions embodied by the policy or plan. Moreover, the diversity of people, interests and activities affected by institutional changes will almost certainly entail a redistribution of benefits from activities in the area, and a redistribution of benefits from government intervention. Ambitious institutions create winners and losers, can shift power positions and complex institutions, in terms of linkages to actors and institutions, and the diversity and technicality of knowledges involved, and they produce those shifts in often unpredictable and opaque manners.

In order to further the discussion on the complex connectivity causing and caused by institutions it is helpful to point out that an institution is both a thing (a tool of coordination which takes a form) and a context for other things (such as ideas, rules or values). Institutions can have a narrative character themselves (this happened, this is what we will do now), they can be underpinned by narratives implicit in the institution itself, and they can relate to and resonate with other narratives circulating in the community (Czarniawska, 1997, 2002). We will see that the connectivity between narratives in or under the institution and narratives held dearly or opposed strongly in the community can have strong implications for the fate of the institution (Wagenaar, 2011).

Some stories have immediate implications for the future, others not. Some come with a clear image of a desirable future, others less so. The presence of such narratives in governance, in the community, and the web of narrative relations which can structure or be structured by the relation between institution, governance configuration and community, will have consequences for the formation and implementation of long-term perspectives in governance. The same set of narratives can instil ideas about the possibilities and limits of governance, on what is governable and what not, hence to what extent governance can move a community towards a future defined in governance.

INSTITUTIONS AND TIME

Coming back to the different types of institutions and their functions in governance, we can now say that institutions *bind time* in specific ways. Binding time, a term common in systems theory, can have several applicable meanings. Time can appear in a particular structure, extending to a particular horizon (forwards and backwards), and it can appear as manageable, in a way that makes other things manageable (Pollitt, 2008; Thygesen, 2022). Laws, by slowing down governance, by encouraging reflexivity, on compatibility with laws and the grounding values embodied by them, can impose time horizons and structure time in the most stringent way, but also other types of institutions can have similar effects (Cosens et al., 2017). Institutions bind time in a cognitive and an organizational sense (Howlett & Goetz, 2014). In both senses, the binding is aspirational, meaning that it depends on the expectation that institutions do create expected effects and hence become *performative*. This means that the structuring effect helps in understanding and organizing time, but that this is a highly suggestive process, relying on persuasion. Whether the goals pursued by the institution can be achieved remains to be seen, even if other implementation tools and infrastructures are present.

The concept of performativity returns later, and so will another key idea which we will meet here already. The slowing down and stabilizing of governance by means of institutions, procedures and more generally the process of differentiation in governance, encourages stability, hence calculations by all actors in governance, and stabilizes expectation in society (Luhmann, 2004). Calculating options and courses of action becomes more realistic. While adaptation and adaptive governance at first sight seem to be weakened by such anchoring effects (through content of institutions, through slow procedures of adoption, implementation, contestation), the stability is also a precondition for adaptation, as it is a precondition for looking forwards and for steering in governance. Grand visions, such as strategies for sustainability transitions, cannot be easily and quickly adopted because of the deliberate anchoring in governance (Van Assche et al., 2021; Van Assche & Verschraegen, 2008). Yet, this anchoring contributes to checks and balances, while the capacity to look forwards and steer in a general direction, with implications for many topics and domains, features of the grand vision, becomes possible because of the same anchoring, and the concomitant stabilization of expectations. Such stabilization enables coordination, calculation, prediction. The creation of stable vantage points, through systems of institutions capable of binding time, creates the possibilities to hold a course, and to adapt (Esposito, 2012).

INFORMAL INSTITUTIONS

In our perspective, formal institutions are those *expected to guide interactions* (Van Assche et al., 2014b). Yet, alternatives to those institutions usually exist, and we call them informal institutions. Formal institutions are not always the written ones, yet in nation states and their bureaucracies, paper becomes necessary, and formality becomes a matter of paper trails and of formally adopted institutions. Paper becomes necessary when the state endorses one role, one form of coordination, and not another one, and wants everyone to remember this. The ascendancy of the nation state as the chief container of power in a larger community made it necessary, in a process of unification, clarification and memorization, to rely on formal institutions as policies, plans and laws (Bernstein, 2011; Peters & Peters, 2002). Once the state backs one institution and formalizes this by declaring on paper that this is so, the threat and promise of state powers tend to relegate alternative coordination mechanisms to the margins.

Informal institutions can survive for a long time, especially where strong local, ethnic or regional traditions exist, as is extensively shown by many studies all over the world (Ellickson, 1991; Ledeneva, 2006). Their deliberate adoption or transformation is difficult, as they are not always visible, and as it is not always clear who has the authority (de facto) to change them. What is possible is a deliberate opening of the formal system for selective informalities, which can then be recognized and formalized (Ramus et al., 2017). This is understandable, as many formal institutions were previously unwritten traditions or rules, and often one form of coordination among others. If informal institutions are formalized, they can acquire legitimacy in a larger community, and the process of formalization can open up possibilities to link and combine with other formal institutions, which can increase the capacity to manage societal complexity, and increase the complexity of the configuration itself in a more manageable manner. Formalization can have these effects because it entails elucidation and homogenization, engendering compatibility and manageability. While informal institutions cannot bind time the same way as formal institutions, a formalization process and connection to or integration in other formal institutions can open up this function. Informal institutions in the form of traditions can be enduring, and project a situation as stable for time eternal, yet the managed transformation of time horizons, the deliberate creation of new complex institutions which can guide a community for the longer term, is unlikely to happen based on informality alone (Greif, 1994, 2014).

Embeddings and Alternatives

Complex institutions tend to rely on informal institutions for their acceptance, implementation and enforcement. Plans work better if they align with community values (*informal as embedding*), and if the future which transpires in or is consciously pursued in the plan does not look too strange for the community it is supposed to serve (Beunen et al., 2022; Miranda & Lerner, 1995). Conversely, if new formalities ignore informalities close to the heart of many, this is likely to generate resistance, backlash and possibly counterstrategy.

At the same time, a multiplicity of coordination forms likely exists in the community. Alternatives for the officially sanctioned form of coordination thus always exist (*informal as alternative*) (Hayoz & Giordano, 2013; Helmke & Levitsky, 2004). The presence of alternatives or complements can be helpful for the implementation of the institution, or not. It can provide welcome *redundancy* in the system, embodying different ways to achieve a goal, to achieve coordination (Howlett, 2019; Kharrazi et al., 2020; Low et al., 2003). Old embeddings of formality can become alternatives to formality, while others vanish or languish once formality is imposed in some sense. The fate of the informal institutions hinges on the relation with formality, and the success of the formal institution itself. If it does not work, or if it leaves large gaps, where terrain remains de facto ungoverned, or partial goals are not really pursued, this leaves large spaces for informality, as well as for processes of formalization (Innis & van Assche, 2022; Van Assche, 2013).

Adopting *new* formal institutions can best be informed by both embeddings and alternatives. If actors adopting a new formal institution are aware of the presence of alternatives and embeddings, of their effects, their pros and cons, then a conscious decision becomes possible with regards to the preferable relation between formal and informal. Informal institutions (just as local knowledge) can represent a public good, but not necessarily. They can be associated with unwanted informal actors, or unwanted powers of formal actors, while elsewhere they can reinforce questionable ethnic divisions or undesirable forms of patronage and inequality (Casson et al., 2010).

In Bogotá, Colombia, a large city, for many years people living in poverty searched the trash for recyclables. At some point the municipal government opted to formalize and regulate their activities, provided uniforms, gloves, carts, and thus in a short time and with a small amount of investment established the city's first recycling system which later evolved its own policies and regulations.

Dead Institutions

Dead institutions are like zombie actors, but more numerous. They are formal institutions that lost teeth. They were not implemented or enforced for a while, and as actual coordination moved in a different direction, using different tools, inserting the old institution in a new form of coordination proved hard (Van Assche et al., 2014a). It is also possible that the formal institution never really worked, that it had little effect, and inspired little trust, or that legitimacy was questioned, or the choice of goals and direction. Dead institutions can be dead on arrival because backlash immediately followed their adoption, without however leading to an official repeal. They can be dead, even if initial support was strong, because resources were lacking and implementation was so slow that the conditions changed, so slow also that the speed itself became a sign of failure. Lack of implementation then became a symbol for poor quality or the inappropriateness of the ideas and inefficacy of the coordination tools (Pressman & Wildavsky, 1979).

Simple rules can become dead institutions. This can happen if their enforcement is neglected or if there is little support for them (Mathur, 2016). Yet becoming a dead institution happens more easily to complex plans or policies. If coordination stops using that institution, it is not easy to restore it, as coordination might have collapsed or taken a different course, with few actors considering the now dead institution as a legitimate and functional tool of coordination. If connectivity with actors and other institutions is lost, trust is gone, and resources will move elsewhere. Coordination, on its new course, will revolve around different ideas, rules, possibly actors. It can be noted that the death of one institution might trigger the creation of a new one, not only a resorting to existing informality, and it might cause the organization of a new actor coalition, or the mobilization of new resources around a new goal (not only a new route to the old goal).

Dead institutions can be a problem, but they can also be useful. They can be revived, and that can be positive or negative for governance and for sustainability transitions (Van Assche et al., 2019). The fact that its binding character was not officially lost makes it possible to bring it back to life, although the new context will make for new effects. One can argue that a revival will only work when a powerful (coalition of) actor(s) sees a use in it, and if they are able to connect the revenant to current modes of coordination. Which might require a modification of the dead institution. The revival might be positive when new uses for the old tool became visible over time, or when the relevance of the initial goal finally became clear. Another reason for the sudden revival of a dead institution is the survival of supporting actors, and the opening up of a window of opportunity (due to political shifts, shifting resource flows, changing priorities at higher levels, or failure of alternative policies).

Dead institutions can contribute to the archive of policy options, to the positive redundancy discussed earlier. Ending up on a shelf is not such a bad thing if people remember there is a shelf, and if current problems are regularly checked against the catalogue of tools on and off the shelf. The problem of lacking cohesion is often not a problem, precisely because the dead institution is dead, because it is not integrated in domains of decision-making, not connected to other institutions that are implemented, and that are partly contradictory with the returning institution (Hartley & Howlett, 2021; Lavie et al., 2010; Seo & Creed, 2002). Contradictions can resolve themselves, and even if this is not the case they can be buffered, as when the two seemingly conflicting institutions operate without real connectivity or competition (in different domains, for different topics and occasions) (Eisenstadt, 1958). What can be problematic is that dead institutions can increase complexity and ambiguity and could be used to weaken more novel and adapted ones.

Formal/Informal Configurations

Informal institutions can have positive and negative effects in governance; yet entirely relying on formal institutions is not realistic, as coordination is needed in practice even where formal institutions do not exist, or do not work. Formal institutions, moreover, especially complex ones, need an anchoring in a landscape of informality, to create support and detailed implementation and enforcement options (Gel'man, 2004; Grzymala-Busse, 2010; Helmke & Levitsky, 2004; Hillier, 2000; Lauth, 2000; Ledeneva, 2006). Rather than assessing the value of formal or informal institutions separately, we argue that it is best to look at the configuration of formal and informal institutions in a community, and then assess the functionality of that configuration as a whole. When we speak of a configuration, we mean that one side can only be understood in reference to the other, that the two sides co-evolve, and that the whole can be considered a unity, with its own features, behavior and evolutionary path.

Informal institutions, as observed by Helmke and Levitsky (Helmke & Levitsky, 2004) and others, can indeed have a range of effects on the functioning of formal institutions, while formal and informal institutions respond to each other. The domain available for informality has a dynamic boundary with formality, while formal institutions can be complemented, undermined, reinforced, replaced by informal ones. We believe, in line with political anthropology, that more relations are possible, and can be observed easily. The effect of one on the other, of informal on formal, can be noticed only much later, further away, in space, domain or topic (Miranda & Lerner, 1995). The same applies to the interplay between formal institutions, where synergies or conflicts, or simple interactions in effects, between institutions can often be understood much later, and elsewhere. Hence our argument that we have to understand formal/informal as a unity which functions in a unique way in each community, with unique effects, which have to be assessed (Van Assche, 2013). The co-evolution of formal and informal, in adaptation to changing environments, accounts for this unique character, while the functioning of the formal/informal configuration has to be judged against its effects on an environment, on the community.

In such an assessment of the formal/informal configurations, a substantial part of an assessment of 'good governance' (see later), we distinguish three basic criteria:

• Does it deliver the goods?

- Does it maintain the pattern of specialization and differentiation?
- Does it allow for structured self-transformation?

These criteria distil our most basic perspective on good governance, and the sources of that perspective are diverse, yet the existence of public or common goods is, indeed, a commonplace in the literatures on politics, policy and administration, on community development and planning, and in geography and anthropology, while the second and third criteria signal a respect for the systems theory of Niklas Luhmann, whose political theory operates on the same premises (Luhmann, 1990, 1995). We also refer once more to Niccolò Machiavelli, who underlined the first and third points as crucial for the quality and survival of a polity, and who highlighted the benefits of differentiation for adaptive governance (Machiavelli et al., 1997).

These three points do not suffice for a full assessment of 'good governance' in a particular context, and the three questions will sprout new ones. The question of public goods cannot be answered so easily, as perfect agreement on a set of public goods and goals might be aspirational, and as those goods can shift shape while we speak. Similarly, the presence of rules to change the rules does not guarantee structured self-transformation, and the idea of 'structure' here can mean peaceful or uneventful but can also positively include a measure of dissensus and even conflict. Furthermore, a pattern of differentiation and specialization might be highly intricate and evolved, yet susceptible to critique on several grounds – moral, economic, political and simply practical. We develop the idea of good governance later, but for now we emphasize that a particular position for informal institutions cannot be taken a priori.

SITES AND ARENAS

Decisions are not always clear. This can be taken to mean that the content of the decision is not entirely clear for the observers of the decision, or even the deciders, and it can mean, more radically, that it is often not clear whether a decision was taken at all (Eggertsson, 2005; Hulliung, 1983). Many things can happen without a real decision, and many things in governance happen without a communication that can be clearly labeled as a decision. Decisions and their content might be more clearly traced a posteriori. The lack of clarity can stem from the fact that not all decisions are taken according to the specified criteria in a governance system, nor from their suboptimal or misdirected communication afterwards (Van Assche et al., 2014a). There is the possibility that the makers of the decision did not single out the communicative event as a decision, rather as a part of everyday business, or something that happened, or even something that was not observed. Another reason is that the *site* of decision-making might not be the one expected for a decision in governance. Not all decisions take place in a recognized governance arena, and not everything decided in that arena is ultimately recognized as a decision, as not all procedures might have been followed, and as power relations in the arena at the moment might not have reflected what happened elsewhere (Van Assche et al., 2020).

The couplings between site, arena and decision in governance are, as with many other things in governance, contingent. Sites of decision-making might be loosely coupled with each other, and loosely coupled with the rest of the governance system (Benz & Eberlein, 1999). Sites might be prescribed in governance, or not, or only for a subset of decisions. While decisions of a certain kind might be expected to take place in a predefined site, or not (Van Assche et al., 2020). Ad hoc decisions might still be recognized as decisions, or they might be functioning as decisions, without official recognition as such; they can still lead to other decisions which do fit the formal criteria of decision-making, and these traces, legacies, can enable the observer to recognize a key decision a posteriori. Key decisions which are not taken according to the formal procedures can indirectly lead to formal institutions, yet also to informal institutions which can be influential in governance. Here, one can note that informality is not the same as marginality, and that elite networks, key formal actors, can coordinate through the use and production of informal institutions which thus stand a better chance to steer the use of formal institutions. Hence, the idea that informality extends to rules to interpret the rules, select the rules, break the rules, ignore them, and hence the idea that collectives can be governed by means of people who play both formal and informal roles, utilizing both formal and informal institutions.

A site of decision-making can be *a place, a moment, or an organization.* It can literally be a place, e.g. a governmental building, a building with strong civic significance or a movable place, where a stable set of actors meet on a regular basis. The time can be important, as decision-makers can only meet on specific moments, either on a regular basis, think of monthly meetings of a parliament or dedicated times for voting on problems, but it can also be at moments that are specifically planned to negotiate and agree on new institutions, such as the conventions of the United Nations. The site can require all three together (place, time, organization), or can suffice with two to function as a site. Decisions can be taken somewhere else, but should be presented at a recognized site, receive the stamp of approval, and henceforth be presented as taken at that site (Ahrne et al., 2016; Crespy et al., 2007).

Decision-making sites can be specific for one decision domain, even a topic, or they can accommodate decision-making for a community. They can be restricted to the political domain, with sites and actors clearly linked to processes of election, representation more generally, and participation, or sites can be located additionally in the sphere of administration, not merely executing or informing decisions. They can be located at the interface of political and other forms of organization, where elected officials and representatives of non-state organizations, for profit and non-for-profit, deliberate on appropriate forms of regulation (as in civil society models of democracy). In highly participatory systems of governance, sites can be more diverse and open (Fischer, 2012). Each site can represent a unique balancing of participation and representation and a different kind of encounter, a unique power relation, between those elected by people and (some of) the people themselves (Purdy, 2012). This is, of course, another description of the phenomenon of governance, as in practice who is involved in decision-making will be associated with the recognized sites of decision-making, which in turn reflect basic assumptions on who should be involved.

Some domains of governance have a clearly recognizable set of sites, others not. This can include a clearly defined arena. Arenas for us are institutionalized sites of decision-making, formal or informal. As we know, informal arenas cannot lead directly to formal decisions (Meadowcroft, 2007). Arenas are most likely combining different features of sites: they impose their own temporality, membership and place. The relation is stable, or assumed stable, and the decisions taken can take on the character of formal institutions more directly (possibly further stamps of approval are required, and a legal green light). Arenas can be established by decree, that is, at once, by a higher power, or they can evolve, and slowly acquire their stable set of relations.

Actors can be arenas, and this complex identity is useful for the functioning of governance, for the linking of levels of governance and the linking of governance and community (Crespy et al., 2007; Duit et al., 2010). A municipality can act, and so can a chamber of commerce, a company or an NGO, while each have an internal complexity which has aspects of competition, of diverse and dissonant constituent parts (Krehbiel, 1918). A municipality is an arena in the sense literal to us, that is, a governance arena, as it produces collectively binding decisions and operates on a combination of participation and representation. From a micro-perspective, the municipality can look like a political arena, with a focus on internal decision-making, histories of competition and collaboration between actors making up the municipality.

In some places, the arena is entirely political, elected, elsewhere, and more common, it is a combination of administrative, political and civic actors which play a role in the arena (Schatzki, 2014). If we zoom out, however, and adopt a macro-perspective, we can observe a different logic at play, a different environment, with new arenas becoming visible at higher levels of governance. At that macro-scale, the municipality performs a unity of voice, purpose and identity, which is not visible from the micro-perspective. We know that only in some cases unity is consciously decided upon, with leadership representing the municipality elsewhere and carefully constructing positions and narratives which are entirely grounded in the decision-making visible in the micro-perspective. Often, this is not the case, and 'the municipality' functions as a unity under more conditions, through more creative or individualist leadership, through decisions that need to be taken without continuous scrutiny by the micro-arena, in an unfolding role the municipality *has* to play, or through reactions of others who ascribe a unity of voice to it (Crespy et al., 2007; Healey, 2006).

The appearance of the municipality as arena or as actor does not hinge entirely on scale or perspective; it is also a matter of occasion. Under defined circumstances, a municipality can emphasize its unity, or be perceived more easily as unity, as an actor trying to act. The occasions on which this happened are not always the moments where the local government must deal with higher-level or neighboring government or polities (Crespy et al., 2007; Diduck, 2010; Hooghe & Marks, 2001). They can also be moments where internal unity has to be emphasized: we, the municipality, as the embodiment of the people, or, where their own citizens have to be addressed in one clear voice, possibly a voice of authority, of memory and shared values. Certain topics warranting more certainty, steering or gravitas can trigger the appearance of the voice of unity, the appearance of the collective as actor, even in dealing with the collective itself, the collective from which it emanated (Duit et al., 2010; Fischer, 2012). This is only possible because of the combination of participation and representation, where a distance between citizens and their representatives is created, yet it can also occur in highly participatory systems, when the community reminds itself, in participatory arenas, of the values it might have forgotten, or the decisions that might have undermined itself.

Evolutionary processes are at work once again. Groups can become actors which engender arenas; sites can become arenas, and arenas can be reduced to actors. Organizations can lose power and status as arenas, and groups can splinter into a set of competing organizations which never agree on an arena to come to collectively binding decisions. If there is no starting point in a shared recognition of a form of co-existence, of a community in the most basic sense, and if the identities and perspectives of other actors are dismissed, then the formation of stable arenas, and of governance as such, is unlikely.

Procedures

Procedures are a specific kind of institution. They unfold the preparation, taking and implementation of decisions and institutions in time, by defining steps, conditionalities, time frames, or connectivity. Procedures can be formal or informal, and they are institutions insofar as they do not merely describe, but also prescribe: these are the steps that *have* to be taken to take a decision, assess the result of a plan, foster inclusion in a policy, bring the relevant expertise on board (Duit, 2015; Duit et al., 2010). Procedures thus play an important role in the binding of time in and through governance: time is structured, and segments of time are connected to knowledge, to other institutions, to selections of actors, to analyses of and interventions in the community. Procedures are thus prime tools to bind time, and this entails a linking of the worlds of governance and the community at large, where a hyper-structuring of governance can be considered a buttressing against the vicissitudes of life. In other words: over-structuring of time, place, knowledge, action through procedures helps to bolster an order which all know to be challenged once confronted with the real world of implementation. The suggestion of certainty and predictability can be performative, in the sense that the rhetoric and the appearance of structure *in governance* suggest that such structure and predictability in the world outside governance is possible (Feldman & Pentland, 2003).

Procedures do not only suggest simplicity, they also help in reality to process and reduce complexity. That complexity is both internal and external to governance. Complex governance systems come with great powers of observation and coordination, but also require a great amount of internal coordination, in order to make coordination of action in the community possible, and procedures are means to achieve this (Duhigg, 2012; Spillane, 2012). Niklas Luhmann speaks of the burden of administrations to manage their internal complexity, but also of the value of that complexity to produce refined maps and understandings of the world upon which it can act, as well as sophisticated tools to change that world (Luhmann, 1995). If procedures harden, and become immune to scrutiny, the realities upon which they are predicated might have changed, and new problems might be invisible for them.

Procedures enable the reproduction of organizations and governance configurations when facing both internal and external complexity (Duit et al., 2010). In times of crisis, procedures might keep governance and its organizations going, even when no ready answers are available, when the connection with the community is tenuous, or when even the basic observation of the situations is imperiled. Under such circumstances, mere survival of the configuration can take precedence over the quality of governance. At other times, lacking quality of governance can lead to a questioning of the configuration and its procedures, and a change in system. The replacement of political leadership, and even administrative leadership, however, does not necessarily bring about a change in procedures, as the procedural sources of rigidity might not be easily discerned, as some actors still identify with the old procedures, and because complex institutions require complex procedures for their formation, implementation and revision (Spillane, 2012). This means that the invention of truly different procedures is extremely difficult, as the current procedures, carrying a complex coordination task, evolved slowly. Even if they are not surviving or copied in their entirety, shorter chains of instructions, fragments of longer procedures become, consciously or unconsciously, models for others, under new leadership (Easterly, 2013).

Procedures regulate the application of other rules and the coordination of rules. They maintain the temporal, spatial and conceptual hierarchies in governance. They structure which place comes first, which form of knowledge, which question or problem, or which department. As such, procedures contribute to the process of making things governable, but they also interfere, at the same time, in power relations and patterns of inclusion and exclusion in governance and community (Duhigg, 2012). They create blind spots which proliferate when procedures proliferate, and they reduce flexibility when the production of certainty is more important than the quality of ongoing observation (and adaptation). Procedures thus help governance to reproduce itself, while fostering a tendency to reduce reflection, thinking, observation and adaptation. Long procedures furthermore are costly and slow, with the chance that the world moved on beyond the problems and opportunities assumed, the chance that the real-life coordination options available in the unfolding of the procedure are different from what was envisioned at the outset (Brunsson, 1989).

Procedures apply to the functioning of sites and arenas, while sites and arenas decide on procedures used, institutions used in the solution of problems. Procedures structure the functioning of administrative organizations, and the goal of the organization can be to monitor, implement or suggest procedures, rather than offering substantive arguments for courses of action. The governance system as a whole stabilizes itself procedurally, as the structure of actors and institutions (even if many institutions incorporate and foster other procedures) does not unfold itself over time without procedures (Brunsson, 1989; Duit et al., 2010; Van Assche et al., 2014a).

Multi-level Governance

Governance almost always exists in levels, and, often, these levels correspond with spatial scales. Levels and scales of governance crystallize over time, meaning that in most areas there was no initial design in which all levels and scales were defined (Benz & Eberlein, 1999; Hooghe & Marks, 2001). Such a starting point of evolution rarely exists, but even where it does seem to be real (as in radical reconstructions of the polity, as in the early USSR), evolution does start as soon as the institutional design is off the drawing board. Evolution here is once again co-evolution, in this specific situation between the different levels of governance. What happens at one level cannot be understood without reference to the others. What is possible at one scale is partly a result of the linkages with the other scales, with the degrees of freedom, of autonomy delineated at higher levels, but also the signals coming from lower levels of governance (Armitage, 2008; Van Assche et al., 2014a). Sometimes, levels can be created fast, as an initiative at the other level, or as an initiative stemming from the same level, but finding acceptance in the others. The levels continue to shape each other, formally and informally.

Competition between levels is possible, where each tries to expand its autonomy, its power, its resources, its perceived importance for citizens and for key non-governmental actors (Benz & Eberlein, 1999; Healey, 2006). Sometimes, higher levels have the power to get rid of, to simply abolish, lower levels of governance, but this rarely happens. Exceptions include situations where regional governance structures are dismantled, because neither local governance nor national governance find them useful, because they are seen as competitors, and when fewer direct links with voting or participating citizens exist. It has to be noted that some form of 'local' governance tends to emerge, even if formal municipalities are absent, and that a weakness of local governance tends to be compensated for by a more active and engaged regional level. What is local, and what needs to be organized locally, depends on time and place, and on the way different levels are articulated in governance (Crespy et al., 2007).

This also means that governance is rescaled regularly. Neo-liberal discourses and their global influence play a role, but so do many other factors. The powers between levels can shift, and so can the selections of topics and domains per level (Swyngedouw, 2000). Regional governance can slowly form in a comprehensive form, so that new futures for the region can be considered, starting from one governance domain or topic, say, transportation, water management or waste collection. In the other direction, levels of governance can be surviving in a hollowed-out form, making visioning impossible, except for one surviving policy domain (say, water governance). A perfect configuration of levels does not exist, as what works has to be adapted to the context and be realistically achievable from the starting point of the current structure of levels (Swyngedouw, 2004).

Rescaling takes place all the time and this rarely happens in simple one-directional processes. 'Downloading' of responsibilities to local governments, or to citizens in local participation processes, is certainly real, and linked to neo-liberal tendencies, but each polity, each multi-level system, where downloading happens will produce a unique version, with relations between levels never approaching a simple model of increasing local responsibilities and withdrawing governments (Kern & Bulkeley, 2009). Indeed, the neo-liberal emphasis on smaller, more accountable government, was often made for governmental actors focused on accounting rather than their substantive tasks, and in many cases did not shrink government, but shifted the emphasis of its activity to self-observation and controls. Downloading rarely happens without strings attached, and a rhetoric of localism or decentralization does not mean that this becomes reality for all governmental actors, for all tasks and domains (Douglas, 2005; Swyngedouw, 2005). Calls for greater autonomy of smaller organizational and territorial units do not mean that those units will be allowed to exercise that autonomy, especially when this goes against the ideology of the center. Moreover, processes of decentralization in one domain or topic of governance often coincide with the opposite, with reinvigorated centralization.

Processes whereby decision-making is taking place at international levels, such as the European Union or the United Nations, can add new levels to governance, but here too the interplay between processes at different levels is often more complex and more difficult to observe than often assumed (Kjaer, 2010). Implementation of international agreements is a process of interpretation and political struggle, whereby differences between countries not only influence the process of implementation at the national, regional of local levels, but also trigger reflections, discussions and further decision-making at the supranational level. This supranational level therefore becomes yet another site for strategizing, power-knowledge dynamics and institutional change, whereby most processes are directly or indirectly coupled with a multitude of processes going on at lower-level sites. And just like the municipality that shifts from an arena of decision-making to a seemingly unified actor once one zooms out to the macro-level, we can observe that at the international level countries can become actors. Countries in such a context are seemingly representing national interests, but in practice this will, in various ways, always be a representation of a diversity of actors, interests and perspectives, whereby some gain more attention and influence than others.

What makes the co-occurrences of levels more complex and interesting is that this can happen *while new scales form*, new forms of regional collaboration between municipalities, new governance structures at a larger scale for one topic, one service, dealing with one problem (Kjaer, 2010; Swyngedouw, 2004, 2005). This might not be recognized as shifts in multi-level governance, since the usually recognized levels are those of comprehensive governance, but they are. They will alter the evolution of the other levels, shift the processes of co-evolution between the levels; how much this is the case will again depend on the case. If a new regional structure for water governance appears, this will likely have effects for what municipalities can do for a range of topics, particularly if this community is situated in a very wet or dry area and if many activities there hinge around the presence/absence of water.

Once a level of governance is there, it is hard to erase. One reason can be the organizational form it takes, the stability of new arenas, the effectiveness of coordination in and around the new level. Once actors come into existence, or redefine themselves to operate at the new scale, organizations, arenas, memories, forms of coordination, this tends to keep the level in place. Similarly, if streams of resources shift because of and through the new level, if interests and discourse coalitions form which operate mostly at the level, it tends to stay in place. Each level will develop its own mode of relating to actors, discourses, resources; while entities at the same level might lead a very different existence. A region might reflect a social or cultural identity, or not; it might reflect a long history of coordination, or not (this theme will be developed later).

Arguments about ideal, more rational, more just, more efficient governance configurations must be taken with a pinch of salt. Not in the sense that improvements are not possible, but in the sense that those arguments can hide many others, and in the sense that no configuration is perfectly just, rational or efficient. Levels of governance rescale for a multitude of reasons, one of them being the prestige of 'innovation' itself, or the perceived forcefulness and acuity of those promoting or organizing the rescaling (Swyngedouw, 2005). Efficiency only makes sense when the functions of the different levels are reduced to a limited set of activities, products or services, rationality can be understood in many ways, and the same applies to justice, whereby shifts between levels can come with new patterns of inclusion and exclusions, but also new sensibilities for older forms of exclusion, inequality, transparency, democracy, expertise, etc.

ACTOR-INSTITUTION CONFIGURATIONS

Just like formal/informal configurations, actor/institution configurations function as one entity. As they emerge, a logic or mode of reproduction develops (North, 2005; Van Assche et al., 2014a). They reproduce and have to be assessed as a unity (see above). Does the configuration deliver the public goods? The level of differentiation? Mechanisms of self-transformation? Under 'public goods' we have to understand here more than 'services,' and more than public goals defined in policies and places, even more than the substance of a comprehensive strategy, which can be taken as a structured set of pursued public goods. One also has to think of the values embraced in the community and of the qualities of governance itself espoused.

Complexity can gradually increase: actors can be added, institutions can be produced and used, more forms of knowledge can be included in decision-making and administration, procedures can be developed, new domains can be delineated, or more topics can attract coordination in governance. Co-evolution is the key: actors co-evolve, and so do institutions, and actors and institutions (North, 1991, 2005). Actors and institutions shape each other to the extent that their change and behavior cannot be understood without reference to the others, and to the overarching system, the configuration. New actors can emerge in governance, or first in the community, or existing groups and organizations can be enrolled and start to function as an actor. We already discussed that the recognition as an actor is not always easy, and that the observation of an actor can also be difficult (Eggertsson, 2005). A group might have existed for a long time, and might not be interested in influencing governance, yet cultural shifts and a new form of organization of the group might give it a new lease on life, a renewed purpose and a new impact on governance, even when there is no participation visible through defined roles in committees, councils and other decision-making bodies or arenas (Steinmo et al., 1992).

Configurations, as we know, draw on and develop their embeddings in informal institutions. This process will be further analysed in several places in this book, as it is relevant and in fact central to the understanding of the embeddings of governance systems in communities, and the possible impacts of governance strategies on the community. Informal institutions can be sources of legitimacy, of trust and power, as well as drivers of efficiency and tools of adaptation and feedback. They can be linked to informal arenas, but even where this is not the case they can connect governance and community in more fine-grained ways (Greif, 2006; Steinmo et al., 1992). The interplay between formal and informal institutions discussed earlier means that new formal institutions can find support in old informal institutions (which might have inspired the new formality), but also that new informal institutions can form, in response to formal change and the resulting pressures and opportunities in the community (Van Assche, 2013).

Not all that happens in a community is coordinated through governance, and that is not a problem. Not all action is collective action, not all decisions have to be collectively binding. Problems arise when topics (and associated activities and resources) that are supposed to be governed by formally recognized configurations are in fact subjected to private governance, criminal governance or what we call *shadow governance.* This is a form of governance where several configurations co-exist that are not supposed to co-exist. This is a problem even if the alternative configuration does not represent private or factional interests, and where it might have emerged because the formal authority (and its governance configuration) neglected an area and was unable to bring order and public goods. It is a problem because the formal status of one configuration and its institutions are bound to hamper coordination in the area marked by shadow governance, and because the shadowy area is unable to connect to the center of power, its resources and its sources of legitimacy. In many developing countries, rural and natural areas and conflict regions tend to develop forms of shadow governance (Hope, 2009; Robinson et al., 2010). One additional reason is that actors might be involved that are not recognized by central government, for ideological or other reasons.

People can identify with an actor-institution configuration, see it as essential to the community, as part of its identity, the cause of its stability, prosperity, fairness, or other values held dearly. Configurations at the national level started to dominate in the 19th century, with the growing dominance of the nation state and its bureaucracies. Political parties developed at that time, as inheritors of older factional identities and interests. Parties, similarly to local governments, can function as actors, as an arena, as a carrier of ideology and producer of ideology. Parties are emergent actors that could have functioned outside democracy. The forming configuration of early democracies made it possible for them to function in a system of regulated competition and collaboration, with the implied promise of longer-term participation, and influence. They thus represent nodes of *knots* in governance, around which sets of tight couplings form. And such evolution becomes possible when roles in governance differentiate from each other and from the roles of the people and organizations (which are now actors) in daily life (Deeg & Jackson, 2007).

Configurations thus have identities and a specific mode of reproduction. Besides the formal mechanisms to change the configuration, informal rules exist, as well as constraints which cannot be described as rules but which are the result of the co-evolutions in the configuration. Some changes become hard to imagine or organize from within a configuration at one point in time, and these limitations are features of the mode of self-reproduction of the configuration, while that mode itself is never completely visible from within the system. Changing features or elements of a governance configuration can have implications or reverberations in many other parts of the system, because of the multiplicity of connections coming out of a history of co-evolutions (Deeg & Jackson, 2007). The effect of a change in one spot can be amplified because of the transformations it can cause elsewhere; a rejuvenated actor might reinterpret a coalition, its use of institutions, which leads to a new institution, changing distribution of resources, which creates resistance, which is the foundation for the formation of a new actor ...

Self-transformation in actor-institution configurations thus never stops, and within this self-transformation structures and elements shape each other in the process. We can call, referring again to Niklas Luhmann, the unity and identity of the process its unique *autopoiesis*. Autopoiesis, a term originally coined by biologists Varela and Maturana, is the form of self-organization typical for life, but also for social systems (such as governance systems) (Maturana & Varela, 1987). Autopoietic systems reproduce themselves based on their own elements, structures and procedures, so any change that is triggered by an environment, or deliberated internally, has to do so taking into account the nature of that autopoiesis. In governance, new structures can be designed, new procedures, new arenas, institutions, forms of policy integration, yet this only works if the old system is the starting point, taking into consideration its tools and abilities to change, its power relations, its set of actors and institutions, and its embedding in society (Brans & Rossbach, 1997; Paterson & Teubner, 1998). *Tabula rasa* institutional design almost never works, and where it did seem to work it tends to be accompanied by untold stories of lost institutional capacity and of governance breakdown. Any biography of Lenin, Stalin or the early USSR can serve as witnesses.

REFERENCES

Ahrne, G., Brunsson, N. & Seidl, D. (2016). Resurrecting organization by going beyond organizations. *European Management Journal*, *34*(2), 93–101. https://doi .org/10.1016/j.emj.2016.02.003

Albert, M. & Hilkermeier, L. (2004). *Observing international relations: Niklas Luhmann and world politics*. Routledge.

Armitage, D. (2008). Governance and the commons in a multi-level world. *International Journal of the Commons*, *2*(1), 7–32.

Beck, S., Jasanoff, S., Stirling, A. & Polzin, C. (2021). The governance of socio-technical transformations to sustainability. *Current Opinion in Environmental Sustainability*, *49*, 143–152. https://doi.org/10.1016/j.cosust.2021.04.010

Benz, A. & Eberlein, B. (1999). The Europeanization of regional policies: Patterns of multi-level governance. *Journal of European Public Policy*, *6*(2), 329–348. https:// doi.org/10.1080/135017699343748

Berkes, F., Colding, J. & Folke, C. (2008). *Navigating social-ecological systems: Building resilience for complexity and change*. Cambridge University Press.

Bernstein, S. (2011). Legitimacy in intergovernmental and non-state global governance. *Review of International Political Economy*, *18*(1), 17–51.

Bettini, Y., Brown, R. R. & de Haan, F. J. (2015). Exploring institutional adaptive capacity in practice: Examining water governance adaptation in Australia. *Ecology and Society*, *20*(1), 47.

Beunen, R. & Patterson, J. (2016). Analysing institutional change in environmental governance: Exploring the concept of 'institutional work'. *Journal of Environmental Planning and Management*, 1–18.

Beunen, R., Van Assche, K. & Gruezmacher, M. (2022). Evolutionary perspectives on environmental governance: Strategy and the co-construction of governance, community and environment. *Sustainabilty*, *Special Issue*, *14*(16), 1–18.

Brans, M. & Rossbach, S. (1997). The autopoiesis of administrative systems: Niklas Luhmann on public administration and public policy. *Public Administration*, *75*(3), 417–439.

Brunsson, N. (1989). Administrative reforms as routines. *Scandinavian Journal of Management*, *5*(3), 219–228. https://doi.org/10.1016/0956-5221(89)90028-6

Caiden, N. & Wildavsky, A. B. (1980). *Planning and budgeting in poor countries*. Transaction Publishers.

Candel, J. J. & Biesbroek, R. (2016). Toward a processual understanding of policy integration. *Policy Sciences*, *49*(3), 211–231.

Casson, M. C., Della Giusta, M. & Kambhampati, U. S. (2010). Formal and informal institutions and development. *World Development*, *38*(2), 137–141. https://doi.org/ 10.1016/j.worlddev.2009.10.008

Chaffin, B. C. & Gunderson, L. H. (2016). Emergence, institutionalization and renewal: Rhythms of adaptive governance in complex social-ecological systems. *Journal of Environmental Management*, *165*, 81–87. https://doi.org/10.1016/j.jenvman.2015 .09.003

Cosens, B. A., Craig, R. K., Hirsch, S. L., Arnold, C. A. (Tony), Benson, M. H., DeCaro, D. A., Garmestani, A. S., Gosnell, H., Ruhl, J. B. & Schlager, E. (2017). The role of law in adaptive governance. *Ecology and Society : A Journal of Integrative Science for Resilience and Sustainability*, *22*(1), 1–30. https://doi.org/10.5751/ES-08731-220130

Crespy, C., Heraud, J.-A. & Perry, B. (2007). Multi-level governance, regions and science in France: Between competition and equality. *Regional Studies*, *41*(8), 1069–1084. https://doi.org/10.1080/00343400701530840

Crozier, M. (2009). *The bureaucratic phenomenon*. Transaction Publishers.

Czarniawska, B. (1997). Learning organizing in a changing institutional order: Examples from city management in Warsaw. *Management Learning*, *28*(4), 475–495. https://doi.org/10.1177/1350507697284006

Czarniawska, B. (1998). *A narrative approach to organization studies*. Sage.

Czarniawska, B. (2002). *A tale of three cities, or the glocalization of city management*. Oxford: Oxford University Press.

de Roo, G., Hillier, J. & Wezemael, J. van. (2012). *Complexity and planning systems, assemblages and simulations*. Ashgate.

Deeg, R. & Jackson, G. (2007). Towards a more dynamic theory of capitalist variety. *Socio-Economic Review*, *5*(1), 149–179. https://doi.org/10.1093/ser/mwl021

Diduck, A. (2010). The learning dimension of adaptive capacity: Untangling the multi-level connections. In D. Armitage & R. Plummer (eds.), *Adaptive capacity and environmental governance* (pp. 199–221). Springer. https://doi.org/10.1007/978-3-642-12194-4_10

Douglas, D. J. A. (2005). The restructuring of local government in rural regions: A rural development perspective. *Journal of Rural Studies*, *21*(2), 231–246. https://doi.org/10.1016/j.jrurstud.2005.01.003

Duhigg, C. (2012). *The power of habit: Why we do what we do in life and business*. Random House Publishing Group.

Duit, A. (2015). Resilience thinking: Lessons for public administration. *Public Administration*, *94*(2), 364–380.

Duit, A., Galaz, V., Eckerberg, K. & Ebbesson, J. (2010). Governance, complexity, and resilience. *Global Environmental Change*, *20*(3), 363–368.

Easterly, W. (2013). *The tyranny of experts: Economists, dictators, and the forgotten rights of the poor*. Basic Books.

Eggertsson, T. (2005). *Imperfect institutions: Possibilities and limits of reform*. University of Michigan Press.

Eisenstadt, S. N. (1958). Internal contradictions in bureaucratic polities. *Comparative Studies in Society and History*, *1*(1), 58–75. https://doi.org/10.1017/S0010417500000098

Ellickson, R. (1991). *Order without law. How neighbors settle disputes*. Harvard University Press.

Esposito, E. (2012). The time of money. In *The Illusion of Management Control: A Systems Theoretical Approach to Managerial Technologies* (pp. 223–236). Springer.

Feldman, M. S. & Pentland, B. T. (2003). Reconceptualizing organizational routines as a source of flexibility and change. *Administrative Science Quarterly*, *48*(1), 94–118. https://doi.org/10.2307/3556620

Fischer, F. (2012). Participatory governance: From theory to practice. In D. Levi-Faur (ed.), *The Oxford Handbook of Governance*. Oxford University Press. https://doi.org/10.1093/oxfordhb/9780199560530.013.0032

Gel'man, V. (2004). Unrule of law in the making: The politics of informal institution building in Russia. *Europe-Asia Studies, 56*(7), 1021–1040.

Greenwood, R., Hinings, C. R. & Ranson, S. (1975). Contingency theory and the organization of local authorities. Part I: Differentiation and integration. *Public Administration, 53*(1), 1–23. https://doi.org/10.1111/j.1467-9299.1975.tb00202.x

Greif, A. (1994). Cultural beliefs and the organization of society: A historical and theoretical reflection on collectivist and individualist societies. *Journal of Political Economy, 102*(5), 912–950. https://doi.org/10.1086/261959

Greif, A. (2006). *Institutions and the path to the modern economy: Lessons from medieval trade.* Cambridge University Press.

Greif, A. (2014). Do institutions evolve? *Journal of Bioeconomics, 16*(1), 53.

Griffiths, J. (2003). The social working of legal rules. *Journal of Legal Pluralism, 48*(1), 1–84.

Grzymala-Busse, A. (2010). The best laid plans. The impact of informal rules on formal institutions in transitional regimes. *Studies in Comparative International Development, 45*(3), 311–333.

Haahr, J. H. & Walters, W. (2004). *Governing Europe: Discourse, governmentality and European integration.* Routledge.

Hartley, K. & Howlett, M. (2021). Policy assemblages and policy resilience: Lessons for non-design from evolutionary governance theory. *Politics and Governance, 9*(2).

Hayoz, N. & Giordano, C. (2013). *Informality in Eastern Europe.* Peter Lang.

Healey, P. (2006). Transforming governance: Challenges of institutional adaptation and a new politics of space1. *European Planning Studies, 14*(3), 299–320. https://doi.org/10.1080/09654310500420792

Helmke, G. & Levitsky, S. (2004). Informal institutions and comparative politics: A research agenda. *Perspectives on Politics, 2*(04), 725–740. https://doi.org/doi:10.1017/S1537592704040472

Hillier, J. (2000). Going round the back? Complex networks and informal action in local planning processes. *Environment and Planning A, 32,* 33–54.

Hooghe, L. & Marks, G. (2001). *Multi-level governance and European integration.* Rowman & Littlefield.

Hope, K. R. (2009). Capacity development for good governance in developing societies: Lessons from the field. *Development in Practice, 19*(1), 79–86. https://doi.org/10.1080/09614520802576401

Howlett, M. (2019). Procedural policy tools and the temporal dimensions of policy design. *International Review of Public Policy, 1*(1), article 1. https://doi.org/10.4000/irpp.310

Howlett, M. & Goetz, K. H. (2014). Introduction: Time, temporality and timescapes in administration and policy. *International Review of Administrative Sciences, 80*(3), 477–492. https://doi.org/10.1177/0020852314543210

Hulliung, M. (1983). *Citizen Machiavelli.* Princeton University Press.

Innis, P. G. & van Assche, K. (2022). The interplay of riskscapes and objects in unplanned settlements in Monrovia. *Geoforum, 136,* 1–10. https://doi.org/10.1016/j.geoforum.2022.07.015

Kern, K. & Bulkeley, H. (2009). Cities, Europeanization and multi-level governance: Governing climate change through transnational municipal networks*. *JCMS: Journal of Common Market Studies, 47*(2), 309–332.

Kharrazi, A., Yu, Y., Jacob, A., Vora, N. & Fath, B. D. (2020). Redundancy, diversity, and modularity in network resilience: Applications for international trade and implications for public policy. *Current Research in Environmental Sustainability*, *2*, 100006. https://doi.org/10.1016/j.crsust.2020.06.001

Kjaer, P. (2010). *Between governing and governance. On the emergence, function and form of Europe's post-national constellation*. Hart Publishing.

Krehbiel, E. (1918). The European Commission of the Danube: An experiment in international administration. *Political Science Quarterly*, *33*(1), 38–55. https://doi.org/10.2307/2141879

Lauth, H.-J. (2000). Informal institutions and democracy. *Democratization*, *7*(4), 21–50. https://doi.org/10.1080/13510340008403683

Lavie, D., Stettner, U. & Tushman, M. L. (2010). Exploration and exploitation within and across organizations. *Academy of Management Annals*, *4*(1), 109–155. https://doi.org/10.5465/19416521003691287

Lawrence, T. B., Suddaby, R. & Leca, B. (2009). *Institutional work: Actors and agency in institutional studies of organizations*. Cambridge University Press.

Ledeneva, A. (2006). *How Russia really works. The informal practices that shaped post-Soviet politics and business*. Cornell University Press.

Low, B., Ostrom, E., Simon, C. & Wilson, J. (2003). Redundancy and diversity: Do they influence optimal management. In *Navigating Social-Ecological Systems: Building Resilience for Complexity and Change*, pp. 83–114.

Luhmann, N. (1990). *Political theory in the welfare state*. Mouton de Gruyter.

Luhmann, N. (1995). *Social systems*. Stanford University Press.

Luhmann, N. (2004). *Law as a social system*. Oxford University Press.

Luhmann, N. (2018). *Organization and decision*. Cambridge University Press.

Luhmann, N., Ziegert, K. A. & Kastner, F. (2004). *Law as a social system*. Oxford University Press.

Machiavelli, N., Bondanella, J. C. & Bondanella, P. E. (1997). *Discourses on Livy*. Oxford University Press.

Mathur, N. (2016). *Paper tiger*. Cambridge University Press.

Maturana, H. R. & Varela, F. J. (1987). *The tree of knowledge. The biological roots of human understanding*. Shambhala Publications.

McCormick, J. P. (2006). Contain the wealthy and patrol the magistrates: Restoring elite accountability to popular government. *American Political Science Review*, *100*(2), 147–163. https://doi.org/10.1017/S0003055406062071

Meadowcroft, J. (2007). Who is in charge here? Governance for sustainable development in a complex world*. *Journal of Environmental Policy & Planning*, *9*(3–4), 299–314. https://doi.org/10.1080/15239080701631544

Miranda, R. & Lerner, A. (1995). Bureaucracy, organizational redundancy, and the privatization of public services. *Public Administration Review*, *55*(2), 193–200. https://doi.org/10.2307/977185

North, D. C. (1990). *Institutions, institutional change and economic performance*. Cambridge University Press.

North, D. C. (1991). Institutions. *Journal of Economic Perspectives*, *5*(1), 97–112. https://doi.org/10.1257/jep.5.1.97

North, D. C. (2005). *Understanding the process of economic change*. Princeton University Press.

North, D. C., Wallis, J. & Weingast, B. (2009). *Violence and social orders. A conceptual framework for interpreting recorded human history*. Cambridge University Press.

Ostrom, E. (1990). *Governing the commons: The evolution of institutions for collective action*. Cambridge University Press.

Ostrom, E. (2005). *Understanding institutional diversity*. Princeton University Press.
Ostrom, E. (2014). Do institutions for collective action evolve? *Journal of Bioeconomics*, *16*(1), 3–30.
Paterson, J. & Teubner, G. (1998). Changing maps: Empirical legal autopoiesis. *Social & Legal Studies*, *7*(4), 451–486.
Peters, B. G. & Peters, G. (2002). *Politics of bureaucracy*. Routledge.
Pollitt, C. (2008). *Time, policy, management: Governing with the past*. Oxford University Press.
Pressman, J. L. & Wildavsky, A. B. (1979). *Implementation: How great expectations in Washington are dashed in Oakland* (2nd edn.). University of California Press.
Purdy, J. M. (2012). A framework for assessing power in collaborative governance processes. *Public Administration Review*, *72*(3), 409–417. https://doi.org/10.1111/j.1540-6210.2011.02525.x
Ramus, T., Vaccaro, A. & Brusoni, S. (2017). Institutional complexity in turbulent times: Formalization, collaboration, and the emergence of blended logics. *Academy of Management Journal*, *60*(4), 1253–1284. https://doi.org/10.5465/amj.2015.0394
Robinson, E. J. Z., Kumar, A. M. & Albers, H. J. (2010). Protecting developing countries' forests: Enforcement in theory and practice. *Journal of Natural Resources Policy Research*, *2*(1), 25–38. https://doi.org/10.1080/19390450903350820
Rosenfeld, M. (2000). The rule of law and the legitimacy of constitutional democracy. *Southern California Law Review*, *74*, 1307.
Schatzki, T. (2014). Practices, governance and sustainability. In *Social practices, intervention and sustainability* (pp. 15–30). Routledge.
Seo, M.-G. & Creed, W. E. D. (2002). Institutional contradictions, praxis, and institutional change: A dialectical perspective. *Academy of Management Review*, *27*(2), 222–247. https://doi.org/10.5465/amr.2002.6588004
Spillane, J. P. (2012). *Distributed leadership*. John Wiley & Sons.
Stead, D. & Meijers, E. (2009). Spatial planning and policy integration: Concepts, facilitators and inhibitors. *Planning Theory & Practice*, *10*(3), 317–332.
Steinmo, S., Thelen, K. & Longstreth, F. (1992). *Structuring politics: Historical Institutionalism in comparative analysis*. Cambridge University Press.
Swyngedouw, E. (2000). Authoritarian governance, power, and the politics of rescaling. *Environment and Planning D: Society and Space*, *18*(1), 63–76. https://doi.org/10.1068/d9s
Swyngedouw, E. (2004). Globalisation or 'glocalisation'? Networks, territories and rescaling. *Cambridge Review of International Affairs*, *17*(1), 25–48. https://doi.org/10.1080/0955757042000203632
Swyngedouw, E. (2005). Governance Innovation and the citizen: The Janus face of governance-beyond-the-state. *Urban Studies*, *42*(11), 1991–2006. https://doi.org/10.1080/00420980500279869
Thelen, K. (2004). *How institutions evolve. The political economy of skills in Germany, Britain, the United States, and Japan*. Cambridge University Press.
Thygesen, N. T. (2022). Moving ahead: How time is compressed and stretched in strategy work. *Journal of Organizational Change Management*, *35*(6), 916–935. https://doi.org/10.1108/JOCM-07-2021-0198
Van Assche, K. (2013). Visible and invisible informalities and institutional transformation. Lessons from transition countries: Georgia, Romania, Uzbekistan. In N. Hayoz & C. Giordano (eds.), *Informality and post- socialist transition*. Peter Lang.

Van Assche, K. & Djanibekov, N. (2012). Spatial planning as policy integration: The need for an evolutionary perspective. Lessons from Uzbekistan. *Land Use Policy*, *29*(1), 179–186. https://doi.org/10.1016/j.landusepol.2011.06.004

Van Assche, K. & Verschraegen, G. (2008). The limits of planning: Niklas Luhmann's systems theory and the analysis of planning and planning ambitions. *Planning Theory*, *7*(3), 263–283.

Van Assche, K., Beunen, R. & Duineveld, M. (2014a). *Evolutionary governance theory: An introduction*. Springer.

Van Assche, K., Beunen, R. & Duineveld, M. (2014b). Formal/informal dialectics and the self-transformation of spatial planning systems: An exploration. *Administration & Society*, *46*(6), 654–683. https://doi.org/10.1177/0095399712469194

Van Assche, K., Beunen, R., Holm, J. & Lo, M. (2013). Social learning and innovation. Ice fishing communities on Lake Mille Lacs. *Land Use Policy*, *34*, 233–242. https://doi.org/10.1016/j.landusepol.2013.03.009

Van Assche, K., Gruezmacher, M. & Deacon, L. (2019). Land use tools for tempering boom and bust: Strategy and capacity building in governance. *Land Use Policy*, 103994.

Van Assche, K., Hornidge, A.-K., Schlüter, A. & Vaidianu, N. (2020). Governance and the coastal condition: Towards new modes of observation, adaptation and integration. *Marine Policy*, *112*. https://doi.org/10.1016/j.marpol.2019.01.002

Van Assche, K., Verschraegen, G., & Gruezmacher, M. (2021). Strategy for collectives and common goods: Coordinating strategy, long-term perspectives and policy domains in governance. *Futures*, *128*, 102716. https://doi.org/10.1016/j.futures.2021.102716

Wagenaar, H. (2011). *Meaning in action: Interpretation and dialogue in policy analysis*. M. E. Sharpe.

4. Governance paths as history and infrastructure for transition

GOVERNANCE PATHS

Let us remind ourselves that all elements of governance co-evolve. They shape each other over time. Actors and institutions, both formal and informal, are a product of this co-evolution. As domains, arenas and levels of governance are emerging outcomes of evolutionary processes. These we can consider structures as they constrain further evolution in a particular way and tend to be more stable. It is good to realize that those structures come out of the same evolution as elements and processes, and that nothing stops evolving (Beunen et al., 2015; Van Assche, Beunen, et al., 2014).

The idea of evolution transpiring here is explicitly not a Darwinian one, with experiments leading to selection and survival of the fittest. Things survive for a variety of reasons, including their inclusion in a configuration. The process of coordination, as well as processes of differentiation, entail that things *have* to respond to each other, and that patterns of response are easier to stabilize than to change. If coordination stops, this harms all involved. Awareness of this principle by all actors, and in the community, is another reason for survival of actors, institutions and other elements and structures of governance.

Each community, therefore, is marked by its own, unique *governance path*. A governance path is *not* a synonym for the history of formal politics and/or administration. It is an evolution, marked by key events, junctures and demarcated phases (Greif, 2014; Ostrom, 2014; Thelen, 2004; Van Assche, Beunen, et al., 2014). The evolution is sometimes gradual, sometimes invisible, but also showing fits and starts, shocks and rapids. A path is marked by sets of relations, modes of reproduction and adaptation, which are only partly transparent for both insiders and outsiders. In multi-level governance, each level has a configuration, hence a path. What is unique is the configuration in its transformation over time, and the mode of self-transformation. Outside forces are always there, but in the end governance only works if transformation is self-transformation. As in other autopoietic systems, if external forces impose a change this needs to make sense in terms of the configuration. It requires interpretation in terms of the system in order to make that sense (Brans &

Rossbach, 1997; Luhmann, 2008; Seidl, 2016; Teubner, 1988). Otherwise, formal change is de facto a breakdown of coordination. Shocks do not always cause such a breakdown; an initial lack of systems response does not always spell doom. After a shake-up, a restructuring can follow, stemming from unseen or formerly marginal sources of self-transformation.

Evolution in governance is always co-evolution, whereby different elements and structures co-evolve. Co-evolution in the radical sense proposed here recognizes the importance of processes of *emergence*. Systems theorist Ludwig von Bertalanffy (Van Assche, Verschraegen, et al., 2019; Von Bertalanffy, 1968) was one of the first to develop this idea, seemingly going against the second law of thermodynamics, which insists on the increase of entropy or disorder over time. Of course, the evolution of life is one long illustration of processes of emergence, of more and more complex orders developing in living systems, and the history of differentiation in society serves as another grand example, as complex systems evolve, which not only structure but *create* the societies we experience as natural. Emergence is not only a matter of increasing complexity, but also of novelty: new identities and a new unity at a higher level of complexity emerges, with a new mode of reproduction (Chaffin & Gunderson, 2016; Kaufmann, 2013; Kjaer, 2010). Cells are autopoietic systems, but so are humans, in their complex interplay between cells (Maturana & Varela, 1987). Social systems, like organizations, are more than a collection of individuals, and so are governance systems and communities (Fuchs, 2001; Luhmann, 1995; Seidl, 2016).

The importance of processes of emergence in governance does not mean that local self-organization always remains essential in governance paths. Nor does it mean that the configuration started in a democratic manner. It does mean that there is *no firm ground* within or underneath the system. There is no natural order of things which underpins a governance configuration and causes it to evolve in a particular manner. Each governance path, each form of social organization, is contingent and constructed, even if many governance ideologies pretend to circle around natural rights, ancient identities or rational practices (Fuchs, 2001; Greif, 2006). Governance and its communities mask their own contingency by means of stories of origin, universal values or a uniqueness that is not further explained. Governance configurations compensate for the lack of natural grounding by making distinctions, creating structures and by differentiating rules and roles (Luhmann, 1989).

Such a distinction can produce further distinctions and they can be layered. Basic distinctions can be made regarding other distinctions, and here we recall the governance dimensions. The governance dimensions taken together create a semantic and organizational space, a space where options for governance become visible, where choices can be made regarding transformation of the system. In a governance path these dimensions evolve, and governance systems can develop reflexive capacity to recognize these evolving dimensions, and learn from their history.

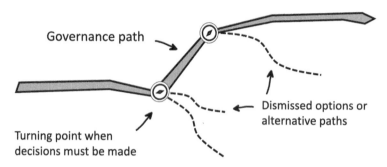

Governance path

Dismissed options or alternative paths

Turning point when decisions must be made

Figure 4.1   Governance configurations and governance paths[1]

Emergence in the case of governance thus means growing complexity in terms of differentiation of the system, and in terms of emerging actors (Chaffin & Gunderson, 2016; Duit et al., 2010; Luhmann, 1995). Actors and institutions differentiate, and their reproduction creates the need for more and changing actors and institutions. Dimension, domains, topics and arenas differentiate, and transform slowly. This differentiation creates both rigidity and flexibility in the system: more entities play a role, which reduces flexibility in interpretations, responses and coordination (Greif, 2006; Kjaer, 2010; Steinmo et al., 1992). Yet on the other hand it increases the number of possible forms of response to change or signals generally, and in the possible forms of coordination. The rigidity stems from the difficulties to respond creatively, as the presence of many actors and institutions creates the need for compromise, for design by committee which can tend to old averages, and for procedures. The flexibility stems from the fact that creativity can also emerge from the interplay between actors and institutions and the differentiation of topics and domains, where specialized knowledge can be applied, and where discussion can lead to innovation.

---

[1]   Actor-institution configurations evolve, transforming themselves and the governance system they are part of. This transformation slowly creates a trajectory we refer to as a governance path. As governance evolves, as certain decisions are taken, certain futures envisioned, and others excluded in practice or deliberately dismissed, the path is created. In retrospect, the governance system is able to identify those key moments, turning points that shifted the path of collective decision-making. It can learn from its past, from its history of decision-making.

As we consider governance as politics in a broad sense, its path also relates to the larger pattern of differentiation in society. Governance changes reflect new patterns of differentiation in society (new professions, interest groups or ideologies), while governance can also alter these patterns of differentiation. How the two directions play out depends on the way governance system and community relate (Luhmann, 1995). It also depends on the dominant patterns of differentiation in society, and the political ideas and aspirations of the emerging entities. If professional groups develop identities and lobbies that scale up and organize, across territories, this will have different consequences for governance than an evolution where cities increase their autonomy and unity vis-à-vis kings and aristocracy.

In order to better grasp the different couplings between society and governance we will differentiate between several models of democracy in the following chapter. Each of these models embodies an (idealized) relation between patterns of differentiation in society and in governance and can therefore be used as an analytical tool in the study of governance paths. These models are necessarily simplifications of the actual patterns of differentiations, decision-making and relation between society and governance. The actual relations between societal organization and governance are of course much more varied and complex than is widely shown in studies in sociology, political science and other disciplines (see also Chapter 2). Yet for the moment it can suffice to notice the two connected patterns of emergence and differentiation, in governance and community, and the variation in the connection.

Direction of Governance Paths

Most internal and external observation and studies of governance take place at later stages of evolution, and this has consequences. In these analyses, including often ours, rigidities are emphasized. We develop the theme of rigidity, flexibility and their sources in governance evolution later in this book, as well as the implications for strategy, yet we now need to emphasize that at all stages there is both rigidity and flexibility and that changing direction, and therefore developing a path, remains possible.

In the early stages of governance formation, more studied by historians than by sociologists and policy scientists, there is already a combination of flexibility and rigidity, even if many rigidities, such as path dependencies, develop over time (Graeber & Wengrow, 2021). Initially, when governance is crystallizing, flexibility can stem from the fact that many of the procedures and specializations that develop later are not present yet, so creative responses and radical decisions are more likely. At the same time, shocks can be more common, in the unstable environments where governance is forming (see Chapters 2 and 3). Furthermore, the newly developing governance systems can be more vulnerable to such shocks. In terms of rigidities, one can mention for such initial phases of governance evolution that *deliberate* steering in a different direction is more difficult, as many possible tools are not yet developed and introduced. Moreover, a less differentiated governance system (and society) can mean that individuals can dominate decision-making in many domains, and the limitations of these individuals also represent rigidities in governance. Niccolò Machiavelli, looking back at the history of Florence and Italy, and elsewhere analysing the vagaries of the Roman republic, makes the point that polities are often founded by breaking the rules of the existing order, with key actors doing things that would be reprehensible in the light of later history, in the light of the values and institutions marking the community later (Machiavelli, 1996; Machiavelli et al., 2008).

Whatever dominates, flexibility or rigidity, a governance path always develops and evolves, and a community can change direction. This is certainly a metaphorical notion, referring to the possibility to change more than a few elements in governance, to instigate change in the community. This can be seen more easily when clear goals and aspirations develop, in the community and in the governance system itself. The idea of changing course can more easily form when there is an idea of a current state of the community, its qualities and issues, and of a possible change in direction. Such awareness often hinges on the formation of ideas of common goods and goals, where a new direction can be a restructured set of such goods and goals, or a new way of moving in that direction if the community is disappointed in the way it is pursuing its perceived core values.

Changing course can emerge from various drivers, such as economic necessity, cultural change, renewed reflection on values, or circumstances. It can cause or be caused by a radical shift in the governance configuration, but not necessarily so. The critique which might precede a desired shift in course, a new path, might focus on the governance system, which is assumed to need an overhaul, a clean-up, an infusion with a new ideology or a mopping up of traces of old ideologies. It can revolve around a different desired balance between participation or representation, or a new kind of participation, involving different people on different topics in different arenas. Alternatively, the focus of critique can be the set of values and associated goals previously embraced in the community, under the assumption that the current machinery of governance does not need a rebuild to move in a different direction.

The process of gradual recognition of a shared identity and interest, of a unity, and a collective sharing of public goods, can be a slow process. The awareness of unity and the awareness of a possible change in direction do not always coincide, yet one tends to be a precondition for the other. One can also interpret this process as a gradual transformation of an arena into an actor – which simultaneously retains its role as arena. The structure of the arena, and of the governance configuration around it, does not necessarily reflect the unity or disunity of a community or of governance. A regional council can be a place to spy on neighboring communities, elsewhere it can reflect and create a regional (or metropolitan) identity, or it can be an arena to define and pursue public goods. Medieval cities and their relation to nobility offer another illustration of such a process, where a civic unity developed around increasing autonomy vis-à-vis the aristocracy, while elements of that aristocracy discerned the opportunities offered by cities and transformed itself to actors *in* (as opposed to outside and against) urban governance. Medieval poems such as 'How one shall govern a city' expressed these values of autonomy, internal differentiation and harmony (Boodt, 2019).

In Hegelian terms, we can say that in governance the community becomes aware of itself, and this growing awareness is at the same time a process of creation. The awareness present in the governance system and the existence of such a system are then helpful in guiding its further development. The need to take collectively binding decisions tends to trigger a reflection on the community, its environment, its past and its possible futures, while experience with governance, and its devising of new tools and distinctions, emboldens communities to think they can steer themselves towards more desirable futures.

TIME AND SPACE IN GOVERNANCE

Rhythms and Cycles

Governance systems make the world governable through inventing stable grounds for themselves. This extends to the structuring of time. In the multiplication of governance elements, time scales, rhythms and cycles multiply. Each is intended to enable organization, yet multiplication makes coordination harder (Howlett & Goetz, 2014; Pollitt, 2008). A level, an arena, a domain or an actor might have its own time horizon, its own rhythm and cycles. The temporalities of the elements can be a product of internal activity, but also stem from coupling with the broader social or ecological environment. The cycles and rhythms of ecological systems can dictate human activity, with implications for its governance (Van Assche, Verschraegen, et al., 2019). The way a religion creates temporal distinctions in a year might be partly coupled to its narratives, partly to the cycles of nature, and the manner of this temporality affects governance beyond religion, stems from a particular coupling between religion and politics, a particular embedding of religion in society.

The temporality of the governance system itself can dictate its own rhythms (election cycles, meeting times, procedures) and it should not be forgotten that governance is not only coordinating activities in its environment, but is an activity itself, which takes time, requires coordination and needs resources.

The concept of social-ecological systems, and the grounding concept of nested systems, make it clear that the temporality of a system cannot be seen in isolation (Chaffin & Gunderson, 2016; Van Assche, Verschraegen, et al., 2019). The temporality is almost certainly a product of the interplay between different systems; in our analysis the interplay between governance, community and the encompassing social-ecological systems. Temporality, in other words, is almost always hybrid, and the necessity for a particular set of temporal distinctions can rarely be traced back to the functional requirements of one system.

We have spoken already of *procedures* as devices to organize time in order to manage complexity, and here we are on the terrain of governance properly, as we are speaking of tools deliberately devised in governance for governance. Procedures reduce complexity in a double sense. First, they split the resolution of problems and the achievement of goals into smaller steps, each potentially marked by its own form of coordination. This means that the procedure can reduce the complexity of coordination by dividing an issue in a set of discrete coordination problems. Second, they allow for a management of cognitive complexity, by potentially linking steps with different sorts of knowledge useful for the analysis and resolution of sub-problems. It can be noted that the reduction of a larger problem into smaller problems, the reduction of a topic into sub-topics, the specialization and differentiation of administration and its experts, and the creation of procedures are tightly coupled and mutually reinforcing processes. New departments with new expertise can handle sub-topics with great clarity, can develop their own procedures and can be incorporated as distinct steps of procedures addressing overarching issues (Georghiou et al., 2014; Lawrence et al., 2015).

Procedures themselves take time. They make temporal distinctions in the governance process of a topic, but they can also have the intention to introduce such distinctions in their environment. That is, the procedure in governance can have effects on organizational processes in the community, as people anticipate governance procedures to plan (asking for a building permit, a business license) (Luhmann, 1997) but, more importantly, there can be an intention behind the procedure, to reorganize activities in society, under new temporalities (Luhmann, 1990; Van Assche et al., 2020). One can think of permit procedures in environmental legislation that are partly intended not to conserve the environment directly, but to slow down decision processes in business and administration regarding sensitive areas. In an elementary example, one can think of school policies, adjustments to the school year, revisions to the curriculum. Outside the regimented school environment, governance and its procedures structure time in innumerable ways, from the opening times of shops, to work and vacation times, and investments in infrastructure that is not ready for a while and, once finished, creates new time-spaces.

Introducing new processes of participation, under different names, such as co-production, deliberation and the name governance itself, creates new couplings between the temporalities of governance and society. Public participation sessions can be visited mostly by those directly affected by a decision on the agenda, and those who have the time and interest to attend (Delina & Sovacool, 2018; Fung, 2006). More generally, participation processes reflect the temporalities of governance rather than society. If decision-making is only possible under conditions imposed by governance, and if the result of a participation process needs to be recognized as a legitimately binding decision in and by governance, this thoroughly shapes the participation from the start, in terms of temporality and in terms of content. In the other direction, direct participation does offer the potential for governance to observe dissonances in the temporalities assumed by the policy and its procedures, and the temporalities relevant to resolution of a societal issue.

Most likely, if such observation occurs, what happens is a reinterpretation of the dissonance and the issue, in such a way that decision-making in the existing configuration can continue. 'We hear that we respond too slowly to complaints.' 'We grasp that we do not offer services in a flexible manner.' The answer must be acceptable and feasible for current governance, and its pattern of slowing down and speeding up deliberation. If actors know that courts can shoot down a proposal coming up in participatory sessions, if they know that the expertise and resources are not there, that the proposal will be opposed by others not at the table, or that it might undermine established practices of coordination and possibly checks and balances, a reinterpretation of the proposal might still move forward. Citizens active in participation processes, on their side, often miss the insight in the temporality and overall complexity of governance, while actors are often less inclined to make that complexity transparent (Gunder & Hillier, 2009; Parés et al., 2012; Suddaby & Panwar, 2022).

Time Horizons

Time horizons are not the same as rhythms or procedures, but they are aspects of temporality which are coupled to both of them. The multiplication of temporalities in and outside governance complicates synthesis of ideas into visions, and the development of shared stories about the future and a set of institutions bringing about that future. Time horizons can be created consciously, for particular institutions and arenas, and they can simply exist, because the features of the autopoiesis of the system combine to create a vision of the future up to a certain distance (Verlin, 2021). Procedures can create time horizons, as the well-known complaints about elections and democratic myopia can testify. Policies, laws and plans can create their own time horizons, hopefully enabling them to fulfill their task without stranding in uncertainty. Furthermore, time horizons are partly a result of the issue at hand, its couplings to social and ecological systems, and partly because the temporalities within governance need to be coordinated (Elliott, 2021; Lawrence et al., 2015).

In collective strategy, a new time horizon *has* to be constructed (Van Assche et al., 2021). This new time horizon challenges existing ways of coordination (Brace & Geoghegan, 2011). First, in order to move the community in a direction desired by the community, the alternative future will be located somewhere else than the time horizons of other policies, and the chances are slim that the time horizon of this synthesis will coincide with the existing collection of horizons pertaining to the coordinated actors and institutions. Second, the policy tools that have to be coordinated, and partly developed, to make the strategy applicable will have to be adjusted, in many cases, and the new temporality of the strategy has to trigger increased reflection on existing tools (see later).

Understanding and mapping the multiplicity of time horizons and temporalities in the governance system and the community is very useful, in the understanding that such mapping cannot be comprehensive, that new temporalities might emerge (a new resource, market) and that some temporalities might not be revealed ('election' of new bosses in criminal-political networks) (Bowden et al., 2019; Zerubavel, 2003). Some actors, engaged in strategy formation, are more shaped by time horizons, or wedded to a certain temporality, than others. Some are more sensitive to the temporalities in governance, others more to those of the wider society. Some try to impose their temporality more on others (we are *all* obliged to fulfill the five-year plan) or impose it on shared visions (whatever comes out of this visioning exercise, nothing happens in the city during cotton harvest). Some arenas construct and impose their own temporalities or horizons.

Institutions, both used and produced in governance, can anchor, fragment, coordinate or favor certain temporalities (Howlett, 2019; Howlett & Goetz, 2014). If five-year plans structure potentially all activity in governance, or if a polity is used to 30-year plans for infrastructure investment, these features, the familiarity with these time horizons, and their coupling with other institutions, enable and constrain the constructions of futures through other institutions and with other actions. Volatile decision-making processes and unpredictable or contradictory processes in society can be stabilized through policies, plans and laws. Institutions can enable long-term perspectives in society and with actors in governance, but they can also disrupt existing forms of longer-term thinking by imposing procedures with other time horizons and different governance temporalities (Christie & Algar-Faria, 2020; Howlett & Rayner, 2013).

Time horizons can come with narratives or produce narratives. These narratives can further drive coordination, or the strategizing of actors (Cunliffe et al., 2004; Kay, 2006). The narrative can also simply be: no change is expected, no change is reasonable or feasible, the future is a continuation of the present. The narratives can be inspired by a relation to the ecological environment, inspire such relation, or they can emerge slowly through interactions within governance (slowly building up to a shared story which then starts to play a role in coordination). Conversely, narratives about self, environment, past and future can create time horizons in governance, in particular domains, arenas, for certain topics, with some actors, in selective institutions.

Space

Just as with time, space needs to be parceled up to make it governable. Distinctions have to be introduced (Jessop, 1996). This can be through the delineation of area-based arenas and actors (e.g. administrative divisions) or through the functioning of particular domains of governance (water systems imposing their spatiality) (Brace & Geoghegan, 2011). The partition of space can come before other distinctions, or after. The focus of decision-making can be the actual use of space, or it can be something else that comes with spatial implications or requirements (Bowden et al., 2019).

When considering space, spatial planning deserves specific attention because of its focus on spatial organization and its specific forms of coordination within a governance system (Van Assche, Duineveld, et al., 2014; Van Assche et al., 2013). *Spatial planning* is, for us, spatial governance, the coordination of policies and practices affecting the organization of space. Spatial planning is an attempt at policy integration in already highly differentiated systems of governance. Spatial planning comes under many different labels and in even more forms (Van Assche et al., 2013). It has gradations in comprehensiveness. It can be a policy domain, but also an activity part of other policy domains.

Furthermore, planning can occur throughout the governance system, or only at certain levels of governance, or for certain topics. In a similar way integration can be a widely shared ambition or can be the focus of a limited set of policies. Spatial planning can happen by producing plans and design, but this is not always the case. Institutions with spatial implications can be coordinated with an eye on those spatial implications, but these spatial implications can also be ignored or overlooked in the policy process. Moreover, even when place-based policies (think economic development, heritage policy, or place branding) are articulated, this does not mean that a plan, as in a graphic document outlining the future of an area, has to be the basis. We return to this idea in later chapters, in part because community strategies, the focus of this book, often tend to be reduced to spatial plans.

Narrative can play a role in several ways in the organization of space (Hoch, 2016; Sandercock, 2003; Throgmorton, 1996). Narratives *about* an area can inspire policies to protect it, or to use it in a different way. Narratives about people who happen to live in that area, their plight, their oppression, or their strong ethnic or religious identity can lead to spatially defined governance changes, or even to a separate governance configuration for that area (giving more autonomy to a locally dominant ethnicity, which then proceeds to introduce more changes to the configuration). Such narratives can be present in governance, enabling self-transformation guided by existing governance tools, or they can come in with a bang, when for example local mobilization along ethnic lines suddenly replaces other identifications (as socialist, Catholic) (Jessop, 1996; Verloo, 2018). Such a bang could often still be accommodated by the existing configuration, but if latent or overt resistance against the revolutionary redefinition obstructs further change, a destabilization, a collapse of governance, can follow.

GOVERNANCE FRAGMENTATION

Differentiation is automatically fragmentation of governance. This fragmentation creates a counter-balance for coordination (Greenwood et al., 1975). Besides this general form of fragmentation, the contingent evolution of different elements of governance, the difficulty of keeping an overview of all ongoing changes and of internal complexity, creates particular forms of fragmentation (Esmark, 2009; Thompson, 1961). Fragmentation means two things for us: on the one hand, disconnect and dissonance, and on the other hand, only partly understood selectivity in terms of time, space and topics. Not everything is covered by governance, as we know, and this is not necessarily a problem, but the selectivity is never entirely the product of intentional selectivity, of a deliberate focus on this topic, that area, this time period. This means that some things assumed to be covered are less so, and that elsewhere there is a density of governance activity. This difference we call fragmentation (the second meaning).

Institutions might relate to each other and to overarching ambitions that drive the development of these institutions, particularly if they are part of a strategy. In practice, the focus of institutions might be much more fragmented, and even institutions that were initiated from a shared ambition might start to diverge over time. Plans for example can lack a systematic reference to policies, policies to laws, laws to laws, etc. Such references might be necessary to pursue the goals of each institution separately, and the goal of the combination of institutions as it was intended. If plans are supposed to reflect changes in laws, but they don't, or if they have the status of laws, but other laws do not change, this can create a disconnect and conflict and disrupt and undermine the strategy. If local policies change incrementally, but a regional policy or more comprehensive policy does not reflect these changes, the legitimacy of either can be questioned, governance becomes more fragmented or comes to a halt (Christensen et al., 2016; Papadopoulos, 2000). Each of the institutions can be abused by 'bad actors,' deploying the disconnect, choosing the one most beneficial, interpreting it loosely, and counting on weak enforcement or sympathetic courts that will notice the disconnect.

Individual decisions can lack reference to the appropriate policies, plans or laws, that is, the ones supposed to guide the decision-making. If such explicit reference and therewith a tight coupling is lost, the elements can evolve more easily their own way. Once a broad environmental policy is disconnected from water governance in practice, the new policies articulated to water governance will be a product of the context of water governance and the integration of water into a series of other environmental topics becomes harder and harder. That is, more external pressure will have to be applied with increasing chance of shocks and loss of coordination (Kooiman & van Vliet, 2000). If a decision is disconnected from the policies supposed to guide it, that decision can still be legitimate as it is the result of otherwise legitimate governance procedures (the ones still recognized as governing decision-making), and if the supposedly guiding policy is itself disconnected in practice from supposedly coupled policies (in coordination) or mother policies (in hierarchy), then this double disconnect is bound to cause fragmentation in governance. The disconnect between decisions, policies and guiding institutions is a very common phenomenon in many places and many domains of governance and it makes it hard to see what is actually governed and what can be governed.

Institutions of a more complex, strategic nature can therefore lack the coordination with other institutions, actors, domains or arenas (and narratives, as we will see later) that could enable them to function as strategy (Van Assche et al., 2021; Van Assche, Gruezmacher, et al., 2019). Worse, the chances are that the coalition of strategizing actors is only half aware of those disconnects, of the pattern of fragmentation, and therefore of the coordination problems that will be encountered when articulating and implementing the strategy. *Mapping the disconnects*, the fragmentation can therefore be a fruitful exercise, though possibly tedious, in preparation of more ambitious collective strategies that will require the coordination of a multiplicity of policies tools and topics (Gruezmacher & Van Assche, 2022; Vranken, 2001; Widerberg, 2016). This brings back home the point that the organizational memory and the memory of the governance system as a whole are important enabling factors for collective strategy. Not only because it is important to remember which tools were used before, which goals were pursued, and which strategies were tried, but also to recall where disconnects are likely to lurk and creating obstacles. Memory helps to prevent disconnect and fragmentation, to trace it, and to overcome it by giving insight into the pallet of tools and the history of their use.

Shards

Time, space and the discursive realm are never entirely covered by governance, as we know. Not everything gets the same attention (Howlett & Rayner,
2007; Jessop, 1996). Certain times, topics or spaces receive more attention,
create a higher density of decision-making. Sometimes this leads to new
configurations, or to a clustering of activity, actors and institutions, within an
existing configuration (Jessop, 2020). Such a form of fragmentation, as we
just discussed, is not necessarily a problem; selectivity is natural and necessary. The manifestation of fragmentation can, however, create coordination
problems, if hitherto disconnected topics have to be connected, or if densely
governed and neglected topics, areas or domains are brought into contact. It
can also enhance innovation, as neglected areas and unexpected contacts can
force the search for new solutions or for new forms of coordination, possibly
for enhancing the governance of the neglected topics, possibly redefining
collective goals and retooling institutions with that in mind.

The denser fragments can emerge when existential problems arise, when
discourses compete, when a new future is crystallizing, when new ideas of
problems require a new form of coordination or the inclusion of more actors,
more forms of knowledge, or more couplings between institutions (Fenger
et al., 2012). In terms of psychoanalyst Jacques Lacan, the denser shard, in
a broader pattern of fragmentation and disconnect, can function as a *point de
capiton*, or quilting point, where a new discourse touches ground (Gunder &
Hillier, 2009; Lacan & Fink, 2006). Bigger discourses and narratives on governance, on collective goals and shared values, on identity and desired futures,
touch the lives of people in the community only selectively, and in order to
remain persuaded, a persuasion which is necessary to keep communities supporting the governance configuration, they need to see something, experience
something, beyond political and bureaucratic rhetoric. Things are happening
in those shards that receive attention from governance, where governance
is denser, and where likely significant decisions are taken, with significant
impact on the lives and the environment of people (Zhao, 2020). If people
see more trees on the street, and a new urban forestry department, working
in conjunction with the planning department, the rhetoric about sustainability
might make more sense.

In Lacanian perspective, this persuasion only works when it is also
self-persuasion, when both those who govern and those who are governed
suspend critical judgment, pretend that indeed, sustainability is important, and
the trees not only symbolize but also create a more sustainable community. We
all pretend we know what we are talking about and we pretend we are talking
about the same thing, which helps to keep communication going, and to maintain basic trust in the governance system (Richards, 2007; Wagenaar, 2015).

In terms of classic psychoanalysis, that is, Freudian terms, we can speak of *cathexis*, or affective investment by a community in certain narratives, topics and discursive shards, which can translate into the appearance of governance shards. We would argue, in line with the previous paragraphs, that not all shards of denser governance are cathectic, that they can have other origins, but to function as *point de capiton* such intensity of collective affect is required (Gunder & Hillier, 2009).

Some shards, because of cathexis, and/or because of a perception as 'model-governance,' can extend themselves; they can sprout rhizomes, connect to and even take over other shards, topics or whole domains. Alternatively, they can remain disconnected experiments and solutions, forgotten in a bigger story.

REFERENCES

Beunen, R., Van Assche, K. & Duineveld, M. (2015). *Evolutionary governance theory: Theory and applications.* Springer.

Boodt, M. D. (2019). 'How one shall govern a city': The polyphony of urban political thought in the fourteenth-century duchy of Brabant. *Urban History, 46*(4), 578–596. https://doi.org/10.1017/S0963926818000731

Bowden, V., Nyberg, D. & Wright, C. (2019). Planning for the past: Local temporality and the construction of denial in climate change adaptation. *Global Environmental Change, 57,* 101939. https://doi.org/10.1016/j.gloenvcha.2019.101939

Brace, C. & Geoghegan, H. (2011). Human geographies of climate change: Landscape, temporality, and lay knowledges. *Progress in Human Geography, 35*(3), 284–302. https://doi.org/10.1177/0309132510376259

Brans, M. & Rossbach, S. (1997). The autopoiesis of administrative systems: Niklas Luhmann on public administration and public policy. *Public Administration, 75*(3), 417–439.

Chaffin, B. C. & Gunderson, L. H. (2016). Emergence, institutionalization and renewal: Rhythms of adaptive governance in complex social-ecological systems. *Journal of Environmental Management, 165,* 81–87. https://doi.org/10.1016/j.jenvman.2015.09.003

Christensen, T., Lægreid, P. & Rykkja, L. H. (2016). Organizing for crisis management: Building governance capacity and legitimacy. *Public Administration Review, 76*(6), 887–897. https://doi.org/10.1111/puar.12558

Christie, R. & Algar-Faria, G. (2020). Timely interventions: Temporality and peace-building. *European Journal of International Security, 5*(2), 155–178. https://doi.org/10.1017/eis.2019.27

Cunliffe, A. L., Luhman, J. T. & Boje, D. M. (2004). Narrative temporality: implications for organizational research. *Organization Studies, 25*(2), 261–286. https://doi.org/10.1177/0170840604040038

Delina, L. L. & Sovacool, B. K. (2018). Of temporality and plurality: An epistemic and governance agenda for accelerating just transitions for energy access and sustainable development. *Current Opinion in Environmental Sustainability, 34,* 1–6. https://doi.org/10.1016/j.cosust.2018.05.016

Duit, A., Galaz, V., Eckerberg, K. & Ebbesson, J. (2010). Governance, complexity, and resilience. *Global Environmental Change, 20*(3), 363–368.

Elliott, R. (2021). Insurance and the temporality of climate ethics: Accounting for climate change in US flood insurance. *Economy and Society, 50*(2), 173–195. https://doi.org/10.1080/03085147.2020.1853356

Esmark, A. (2009). The functional differentiation of governance: Public governance beyond hierarchy, market and networks. *Public Administration, 87*(2), 351–370. https://doi.org/10.1111/j.1467-9299.2009.01759.x

Fenger, H. J. M., Bekkers, V. J. J. M. & Fenger, M. (2012). *Beyond fragmentation and interconnectivity: Public governance and the search for connective capacity.* IOS Press.

Fuchs, S. (2001). *Against essentialism: A theory of culture and society.* Harvard University Press.

Fung, A. (2006). Varieties of participation in complex governance. *Public Administration Review, 66*(s1), 66–75. https://doi.org/10.1111/j.1540-6210.2006.00667.x

Georghiou, L., Edler, J., Uyarra, E. & Yeow, J. (2014). Policy instruments for public procurement of innovation: Choice, design and assessment. *Technological Forecasting and Social Change, 86*, 1–12. https://doi.org/10.1016/j.techfore.2013.09.018

Graeber, D. & Wengrow, D. (2021). *The dawn of everything: A new history of humanity.* Penguin UK.

Greenwood, R., Hinings, C. R. & Ranson, S. (1975). Contingency theory and the organization of local authorities. Part I: Differentiation and integration. *Public Administration, 53*(1), 1–23. https://doi.org/10.1111/j.1467-9299.1975.tb00202.x

Greif, A. (2006). *Institutions and the path to the modern economy: Lessons from medieval trade.* Cambridge University Press.

Greif, A. (2014). Do institutions evolve? *Journal of Bioeconomics, 16*(1), 53.

Gruezmacher, M. & Van Assche, K. (2022). *Crafting strategies for sustainable local development.* InPlanning.

Gunder, M. & Hillier, J. (2009). *Planning in ten words or less. A Lacanian Entanglement with Spatial Planning.* Ashgate.

Hoch, C. (2016). Utopia, scenario and plan: A pragmatic integration. *Planning Theory, 15*(1), 6–22.

Howlett, M. (2019). Procedural policy tools and the temporal dimensions of policy design. *International Review of Public Policy, 1*(1), article 1. https://doi.org/10.4000/irpp.310

Howlett, M. & Goetz, K. H. (2014). Introduction: Time, temporality and timescapes in administration and policy. *International Review of Administrative Sciences, 80*(3), 477–492. https://doi.org/10.1177/0020852314543210

Howlett, M. & Rayner, J. (2007). Design principles for policy mixes: Cohesion and coherence in 'new governance arrangements'. *Policy and Society, 26*(4), 1–18. https://doi.org/10.1016/S1449-4035(07)70118-2

Howlett, M. & Rayner, J. (2013). Patching vs packaging in policy formulation: Assessing policy portfolio design. *Politics and Governance, 1*(2), 170–182. https://doi.org/10.17645/pag.v1i2.95

Jessop, B. (1996). Interpretive sociology and the dialectic of structure and agency. *Theory, Culture & Society, 13*(1), 119–128. https://doi.org/10.1177/026327696013001006

Jessop, B. (2020). The governance of complexity and the complexity of governance. In B. Jessop (ed.), *Putting civil society in its place: Governance, metagovernance*

and subjectivity. Policy Press. https://doi.org/10.1332/policypress/9781447354956
.003.0002

Kaufmann, M. (2013). Emergent self-organisation in emergencies: Resilience rationales in interconnected societies. *Resilience, 1*(1), 53–68.

Kay, A. (2006). *The dynamics of public policy: Theory and evidence.* Edward Elgar Publishing.

Kjaer, P. (2010). *Between governing and governance. On the emergence, function and form of Europe's post-national constellation.* Hart Publishing.

Kooiman, J. & van Vliet, M. (2000). Self-governance as a mode of societal governance. *Public Management: An International Journal of Research and Theory, 2*(3), 359–378. https://doi.org/10.1080/14719030000000022

Lacan, J. & Fink, B. (2006). *Ecrits: The first complete edition in English.* W. W. Norton & Co.

Lawrence, J., Sullivan, F., Lash, A., Ide, G., Cameron, C. & McGlinchey, L. (2015). Adapting to changing climate risk by local government in New Zealand: Institutional practice barriers and enablers. *Local Environment, 20*(3), 298–320. https://doi.org/ 10.1080/13549839.2013.839643

Luhmann, N. (1989). *Ecological communication.* University of Chicago Press.

Luhmann, N. (1990). Technology, environment and social risk: A systems perspective. *Industrial Crisis Quarterly, 4*(3), 223–231. https:// doi .org/ 10 .1177/ 108602669000400305

Luhmann, N. (1995). *Social systems.* Stanford University Press.

Luhmann, N. (1997). Limits of steering. *Theory, Culture & Society, 14*(1), 41–57. https://doi.org/10.1177/026327697014001003

Luhmann, N. (2008). The autopoiesis of social systems. *Journal of Sociocybernetics, 6*(2), 84–95.

Machiavelli, N. (1996). Il Principe. In D. Wootton (ed.), *Modern political thought: Readings from Machiavelli to Nietzsche.* (pp. 6–57). Hackett.

Machiavelli, N., Bondanella, J. C. & Bondanella, P. E. (2008). *Discourses on Livy.* Oxford University Press.

Maturana, H. R. & Varela, F. J. (1987). *The tree of knowledge. The biological roots of human understanding.* Shambhala Publications.

Ostrom, E. (2014). Do institutions for collective action evolve? *Journal of Bioeconomics, 16*(1), 3–30.

Papadopoulos, Y. (2000). Governance, coordination and legitimacy in public policies. *International Journal of Urban and Regional Research, 24*(1), 210–223.

Parés, M., Bonet-Martí, J. & Martí-Costa, M. (2012). Does participation really matter in urban regeneration policies? Exploring governance networks in Catalonia (Spain). *Urban Affairs Review, 48*(2), 238–271. https://doi.org/10.1177/1078087411423352

Pollitt, C. (2008). *Time, policy, management: Governing with the past.* OUP Oxford.

Richards, B. (2007). *Emotional governance: Politics, media and terror.* Springer.

Sandercock, L. (2003). Out of the closet: The importance of stories and storytelling in planning practice. *Planning Theory and Practice, 4*, 11–28.

Seidl, D. (2016). *Organizational identity and self-transformation. An autopoietic perspective.* Routledge.

Steinmo, S., Thelen, K. & Longstreth, F. (1992). *Structuring politics: Historical institutionalism in comparative analysis.* Cambridge University Press.

Suddaby, R. & Panwar, R. (2022). On the complexity of managing transparency. *California Management Review, 65*(1), 5–18. https:// doi .org/ 10 .1177/ 00081256221128766

Teubner, G. (1988). *Autopoietic law: A new approach to law and society.* Walter de Gruyter.

Thelen, K. (2004). *How institutions evolve. The political economy of skills in Germany, Britain, the United States, and Japan.* Cambridge University Press.

Thompson, V. A. (1961). Hierarchy, specialization, and organizational conflict. *Administrative Science Quarterly, 5*(4), 485–521. https://doi.org/10.2307/2390618

Throgmorton, J. (1996). *Planning as persuasive story-telling.* University of Chicago Press.

Van Assche, K., Beunen, R. & Duineveld, M. (2014). *Evolutionary governance theory: An introduction.* Springer.

Van Assche, K., Beunen, R., Duineveld, M. & de Jong, H. (2013). Co-evolutions of planning and design: Risks and benefits of design perspectives in planning systems. *Planning Theory, 12*(2), 177–198. https://doi.org/10.1177/1473095212456771

Van Assche, K., Beunen, R., Gruezmacher, M., & Duineveld, M. (2020). Rethinking strategy in environmental governance. *Journal of Environmental Policy & Planning,* 1–14.

Van Assche, K., Duineveld, M. & Beunen, R. (2014). Power and contingency in planning. *Environment and Planning A, 46*(10), 2385–2400.

Van Assche, K., Gruezmacher, M. & Deacon, L. (2019). Land use tools for tempering boom and bust: Strategy and capacity building in governance. *Land Use Policy,* 103994.

Van Assche, K., Verschraegen, G. & Gruezmacher, M. (2021). Strategy for collectives and common goods. Coordinating strategy, long term perspectives and policy domains in governance. *Futures, 128*(5).

Van Assche, K., Verschraegen, G., Valentinov, V. & Gruezmacher, M. (2019). The social, the ecological, and the adaptive. Von Bertalanffy's general systems theory and the adaptive governance of social-ecological systems. *Systems Research and Behavioral Science, 36*(3), 308–321. https://doi.org/10.1002/sres.2587

Verlin, J. (2021). Humanitarian planning and localised temporalities: The Haitian case. *Global Policy, 12*(S7), 68–79. https://doi.org/10.1111/1758-5899.12978

Verloo, N. (2018). Social-spatial narrative: A framework to analyze the democratic opportunity of conflict. *Political Geography, 62,* 137–148. https://doi.org/10.1016/j.polgeo.2017.11.001

Von Bertalanffy, L. (1968). *General System Theory.* George Braziller.

Vranken, J. F. (2001). European urban governance in fragmented societies. In *Governing European Cities.* Routledge.

Wagenaar, H. (2015). 22 transforming perspectives: The critical functions of interpretive policy analysis. *Handbook of Critical Policy Studies,* 422.

Widerberg, O. (2016). Mapping institutional complexity in the Anthropocene. In *Environmental Politics and Governance in the Anthropocene.* Routledge, London, 81–102.

Zerubavel, E. (2003). *Time maps: Collective memory and the social shape of the past.* University of Chicago Press.

Zhao, Y. (2020). Folding Beijing in Houchangcun Road, or, the topology of power density. *Urban Geography, 41*(10), 1247–1259. https://doi.org/10.1080/02723638.2020.1850046

5.   The realm of discourse: stories and concepts in governance and community

KNOWING AND ORGANIZING

Knowing helps to organize and vice versa (Foucault, 1994, 2003; Van Assche et al., 2014; Voß & Freeman, 2016). As governance pertains to a community, how it wants to organize itself, and develop in a desirable direction, a variety of forms of knowledge will be at play. Many forms of expert knowledge will play a role, in administration, and through advisors, consultants, contractors, academics (Collins & Evans, 2002; Fischer, 2000; Latour, 2004; Turner, 2013). Many stories about the community, the good community, history, place, about good governance co-exist (Anholt, 2009; Czarniawska, 1997; Putnam, 2000), many versions of local knowledge, traditional or otherwise, about what is happening, what could and should happen (Canagarajah, 2002; Fischer, 2000; Geertz, 1983; Van Assche & Hornidge, 2015). As governance produces collectively binding decisions, the collective needs to agree, and a diversity of knowledges requires selection and integration.

'Knowledge' we understand broadly, therefore, and this is not, in our view, a matter of personal preference or general theoretical orientation, but a necessity if we want to understand how governance works, how it can develop long-term visions and how it can transform itself and society. We need to understand knowledge broadly because of the connections between knowing and organizing, which will be slowly developed in the following chapters, because of the importance and variety of learning processes (see the Chapters 8 on change and 10 on strategy), and because visions of the long term can never be simply an accumulation of expert knowledge. Other forms of knowledge will have to be integrated, and *narratives* (see below, this chapter) will be required to integrate knowledges in a form that is persuasive, cohesive and enabling policy integration (Boal & Schultz, 2007).

Expert knowledge, narratives, local knowledge are considered knowledge, without privileging any of them. Each type of knowledge lodges a great internal variety of perspectives, harbors contradictions and tensions, resists

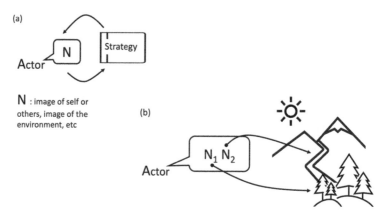

Figure 5.1   Narratives, environment and future[1]

integration, can be used and abused. None of them gives direct access to reality or reflects historical experience or social identity in an immediate way. Expert knowledge can refer to knowledge produced in academic disciplines, but also to knowledge acquired through special, clearly defined experiences, fulfilling recognizable roles in practice. Experts become experts when they are recognized as such, when a distinction is made with lay knowledge (Easterly, 2013). Local knowledge can be opposed to the expertise in administration or academia or in specialized firms, yet local knowledge itself is a complex phenomenon, where experts can also be recognized (Canagarajah, 2002; Geertz, 1983). In other words, overlapping distinctions can occur: local/supra-local, expert/lay, and in governance/outside governance (or in administration/outside administration). In our view, much confusion regarding knowledge, many competing claims, can be traced back to these overlapping distinctions, which are problematically reduced to the local/expert knowledge distinction (Figure 5.2).

Communities have histories that leave traces, governance systems have histories, and knowledges have histories. Those histories will entangle, and what is now expert knowledge, in a governance system, is bound to contain traces of what used to be local knowledge, while current local knowledge will

---

[1]   (a) Actors in governance can produce and subscribe to narratives that portray images of self, of others and of the environment. These narratives inform imagined futures and can shape strategy, while at the same time strategies can influence the narratives. Narratives are partial views, they never offer direct access to a unified reality or objective history. (b) Narratives about the environment shape and are shaped by the interactions actors establish with their surroundings. Narratives can imply shared values, goals and ways of organizing.

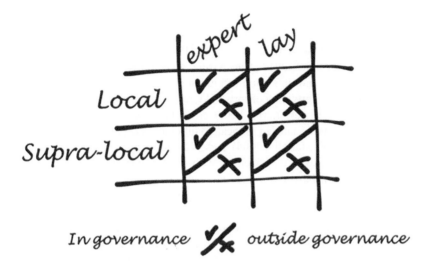

Figure 5.2   Overlap between types of knowledge and governance²

incorporate many insights from expert knowledge, or from knowledge which used to be expertise (Van Assche & Hornidge, 2015). It is common to find situations where local knowledges are shaped by the perspectives of groups not living there anymore. And it is logical to find traditional knowledge, that is knowledge associated with a particular group and its (ritual, mnemonic, ecological, medical, military) traditions, which partly survives those traditions, and becomes generally local, or transforms into recognized expert knowledge (often through establishing new connections), while some of the traditional knowledge was a practical adaptation to an environment left behind a long time ago. Thus, if we rely on the simple distinction local/expert knowledge, and ignore the overlaps with other distinctions just mentioned, we still must recognize that local knowledge is a combination of ad hoc adaptations to an

---

²   Knowledge can take different overlapping forms; categorizing knowledge in a way that excludes overlaps is impossible. Old expert knowledge can appear as local knowledge, traditional knowledge can be supra-local and overlap with what defines expert roles elsewhere. We can easily recognize expert knowledge and lay forms of expertise. Most manifestations of knowledge can thus be labeled in several ways and can be expressed or institutionalized ingovernance, yet as governance responds to its environment, what is excluded can have indirect effects.

(old) environment, (old) traditional knowledge and (old) expertise, and that they will be entwined in complex patterns (Clark & Murdoch, 1997; Van Assche & Hornidge, 2015).

Many discussions on what counts as 'real' local knowledge, or for that matter 'real' expert knowledge are thus rather pointless, or part of a play for power in the governance system (Escobar, 1998; Newman & Clarke, 2018; Turner, 2013; Turnhout, 2018; Van Assche & Hornidge, 2015). This is the case because of the multiplication of hidden distinctions mentioned, because of the evolution and entwining of sorts of knowledge, the prevalence of hybridization, and because *ascription* is key. Certain facts, narratives, perspectives, conceptual relations are labeled as local, traditional, as expertise, as adapted or adaptive (Jasanoff & Martello, 2004). Actors deploy some forms of knowledge and label them in a way they identify with some forms and not others, and this influences their labeling of that knowledge (Cetina, 2007; Van Assche et al., 2013). Sometimes, those labels are recognized or not, sometimes the role advocated for knowledge under that label is recognized or not. This selection, reorganization and labeling of knowledge is the politics and the micro-politics of knowledge one can find in any governance system, a theme we develop in this and following chapters. What is important to highlight now is that privileging any sort of knowledge a priori, or universally, makes no sense, nor does it help to understand governance or to improve it. What can be said generally is that each governance system embodies a pattern of inclusion and exclusion of forms of knowledge, that some of these patterns are adaptive and legitimate while others are problematic, and that each governance system should have the *potential* to open for any kind of knowledge.

KNOWLEDGE AND DISCOURSE

Even if certain scientists have universalist ambitions or beliefs, in governance their expertise meets other forms of knowledge, including other forms of expertise. These can include or be instrumentalized for different values, towards different ambitions, leading to different recommendations. Different questions in governance will pop up depending on the sorts of knowledge present and absent, different methods, problem definitions, diverging answers, priorities, but even different understandings of subjects and objects (see below).

We follow Michel Foucault and interpretive policy analysis in seeing all forms of knowledge as *discourse*, and most of them either narratively structured or underpinned by assumptions which link up to a narrative form (Foucault, 1972, 1980). A *discourse* for us is a set of concepts and their relations which makes particular parts or aspects of reality accessible for us. Knowing is impossible without discourse and discourse is a product of a collective, one can say of a discursive community. Discourse creates realities and

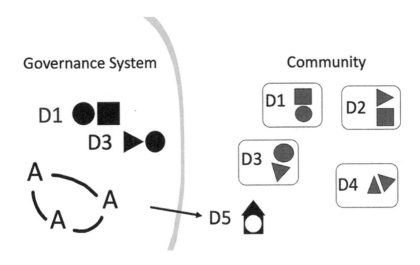

Figure 5.3   Transformation of discourses through governance[3]

makes them navigable for us. Discourses are thus social constructions, but this does not mean that just any construction is possible. A community lives in an environment, shares values, pursues goals, specializes in certain activities, develops forms of organization, and this has to remain compatible with the discourses held to be true, while those discourses will trigger further processes of organization, lead to the emergence of new values, adaptations of and to that environment, etc. (Van Assche et al., 2022) (see Figure 5.1b).

Each discourse is a *selection* of features. Alternative selections exist and each selection highlights and hides certain elements and relations. Patterns of inclusion and exclusion are always there, and blind spots cannot be avoided. The same environment, the same situation, can be constructed in different ways that remain functional, yet using different concepts, different relations, different emphases and different assumptions (Foucault, 1972). Discourses can be narrow or broad in focus, conceptually closed or even hostile to others,

---

[3]   Different features of discourses (D) found in the community can be incorporated by actors (A) into the governance system and then changed, amplified, combined, etc. Governance configurations reflect, modify, combine and weaken discourses in the community and they can create new discourses (D5).

or rather open and flexible in connecting to others, to construct deeper truths or broader perspectives (Figure 5.3).

Discourses can form *coalitions* that reinforce each other's truth in governance, and exist in *configurations* in the community at large, similarly reinforcing truths, leading to the sharing of values, problem definitions and solution orientations (Hajer, 1995; Van Assche et al., 2012). Governance configurations reflect, modify, combine and weaken discourses in the community and they can create new discourses. Discourse coalitions can start as actors forging coalitions or as discourses linking or merging, after which actor coalitions come into being. Those coalitions can eventually produce new identities, or they can simply remain convenient combinations of ideas and/or actors.

Discourses or discursive fragments can travel, mutate and combine (Bal, 2002). Traveling discourse can be interpreted as learning. Giving the discourse agency makes sense as well, as some travels are made possible not just by the desire of some to learn, but by the structure and function of a particular discourse or fragment or by infrastructures and technologies of reproduction of discourses (print, internet, diplomatic networks, trade routes …). Discourses *always* co-evolve with others. They cannot be understood without reference to others, even in the case of the most encompassing and/or closed discourses.

KNOWLEDGE AND NARRATIVE

Narratives make the world understandable and make discourses persuasive (Czarniawska, 2004; Gabriel, 2000; Throgmorton, 1996; Van Assche et al., 2014). They have an internal logic and structure that makes things familiar, seemingly transparent, intuitive or persuasive. Narrative structures in knowledge or underpinning knowledge can be easy to discern, or not. Assumptions in discourses can derive from accepted narratives, or, vice versa, narratives can assemble elements from a wide-ranging set of discourses. Narratives can also create connections between different discourses, thereby stabilizing all of them, so a discursive configuration forms (Bal et al., 2009). Narratives impart structure and account for recurring figures: episodes, introduction and conclusion, a quest, dramatic twists, a foreground, a forgotten history, scapegoats, heroes and villains, ideal communities, a balance between humans and environment, a relation between immanent and transcendent, or forces of nature gathering (Bal et al., 2009). Not all elements and structures need to be universal (as early 20th-century theorists of narrative would want), but the idea of narrative itself, as a structuring principle, an engine of elements becoming recurrent and familiar, and as a force of persuasion and naturalization, we do believe to be universal (Culler, 2002).

In governance, forms of knowledge tend to morph into narratives, in order to persuade other actors, the community at large, and in order to obtain a position in governance, a spot around the table, or a codification in institutions (Boal & Schultz, 2007; Throgmorton, 1996). The nature of governance itself, as the making of collectively binding decisions, but also as the persuasive performance which needs to take place before that, naturally triggers the use or production of narratives. Here one can think of narratives about the good community, the dramatic problem, the recognizable villain, the glorious future, the enemies in and of the community, or a threat to the 'true' nature of the community and its values (Culler, 1975, 2002).

Even a cursory look at political debates or media coverage of specific governance issues reveals various narratives and their influence on public debates, decision-making and the interpretation of various policies. The various narratives on global warming and climate change and their coverage in media are, for example, widely studied (Barkemeyer et al., 2017; Hase et al., 2021; McComas & Shanahan, 1999), but the presence and impact of different and often competing narratives can also be seen when looking at more specific issues, such as the European agricultural policy (Potter, 2006) or the policies and practices of reducing emissions from deforestation and forest degradation (REDD+) (Hiraldo & Tanner, 2011). Governance itself can therefore be considered an engine of narratives. Narratives can be used or constructed to persuade other actors or the community, and narratives can be devised to bridge or highlight differences, recognize common goods, or to find desirable and shared futures. Certain institutions can take the form of a story themselves; strategies are among those.

Narratives can link to existing social or spatial identities (Anholt, 2009; Czarniawska, 1997; Elias & Scotson, 1994). They can lean on accepted versions of history, which are narratives themselves. Furthermore, narratives on history, place and group can shape each other: a social identity incorporates references to a shared history, to enemies and friends, to places left, visited, and places where roots were struck (Lewicka, 2008; Van Assche et al., 2009). A place means something by reference to the people and groups living there, moving in and out, sharing a history there. Not all histories are histories of groups and places, but omitting references to them would make the narrative hard to understand, and group (or national, regional, local) histories do establish tight couplings to places and concepts of social identity.

Narratives playing out in governance can be influenced by a variety of identities. Here one can think of the identities of professional groups, cultural, ethnic, or religious identities (groups), party identities, organizational identities, or disciplinary identities. Even disciplines are more than perspectives

Types of Knowledge

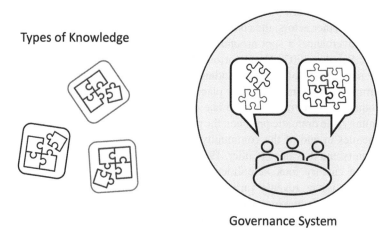

Governance System

Figure 5.4   Knowledge, narratives and governance[4]

on reality; they also take on the character of organization and they are social groups, with their own narrative identities (Czarniawska, 2012). Each governance system will always have different narratives around the table, in politics, administration, or in participatory settings. Each system will also be marked by older narratives in its structures, institutions, and in its procedures. Party identities might have structured still existing participatory settings or checks and balances, and professional identities might have structured departments and plan formation. These identities might still be very present, or might be long gone, leaving traces in governance that might not be recognized by its participants anymore.

Especially if connected to identities, narratives can invest decisions, courses of action, with *affect*, either positive or negative, and either inclusive or exclusive, and these affects can consequently trigger other affects. If affects are touched, narratives can be triggered, and, conversely, if narratives are recognized, affects can be invoked. Psychoanalysis would argue that affective responses often involve unconscious recognition of narrative scenarios, of situations that were experienced a long time ago, given meaning by shaping them as narrative (Young & Frosh, 2018). A narrative which then shaped identity without the person remaining aware of this (see later for the potential of psychoanalytic interpretations at community level).

---

[4]   Knowledge and narratives are both assembled and disassembled in governance. The pressure of decision-making and the presence of competing and complementary discourses fuels discursive dynamics. Discourses cannot be understood without reference to others, and governance is a site where discursive coalitions form.

SPECIAL CONCEPTS AND NARRATIVES

Metaphors

We are surrounded by metaphors, and we form ourselves with metaphors (Barnes & Duncan, 1992; Chandler, 2001; Lakoff & Johnson, 1980). Metaphors, like narratives, assumptions and blind spots, are always there. Metaphors are conceptual connectors, or bridges, linking several discourses, or domains of meaning and meaning production (Danesi, 2013). They can make complex issues understandable, or new objects and situations, by references to known ones, which tend to be situated in other semantic spheres. They use a perspective that formed around the need to make certain things understandable, to explain something else, *or* to shed a new light on it (Danesi, 2013; Sapir & Crocker, 2016).

A new metaphor can create a new meaning, even if there was little confusion before. An organization is a ship, a worker is a bee, a community a beehive. The process can transform the two sides: we can come to understand bees differently, as well as the community. One direction of transformation can be more intentional than the other. The metaphors can be forged anew, by an author, or user of language, trying to communicate something, or they can be found elsewhere, in literature, in policy discourse, in media. They can spread, become prevalent, and can transform perspectives gradually, without people being much aware of them.

Metaphors can spawn other metaphors: the company is a ship; the CEO is the captain. Or they can create other narratives: If the company is a ship, where is it going? They can translate experiences to a narrative structure: Who is, in this situation which makes us feel terrible, slighted, resentful, the villain? The tendency of certain metaphors to create others can be reinforced if they make something understandable that is difficult to grasp through other metaphors, or if they are endowed with special significance by a ruling ideology or a master-narrative which is expected to frame communication on many topics. Ideologies tend to rely on central metaphors (socialist worker bees, socialist sloths) (Throgmorton, 1996).

Each metaphor explains, as any discursive function, by highlighting and hiding, emphasizing and de-emphasizing, connecting and disconnecting. Families of metaphors tend to multiply blind spots. Such cannot be avoided, and long use of metaphors to elucidate one topic can crowd out others, making alternative understandings harder to access. Yet, dominance of a metaphor can also instigate resistance, annoyance, counter-creation of new metaphors, often first in societal margins, or creative circles. Besides the provoking of counter-power by power (see below) the stretching up of metaphors, a common occurrence through extended use, tends to reduce explanatory power, and invite resistance. If everything becomes a ship, and everyone a bee, it does not say much anymore, and parody is imminent.

As governance brings in the complexity of the world, metaphors are handy to help in managing complexity. As diversity of perspectives is essential for good governance, adaptive governance, to maintain differentiation and self-transformation, and discern a representative set of common goods, metaphors can assist in delineating the differences in perspective, but also in finding bridges for collaboration, and making perspectives accessible for each other. As ideologies (see below) can be expected to play a role, their central metaphors will struggle to frame as many topics as possible, to subjugate other actors' narratives under their own. Governance can create metaphors, to sum-marize new narratives, to symbolize new futures or common goods, and it can *test* metaphors, by trying different metaphors, hence angles, in governance and its analysis (Allan, 2007; Coffey, 2016; Doornbos, 2001).

Open Concepts

Just like metaphors, open concepts help to create understanding and interpre-tive flexibility (Chandler, 2001; Kooij et al., 2012). Sustainability, resilience, innovation, but also efficiency, and ultimately 'democracy,' are all examples of open concepts (Gunder & Hillier, 2009). These open concepts grasp big issues through concepts that are broad, flexible, open to various interpre-tations, and to framing by different metaphors. The flexibility allows for coordination as two communicating parties suspend disbelief, pretending they are sure they're talking about the same thing. Performing understanding and agreement is a function of open concepts, and it helps to continue coordination. It enables governance, particularly in conditions where uncertainty and com-plexity prevail. Projection from two sides is possible, and resulting practical problems can be rationalized without opening up the fundamental uncertainty. In the end, we all know what sustainability is, no?

If we are not sure, we produce new open concepts that can be interpreted as objective criteria. If 'sustainability' is not clear, we recognize that there is social, economic, environmental sustainability. This does not mean we know what these things are, or that we are not aware of the tensions and contradic-tions which certainly arise between these different 'aspects' of sustainability. For systems theory, many open concepts hide paradoxes, and the production of new open concepts to veil the open character of the first one is an effort to veil the paradox. Luhmann speaks of *de-paradoxification*, a process which can take a series of conceptual moves, to build layers of seeming certainty upon an essentially paradoxical issue (Luhmann, 2018; Seidl, 2016). In other cases, what is hidden is, in systems terms, more a matter of undecidability.

In the example of sustainability, it is both, as some issues pertaining to it are undecidable, and particular directions of interpretation lead to irreducible contradictions. The concept itself is thus both undecidable and paradoxical, as several ways of specifying it lead to several sets of problems (Roe, 1994).

Psychoanalyst Jacques Lacan speaks of 'point de capiton' (see Chapter 4), referring to signifiers which bestow meaning upon many others, yet, again, in a paradoxical operation suggesting the impossible, namely that a real anchoring of discourse in objective reality is possible (Lacan, 1993). We give ourselves and each other the impression that we know what we talk about, we make the elusive tangible, and we pin it down. In a Lacanian perspective, a master signifier such as 'sustainability' serves as *point de capiton* because there is a nascent collective awareness that things are not going well, that we are not on the right track as a collective. Collective anxiety and collective desire for a safe future, for stability, for an impossible unity and cohesion in the community, coalesce into the formation of new master signifiers which hope to capture that desired future state.

Open concepts thus enable *productive fictions*, and they enable the immediate continuation of coordination. Open concepts and productive fictions are useful in governance and strategy. Policies under the label of sustainability can solve actual problems, can lead to new forms of coordination, to the production and inclusion of new forms of knowledge in governance, and sustainability discourse can bring about greater awareness of more narrowly defined problems in society. Public discourse, discussion and academic debate on sustainability can bring in refinements, modifications, critiques of the concepts, which might make for modified expectations, yet not less urgency in actual problem-solving. Just as the innovation discourse produced a corrective discourse of social innovation, the sustainability discourse led to discussions which exposed its limitations, which brought in resilience thinking, and through internal and external debate evolved to become more cognizant of the complexities of social systems and of governance. Productive fictions can be highly productive, in other words.

Open concepts work best when we're not fully aware we're using them, when they are not continuously scrutinized, or, if so, in a way that suggests method without noticing the open character of the concept. Sustainability is a key example for our story, but one can include resilience, innovation or development easily. Open concepts enable thinking and coordination, yet also require a form of not-thinking. Mats Alvesson (see later), critical management scholar, speaks of functional stupidity (Alvesson & Spicer, 2012). Some open concepts can be situated on the productive side, others much nearer to stupidity. If non-thinking prevails and if this non-thinking is counter-productive, leading to not the best feasible sustainability policy, then scrutiny, unfolding of the paradox, has to take place. Open concepts can start functional, yet if they proliferate non-thinking (especially if accompanied by frantic activity), dysfunctionality lurks around the corner.

Ideology

Ideologies are narratives. They are Big Stories, master narratives or meta-narratives in terms of philosopher Jean-François Lyotard (Lyotard, 1984). They are stories that explain and connect many things at the same time. They offer an experience of unity and an impression of totality in which one can navigate and find a place. Lyotard himself believed that post-modernity (for him starting in the 1980s) embodied the end of grand narratives, as even the communists didn't believe in communism anymore, as few Catholics took notice of the Pope, and as other ideologies had become more a matter of practical organization of life and of governance, without inspiring much belief in their narrative. Catholic political parties survived, but didn't reflect too many Catholic values, rather a set of pragmatic adaptations to practical desires and competing discourses; communists just tried to survive in a system collapsing for all practical purposes.

We tend to disagree on this point and follow Slavoj Žižek and psychoanalysis in asserting that ideologies are always there, that totalizing narratives always play a role in identification of individuals, groups and communities (Žižek, 1989). We also follow Žižek in arguing that ideology is *empty*. It is always a fantasy of wholeness, which was to work with an empty core. Ideology can be highly productive. It can drive communities, unify them, but just as easily divide them and erode checks and balances when ideology is privileged over the values of the prevailing form of democracy.

Some ideologies are more normative than others and some are more comprehensive or totalizing than others. The role of the state or of governance can transpire clearly from the ideology, or less so. With all these differences, ideologies tend to function as meta-narratives, underpinning or producing other stories. The narrative itself can indicate directly how open it is to collaboration with other ideologies, where and how to compete with others. The willingness of an ideology to work in or accommodate to a democratic system makes a big difference, and scholars of governance cannot assume that governance is democratic governance or that where it exists this is a stable state. In democracies, it is worth being careful with assumptions regarding agreement on the value of democracy, or the kind of democracy. Just as it is worth pausing before assuming we share the narrative about what we share as a community, what are common goods, founding values, or narratives inspiring identification.

Ideology can deploy open concepts, metaphors and subservient narrative, and it can function as a master signifier itself. It can invoke a Big Other, an imagined authority which is sanctioning what we, as individuals and as a community, ought to do. In governance, ideologies can structure the whole system, and this can be observed or not. Ideologies can underpin decisions, positions, patterns of inclusion and exclusion, or choice of policy tools. They can create or exist in discursive coalitions and configurations, and they can imbue meaning to layered narratives which leads to perceptions of problems, methods and solutions (see the following chapters).

COMPLEXITY

Complex Institutions and Semiotics

Actors have beliefs, forms of knowledge, and they identify with these forms of knowledge to different degrees while they use them in different manners and to different degrees. They connect identity stories with public goods and issues at hand in unique ways. Actors can represent, in their participation in governance, a carefully managed internal consensus, or they can prefer a rapid, affect-laden response to events in the community and within governance. This means that actors use and interpret institutions according to their own understandings of the world and of the situation and its requirements. These understandings are based on a unique mix of knowledges, a discursive configuration which is in some ways personal, and in many ways reflecting a community, and a group represented. Actors come to different interpretations of what constitutes a problem, and argument, evidence or a solution, and in these interpretations, ideologies, narratives, various discourses, forms of local and expert knowledge always blend, and the exact nature of the blend is unknowable.

Complex institutions, such as plans and strategies, can connect to many stories, forms of knowledge, and to many other institutions (Eco, 2020). Each of those institutions can be interpreted in different ways, and the same goes for their effects. For the interpretation theory of C. S. Peirce (Peirce, 1958), or Peircean semiotics, the work of interpretation is the developing of signs, and in the case of complex institutions there is a lot of work to do. The work of interpretation never stops, and with complex institutions, interpretation has several dimensions: an ongoing unfolding of the institution, interpretation of the meaning and the possible use (Niederdeppe et al., 2014). And, second, an ongoing reinterpretation in an always shifting governance and societal context. The institution itself is thus *text and context*, system of signs and a sign itself (Eco, 2019).

Such a distinction is not a trivial one, as it can help to understand the way that complex plans and strategies are used, the forms of knowledge it connects to, and the support or resistance it will generate. A particular policy can become a reviled symbol of an opposing ideology (Cohen, 1969). A type of institution, say, a plan, can already trigger resistance, on ideological grounds or because a particular idea is alarming, invested with negative affect, or because it represents a disconnect with a perceived truth. A series of perceived effects of an institution, perceived failures to coordinate, or coordination successes with effects disapproved of, can turn the institution into a symbol of something that looks negative in the discourses that frame the perspective of a set of actors, which can then form a coalition, an organized opposition. A perceived failure of a strategy can generate a web of negative associations around one of its key words, or, a rhetorical reframing of the strategy by opponents can generate a new key word which can rally resentment more easily.

Looking at the strategy as a micro-world, different readers, even if unfamiliar with it and not assigning a meaning to the strategy, will make different connections, will find some parts harder to understand than others, will read different intentions (Eco, 1984). Some of the arguments presented in the strategy will be read as evidence, while others will diagnose it as ideology, or a locally held narrative; what some readers see as a method of investigation used looks to others like an acceptable but analytically indifferent way of structuring the text.

Certainty and Selectivity

In modernist statecraft, certainty and probability took central place in decision-making (Luhmann, 2002; Scott, 1998). Actors and their assistants were supposed to come up with facts, and the resulting decisions and institutions were supposed to be supported by the facts. Or, actors were supposed to state their desires clearly, and in governance these could be confronted with each other and the facts, leading to rational and fair decisions, to imperfect but optimal outcomes. Such deliberation was expected to banish the negative effects of ideology, factionalism, self-interest and ignorance. Governance would be efficient and fair. 'Evidence-based' policy was thus promoted and at points in time by both the political left and right, in both western countries and the global south, in welfare states, neo-liberal polities and communist regimes.

Even where high modernist ambitions to define the perfect organization of society and space were not embraced, and where scientific certainty to bring about such a perfect state was not expected, uncertainty was understood as something that could be and should be managed in a rational way. Where perfection and certainty are not possible, probabilities rule. Risk, threat and opportunity thus come to dominate decision-making, and they are translated into numbers; as numbers, in Enlightenment thinking, are the signs that are supposed to reflect reality most accurately (Hacking, 1990). The proliferation of indicators, quantitative assessments, accounting modes, the proclaimed need for transparency, efficiency, and the actual need for policy coordination then led to a proliferation of quantitative measurements of the world, the governance process and its outcomes. And it required and produced a simpli-fication and homogenization of understandings of the world, governance and outcomes to make this quantification work.

We know by now, however, that the delineation of facts, problems, accept-able methods of analysis, organization, or intervention, are always contingent, evolving and, in governance, co-evolving. Once accounting is introduced for one domain of governance, for one topic, it will trigger calls for its introduc-tion elsewhere. Once accounting is introduced everywhere, it will generate a perceived need for accounting standards (Robson & Bottausci, 2018). The selection of knowledges that produce acceptable evidence, and the selectivity of each of those knowledges, remains unquestioned, while contingency rules here as well. If these contingencies are naturalized, new opacities are created, which can be used and abused by those in power, those who *are* aware of the contingent nature of knowledge use in governance – including the knowledge used to assess governance. Moreover, the reinterpretation of knowledge, of institutions and of past and present (what are problems, questions, assets) tends to entangle.

Certainty and evidence-based decision-making in a literal sense is not possi-ble because the selectivity of knowledges in governance is shifting all the time. Even if some forms of knowledge are more entrenched than others, associated with powerful actors and important institutions, this does not provide enough stability (in any form of democratic governance) to come naturally to stable facts that can support decisions in the longer run. Certain versions of history, of assets, of problems might be shared, yet this will not last for long, as both interests and interpretations change, and as new interpretations can come from many sides. A new value can inspire a re-evaluation of history, which leads to a reassessment of a policy, etc.

This instability in the selection and use of knowledges in governance does not make governance for the long run impossible, nor efficient governance, nor democracy. It does mean that governance is easier if people share values and stories, and if people are used to certain forms of governance and its tools. It also means that the slowing down of governance is important (as through law), its checks and balances, and that routines and decisions themselves perform functions of non-thinking, enabling productive fictions.

STRATEGY AND OBSERVATION

As the future is per definition unknowable, and as coordination and policy integration are per definition imperfect, strategy is bound to be difficult. At the same time, different observations, made in different perspectives, leaning on different knowledges, can tell us that strategy is utterly necessary, that governance for the short term cannot be allowed to exclude anything else. This already is an argument for *adaptive* strategy. As we know, operating based on a strategy that is regularly assessed, discussed, adapted, is very different from absent strategy. It also points already at the need for a shared long-term perspective, a narrative which can be forged, which can link to existing narratives, and underpin the strategy. And it hints at the importance of *choices*.

Decisions are per definition jumps across an abyss of irreducible uncertainty, and strategies even more so. Deliberate choices in strategy help in selecting the forms of knowledge prioritized in strategy, and the continuous management of uncertainty. Further, this suggests that awareness of the temporality of processes subjected to strategy is a key factor for success, and that these must be coordinated with the temporality of governance itself. This implies, among other things, that random choices of duration, and random targets of achievement, are not the best idea.

It is worthwhile here to take a step back and remind ourselves that knowledge in governance has to start from observation. Governance systems observe their societal environment, and vice versa. Actors observe other actors in governance, as well as the community. Observations start from distinctions: something is either this or that. The insights from social systems theory can be useful here, as this distinguishes between first-order observations and second-order observation (Fuchs, 2001; Luhmann, 1995). *First-order observations* observe an environment, *second-order observation* observes how other observers make and apply distinctions. In governance, second-order observation of society is possible, through the combination of political and administrative actors, and their advisors. Such second-order observation of governance is useful to grasp how environments are observed and understood and how these observations are reflected in governance; in other words, how the relation between knowing and organizing is functioning. These second-order observations are a way to open governance for additional observation points and to a more diverse set of perspectives, and are useful to identify blind spots. Hence, second-order observations help in fostering reflexivity and to adapt governance.

The configuration of governance and its evolution determines what kind of observations are made by governance or entering governance. A lack of observation can ignore or create problems. New arenas, domains, themes, actors might restructure observation.

The importance of the multiplicity and quality of observations can also be linked to the idea of evidence-based policy (Head, 2010) or to procedures such as environmental impact assessments (Morgan, 2012) that not only bring in expertise but also expand the modes and field of observation. Their true value does not lie in the fact that they can or should determine decisions, but in the fact that additional observations are brought to the fore, which at least stimulate additional reflection, even in cases where evidence or assessments are in the end put aside. We can add that allowing for truly second-order observation can help to transform first-order observation, and that not all external expertise represents second-order observation.

Ecological problems tend to proliferate because they are not observed, not voiced, or because those who raise concerns are not heard or are ignored. In even more extreme situations, environmental concerns, or the people voicing these concerns, are silenced, or obstructed via alternative facts and the creation of doubt (Oreskes & Conway, 2010).

Warnings about environmental issues go back a long way and this is particularly true for some of the largest sustainability challenges such as climate change or biodiversity decline. One of the most well-known examples of such warnings is the report 'The limits to growth' (Meadows et al., 1972). Although the report gained a lot of attention and did trigger societal debates and the formulation of policies, over time the warning could not prevent the crossing of various planetary boundaries (Steffen et al., 2015). On a smaller scale the negative impact of livestock farming in the Netherlands is another example. Although experts and politicians in the 1970s and 1980s had already issued warning about the negative impacts of cattle, pigs and chickens in the Netherlands (Lamers, Leon, n.d.), policies mainly focused on technical solutions, weakening regulation, and facilitating livestock farmers, making problems more entrenched and more difficult to address, evolving into a situation in which not only the environment and public health are at risk, but the problem also causes significant economic damage (Beunen & Kole, 2021; Erisman et al., 2021).

Strategy for the long term will benefit from a deepening and broad sharing of awareness regarding the observational qualities of governance, of its sites of observation, its dominant distinctions, framing metaphors, ideologies and open concepts, and its modes of self-observation. Even if the final decisions on strategy are the domain of a few, it is not advisable to compartmentalize administration and governance as such to such an extent that most are aware of only a small part of the procedure, of only a few of the goals, of only a fraction of intentions, and that few can participate in truly essential discussions on the forms of observing and knowing which have propelled and shaped the strategy process. If this is the case, limitations are unknown to most, and this might include leadership, as they might assume others took care of this knowing. Furthermore, the big message, necessary to render strategy cohesive and persuasive, can veil, even with the bringers of the message, its inherent limitations and uncertainties (Boal & Schultz, 2007).

The imperfection of checks and balances, the design of most governance systems, democratic and otherwise, ensures that factionalism is never excluded, that strategists thinking about the future of the community also think about their own future and that of their party. All this makes for a difficult balancing act when speaking of common goods, and, closer to our current topic, when discerning and openly acknowledging latent ideologies, privileged forms and sites of observation, favored institutions, and other limitations of observation and self-observation.

A CONCLUDING NOTE

Knowledge is knowledge of something, and that something is a reality. The production of knowledge is the reinforcement of certain versions of reality, as that production can only take place if some assumptions regarding reality and its investigation are *not* scrutinized. Hence, while knowledge can transform our understanding of reality, this is rarely radical, and the limits of the intervention are rarely transparent. In governance, a basic reality must be shared before governance becomes realistic, while governance must power to transform that reality (Shore et al., 2011). The following chapters will explore processes of change and stability in governance, yet the ideas introduced in this chapter allow us to observe that the creation of a shared reality is both enabled and rendered more difficult in governance. Indeed, the creation of unity is more difficult when diversity is made visible, yet governance also possesses various tools to change reality for many, to make subjects more similar, and to naturalize what is contingent (see Chapter 8) (Culler, 2002). When shared narratives, ideologies and similar identities are in place, the hardening of realities is relatively easy, and the difficulties for introducing transition strategies are entirely contingent on the nature of the locally dominant narratives and identities. When governance is strategic in naturalizing what could have been different, and what was the product of power/knowledge interactions in governance itself, then one can say that governance is successful in creating its own support, in creating the conditions for future success. This, we will note, can be helpful for transition strategy, yet it also brings into focus the ethical dilemmas of just transition.

REFERENCES

Allan, C. (2007). Exploring natural resource management with metaphor analysis. *Society and Natural Resources*, *20*(4), 351–362.

Alvesson, M. & Spicer, A. (2012). A stupidity-based theory of organizations. *Journal of Management Studies*, *49*(7), 1194–1220.

Anholt, S. (2009). *Places: Identity, image and reputation*. Palgrave Macmillan.

Bal, M. (2002). *Travelling concepts in the humanities: A rough guide*. University of Toronto Press.

Bal, M., Boheemen, C. van & ebrary Inc. (2009). *Narratology introduction to the theory of narrative* (3rd edn.). University of Toronto Press.

Barkemeyer, R., Figge, F., Hoepner, A., Holt, D., Kraak, J. M. & Yu, P.-S. (2017). Media coverage of climate change: An international comparison. *Environment and Planning C: Politics and Space*, *35*(6), 1029–1054. https://doi.org/10.1177/0263774X16680818

Barnes, T. J. & Duncan, J. S. (1992). *Writing worlds. Discourse, text and metaphor in the representation of landscape*. Routledge.

Beunen, R. & Kole, S. (2021). Institutional innovation in conservation law: Experiences from the implementation of the Birds and Habitats Directives in the Netherlands. *Land Use Policy*, *108*, 105566.

Boal, K. B. & Schultz, P. L. (2007). Storytelling, time, and evolution: The role of strategic leadership in complex adaptive systems. *The Leadership Quarterly, 18*(4), 411–428. https://doi.org/10.1016/j.leaqua.2007.04.008

Canagarajah, S. (2002). Reconstructing local knowledge. *Journal of Language, Identity & Education, 1*(4), 243–259. https://doi.org/10.1207/S15327701JLIE0104_1

Cetina, K. K. (2007). Culture in global knowledge societies: Knowledge cultures and epistemic cultures. *Interdisciplinary Science Reviews, 32*(4), 361–375. https://doi.org/10.1179/030801807X163571

Chandler, D. (2001). *Semiotics: The basics*. Routledge.

Clark, J. & Murdoch, J. (1997). Local knowledge and the precarious extension of scientific networks: A reflection on three case studies. *Sociologia Ruralis, 37*(1), 38–60.

Coffey, B. (2016). Unpacking the politics of natural capital and economic metaphors in environmental policy discourse. *Environmental Politics, 25*(2), 203–222.

Cohen, A. (1969). Political anthropology: The analysis of the symbolism of power relations. *Man, 4*(2), 215–235. https://doi.org/10.2307/2799569

Collins, H. M. & Evans, R. (2002). The third wave of science studies: Studies of expertise and experience. *Social Studies of Science, 32*(2), 235–296. https://doi.org/10.1177/0306312702032002003

Culler, J. (1975). *Structuralist poetics: Structuralism, linguistics and the study of literature*. Routledge.

Culler, J. (2002). *Barthes: A very short introduction*. Oxford University Press.

Czarniawska, B. (1997). *Narrating the organization. Dramas of institutional identity*. University of Chicago Press.

Czarniawska, B. (2004). *Narratives in social science research*. Sage.

Czarniawska, B. (2012). Organization theory meets anthropology: A story of an encounter. *Journal of Business Anthropology, 1*(1), article 1. https://doi.org/10.22439/jba.v1i1.3549

Danesi, M. (2013). On the metaphorical connectivity of cultural sign systems. *Signs and Society, 1*(1), 33–49. https://doi.org/10.1086/670164

Doornbos, M. (2001). 'Good governance': The rise and decline of a policy metaphor? In *Changing the Conditions for Development Aid*. Routledge.

Easterly, W. (2013). *The tyranny of experts: Economists, dictators, and the forgotten rights of the poor*. Basic Books.

Eco, U. (1984). *The role of the reader: Explorations in the semiotics of texts* (vol. 318). Indiana University Press.

Eco, U. (2019). 2. Function and sign: Semiotics of architecture. In *2. Function and sign: Semiotics of architecture* (pp. 55–86). Columbia University Press. https://doi.org/10.7312/gott93206-004

Eco, U. (2020). Social life as a sign system. In *Fashion Theory* (2nd edn.). Routledge.

Elias, N. & Scotson, J. L. (1994). *The established and the outsiders: A sociological enquiry into community problems*. Sage.

Erisman, J. W., de Vries, W., van Donk, E., Reumer, J., van den Broek, J., Smit, A., Kerklaan, J. & van Schayck, P. (2021). *Stikstof: De sluipende effecten op natuur en gezondheid*. Stichting Biowetenschappen en Maatschappij. Uitgeverij Atlas.

Escobar, A. (1998). Whose knowledge, whose nature? Biodiversity, conservation and the poltical ecology of social movements. *Journal of Political Ecology, 5*(1), 53–82.

Fischer, F. (2000). *Citizens, experts and the environment. The politics of local knowledge*. Duke University Press.

Foucault, M. (1972). *The archaeology of knowledge & the discourse on language*. Pantheon Books.

Foucault, M. (1980). *Power/knowledge: Selected interviews and other writings, 1972–1977*. Pantheon Books.

Foucault, M. (1994). *Power. Essential works of Foucault 1954–1984. Volume 3*. The New Press.

Foucault, M. (2003). *Society must be defended: Lectures at the Collège de France, 1975–76*. Allen Lane/The Penguin Press.

Fuchs, S. (2001). *Against essentialism: A theory of culture and society.* Harvard University Press.
Gabriel, Y. (2000). *Storytelling in organizations. Facts, fictions, and fantasies.* Oxford University Press.
Geertz, C. (1983). *Local knowledge: Further essays in interpretive anthropology.* Basic Books.
Gunder, M. & Hillier, J. (2009). *Planning in ten words or less. A Lacanian entanglement with spatial planning.* Ashgate.
Hacking, I. (1990). *The taming of chance* (vol. 17). Cambridge University Press.
Hajer, M. A. (1995). *The politics of environmental discourse: Ecological modernization and the policy process.* Clarendon.
Hase, V., Mahl, D., Schäfer, M. S. & Keller, T. R. (2021). Climate change in news media across the globe: An automated analysis of issue attention and themes in climate change coverage in 10 countries (2006–2018). *Global Environmental Change, 70,* 102353. https://doi.org/10.1016/j.gloenvcha.2021.102353
Head, B. W. (2010). Reconsidering evidence-based policy: Key issues and challenges. *Policy and Society, 29*(2), 77–94.
Hiraldo, R. & Tanner, T. (2011). Forest voices: Competing narratives over REDD+. *IDS Bulletin, 42*(3), 42–51. https://doi.org/10.1111/j.1759-5436.2011.00221.x
Jasanoff, S. & Martello, M. (2004). *Earthly politics: Local and global in environmental governance.* The MIT Press.
Kooij, H.-J., Van Assche, K. & Lagendijk, A. (2012). Open concepts as crystallization points and enablers of discursive configurations: The case of the Innovation Campus in the Netherlands. *European Planning Studies,* 1–17. https:// doi .org/ 10 .1080/ 09654313.2012.731039
Lacan, J. (1993). *The seminar of Jacques Lacan, Book 3: The psychoses 1955–1956* (pp. x, 341). W. W. Norton & Company.
Lakoff, G. & Johnson, M. (1980). *Metaphors we live by.* University of Chicago Press.
Lamers, L. (n.d.). *De kool, de geit en het mestbeleid,. Waarom het wensdenkende mestbeleid niet werkte.* Landwerk.
Latour, B. (2004). *Politics of nature. How to bring the sciences into democracy.* Harvard University Press.
Lewicka, M. (2008). Place attachment, place identity, and place memory: Restoring the forgotten city past. *Journal of Environmental Psychology, 28*(3), 209–231. https://doi.org/10.1016/j.jenvp.2008.02.001
Luhmann, N. (1995). *Social systems.* Stanford University Press.
Luhmann, N. (2002). *Risk. A sociological theory.* Aldine Transaction.
Luhmann, N. (2018). *Organization and decision.* Cambridge University Press.
Lyotard, J. F. (1984). *Postmodern condition: A report on knowledge.* Manchester University Press.
McComas, K. & Shanahan, J. (1999). Telling stories about global climate change: Measuring the impact of narratives on issue cycles. *Communication Research, 26*(1), 30–57. https://doi.org/10.1177/009365099026001003
Meadows, D. H., Randers, J. & Meadows, D. L. (1972). The limits to growth (1972). In *The Limits to Growth (1972)* (pp. 101–116). Yale University Press. https://doi.org/ 10.12987/9780300188479-012
Morgan, R. K. (2012). Environmental impact assessment: The state of the art. *Impact Assessment and Project Appraisal, 30*(1), 5–14. https://doi.org/10.1080/14615517.2012.661557
Newman, J. & Clarke, J. (2018). The instabilities of expertise: Remaking knowledge, power and politics in unsettled times. *Innovation: The European Journal of Social Science Research, 31*(1), 40–54.
Niederdeppe, J., Shapiro, M. A., Kim, H. K., Bartolo, D. & Porticella, N. (2014). Narrative persuasion, causality, complex integration, and support for obesity policy. *Health Communication, 29*(5), 431–444. https:// doi .org/ 10 .1080/ 10410236 .2012 .761805

Oreskes, N. & Conway, E. M. (2010). *Merchants of doubt: How a handful of scientists obscured the truth on issues from tobacco smoke to global warming.* https://philpapers.org/rec/OREMOD

Peirce, C. (1958). *Values in a universe of chance: Selected writings of Charles S. Peirce.* Doubleday.

Potter, C. (2006). Competing narratives for the future of European agriculture: The agri-environmental consequences of neoliberalization in the context of the Doha Round. *The Geographical Journal, 172*(3), 190–196. https://doi.org/10.1111/j.1475-4959.2006.00210.x

Putnam, R. D. (2000). *Bowling alone: The collapse and revival of American community.* Simon & Schuster.

Robson, K. & Bottausci, C. (2018). The sociology of translation and accounting inscriptions: Reflections on Latour and accounting research. *Critical Perspectives on Accounting, 54*, 60–75. https://doi.org/10.1016/j.cpa.2017.11.003

Roe, E. (1994). *Narrative policy analysis: Theory and practice.* Duke University Press.

Sapir, J. D. & Crocker, J. C. (2016). *The social use of metaphor: Essays on the anthropology of rhetoric.* University of Pennsylvania Press.

Scott, J. C. (1998). *Seeing like a state: How certain schemes to improve the human condition have failed.* Yale University Press.

Seidl, D. (2016). *Organizational identity and self-transformation. An autopoietic perspective.* Routledge.

Shore, C., Wright, S. & Però, D. (2011). *Policy worlds: Anthropology and the analysis of contemporary power.* Berghahn Books.

Steffen, W., Richardson, K., Rockström, J., Cornell, S. E., Fetzer, I., Bennett, E. M., Biggs, R., Carpenter, S. R., de Vries, W., de Wit, C. A., Folke, C., Gerten, D., Heinke, J., Mace, G. M., Persson, L. M., Ramanathan, V., Reyers, B. & Sörlin, S. (2015). Planetary boundaries: Guiding human development on a changing planet. *Science, 347*(6223), 1259855. https://doi.org/10.1126/science.1259855

Throgmorton, J. (1996). *Planning as persuasive story-telling. The rhetorical construction of Chicago's electric future.* University of Chicago Press.

Turner, S. P. (2013). *The politics of expertise.* Routledge.

Turnhout, E. (2018). The politics of environmental knowledge. *Conservation and Society, 16*(3), 363–363.

Van Assche, K. & Hornidge, A.-K. (2015). *Rural development: Knowledge and expertise in governance.* Wageningen Press.

Van Assche, K., Beunen, R. & Duineveld, M. (2012). Performing success and failure in governance: Dutch planning experiences. *Public Administration, 90*(3), 567–581. https://doi.org/10.1111/j.1467-9299.2011.01972.x

Van Assche, K., Beunen, R. & Duineveld, M. (2014). *Evolutionary governance theory: An introduction.* Springer.

Van Assche, K., Beunen, R., Duineveld, M. & de Jong, H. (2013). Co-evolutions of planning and design: Risks and benefits of design perspectives in planning systems. *Planning Theory, 12*(2), 177–198. https://doi.org/10.1177/1473095212456771

Van Assche, K., Devlieger, P., Teampau, P. & Verschraegen, G. (2009). Forgetting and remembering in the margins: Constructing past and future in the Romanian Danube Delta. *Memory Studies, 2*(2), 211–234. https://doi.org/10.1177/1750698008102053

Van Assche, K., Duineveld, M., Beunen, R., Valentinov, V. & Gruezmacher, M. (2022). Material dependencies: Hidden underpinnings of sustainability transitions. *Journal of Environmental Policy & Planning, 24*(3), 281–296. https://doi.org/10.1080/1523908X.2022.2049715

Voß, J.-P. & Freeman, R. (2016). *Knowing governance: The epistemic construction of political order.* Springer.

Young, L. S. & Frosh, S. (2018). Psychoanalysis in narrative research. In *Methods of Research into the Unconscious.* Routledge.

Žižek, S. (1989). *The sublime object of ideology.* Verso.

6. Power and knowledge in governance: enabling, structuring and hindering transitions

POWER OMNIPRESENT IN GOVERNANCE

Power is that which can move things, achieve things or block things and hence one of the topics that has gained a lot of attention in the literature on governance. Power has been conceptualized, defined and studied in many different ways and there is a tradition of literature that goes back to key thinkers such as Foucault (Foucault, 1979, 1980, 1998), Nietzsche (Glenn, 2004), Machiavelli (Machiavelli, 1988) to Plato (Smith, 2000). A key message that stems from all this literature is that power exercised in and through governance cannot be simply force or coercion. Hence attention is also paid to the ways in which power is intertwined with knowledge, and in the various ways in which power can be seen as a potentiality that is located in networks of discourses and materialities and in the relations between structures and elements and subjects and objects (Borch, 2005; Pottage, 1998; Van Assche, Duineveld, et al., 2014). That power is much more than simple coercion immediately becomes clear if one looks at governance practices. The threat of violence or of coercion might work better than violence or coercion itself; law cannot work if coercion is needed all the time and one cannot force everybody to do something all the time, nor can one regulate everything. The functioning of power is also visible in the narratives that are shared about the environment, about governance, or about certain issues or actors in governance (Bourdieu, 1991; Czarniawska & Gagliardi, 2003; Flyvbjerg, 1998; Van Assche et al., 2017).

Power is inherent to politics, opposition, strategy, patterns of inclusion and exclusion, and to the various ways in which knowledge is developed and used (Asimakou, 2009; Fischer, 2000; Law, 1990; Turner, 2013). Power is something that is ascribed to actors, to institutions, to specific tools, to parts of the governance systems, or the overall system of governance, and it is a mechanism that is visible in interactions between actors and between actors and other elements of the governance systems of its environment (Acemoglu & Robinson, 2013; Armstrong & Bernstein, 2008; Clegg, 1989; Mahoney &

Thelen, 2010). Power produces and is inscribed in realities, discourses, knowledge, subjects, objects and values, and pushes others into the background. The tools of policy, including all institutions, are tools of power, as they can make things happen, in governance and in the community. They guide behavior (Acemoglu & Robinson, 2013; Escobar, 1984; Foucault, 1980). Coordinating is guiding, and coordination will include elements of prohibition, encouragement and dissuasion, as our brief prior discussion of policy tools revealed.

One cannot avoid or evade power: things need to happen in a coordinated fashion, and others have to be stopped or prevented. Activities take place without governance in sight, but governance decides what is possible. If people believe in the institutions designated to regulate an activity, coordination according to the institution will be easier. If institutions are *never* enforced, then the expectation will become that governance does not work, that it is not necessary to comply or to use it to guide coordination. If exceptions are perceived as random or unfair, legitimacy will also be undermined and if non-compliance is blatant and rule-breakers are proud of it, this can signal a collapse of the whole governance system (Cleaver & Whaley, 2018; Escobar, 1984; Van Assche et al., 2011).

Counter-power tends to follow power; actions cause reactions. A big policy push unwanted in a community will create a backlash or simmering resentment which will explode when conditions are ripe. This means that in governance, and through governance, careful and measured use of power is of the essence. As reactions can be partly anticipated, Foucault speaks of 'gymnastics' (Foucault, 1979). If the exercise of power is not observed, the chances of counter-powers appearing are slimmer. The same applies to strategy. Strategy, if observed, and if the aims or results are not to the liking of other actors or groups in the community, will provoke counterstrategy. If the strategy remains hidden, counterstrategies are less likely to appear (Flyvbjerg, 1998; Luhmann, 1997; Valentinov et al., 2019). The questions multiply here, as hiding community strategy from the community is a tricky strategy, and one fraught with ethical dilemmas.

The ability to make people believe something, to persuade them, to reframe their perspective or understanding, or to make something look natural that is contingent, is power. Citizens, and actors in governance, act on things they believe consciously, things they take for granted or can be convinced of. Stories can give cohesion to an explanation, a situation, a past and a future. Localizing explanations, linking to local knowledge, can make policies more practical but also more persuasive if locals define themselves as local. The persuasive aspect can take over the adaptive or corrective aspects of localizing narratives, and can serve to keep actors in power, rather than solving problems. Similarly, ideologies, as master-narratives, can be sincerely believed as the most appropriate direction for the community, bringing forth a better future by means of superior modes of governance, and the same ideologies can serve to keep individuals and factions in power (Henry, 2011; Therborn, 1999). Neo-liberal ideas about business, trade and small government upheld by conservative parties are the main reason why in certain places in North America conservative parties have been in power for decades and liberal party candidates have no chance of being elected. People can grasp something as reality because of learning and non-learning, critical thinking and imitation, persuasion and coercion, because of the seduction of identity and the pressure to conform.

People believe things more easily and do things more readily when they trust that the system of governance works, is legitimate and makes sense. People believe and act when they trust the person representing a role in the system even if they do not entirely understand the details of the role or the knowledge applied or the structures of roles (Burchell et al., 1991; Stern, 2008). Trust in a person can blend into trust in the system (or if one prefers confidence in the system), and conversely trust in the system, together with a recognized role in the system, can confer trust to the person (de Vries et al., 2015; Rousseau et al., 1998). Trust in the system is easier to maintain if the procedures of representation and participation are trusted; that is, if the system is recognized as representing the interests of the community (even if imperfectly) and not as an opposing power, perpetuating itself for its own sake, or representing the interests of a despised elite (see above) (Hardin, 1999; Luhmann, 2018).

Power and Policy Tools

Policy tools work best if people believe in them. The reasons for such trusting or positive interpretation can be manifold. Citizens (and actors in governance) might be familiar with them, might have seen positive results, or might support the goals for which the policy tools are used. The tools, furthermore, might be associated with a preferred ideology or exalted form of expertise. They are perceived to fit well in the governance system, to further a real common good that is readily accepted. People do *not* believe in a policy tool for similarly diverse reasons. The type of tool can annoy them, the person presenting it at a public meeting, the graphic presentation looking too artistic or bureaucratic, the cost (to prepare a strategy, order a study, organize a participation process), the ideology *presumed* to hide beneath the surface of stated good intentions and neutrality (Clark & Newman, 1997).

People interpret a policy tool, including all types of institutions, depending on their ideology, their place and historical narratives, the sign systems they are familiar with, their level of education, social and cultural identity, their mood, the rhetoric in media and politics (Yanow, 2007; Žižek, 1989). The political and societal debates about taxes as policy tools, and more recently the growing aversion against tax exemptions for aviation and fossil fuels, clearly show the different ways in which ideology is related to policy tools. Planning is another example that shows how the way in which people see and understand planning strongly influences if and how they accept it as a (meta-) tool for governance (Gunder & Hillier, 2009; Shepherd et al., 2020). Dominant metaphors, persuasive images, impressive numbers can all contribute to the positioning vis-à-vis a policy tool that *is already supposed to take these diverse positions into account.* In practice, this is never possible, and no combination of participation and representation can gauge public opinion to such an extent that interpretive shifts and fissures *after* presentation or application of the tool can be avoided (Gunder, 2010).

Many links between ideology and policy tools can be recognized, yet these connections change over time, as testified by ever-shifting debates on existing and new policy tools. If an ideology is opposed to planning, people identifying with it will not appreciate one instance of a plan, even if it could benefit them. If people identify as a group that was mistreated by a governance system or, worse, those in power, they are more likely to dispute the benefits and legitimacy of whatever policy produced. If people mistrust a particular branch of government, or domain of governance, or one governmental actor, then any policy tool emanating from there or used there might be felt as coercion. If governance is understood as performance, as theatre, then different roles can be invented or taken on, and resistance can be feigned, to get a better bargain (Hillier, 2000). If taxes and subsidies are seen as evil in the reigning ideology, then policies relying on taxes tend to be opposed even if the goal is appreciated. If locals are always right, then regional planning will be less than welcome (Boddy & Hickman, 2018). If laws are seen to benefit supposedly privileged groups, the law will be seen as unjust, and its enactment as a confirmation of the story about elite power. Stories shape calls for policy and responses to policy (Czarniawska & Gagliardi, 2003).

POWER/KNOWLEDGE

For Michel Foucault, knowledge is power (Foucault, 1980). Knowing things is helpful in governance, while controlling what people believe gives you power. This happens through rhetoric in election times, but once in power for a while, one can use all the tools of governance to shape the thought of citizens (Foucault, 1980). Once in power the rhetoric in the next election period can be amped up and take the shape of promises, knowledge claims (we know how things work), where results can be pointed at. In totalitarian regimes, propaganda is deemed okay by those in the sphere of governance, and ministries, research institutes, media, schools can become propaganda machines. Science can become ideological, can be used to present the political order as a natural order (Ledeneva, 2006). Only certain methods to produce knowledge are acceptable, some assumptions, some lines of reasoning, and some outcomes and diagnoses. Only certain forms of learning are promoted, only certain media are allowed and, in there, only certain narratives, topics, people and angles.

Foucault acknowledged that discourse holds power over the strategist. The strategist attempting to control minds, deciding what is real and desirable for citizens, never escapes the power of discourse. Think of a wine merchant focusing on pinot noir, rather than others, what is the story behind her intention? Why choose the profession at all? Why be annoyed with customers asking for alternatives? In line with psychoanalysis, we argue that people are never entirely transparent to themselves. From within discourse, the structure of that discourse is never entirely visible, let alone alternative interpretations of the topic of discourse. Foucault, as with many other academic writers and otherwise, observed that strategizing itself can become an addictive habit or, more precisely, a self-reinforcing habit. Power corrupts, indeed, and losing power is painful, albeit a different issue. The game of strategy itself takes hold over the strategist, and the search for other actors' strategies leads unavoidably to some discovery, a pin prick to develop new strategy, etc., *ad infinitum.* In this game, the desire to strategize has taken a hold on the strategist, to the extent that the initial reality can be suspended or lost.

Governance is inherently about power and knowledge (Van Assche et al., 2017). If knowledge enters governance, it is promised power and the powers of governance make it productive in terms of knowledge. Governance thus triggers competition, selection, production, coordination of forms of knowledge (see the previous chapter). All of those are structurally tangled up with power. The most encompassing form of knowledge, bestowing powers of coordination and legitimacy, is the model of the world and the community that is operated upon in governance. That model does not always exist as a unity. It can be a plurality, and competition can prevent the formation of a shared understanding (Voß & Freeman, 2016; Yanow, 2003). If it exists, it supports nested narratives, a discursive coalition, a combination of privileged expert knowledges, privileged because they seem to detail a model already accepted, a reality simply reflected (Dean, 2013; Van Assche et al., 2021).

The selection of actors and the selection of knowledge in governance cannot be separated. Knowledges support each other; they support actors, their power, and they support other knowledges and their actors. For this reason, we speak of power/knowledge configurations in governance. One cannot understand knowledge without reference to power in a governance context, and this context makes the reference specific. In governance, power and knowledge co-evolve in a distinct manner, as the pressure cooker of governance invests potentially all knowledge with power, while all power that can be wielded has to be based on knowledge and will trigger the production of new knowledge (Beunen et al., 2015; Van Assche, Beunen, et al., 2014).

Resources and Things

Power in governance is ultimately aimed at control over the making of collectively binding decisions, thus the shaping of the collective. This also entails control over resources, including access to resources, distribution of resources, and distribution of benefits emanating from resources. A resource or an asset can bestow power and power can materialize control over resources (Van Assche et al., 2017). However, something *becomes* a resource in a particular perspective. Actors can embrace or develop discourse, which entails an understanding of resources and how to exploit them and an understanding of value and how to create it. They can develop, in other words, the perspective that can make something an asset or resource, or, elsewhere, they can create a perspective on a recognized resource that can shift its use and valuation (Alevizou et al., 2016; Van Assche & Gruezmacher, 2022). Expertise can create value in an obvious sense, yet the narratives about the resource, or about the role of the resources in the development of the community, hold power. Resources or assets can thus wield power via ideologies, via the narratives of identity and value the resources imbue, via actors identifying with those narratives (Van Assche & Lo, 2011).

Discourses can directly center on resources, and can influence governance because of that – the resource is widely understood to hold the key to prosperity. Yet discourses on very different things can have an impact on the valuation of resources in a community, in its governance system (Van Assche et al., 2017). The importance of resources does not break the hold of power/knowledge configurations in other words. Narratives of value drive power/knowledge transformation. As values and narratives of value change, so do power/knowledge configurations. Internet access is a service that is highly valued, but that was not the case in the 1980s when the internet was in its infancy. If an internet company can guarantee remote regions access to the internet, that company will likely be given a special place at the negotiating table when it comes to infrastructure development in the region. It's important to keep in mind here that value can be attributed in different dimensions, not only in monetary terms.

Power/knowledge configurations drive the production of objects and subjects in governance (Duineveld et al., 2013; Kooij, 2014). This can be a result of conflict, of collaboration or of exploration. The needs of governance to come to decisions, to achieve goals, to decide on goals, to coordinate and come to an understanding, as well as to represent others and their understandings, puts a continuous pressure on the production of new meaning in governance.

This can entail the recognition of new assets and values, but also of new things and new social identities, or perspectives on the world associated with a group. Not all subjectivities are produced in governance, but all who become represented in governance will certainly transform, all who participate will change (Ashmore et al., 2001; Elias & Scotson, 1994; Seidl, 2016; Tajfel, 2010; Turnhout et al., 2010; Van Assche et al., 2011; Van Dam et al., 2015).

New objects can lead to new subjects and vice versa. The development of infrastructures, for mobility, water or energy, for example, often comes with the emergence of dedicated infrastructure managers, while groups in governance might create new objects or bring attention to things previously not observed, or not given concern. New subjects can lead to new versions of identity politics, but also to a range of narratives touching on other topics of governance. Objects and subjects can gradually emerge, and irreversibility can be created in many infinitesimal steps. New objects can be truly internally constructed, entirely a product of governance, its conflict, collaboration, learning, its recombination of knowledges, or they can come through widely circulating semantics (Brans & Rossbach, 1997; Seidl, 2007). The learning and creativity can be intentional, or not. Necessity, the sheer survival of actors or of a configuration, can be the driver of innovation, resulting in new objects and subjects emerging. The self-understanding of the community can shift under pressure, can be creatively reworked without this being observed. In other cases, observation capacity exists, but self-understanding is changed by the drummed-up arguments, and these start to look impressively persuasive when pressures mount.

If a shared identity emerges where none existed, or where a markedly different one existed, and this new identity is expressed in governance, one can expect more discursive production. This will imply new objects and subjects in governance and community. New futures can emerge, in conjunction with objects and subjects and asset redefinition. Those new futures can, in turn, lead to the recognition of new assets and the assertion of new desires (Hillier, 2016; Van Assche & Gruezmacher, 2022).

Is Power Stemming Only From Knowledge?

Power is certainly not stemming from knowledge alone. Power can come from many sources including resources, brute force or connections. Michel Foucault's view – and ours – is rather that all forms of knowledge are underpinned by power relations, that they are underpinning power relations, and that they do have power effects. Seeing new things can alter power relations, yet maintaining a status quo in knowledge, reproducing it, necessarily keeps certain power relations in place. Following Foucault, governance is capable of creating and disciplining citizens, transforming subjectivities, and naturalizing discursively constructed and strategically modified realities (Burchell et al., 1991; Van Assche et al., 2017). All these operations shape the cognitive frames we live by and strategize in. In addition, there is the more direct application of power bestowed upon actors by governance, power by investing and disinvesting, prohibiting, guiding, etc.

For us, the context of governance ties the selectivity of the use and production of knowledge in governance directly to power. The lure of power, as we know, is always there; the promise of reshaping the community based upon one's self-image, one's personal or factional ideal of the community (Swyngedouw, 2000). With power comes responsibility, and with the lure comes the pressure (Machiavelli, 1988). Anything in governance can potentially lead to changes in the community, to changes in the hold governance has over the community, anything can translate into thwarted ambitions and dreams coming true. A small intervention in space, a meaningless speech can acquire meaning beyond measure. A detail can needle citizens, affect their sense of place and identity in unforeseen ways. The lure and the pressure of power that are always present in governance infuse any form of knowledge with the potentiality of power. Alternatively, the potentiality of power subsumes potentially any form of knowledge (Foucault, 1970, 1979).

KNOWING AND ORGANIZING: THE CONFIGURATIONS

Power/knowledge (P/K) and actor/institution (A/I) configurations co-evolve. They can be considered subsystems of the governance configuration. Their tight coupling means that changes in A/I rebound to have effects in P/K and vice versa (Beunen et al., 2015; Van Assche, Beunen, et al., 2014). A new actor will bring in a new perspective, a new understanding of the world, while a new institution will draw on the knowledges available in the system but will shift their selectivity and change power relations accordingly. A new actor might bring in a new perspective on the past or present. It might reshuffle the construction of futures in governance, and, with that, the coordination of policies towards a new emerging future, hence power relations in the present (Van Assche et al., 2011, 2017).

Gaining or losing power can be attributed to many things, yet it is clear that a shift in power will create a new discursive configuration in governance, which will change the use of institutions, which triggers new selectivity in knowledge. Conversely, the production of new knowledge, e.g. through gradual construction of a new object, is most likely to shift power relations, or create openings for entrepreneurial actors to change roles (Allen & Cochrane, 2010; Borch, 2005). Whether a new actor will alter power relations, whether a new discourse will do this, or whether this will affect the inclusion and identification of actors, does not depend on one factor. There will be thresholds and limits, yet those are not universal. They are the product of the system as a whole and of the same evolution which created the configurations. Formal rules will govern the inclusion of new actors in formal arenas, but how aspiring actors come into being, and how the actual participation pattern in governance evolves, is determined by unique sets of formal/informal rules which reflect the character of the configuration as whole (Acemoglu & Robinson, 2013). How objects are constructed, and possibly create new actor coalitions around them, or how old actors create new objects which then trigger new discourse raising vanished actors from the dead, cannot be deduced from a narrow set of parameters. It depends on the whole web of relations typifying a governance system, as well as the needs of the moment.

New stories can bubble up in the community, seeping into governance, rendering the whole configuration powerless. In terms of systems theory, semantics can shift slowly or quickly. Sometimes this maintains governance capacity, if it is made part of governance deliberations. Sometimes, it can render coordination impossible, if it takes the actors by surprise, and their own narratives do not offer an answer. If a number of people suddenly recognize themselves as a group with a shared identity, moreover a group (unsurprisingly) ignored by politics, this can hollow out the rhetoric of governance actors quickly and dramatically. The new identity can lead to political mobilization (or can be a product of political rhetoric), it can cause a breakdown in coordination, or, alternatively, quickly engender a new actor which assumes a role in a system suddenly less questioned once a seat is secured (Dyrberg, 1997; Escobar, 1998).

Sometimes, stories stay the same, but the trust in leadership to turn them into decisions and decisions into new realities is lost. Or, trust in the sincerity of leadership regarding the story is lost – a scandal, a policy failure, the success of a neighboring community opens eyes. Governance capacity can break down. Or, the same stories remain dominant in governance, but a more powerful leader or actor coalition comes in and takes decisions based on fewer institutions – big plans instead of many little policies, enforcement of formality rather than persuasion and informality. Sometimes, stories are stable, but the situation changes, so more direct control is needed. This aligns with the shards idea, areas in space/time where more coordination and fights over coordination occur. A landslide, a mine disaster, or a flooding can happen and if no answers come fast, if the relevance of the configuration looks diminished, new actors might appear or a revolution might be set in motion. The shard can colonize the context, as we saw. A war in a remote province can remake national politics – as in Armenia after the first Nagorno-Karabakh war where the local political elite of the small border region moved to the center of power.

Knowing and Organizing

Power is less visible than actors or institutions. Knowledge is less visible, especially if we go beyond the expert knowledge and expertise that is written down, required by procedures, present in departments, assumed in institutions, or invited around the table. P/K configurations are more elusive than A/I configurations and they are not of the same nature. They are similar *only* in the sense that they are able to articulate into each other within governance, meaning that they are able to enter co-evolutionary paths which shape the way in which communities can take decisions. The co-evolution of the two configurations multiplies possible pathways of evolution; formality, informality and diversity come into play through diverse forms of productivity, unique capacities to connect the different forms of knowledge identified. The co-evolution of A/I and P/K makes it possible for an informal institution to emerge where new knowledges meet old actors, or makes it possible for new expertise to reinforce old narratives that buttress old informalities which can then start to erode old formalities as well as the position of a key actor associated with them. Empirical observation quickly reveals that the connectivities established through multiple co-evolving systems generate a structured contingency of endless variety (Hillier, 2000; Lauth, 2000).

Power/knowledge configurations are much less stable than actor/institution configurations. They introduce uncertainty and unpredictability, as well as adaptation and flexibility. New interpretations of old institutions surface all the time, just like calls for new institutions when the old ones are perceived to fail. P/K makes unexpected combinations of institutions or actors suddenly look natural or logical. It makes strategizing for the long run harder, yet makes short-term tactics easier. Power/knowledge therefore functions as driver of governance evolution (Van Assche, Duineveld, et al., 2014). Without power/knowledge entwining, without the ever-appearing shifts in power relations, ambitions and strategies, and without the intricate connections with discursive shifts, new understandings of self and environment, past and futures, problems and solutions, governance configurations could be much more stable, decisions more predictable, and long-term strategy more rational, cohesive and persistent. In such a situation governance would also be entirely useless, entirely unsuited for human nature, and for the way we relate to our environment.

How we understand something determines how we organize something. How you organize something determines what knowledge is used and produced. Stories structure the production and structuring of other forms of knowledge and stories structure the way we turn that knowledge into reality, through believing, acting, organizing, which is coordinating action by applying structure. Organizing can entail the creation of organizations (say, departments), sites and arenas, procedures, decision tools, but not necessarily all of those. Organizing is the act of structuring itself, and this can lead to the emergence of any of the things just mentioned, depending on the need and goal (what are we organizing, for whom?) and depending on the path the process of organization took (which structures were already created?). Organizing can create structure in different domains at the same time: structuring meaning can structure action simultaneously (while structuring action necessarily requires a prior structuring of meaning).

A process of organization can structure and be structured by distinctions in time and space: do this, or think this, first, do that there. Organization and meaning thus necessarily imply each other, while time and space are contingently deployed. More complex processes of organization will need to unfold over time and space, more distinctions will be applied, more structures developed, and, likely, the entities we call organizations. Those organizations can then develop their own identities and give guidance to their self-production. De Saussure (1989) observed a century ago how signifier and signified could operate and create meaning, only on the basis of double distinctions, made in the continuums of sound and meaning, thus on the basis of a *simultaneous* organization of two fields, which enabled their connectivity.

Actor/institution configurations *are* forms of organizing, and their continuous reproduction is a process of organization. Governance thus deals with several levels of organization. Actors can be organizations, the configuration is an organizational form, and the decisions taken, and institutions produced, are expected to organize the environment of governance, the community and its ecological context. Beyond actual implementation, whatever comes out of governance is changing power relations in the community. This can then translate back in processes of social mobilization and organization, which can drive governance reform. In the self-reproduction of the configurations, power and knowledge are thus *both input and output*, at the level of governance and in between governance and community. Input and output never cease, however authoritarian or rigid the system might be.

Exclusion

Because of the ways that knowing and organizing are linked in governance, exclusion of groups, their perspectives and their interests can be deeply entrenched (Czarniawska, 2001; Czarniawska & Gagliardi, 2003; Tregidga et al., 2013). They might not be represented by an actor, they might not be organized, or they might not be visible in existing participatory settings. Their understandings of problems and assets might not be captured by the experts in administration, nor by the openings to local knowledge which might exist. Current complex institutions, including strategies, might be blind to their existence, while less complex institutions might be predicated upon their absence, meaning that they could be in the crosshairs of their usual activities and routinely ignore what is valuable to them. The complex couplings in co-evolving systems, in the configurations discussed, are the cause of this, as they introduce exclusions, blind spots which are layered and mutually reinforcing (Luhmann, 1989; Neisig, 2021).

That same path, and the same interplay between knowing and organizing, as we will discuss in the following chapters, also introduces flexibility, and openings to end such exclusions. Configurations are never entirely stable, nor perfect, and ripples and fissures in seeming certainties appear all the time. Actors lose interest, lose power, stories lose appeal, knowledge loses validity, and narratives overextend, cause resistance or fall apart. Ideologies stabilize other narratives and actor positions but are never stable themselves. They are reinterpreted, modified, extended through use and observation, and they can gradually lose persuasiveness, even without people noticing it. Then, a threshold is crossed, a moment of awakening occurs, and the whole narrative infrastructure of governance, resting on the master narrative of ideology, can crumble. Or, the persistent failure of one domain of governance, the persistent erosion of narratives underpinning that domain, can turn into a slow erosion of the master narrative.

REFERENCES

Acemoglu, D. & Robinson, J. A. (2013). *Why nations fail: The origins of power, prosperity, and poverty.* Profile Books.

Alevizou, G., Alexiou, K. & Zamenopoulos, T. (2016). *Making sense of assets: Community asset mapping and related approaches for cultivating capacities.* The Open University and AHRC, pp. 43–43.

Allen, J. & Cochrane, A. (2010). Assemblages of state power: Topological shifts in the organization of government and politics. *Antipode, 42*(5), 1071–1089.

Armstrong, E. & Bernstein, M. (2008). Culture, power, and institutions: A multi-institutional politics approach to social movements. *Sociological Theory, 26,* 74–99.

Ashmore, R. D., Jussim, L. & Wilder, D. (2001). *Social identity, intergroup conflict, and conflict reduction.* Oxford University Press.

Asimakou, T. (2009). *Innovation, knowledge and power in organizations.* Routledge.

Beunen, R., Van Assche, K. & Duineveld, M. (2015). *Evolutionary governance theory: Theory and applications.* Springer.

Boddy, M. & Hickman, H. (2018). 'Between a rock and a hard place': Planning reform, localism and the role of the planning inspectorate in England. *Planning Theory & Practice, 19*(2), 198–217.

Borch, C. (2005). Systemic power: Luhmann, Foucault, and analytics of power. *Acta Sociologica, 48*(2), 155–167. https://doi.org/10.1177/0001699305053769

Bourdieu, P. (1991). *Language and symbolic power.* Polity.

Brans, M. & Rossbach, S. (1997). The autopoiesis of administrative systems: Niklas Luhmann on public administration and public policy. *Public Administration, 75*(3), 417–439.

Burchell, G., Gordon, C. & Miller, P. (1991). *The Foucault effect: Studies in govern-mentality*. University of Chicago Press.

Clark, J. & Newman, J. (1997). *The managerial state: Power, politics and ideology in the remaking of social welfare*. Sage.

Cleaver, F. & Whaley, L. (2018). Understanding process, power, and meaning in adaptive governance. *Ecology and Society, 23*(2).

Clegg, S. R. (1989). *Frameworks of power*. Sage.

Czarniawska, B. (2001). Anthropology and organizational learning. In *Handbook of Organizational Learning and Knowledge*, pp. 118–136.

Czarniawska, B. & Gagliardi, P. (2003). *Narratives we organize by* (vol. 11). John Benjamins Publishing.

de Saussure, F. (1989). *Cours de linguistique générale*. Otto Harrassowitz Verlag.

de Vries, J. R., Aarts, N., Lokhorst, A. M., Beunen, R. & Munnink, J. O. (2015). Trust related dynamics in contested land use: A longitudinal study towards trust and distrust in intergroup conflicts in the Baviaanskloof, South Africa. *Forest Policy and Economics, 50*, 302–310.

Dean, M. (2013). *The Signature of power: Sovereignty, governmentality and biopolitics*. SAGE.

Duineveld, M., Van Assche, K. & Beunen, R. (2013). Making things irreversible. Object stabilization in urban planning and design. *Geoforum, 46*, 16–24. https://doi.org/10.1016/j.geoforum.2012.11.026

Dyrberg, T. B. (1997). *The circular structure of power: Politics, identity, community*. Verso.

Elias, N. & Scotson, J. L. (1994). *The established and the outsiders: A sociological enquiry into community problems*. Sage.

Escobar, A. (1984). Discourse and power in development: Michel Foucault and the relevance of his work to the Third World. *Alternatives, 10*(3), 377–400. https://doi.org/10.1177/030437548401000304

Escobar, A. (1998). Whose knowledge, whose nature? Biodiversity, conservation and the poltical ecology of social movements. *Journal of Political Ecology, 5*(1), 53–82.

Fischer, F. (2000). *Citizens, experts and the environment. The politics of local knowledge*. Duke University Press.

Flyvbjerg, B. (1998). *Rationality and power: Democracy in practice*. University of Chicago Press.

Foucault, M. (1970). *The order of things*. Pantheon Books.

Foucault, M. (1979). *Discipline and punish: The birth of the prison*. Penguin Books.

Foucault, M. (1980). *Power/knowledge: Selected interviews and other writings, 1972–1977*. Pantheon Books. https://books.google.ca/books?id=Aqf309sk_EsC

Foucault, M. (1998). *The will to knowledge. The history of sexuality: 1*. Penguin Books.

Glenn, P. F. (2004). The politics of truth: Power in Nietzsche's epistemology. *Political Research Quarterly, 57*(4), 575–583.

Gunder, M. (2010). Planning as the ideology of (neo-liberal) space. *Planning Theory, 9*(4), 298–314.

Gunder, M. & Hillier, J. (2009). *Planning in ten words or less. A Lacanian entanglement with spatial planning*. Ashgate.

Hardin, R. (1999). Do we want trust in government. In M. Warren (ed.), *Democracy and trust* (pp. 22–41). Cambridge University Press.

Henry, A. D. (2011). Ideology, power, and the structure of policy networks. *Policy Studies Journal, 39*(3), 361–383. https://doi.org/10.1111/j.1541-0072.2011.00413.x

Hillier, J. (2000). Going round the back? Complex networks and informal action in local planning processes. *Environment and Planning A, 32*, 33–54.

Hillier, J. (2016). *Stretching beyond the horizon: A multiplanar theory of spatial planning and governance.* Routledge. https://doi.org/10.4324/9781315242255

Kooij, H.-J. (2014). Object formation and subject formation: The innovation campus in the Netherlands. *Planning Theory*, 1473095214527278.

Lauth, H.-J. (2000). Informal institutions and democracy. *Democratization, 7*(4), 21–50. https://doi.org/10.1080/13510340008403683

Law, J. (1990). Power, discretion and strategy. *The Sociological Review, 38*(1_suppl), 165–191. https://doi.org/10.1111/j.1467-954X.1990.tb03352.x

Ledeneva, A. (2006). *How Russia really works. The informal practices that shaped post-Soviet politics and business.* Cornell University Press.

Luhmann, N. (1989). *Ecological communication.* University of Chicago Press.

Luhmann, N. (1997). The control of intransparency. *Systems Research and Behavioral Science, 14*(6), 359–371. https://doi.org/10.1002/(SICI)1099-1743(199711/12)14:6<359::AID-SRES160>3.0.CO;2-R

Luhmann, N. (2018). *Trust and power.* Polity Press.

Machiavelli, N. (1988). *The prince.* Cambridge University Press.

Mahoney, J. & Thelen, K. (2010). *Explaining institutional change: Ambiguity, agency, and power.* Cambridge University Press.

Neisig, M. (2021). The circular economy: Rearranging structural couplings and the paradox of moral-based sustainability-enhancing feedback. *Kybernetes, 51*(5), 1896–1914. https://doi.org/10.1108/K-12-2020-0843

Pottage, A. (1998). Power as an art of contingency: Luhmann, Deleuze, Foucault. *Economy and Society, 27*(1), 1–27.

Rousseau, D. M., Sitkin, S. B., Burt, R. S. & Camerer, C. (1998). Not so different after all: A cross-discipline view of trust. *Academy of Management Review, 23*(3), 393–404.

Seidl, D. (2007). General strategy concepts and the ecology of strategy discourses: A systemic-discursive perspective. *Organization Studies, 28*(2), 197–218.

Seidl, D. (2016). *Organizational identity and self-transformation. An autopoietic perspective.* Routledge.

Shepherd, E., Inch, A. & Marshall, T. (2020). Narratives of power: Bringing ideology to the fore of planning analysis. *Planning Theory, 19*(1), 3–16. https://doi.org/10.1177/1473095219898865

Smith, N. D. (2000). Plato on knowledge as a power. *Journal of the History of Philosophy, 38*(2), 145–168. https://doi.org/10.1353/hph.2005.0082

Stern, M. J. (2008). The power of trust: Toward a theory of local opposition to neighboring protected areas. *Society & Natural Resources, 21*(10), 859–875. https://doi.org/10.1080/08941920801973763

Swyngedouw, E. (2000). Authoritarian governance, power, and the politics of rescaling. *Environment and Planning D: Society and Space, 18*(1), 63–76. https://doi.org/10.1068/d9s

Tajfel, H. (2010). *Social identity and intergroup relations.* Cambridge University Press.

Therborn, G. (1999). *The ideology of power and the power of ideology.* Verso.

Tregidga, H., Kearins, K. & Milne, M. (2013). The politics of knowing 'organizational sustainable development'. *Organization & Environment, 26*(1), 102–129. https://doi.org/10.1177/1086026612474957

Turner, S. P. (2013). *The politics of expertise.* Routledge.

Turnhout, E., Bommel, S. & Aarts, N. (2010). How participation creates citizens: Participatory governance as performative practice. *Ecology and Society, 15*(4), 26.

Valentinov, V., Verschraegen, G. & Van Assche, K. (2019). The limits of transparency: A systems theory view. *Systems Research and Behavioral Science, 36*(3), 289–300. https://doi.org/10.1002/sres.2591

Van Assche, K. & Gruezmacher, M. (2022). Asset mapping 2.0; contextual, iterative, and virtual mapping for community development. *Community Development*, 1–16. https://doi.org/10.1080/15575330.2022.2131861

Van Assche, K. & Lo, M. C. (2011). Planning, preservation and place branding: A tale of sharing assets and narratives. *Place Branding and Public Diplomacy, 7*(2), 116–126. https://doi.org/10.1057/pb.2011.11

Van Assche, K., Beunen, R. & Duineveld, M. (2014). *Evolutionary governance theory: An introduction*. Springer.

Van Assche, K., Beunen, R., Duineveld, M. & Gruzmacher, M. (2017). Power/knowledge and natural resource management: Foucaultian foundations in the analysis of adaptive governance. *Journal of Environmental Planning and Policy, 19*(3), 308–322.

Van Assche, K., Duineveld, M. & Beunen, R. (2014). Power and contingency in planning. *Environment and Planning A, 46*(10), 2385–2400.

Van Assche, K., Duineveld, M., Beunen, R. & Teampau, P. (2011). Delineating locals: Transformations of knowledge/power and the governance of the Danube Delta. *Journal of Environmental Policy & Planning, 13*(1), 1–21. https://doi.org/10.1080/1523908x.2011.559087

Van Assche, K., Verschraegen, G. & Gruezmacher, M. (2021). Strategy for the long term: Pressures, counter-pressures and mechanisms in governance. *Futures, 131*(102758).

Van Dam, R., Duineveld, M. & During, R. (2015). Delineating active citizenship: The subjectification of citizens' initiatives. *Journal of Environmental Policy & Planning, 17*(2), 163–179.

Voß, J.-P. & Freeman, R. (2016). *Knowing governance: The epistemic construction of political order*. Springer.

Yanow, D. (2003). Accessing local knowledge. In M. A. Hajer & H. Wagenaar (eds.), *Deliberative policy analysis. Understanding governance in the network society* (pp. 228–236). Cambridge University Press.

Yanow, D. (2007). Interpretation in policy analysis: On methods and practice. *Critical Policy Studies, 1*(1), 110–122. https://doi.org/10.1080/19460171.2007.9518511

Žižek, S. (1989). *The sublime object of ideology*. Verso.

7. Rigidities in governance and transition: dependencies

DEPENDENCIES IN GOVERNANCE

Governance configurations reproduce themselves and create governance paths. We know that these paths do not allow for just any transformation; they are not entirely flexible. The rigidity and flexibility of governance paths are shaped by different *dependencies* (Beunen et al., 2014; Van Assche et al., 2013; Van Assche, Duineveld, et al., 2021). Dependencies in a governance path never amount to determinacy. There are always sources of and mechanisms providing flexibility. Even if systems seem to be entirely stable and unchangeable, things will happen. Invisible change takes place, and systems can collapse or change direction without external observers being able to predict this. A change in path, as we noticed earlier, is always a matter of a posteriori interpretation. Prior events will appear in hindsight as key events, and seemingly important mechanisms stabilizing the system will appear later as rhetorical facades or paper tigers. An inflection in the governance path can occur to no one, except later, when the configuration has moved on. If there was a collective strategy, or at least an awareness of a direction, then a change of direction can be noticed more easily. Yet, even if there is not clearly articulated direction (say, only a list of services as the self-description of the system) then a change of those services can be understood as a sign of a changing path (Alver Rolo et al., 2021; Van Assche, Djanibekov, et al., 2014).

A configuration is not just a pattern, but also a mode of transformation, a mode of self-transformation. The rigidities in a governance path can only be understood against this background. It is because governance paths modify themselves continuously, because they use their previous state as input for a next iteration, that whatever that previous state entails counts in various ways in the processes of change. Rigidities form because what exists shapes what can exist. Not only does the presence of actors account for rigidity, potentially *anything* in the system can create rigidity, just as flexibility can stem from a wide variety of sources. Rigidities can form because of existing structures, elements, or because of histories of interactions between actors and institutions, between power and knowledge, between the formal and informal, and between configurations of power/knowledge (P/K) and actors/institutions (A/I). Rigidities develop because of resource distributions, and because of material environments providing some of those resources (Alver Rolo et al., 2021; Van Assche, Djanibekov, et al., 2014; Van Assche, Duineveld, et al., 2022).

Dependencies are not just negative constraints. They provide structure and predictability, and create strategic options, asset preservation and identification, as much as they limit options to adapt, to transform or to strategize. They enable as much as they disable, in a similar way that as discourse creates realities by developing structures which stand in the way of alternative understandings. Any structure will reduce the visibility of alternatives and reduce the options for alternatives to develop. This also applies to thinking and organizing in governance, where what is at stake is a continuous reorganization of the community based on continuously changing discourses (Czarniawska, 2014; Van Assche, Djanibekov, et al., 2014). Brakes on change will eventually accumulate as the structures *have to* link (see previous chapter), and as some decisions and institutions have the function to stabilize governance and community (Ansell & Torfing, 2021; Foucault, 1982; Luhmann, 2018).

Evolutionary governance theory distinguishes between *path dependency, interdependency, material dependency* and *goal dependency* as forms of rigidities in the governance path. Path dependencies, as rigidities in self-transformation which can be ascribed legacies from the past, are most fundamental, in the sense that a path develops over time and that, therefore, there are no dependencies, no features of governance at all, without a path and its dependencies. In the following sections, we discuss the different dependencies, their interplay, their meaning for the transformation of governance and the emergence and functioning of strategy. We refer to earlier presentations and elaborations of EGT for more on the dependencies; here, we intend to keep it short, and streamlined with the focus on our story of strategy for transition.

PATH DEPENDENCIES

Path dependencies are legacies from the past which affect the functioning of governance in the present (Avid, 2007; Barnett et al., 2015; Garud et al., 2010; Pierson, 2000; Van Assche, Beunen, et al., 2011). As everything in governance is in a sense a legacy of the past, a path dependency potentially can be anything. Nevertheless, if we understand the task of identifying dependencies as recognizing what is typical in a governance configuration and path, we can be guided by comparing different states of the configuration over time. To structure this search, we distinguish between *cognitive and institutional* path dependencies, relevant and still active legacies in the realms of thinking and of organizing (Van Assche, Duineveld, et al., 2021, 2022). Institutional

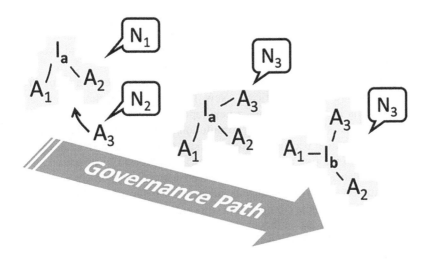

Figure 7.1   Actor-institution configuration and evolution of governance[1]

dependencies stem from a configuration of actors/institutions (A/I); cognitive dependencies stem from a configuration of power/knowledge (P/K). Once again, dependencies are not merely negative limitations; path dependencies stabilize governance paths, maintain values, memories, and checks and balances (Avid, 2007; Van Assche, Duineveld, et al., 2021).

Institutional Path Dependencies

Once domains and arenas are defined, this structure keeps governance on an evolutionary track. Certain themes and activities are prioritized because of the pattern of domains and arenas and the prioritizing of topics emanating from this. Certain places and routines for decision-making become engrained.

---

[1]   Governance paths modify themselves continuously, because they use their previous state as input for a next iteration. Actor-institution configurations can change as a result of a new actor (A3) entering the configuration, with a different narrative (N2), different ideas or perspectives that cause the configuration to create a new narrative for itself (N3) and eventually to change the institution (from Ia to Ib) that coordinates the actors in the configuration.

Meta-rules, including procedures and rules to change the rules, are harder to change than rules themselves; these meta-rules tend to be tightly coupled to an arena, tend to be prone to elaborate procedures, a high bar for change is set in terms of representation and density of argument for change (Scharpf, 1997). If access to an arena is hard or if general access to the configuration is hard, actors in place tend to stay in place, and patterns of inclusion and exclusion tend to remain similar.

If institutions are harder to change, path dependencies stemming from institutions are more significant. New forms of participation might arise easily, shifts in representation, or new topics of governance, yet if much of what happens is anchored in a constitution, then continuous interpretation of that constitution becomes more important than making better rules (as for example with the first amendment of the United States Constitution). Strong interdependencies between actors, between institutions, and between actors and institutions increase path dependencies. On the other hand, if things change, then the whole configuration can unravel or break. The strong ties can withstand pressure but in the presence of a shock or disturbance, the building can turn out to be brittle. For actors tied to a regime that appears all powerful (but which in reality was never really all powerful and really only paranoid) reorientation towards alternative leaders, ideologies and public support is extremely difficult. Institutions do not keep the regime in place if they are not perceived as legitimate or do not have a functional mode of self-reproduction, and they are only accepted as long as the regime is in place (Humphrey, 2002; Ledeneva, 2006).

Elaborate decision premises can both reinforce and soften path dependencies. Long procedures of decision-making, intricate interweaving of expertise, and connectivity to a set of participation sites can all increase adaptivity, yet this doesn't necessarily have to be the case. The procedure itself can impose rigidity and maintain blind spots. The selection of expertise can look diverse, but can actually start from the same assumptions that dominate the decision-making process, and participation can be routinely ignored, rendered harmless or can take place in a homogeneous setting where everyone agrees (Calhoun, 2015; Cooke & Kothari, 2001). The intention of elaborating decision premises, their deliberate design, might stem from caution or from an intention of avoiding harmful decisions, or it might have been envisioned as a means of refining and adapting decisions by tapping into the diverse knowledges in and around governance.

Some actors can transform more easily than others and some can be replaced more easily than others; both distinctions have implications for institutional path dependencies. A political party can be in power for 70 years in a democratic region, yet its internal divisions, structure of representation and its connection to different groups in society might allow for a continuous and even tumultuous process of redefinition. This creates openings, windows of opportunity changing coalition partners in government, thus allowing it to adapt to adaptation and to stay in government longer.

Some actors are hard to get rid of, some administrative actors can be abolished or reformed more easily than others, and some can be missed more lightly than others. Some institutions are harder to change than others. We discussed laws earlier, but one can also think of policies, plans, strategies, leaning on a strong coalition or kept in place by powerful processes of naturalization, and therefore what they try to achieve looks logical, their assumptions look natural (Culler, 1975, 2002). The policy itself can have contributed, over time, to such a process of naturalization (see earlier). Institutional path dependencies stem from both evolution and design (Greif, 2006).

Cognitive Path Dependencies

Once ideas are codified into an institution, they exert influence. Once a form of knowledge is institutionalized, is made part of procedures, entrenched in arenas, embraced by governmental actors, it has an impact and tends to stay. Once a narrative is embedded with a set of actors, it tends to keep its place. An ideology can pervade a whole configuration, or ideological splits can be institutionalized, with polarization becoming a path dependency. Conflicts can reproduce themselves, making it hard to insert new ideas in governance beyond the narratives of the two camps (Brenneis, 1988; J. de Vries & Aalvanger, 2015).

Stories about the past or future can become cemented in governance or tightly associated with key actors, and this might undermine the belief that institutions can be used to switch tracks or that alternative futures might be possible. Narratives can select metaphors and forms of local and expert knowledge which come to dominate governance (Van Assche, Gruezmacher, et al., 2020). Sometimes, the original narrative might have vanished from governance or collective consciousness, yet some of the metaphors, images, discursive fragments, values it produced linger on for generations (Van Assche, Gruezmacher, et al., 2021). Expert knowledge can be structured by narratives that slowly crumble, causing a paradigm shift among experts, but the old expertise and/or the associated narrative can have a long afterlife in the community, and can come back when new participation sites are introduced.

In many former mining communities in western Canada, coal has been long gone. The mining spirit, however, lives on in the mind of the communities and in their governance systems. Collective decisions revolve around the desire to bring back the 'good old days'; the industry. The imposing landscape and the bounteous heritage are sidelined by the prospect of a new mining project, a foreign company, the promise of bringing back economic prosperity by reviving the mines. Mining engineers are revered, former miners are respected while environmentalist or heritage conservation specialists are ignored. Images, narratives and policies thought to support the coal industry are kept, protected, revamped, while initiatives to protect cultural or natural assets might be regarded as hampering progress or a plain waste of time and resources (as opposed to an alternative future).

Discourses, metaphors, narratives, ideologies can keep each other in place, and they can keep actors and institutions in place. One can speak of discursive configurations, families of metaphors, master-narratives and nested narratives. We refer you to the previous chapters on discourse and power/knowledge for more detail.

Cognitive path dependencies have a different relation to the past than institutional path dependencies because institutions do not imagine and interpret themselves but require people to do so. The past certainly leaves traces in many ways, and for EGT literally everything in governance is affected by the past. New actors are most likely transformed by the virtuality, or the expectations, of becoming part of governance. New ideas are molded to become part of proposals for new institutions. Once an actor or institution is in place, it will function in a way pre-structured by governance evolution, by existing formal and informal institutions, dominant narratives, patterns of inclusion and exclusion. The new actor will be observed by others and made part of their strategies in old ways, shaped by governance paths (Friedmann, 1992; Golden, 1992; Zerubavel, 2003).

In discursive domains, old power relations entrench narratives and their use, and shifting power relations can alter inclusion/exclusion of knowledges, the strategic use of narratives (K. Knorr-Cetina, 1999; K. D. Knorr-Cetina, 2013). Governance evolution, furthermore, restructures memory on a regular basis. This concerns the memory of the past of the community, but also institutional memory, the memory of the actors in governance, and of the system as a whole. Social memory and institutional memory will prove essential for strategy, as we will discuss in later chapters. We can mention now that memory is always a selectivity of remembering and forgetting, and that, to remember systematically, and forget methodically, *infrastructures* are needed (Esposito, 2008; Perez-Sindin & Van Assche, 2020). Those infrastructures can include practices of note-taking at meetings, bookkeeping, physical archives, museums, academic exercises, regular reviews of policy reminding what came before, procedures in decision-making reminding all, discussion time and sites with input by keepers of memory, or topics in governance devoted to memory and connectivity with the present, etc. The chapter on looking forward (and back) will further develop our understanding of memory and cognitive path dependencies.

Cognitive legacies are broader than memories. The past affects how many ideas are framed and used or not used in governance. The past can traumatize a community and mark governance. This, too, will invite discussion in later chapters.

Path Dependencies: Interplay

Different path dependencies can reinforce each other or do the opposite. This takes us back to one of evolutionary governance theory's fundamental principles: the interplay of dependencies can produce flexibility. An institution rooted in a narrative can keep that narrative in place; an ideology associated with an informal institution can promote formalization – and can then crowd out other narratives. A key arena can become dominated by a narrative about the community, which then spreads across several domains of governance, and can lead to the production of institutions structured by expert knowledge derived from that narrative. Expert competition in governance can promote hierarchies of expertise (Fischer, 1990, 2000; Latour, 2004; Pierre & Peters, 2000). When these forms of expertise are recombined in a plan, the higher-ranking expertise can inspire key decisions or can generate the first ordering principle of a plan, or the first ordering concept (Van Assche & Hornidge, 2015).

When different path dependencies attenuate each other, even subvert each other, this can have several reasons. One basic set of related reasons is that not everything in a system is tightly coupled or coordinated, not everything is stable, not everything is visible for those in power (Clement, 2013; Drazin & Van de Ven, 1985; Rasche, 2012). An old actor can stay in power in part by adaptation, which can include a rejection of old stories or a radical reinterpretation. An old story promoted by an old actor might have new effects as through strategy and the involvement of other actors in governance. Institutions might be used in a new way, which leads to new governance effects, observation of those effects in the community and in governance, and to a new interpretation of the potential of those institutions. Another reason for an interplay of rigidities that can engender flexibility is that governance systems are never immune to uncertainty coming from the environment, even if the signals coming from the social and ecological environment are selective and are carefully managed (Van Assche et al., 2013; Van Assche, Djanibekov, et al., 2014).

As not all path dependencies serve the same goal nor the same actor and are not part of the same tightly coupled coordination mechanism, responses to change can hitherto bring together disconnected and path dependent governance features into contact, making for a creative clash (Brosius, 2004). Think for example, of a conservative water management bureaucracy and a chamber of commerce ensconced in narrowly defined governance roles that must suddenly deal with each other. The double conservatism makes for a clash and for a breaking open of the thinking and organizing process, which might be less dramatic when more adaptive actors had been forced into contact.

If power relations, domains and institutions maintain a naturalization of narratives and of selected expert knowledges, this will be tough to challenge, unless something in the community happens, dramatic enough to make people reconsider reality (Bal, 1985; Van Assche, Gruezmacher, et al., 2022). At a deeper level, the structure of governance dimensions (see earlier), which is in itself a combination of organizational and semantic histories, tends to evolve slowly. The hardening of realities in and through governance is a process that is hard to avoid, as it pertains to the functioning of governance. If it does not happen, finding common ground is more elusive, and communities might not be amenable to coordination.

INTERDEPENDENCIES

Interdependencies play out between actors and institutions, between institutions, between actors. Interdependence entails that one entity needs the other one to achieve its intended effect or play its intended role. Actors in democratic governance, for example, need others to achieve something and to stay in power (Flyvbjerg, 1998; Fraser & Gerstle, 2005). Actors need institutions in order to do this (Fuenfschilling & Truffer, 2016; Van Assche et al., 2013) and they are coupled with specific forms of knowledge. Interdependencies are visible and active in the present.

Institutions cannot operate in isolation. They need to be considered in networks or configurations of other institutions of the same sort and of other sorts (Latour, 2004; D. C. North, 2008; Van Assche, Verschraegen, et al., 2021a). Rules of formation and rules of combination differ between the types of institutions, yet complex institutions can only function if different types are combined. Rules to combine types of institutions will differ per governance path as well – one can think of the unique roles of law in different planning systems, the unique relations to informality in formal waste management systems or the unique relations between policy domains, and between one policy domain and planning (Greenwood, 2017; Hall & Thelen, 2009; D. North, 2005; Peck & Theodore, 2007).

Interdependencies occur in the discursive realm as well: stories support each other, narratives are nested, and metaphors are related. Some stories need each other in order to look real, true or relevant. How tight these and other interdependencies are cannot always be ascertained easily. Over time interdependencies can become closer, or they can unravel or turn into loose associations or routines which can be broken. An example here is the growing connection between stories about sustainability transitions and those about justice and inclusion, therewith bringing focus to the concept of just transition and the various ways in which this concept can be understood and applied (Bouzarovski, 2022; Wang & Lo, 2021). Stories can also be linked to particular policy tools, and these links can change as well. Actors might coordinate by means of a certain policy tool, and might have become seemingly dependent on that tool, but they might become persuaded that what they really share is a goal, an understanding of a desired state in society, and that other tools might be more useful. Also networks of actors, knowledge and institutions can emerge pushing the use of certain policy tools, a phenomenon Voß and Simons (2014) refer to as instrument constituencies. Furthermore, a metaphor might be tightly coupled to its parental metaphor, and might first appear only with the parent, but after a history of application, testing and stretching, the metaphor might walk alone, and survive beyond the parent (Armstrong & Bernstein, 2008; Shiner, 1982).

Interdependencies can affect the distribution and control over resources. An interdependent network of actors can stay in power by favoring each other in terms of resource distribution, and it can establish patronage networks in society. Interdependence of actors and institutions can also shape the flows of resources, make it difficult to see alternative distributions and flows, and difficult to see which tools could be used to facilitate this (Easterly, 2007; D. C. North et al., 2009). Unfamiliarity with policy tools, and anxiety about collapse of coordination and loss of power, can reinforce the interdependence. If interdependence is not observed, and actors believe they are freely choosing the best policy tools, while relying on a limited set which is not scrutinized, and which is coordinating action beyond what is assumed, then reintroducing flexibility is less likely (Acemoglu & Robinson, 2012; Greif, 2006).

MATERIAL DEPENDENCIES

Governance systems are part of communities that are embedded in social-ecological systems. This creates another layer of influence in two directions, and it creates a new set of dependencies. We see *material dependencies* as impacts of the material environment on the reproduction of the governance system (Van Assche, Duineveld, et al., 2022). Thus, communities can be dependent on their environment in various ways, yet, strictly speaking, only some of those dependencies produce recurring patterns in governance, material dependencies. Many material dependencies do not reflect any direct dependence on a material environment or its resources. Shocks can create material dependencies in a flash, and slowly built infrastructures can very gradually result in such dependencies (Bouzarovski et al., 2015; Killeen, 2007; Renaud et al., 2010).

Resource communities are a clear example of a situation in which the governance systems clearly depend on materiality, both the resource as well as the infrastructures constructed to benefit from that resource. The system of automobility (Urry, 2004) is another example of such material dependency, in which governance systems depend on a specific type of mobility, the infrastructure needed for that mobility, and the organization of space that emerged consequently. This dependency makes certain changes in governance more likely than others, because of the entanglements with discourses, institutions and actors.

We distinguish between *human-made*, *natural* and *hybrid* material dependencies, with natural ones triggered by features of the natural environment (Van Assche, Duineveld, et al., 2022). Infrastructures can directly or indirectly lead to human material dependencies; pollution can become an (often unseen) hybrid material dependency. Natural resources exist in nature, but they become resources because of a social-ecological context; hence, if they trigger material dependencies, they will be hybrid. Since the entanglement between social and ecological systems, or the embedding of communities in their environment is never fully observable, and some features of the environment do not change rapidly or visibly, some material dependencies can become observable only when things go wrong – as with some forms of pollution, not seen, not categorized as pollution or harmful, until its full range of effects comes to the surface, and as with climate change.

Material dependencies never amount to a complete structuring of governance by a material environment. Determinism is not possible, as in the end governance systems are autopoietic and only act upon their own interpretation of the material environment (see above). Material dependencies, however, can be enabling or hampering and can be understood as positive or negative in the perspective of a community strategy. Enabling here is enabling of a development, and positive means positive in the assessment and perspective of the community. We can also add the perspective of anyone interested in sustainability, as a road through the jungle might be a dream for a local government, but not positive in terms of sustainability transitions. It will trigger development in the jungle, new interdependencies, and a path away from sustainability. This has been the case with the large infrastructure interconnectivity initiative in South America, led by Brazil, which not long ago completed the interconnectivity of infrastructure from the east to the west part of the continent and for the first time managed to connect Atlantic Ocean ports with Pacific Ocean ports. As a result of an increased movement of goods through regions of the Amazon rainforest that had been previously extremely remote, different markets are being opened, some detrimental to the conservation of traditional cultures and biodiversity (Castro & Ravena, 2020; Kanai, 2016; Killeen, 2007). The new roads and port infrastructure have brought new actors to the region, pushing for further development, new roads and more infrastructure; the flood gates have been opened.

Material dependencies develop in the grooves of path dependencies and they create new path dependencies. They embody a link with the material environment and are the only dependencies that *require* envisioning the social-ecological system. As this is less observable than the social environment, encompassing more latent complexity, material dependencies can represent unobserved stability, but can also introduce more radical uncertainty. Communities can suddenly hit environmental boundaries that were not seen or conceptualized (Van Assche et al., 2019). The conceptualization and observation of such boundaries can in return have an impact on governance, as with the growing attention for planetary boundaries (Steffen et al., 2015). The understanding of embedding ecosystems, their processes, the entwining with social systems, as well as all effects of new activities, products, forms of resource use and extraction, are always imperfectly observed and understood, and this partial understanding is only selectively present in governance (Ison & Straw, 2020; Luhmann, 1989). Problems with observation of material dependencies can require new forms of knowledge, new actors, but also new arenas. One can think of new environmental problems arising in areas where governance is weak or highly selective in terms of topics – a selectivity commonly inspired by ideology.

Material dependencies develop because of *material events.* Material events are things happening in the environment that affect governance, sometimes slowly, sometimes quickly. Fast and dramatic events, shocks that might be unforeseen, but also slow change that might be unobserved, can lead to material events and to material dependencies. These material dependencies can also come about through the impact of an event on the community or on governance that was not observed. We distinguish therefore between *silent, whispering, vigorous, fading* and *deadly events* (Van Assche, Duineveld, et al., 2022). Deadly events cause collapse, silent ones are unobserved, and could lead to many things, while vigorous events are observed and are in full swing. Fading events are those where memories, but not necessarily effects, fade. Whispering events are heard in few corners of the community and of the governance system, and much work is needed to amplify the whisper, much persuasion is needed before action is taken. The ban of DDT (dichloro-diphenyl-trichloro ethane) in the United States came a decade after its harmful effects had been announced in the publication of Rachel Carson's *Silent Spring* (1962).

Material events can create boundaries internal to governance that remain unobserved for a while, then render an issue ungovernable. And they can produce change in the environment that is not fully observed or understood, but that starts to function as a boundary later on, a poorly understood barrier for old activities and new ambitions. The boundary can also make things ungovernable that seemed amenable to coordination before. As can be expected, chains of cause and effect and multitudes of hybrids appear. Consider changes to natural environments brought by human activities that then trigger other changes that then affect human use. This may happen slowly at first, then crossing a threshold (of profitability, survivability, observed long-term sustainability, fairness), and then leading to conflict, where no conflict resolution mechanisms existed since it was presumed institutions would remain stable and ecosystems predictable.

Material events do not always trigger material dependencies, and the quality of observation in governance and community co-determines what kind of event it becomes, what dependencies develop and to what extent they can be managed.

GOAL DEPENDENCIES

Goal dependencies are effects of the (imagined) future on the present reproduction of governance. In a simple form, we are dealing with quantitative targets and numeric goals, which are often used to integrate policies, drive strategies and link policy domains. Effects can also stem from simple images of the future, or from affects invested in those images: desire, fear, greed, compassion, etc. Complex institutions such as policies and plans are likely to engender complex goal dependencies. Grasping diverse goal dependencies, diverse effects on governance of ideas of and for the future, may be helpful to look beyond the misleading dichotomy of implementation/non-implementation or conformity/non-conformity. Non-implementation does not always signify failure, yet absence of goal dependencies is a failure. Anticipating goal dependencies prior to policy articulation, and continuously observing and managing them during implementation, is advisable.

Goal dependencies come in a staggering diversity. Yet very often the investigation of this diversity, in policy practice and policy academia, is halted because of false dichotomies and simplified models, including the implementation/non-implementation distinction mentioned above (Spicer et al., 2009). Also, the reductive assessment of complex policy to a few effects and goals, or the reduction of local governance itself to the delivery of services, are examples in which the influence of goal dependencies is overlooked (J.-M. Buijs et al., 2009; Innes & Booher, 2010). Non-observation of governance itself, and highly selective observation of effects in the community are not helpful in ascertaining the diversity of effects and of goal dependencies. Goal dependencies can be introduced directly in governance, and they can be reintroduced as the political consequences of effects in the community.

Goal dependencies can include the production of new actors, new objects and new subjects (see later), the production, reuse, reinterpretation, relinking of existing institutions, or the production of knowledge to oppose, modify, specify, localize the plan, etc. It is helpful to consider here the unceasing nature of co-evolution in governance, and the never-ending stream of rein-terpretations of institutions, identity narratives, stories about past and future. Interpretation never ends and strategy never ends. Strategy provokes reinter-pretation of institutions and vice versa, and their interplay contributes to the impossibility of stability in governance (Alver Rolo et al., 2021; Van Assche, Verschraegen, et al., 2021b). New actors come in and modify the effect of an institution. Environments change, are known to offer unseen opportunities to some not present in governance, while new subjectivities come with new per-spectives on the future (Braidotti, 1997). Hence, goal dependencies multiply, diversify and shift continuously (Luhmann, 2004).

The unfolding and observation of goal dependencies takes time. They can work their way through the network of co-evolving entities in governance. Each connection can modify, amplify, oppose the effect of the institution (Perez-Sindin & Van Assche, 2020). This makes goal dependencies hard to manage and renders implementation always more than pushing a button. Continuous observation and steering are needed. If a vision is ambitious and intends to coordinate many other policies, actors and policy domains, then many sources of reinterpretation and resistance can be expected. Many forms of blindness come into play: organizations are partly opaque to each other, the same applies to function systems, while disciplines systematically misin-terpret each other, and different interests and power relations inspire different interpretations and positions (Foucault, 1980; Luhmann, 1993). A diversity of knowledges is likely involved, and the more conceptual that are expected to be connected, the more steps in reinterpretation can be assumed.

Complex policies and plans, in order to work, will need to connect to other institutions, which connect to other institutions in a complex network that makes their articulation and implementation possible (Cilliers, 2001; Innes & Booher, 2010). It is often impossible to discern a priori which institutions need to be harnessed, which ones will be involved later in implementation, and which ones will be triggered in other policy domains, as an indirect consequence of interventions in the community envisioned by the policy. In case of long-term strategies, this process of implementation takes a long time, whereby implementation it is not an execution of a discrete decision, the construction of an object, or a changing of a tax rule, but a process of guidance and coordination of other institutions. The invisible connectivity of indirectly involved institutions, as well as the unpredictability introduced by the inter-vention in the environment and unforeseen effects and responses there, and the uncertainty coming with continuous change in governance itself, combine, over time, to produce ramifications of implementation, in governance and community, which require sharp observational skills by decision-makers (Jessop, 2002; Van Assche, Hornidge, et al., 2020). The reverberations of bringing a new complex institution into the world can be felt far from the site of decision-making, and the observation of those effects needs to be far and wide, in governance and community.

The complexity of governance systems, their built-in redundancies, and the relative autonomy and overlap of governance domains and levels allows for the *multiplication of strategies.* This means that in a community it is not unusual to have various documents with strategic intentions and/or strategic potential. Several complex institutions could be used to move the community in a different direction, several are supposed to envision its long-term future. Some might start from one topic, arena, policy domain and develop a general vision from there, without necessarily considering what might exist elsewhere in the configuration, with strategic ambitions, and without always realizing which institutions already exist and could be coordinated in order to achieve the stated goals. Strategies can be complimentary, can ignore each other, and can be irrelevant as having no effect, and certainly no effect on other institutions with strategic intent (Van Assche, Duineveld, et al., 2021; Van Assche et al., 2013). They can also compete, and overturn key decisions, even in supposedly top-down systems of governance (Carter et al., 2008; Golsorkhi et al., 2010).

The evolutionary slant of EGT helps to trace one more obstacle towards simple implementation of strategies and other complex institutions. The co-existence of competing strategies certainly renders the pattern of goal dependencies of each one more complex, yet the story does not end there. The never-ending of stories is relevant since strategies that were perceived to be abandoned, visions which were seemingly forgotten, either formally replaced or quietly gathering dust as dead institutions, can have complex afterlives. They can live on in other institutions, in organizations, in stories, or in informalities. An old vision can live on in the mind of mid-level administrators who make a career and become influential later on, reviving some of the key principles (Alver Rolo et al., 2021; Beunen et al., 2022).

A few ideas in the old vision can have sparked a discovery of forms of expertise and local knowledge hitherto unknown in administration, forms of knowledge whose presence does not end with the transition to a new vision. One law might have been changed as a direct result of the old vision, and the strategists behind the new vision might have left it alone, ready for use by counterstrategists. Maybe the old vision created an organization intended to be an actor; with new leadership and a new vision, redefinition of the role occurred, but the organization survived, quietly maintaining an identity closely tied to the old vision and old leadership, and cultivating grudges which can turn out to be productive later (Healey, 1996; Kojola, 2020; Van Assche, Duineveld, et al., 2021).

ROLES, IDENTITIES AND DEPENDENCIES

Thinking in terms of roles can deepen our understanding of dependencies. *Roles connect knowledge, power and institutions for actors.* One can distinguish between *self-observed roles, desired roles, formal roles and observed roles.* Desired roles can inspire actor strategy to move in that direction, to do what one would love to do, which can be a matter primarily of self-interest, or imply a genuine interest in the public interest (just giving oneself a different position in promoting it) (Stryker & Burke, 2000). Formal roles, the roles outlined for actors, and for people and organizations in administration and elsewhere in the sphere of governance (whether an actor or not) by means of formal institutions, *almost never coincide* with observed or self-observed roles (Hillier, 2000; Innes et al., 2007; Seidl, 2016). Formal roles come out of a history of differentiation in governance and society, yet the other types of roles are not simple deviations (Esmark, 2009; Luhmann, 2006). They, too, are products of governance evolution.

Actors can become actors because roles are there, or because they can force the creation of a role. Organizations can lose their formal role but continue strategizing and try to redefine their role. Roles change in the interplay between formal, desired, observed and self-observed roles. If the differences between these aspects of roles are significant, notable strategizing can be expected. Where governance is weak, rule of law not too stringent, where some regions are loosely coupled with the rest of the territory, this can give way to shadow governance (Gel'man, 2004; Grzymala-Busse, 2010; Mielke, 2022). More commonly, new informalities mushroom in the shadow of this difference. Where desired roles are starkly different from self-observed roles, pathways to a change in role might exist but might be difficult to access (depending on competition, resources, organizational structures); where self-observed roles diverge greatly from formal roles, paths to formalization might be limited because of competition, institutional breaks, perceived redundancies, ideological resistance, or lack of political courage (Hayoz & Giordano, 2013; Jessop, 2002). Certainly, many other reasons can be added. What remains stable, however, is that these four aspects of roles *cannot coincide*, for all the reasons outlined in the previous chapters, and that this enduring difference is the origin of a pattern of continuous searching, shifting, dissimulating, strategizing, testing, an unstable bricolage which looks stable because of the suspended disbelief in the power of formal institutions.

The difference itself is a driver of change, and there are the changes in governance and environment that create a demand and a desire for role redefinitions. New activities in society might lead to calls for new roles. New forms of expertise might render a new topic governable, which then generates new roles. An organization can exist and take up a role or it might be created when a new role was formally approved. A new role might be approved because of the strategizing by actors who are dissatisfied with their role, or by organizations (or people) aspiring to be an actor (Bohnsack et al., 2016; Bryant, 1995). The new role might be a new job, a new organization, but also a new procedure giving voice to the newly included actor (who just does what it used to do).

Roles are thus evolving; they create new reasons and tools for strategizing and hence further the evolution of roles (and governance configurations). They drive evolution yet anchor and structure governance at the same time. They can provide stability to actors and provide impetus and ambition for change, yet within demarcated paths (Czarniawska & Sevón, 2011; Golsorkhi et al., 2010; Weick & Quinn, 1999). Path dependencies, goal dependencies, interdependencies and material dependencies form in governance paths where power/ knowledge is a major driver of evolution, yet also the interplay between institutions themselves, even in routine situations, leads to change. Rigidities in the governance path form because knowledge, power and institutions connect, and that connection must be forged and navigated by actors. Without actors doing something, nothing happens, starting with the making of institutions.

Actors make institutions and institutions make actors, indeed, and this structuration principle certainly applies to governance, but 'actors' are never simply there (Bohnsack et al., 2016; Brown et al., 2013). They transform, strategize, move in and out, and this process can best be understood by the combination of stability and instability which stems from roles and their impossibility to coincide with themselves. Roles rely on doing something and being allowed to do something, on an understanding of the whole one operates in, and at least a basic sharing of that understanding by others. Stabilizing roles can come from a greater sharing of understanding, a clearer (and formal) permission, from greater activity, more predictable and observable activity (Alvesson et al., 2008; Few, 2002).

When we consider roles in this light, their production of stability and change helps to explain the unique form of contingency of governance paths (see next chapter). They help to see why and how dependencies develop, and how these dependencies are both constraining and enabling. Once a set of roles has crystallized, and only then, a governance configuration can stabilize its path, while maintaining sufficient sources of internal variation and drivers of change.

Identities

Actors desire a certain state of society, of the governance system. Individuals and groups often outside governance hope to become part of it. They construct desired roles, and these roles are structured around narratives of society and environment, of governance and *self* (Haslam, 2004; Hornsey, 2008; Seidl,

2016; Stryker & Burke, 2000). Depending on the relation between these narratives, and depending on the kind of actor (individual, group, organization), different *identity narratives and subjectivities* play a role in the formation of desired roles (G. Ashworth et al., 2007; J. de Vries & Aalvanger, 2015).

What is and what should be acquires a difference, a unique difference, in the interplay between these narratives of self, society, governance and environment. That difference slips naturally into normativity: Should I reproduce the system, or change it? Should I reproduce the system, but change society? Should society change the same, but do we need to alter or protect better the environment? The difference between what is and what should be can become relevant for people and organizations by assuming an actor role in governance, where already a desired role, different from other role aspects, exists (Czarniawska & Joerges, 1997; Ivory, 2013). It can become real by not subscribing to that desired role but constructing a new one, based on unique new observations while stepping into that pre-existing role. The difference can be relevant during the struggle to become an actor but change once an actor position is taken (Czarniawska, 2004; Emihovich, 1995).

It is entirely possible to identify with an organization that is an actor, and it is possible to identify with the governance system as an individual and as an organization. It is also a reality that many individuals and organizations do not envision the nature and functioning of the larger whole they are part of and fulfill a role (Alvesson, 2004; Alvesson & Kärreman, 2007; Alvesson & Spicer, 2012). That larger whole can be the governance system and the social-ecological system one is embedded in, and a blissful ignorance of context, a narrow focus on a small role, makes it easy *not* to reflect on that role, and on the possibilities to change that role, or move between roles. In that case, roles are no drivers of transformation and self-transformation, but in our view this does not apply to actor roles. Being an actor in governance *forces* contact with larger wholes, with competing perspectives, and with the seemingly stable but really shifting sands of role dynamics in governance (see above) (Luhmann, 2018; Van Assche, Duineveld, et al., 2011).

Seeing a larger whole, being able to reflect on one's role, and one's potential influence on governance, thus drives self-transformation and the emergence of normativity. Other linked sources are the identity narratives just mentioned. People can enter an organization with a strong identity, which is or not yet-connected to a desired role. The existence of a strong identity makes it more likely, if connected with acute observation of an always imperfect environment, that a desired role will be constructed at some point, by leadership or by a wider membership not recognizing itself in the work they are doing at the time being (Alvesson & Kärreman, 2007; Downing, 2005; Seidl, 2016). The identity of the organization can be derived largely from a professional identity, which then constructs an image of the environment, of governance and society, based on that identity, the distinctions made, and defines a desired role in governance in that perspective. One can represent an actor that is not well-organized yet takes on the form of organization in the history of participation in governance; that process can reshape the identity narrative of the actor as decisions are forced, through reflection, and it can introduce a split identity, a tension between the new organization and the group it is expected to embody (Alvesson et al., 2008; Czarniawska, 1997).

Identity narratives can be derived from ideology, from ethnic, cultural, place narratives, or from shared economic interests. Identities, or the narratives of 'self' we mentioned above, relate to narratives of governance, society and environment in different ways, ranging from blindness to indifference, resistance, ambition, hope and explosive revolutionary anger (Friedmann, 1992; Stewart Leith, 2010). What is hoped for in society, in governance, can derive from identity narratives, while hopes can lead to assimilation into existing identity narratives and the taking up of existing subject positions (one becomes 'an environmentalist'). If participation in governance becomes a reality, the role dynamics of governance become real and roles are reassembled regularly through adaptation, competition and collaboration processes in governance. For the desired roles, narratives of self, environment and governance can transform, and their connectivity will change, meaning that a desired role can come from a new understanding of environmental problems, leading to new ideas of self, and an aspired role, but a thorough self-reflection (as individual, as organization) can also modify perspectives on the environment, and hence a desired role (Dyrberg, 1997; Van Assche et al., 2008).

Identity narratives thus connect to other narratives, and the ensuing discursive dynamics open avenues for role formation in governance. They create gaps between existing and hoped conditions, in governance and in the world, and create drivers to bridge that gap. Because the nature of governance (and humans) is never perfect, this bridging and the drive to do so perpetuates itself. Identity narratives thus connect power, knowledge, actors and institutions, and help to understand roles in their work keeping governance together and keeping it moving. The autopoietic nature, or identity, of a governance configuration presents a matrix for the evolution of formal and actual roles, while the narrative nature of community, group, individual makes for the evolution of desired roles (Brans & Rossbach, 1997; Dunsire, 1996; Seidl, 2016). Becoming an actor, becoming immersed in governance, creates the irreducible difference between aspired, formal and actual roles which then contributes to self-transformation. All dependencies emerge in this path of evolution, and the sum of dependencies is a different description of the fraction's co-evolution of the different aspects of roles in governance. How new visions land in governance, the goal dependencies which are engendered, result from the overall structure of the configuration, and its mode of self-transformation, which can also be described in terms of the connectivity and dynamics introduced by identities and roles (Seidl, 2016; Valentinov, 2012).

Identity Crisis

Identities can become problematic in governance in a few ways. As one can expect, it depends on the construction of the narrative, and it has to do with the way the narrative (and associated subjectivities and roles) relates to the environment. If a group sees itself as the only true representative of the community, the guardian of its values, the keeper of its only real memory, this does not bode too well (Koch et al., 2021; Warner, 2019). If the identity narrative is explicitly negative about other groups, its role in society, its presence or absence, this is bound to create conflicts (J. R. de Vries et al., 2015). Other groups can be visible or invisible in the identity narrative, and, as we know (see the chapters on discourse and power), some identity narratives can have clear images of and implications for idealized governance, others less so. If identities draw heavily on ideology, the chances are that governance implications are more immediate (Brenneis, 1988; J. de Vries & Aalvanger, 2015).

Identities tend to have different trajectories in governance also depending on their inherent flexibility and their performative flexibility. By which we mean that part of the story can be that the identity has always been the same and should remain the same. This can be combined with an image of an old position in society or in governance, lost, and waiting to be recaptured, or a central current position which is perceived to be natural (because of the narrative) and felt under threat (of groups immediately appearing in a negative light). Alternatively, an idealized past of the group or the community can inspire some flexibility, some possible change, away from a situation perceived as deteriorated, but only in that direction, towards a rigidly constructed and likely unreal past (Gabriel, 2000; Van Assche, Gruezmacher, et al., 2021). Less problematic in democratic systems are identity narratives that acknowledge co-existence with other groups, an acceptance which can be smoothened if identity narrative and narratives of governance share ideas and images of co-existence and collaboration (Bowles et al., 2008).

In the other direction, identities can have a tough time in governance if sitting actors, or narratives shared widely in governance, shed a negative light on one actor, aspired actor, and its identity narrative. Paranoid attitudes, passive aggression, silent formation of coalitions of counter-discourses can block the actor from playing much of a role and can hamper the reproduction of governance. The nature of the identity narrative and of narratives on that nature can of course interact, as when parties perceived as radical enter governance systems populated by actors who have more in common. Identity narratives inspiring a radical overhaul of governance while this sentiment is not shared by the rest of the configuration can count on much resistance, while new narratives earnestly hoping for a collaborative transformation might not be welcomed as much, when the rhetoric of collaboration in governance veils tightly knit coalitions narrowly defining collaboration (Alvesson et al., 2008; Czarniawska, 1997). This last situation illustrates what we call *performative flexibility*: a performance of flexibility, adaptive capacity, collaboration can have a backstage where more rigid understandings of self, governance and community dominate.

Identity Politics

When politics becomes identity politics, when governance becomes overly oriented towards values and futures defined by identities rather than by reflection on issues and articulating adaptive answers (for example 'we must do X because we are Y'), governance paths become more rigid. All dependencies can play a role in this process. We speak thus of identity politics when actors, or a whole configuration, take decisions and produce institutions based largely on narratives of self (G. J. Ashworth & Larkham, 1994; J. de Vries & Aalvanger, 2015).

Identity politics occur when actors compete fiercely, either in formal roles or otherwise. Ethnic, cultural, organizational, party, clan, religious and professional identities can be structured in such a way that others appear immediately as competition, and that the importance of this competition overrides checks and balances (McCoy et al., 2018). Resources might be scarce, but the competitive process cannot be generalized as being about resources; what counts as a resource, why it is important, how competition over resources is supposed to take place, how this fits in governance, how it hinges on discourse, on narrative understandings of self, governance, community and environment. Increasingly one can see that environmental issues, such as climate change, and sustainability more generally, become objects of identity politics (Barnett et al., 2021; Masson & Fritsche, 2021; Unsworth & Fielding, 2014). Moreover, identity politics can be strong without much competition, when a strong and unifying community identity dominates governance and daily life (Dyrberg, 1997; Yashar, 2007).

If governance evolution produces two main factions, and these factions become institutionalized in governance and entrenched in society (say, through the establishment of political parties, and electoral systems which discourage third parties), *polarization* can ensue (Hammer, 2019; Warner, 2019). Moreover, identity politics can create polarization in governance and society, something which seems to occur increasingly also in relation to sustainability challenges. Bitter strife can become normalized. Conversely, strategizing in governance can also include identity politics and polarization, whereby certain parties create and exaggerate differences between views and bolster strife and conflict in order to impact decision-making process. Yet, also when polarization is not on the horizon, when identities are shared and deeply held, they can cause blind spots, various forms of non-thinking, non-observing, of naturalization, neglect of checks and balances (see previous and later chapters). Such situations can occur when a community is tightly coupled to its physical environment or one economic activity, but other paths in this direction are possible (A. E. Buijs, 2009; Gomes et al., 2012; Igoe, 2006). Religious, cultural, ethnic enclaves are examples, or communities with histories of ethnic or religious tensions, where perspectives immunizing themselves against critique were turned into political actors (or sub-territories).

DEPENDENCIES AND THEIR INTERPLAY

Dependencies in governance create rigidities, but not merely constraints. They structure governance evolution, where biding time is essential for maintaining trust in the system, stabilizing expectations and allowing for long-term policy as well as for actors to strategize. For understanding the interplay between the configurations in governance, and the gradual emergence of typical patterns of dependencies, of unique structuring of contingency, one needs to invoke not only the power of rational argument, of finding facts to solve problems, not only of strategy and persuasion, but also, fundamentally, of non-thinking, both strategically used and otherwise (Holmström, 2007; Van Assche, Duineveld, et al., 2014). It is easy to be persuaded, when one believes persuasion is not necessary or not there, that reality is simply as it is. Non-thinking, non-observing, non-strategizing or competing go hand in hand (Alvesson & Sköldberg, 2017). Naturalization of an existing order, of a contingent governance system, of one selective understanding of the environment, one order in society, one version of history, can easily conspire to create a future that is the result of non-thinking and non-learning. We return to this in the next chapter where we re-examine drivers of change (Culler, 1975).

In addition, some beliefs, narratives, ideologies might obscure the fact that governance can do things, can adapt, can further common goods and help societies to face threats. Many elements of governance can start to look like neutral infrastructure, or blend into the background, for a smaller set of topics where decisions are appropriate. While that set can be radically expanded, and the structures of decision-making, the tools of governance could be revised to enable alternative courses of action. Sometimes it is hard to see why something became background for something else, became invisible, while something else looked like it was amenable to collective decision-making. Signals from outside governance can alert actors that new topics might need to be introduced in governance, that a rethinking of aspects of governance is needed, maybe the delineation of a new domain, a new configuration of actors. What can also awaken sleeping systems, reproducing largely on naturalization and routine, is the observation of others strategizing in what seemed to be an immutable and mute background (Culler, 2002).

In the present, interdependencies tend to increase path dependencies, in combination with the processes of discursive naturalization mentioned above (in the sphere of power/knowledge). If, in governance, one cannot imagine alternative forms of coordination for a topic deemed essential, then the focus will be more on safeguarding coordination rather than adapting it. Roles in governance, in their unique linking to identity and other narratives, can both harden and soften path dependencies, as they provide structural couplings between the configurations in governance, and drivers of change. Existing patterns of roles and identities represent path dependency and interdependency yet also enable path creation, as the roles are inherently unstable (Alexander, 2001; Avid, 2007). Some patterns of roles and identities will harden dependencies more than others because of their different structures, internal and external frictions, because of more stable environments.

Material dependencies are as powerful as they can be possibly made or allowed to be within governance. Social-ecological systems cannot be steered by ecological systems and materiality affects governance in ways that must be addressed in governance (Latour, 2004; Law & Mol, 1995; Van Assche, Duineveld, et al., 2022). Strategies to transform relations with the environment, however, will have to be cognizant of the pattern of goal, path and interdependencies now. They will have to be aware of the actual modes of self-transformation (as opposed to the formal self-description), of the actual steering potential and connectivity with society and environment (as opposed to simple hopes for implementation). That way, strategies for sustainability can increase their chances of managing goal dependencies in such a way that what happens in society can be sincerely labelled as 'transition.' We develop these themes in the following chapters, on change, intentional change, and strategy.

REFERENCES

Acemoglu, D. & Robinson, J. (2012). *Why nations fail. The origins of power, prosperity and poverty*. Crown Business.
Alexander, E. R. (2001). The planner-prince: Interdependence, rationalities and post-communicative practice. *Planning Theory and Practice, 2*, 311–324.
Alver Rolo, R., Van Assche, K. & Duineveld, M. (2021). Goal dependencies and steering in governance. The formation of the Argentine Planning Council. *Politics and Governance*.
Alvesson, M. (2004). *Knowledge work and knowledge-intensive firms*. Oxford University Press.

Alvesson, M. & Kärreman, D. (2007). Unraveling HRM: Identity, ceremony, and control in a management consulting firm. *Organization Science, 18*(4), 711–723. https://doi.org/10.1287/orsc.1070.0267

Alvesson, M. & Sköldberg, K. (2017). *Reflexive methodology: New vistas for qualitative research.* SAGE.

Alvesson, M. & Spicer, A. (2012). A stupidity-based theory of organizations. *Journal of Management Studies, 49*(7), 1194–1220.

Alvesson, M., Lee Ashcraft, K. & Thomas, R. (2008). Identity matters: Reflections on the construction of identity scholarship in organization studies. *Organization, 15*(1), 5–28.

Ansell, C. & Torfing, J. (2021, May). *Public governance as co-creation: A strategy for revitalizing the public sector and rejuvenating democracy.* Cambridge Core; Cambridge University Press. https://doi.org/10.1017/9781108765381

Armstrong, E. & Bernstein, M. (2008). Culture, power, and institutions: A multi-institutional politics approach to social movements. *Sociological Theory, 26*, 74–99.

Ashworth, G. J. & Larkham, P. J. (1994). *Building a new heritage: Tourism, culture and identity in the new Europe.* Routledge.

Ashworth, G., Graham, B. & Tunbridge, J. (2007). *Pluralising pasts: Heritage, identity and place in multicultural societies.* Pluto Press.

Avid, A. P. (2007). Path dependence: A foundational concept for historical social science. *Cliometrica, 1*, 91–114.

Bal, M. (1985). *Narratology: Introduction to the theory of narrative.* University of Toronto Press.

Barnett, J., Evans, L., Gross, C., Kiem, A. S., Kingsford, R. T., Palutikof, J. P., Pickering, C. M. & Smithers, S. G. (2015). From barriers to limits to climate change adaptation: Path dependency and the speed of change. *Ecology and Society, 20*(3), 5.

Barnett, J., Graham, S., Quinn, T., Adger, W. N. & Butler, C. (2021). Three ways social identity shapes climate change adaptation. *Environmental Research Letters, 16*(12), 124029. https://doi.org/10.1088/1748-9326/ac36f7

Beunen, R., Van Assche, K. & Duineveld, M. (2014). *Evolutionary governance theory.* Springer.

Beunen, R., Van Assche, K. & Gruezmacher, M. (2022). Evolutionary perspectives on environmental governance: Strategy and the co-construction of governance, community and environment. *Sustainabilty,* (14).

Bohnsack, R., Pinkse, J. & Waelpoel, A. (2016). The institutional evolution process of the global solar industry: The role of public and private actors in creating institutional shifts. *Environmental Innovation and Societal Transitions, 20*, 16–32.

Bouzarovski, S. (2022). Just transitions: A political ecology critique. *Antipode, 54*(4), 1003–1020. https://doi.org/10.1111/anti.12823

Bouzarovski, S., Bradshaw, M. & Wochnik, A. (2015). Making territory through infrastructure: The governance of natural gas transit in Europe. *Geoforum, 64*, 217–228.

Bowles, S., Gintis, H. & Gustafsson, B. (2008). *Markets and democracy: Participation, accountability and efficiency.* Cambridge University Press.

Braidotti, R. (1997). Meta (l) morphoses. *Theory, Culture & Society, 14*(2), 67–80.

Brans, M. & Rossbach, S. (1997). The autopoiesis of administrative systems: Niklas Luhmann on public administration and public policy. *Public Administration, 75*(3), 417–439.

Brenneis, D. (1988). Telling troubles: Narrative, conflict and experience. *Anthropological Linguistics*, 279–291.

Brosius, J. P. (2004). Indigenous peoples and protected areas at the World Parks Congress. *Conservation Biology*, *18*(3), 609–612. https://doi.org/10.1111/j.1523-1739.2004.01834.x

Brown, R. R., Farrelly, M. A. & Loorbach, D. A. (2013). Actors working the institutions in sustainability transitions: The case of Melbourne's stormwater management. *Global Environmental Change*, *23*(4), 701–718.

Bryant, C. R. (1995). The role of local actors in transforming the urban fringe. *Journal of Rural Studies*, *11*(3), 255–267. https://doi.org/10.1016/0743-0167(95)00020-N

Buijs, A. E. (2009). Lay people's images of nature: Comprehensive frameworks of values, beliefs, and value orientations. *Society & Natural Resources: An International Journal*, *22*(5), 417–432.

Buijs, J.-M., Eshuis, J. & Byrne, D. (2009). Approaches to researching complexity in public management. In *Managing complex governance systems* (pp. 51–69). Routledge.

Calhoun, C. (2015). *Democratizing inequalities: Dilemmas of the new public participation*. NYU Press.

Carson, Rachel. (1962). *Silent spring*. Houghton Mifflin.

Carter, C., Clegg, S. R. & Kornberger, M. (2008). *A very short, fairly interesting and reasonably cheap book about studying strategy*. SAGE.

Castro, P. P. C. & Ravena, N. (2020). Neo-developmentalism and regional integration: IIRSA impact in the environmental agenda in the Amazon. In *Ecosystem and Biodiversity of Amazonia*. IntechOpen.

Cilliers, P. (2001). Boundaries, hierarchies and networks in complex systems. *International Journal of Innovation Management*, *5*(02), 135–147.

Clement, F. (2013). For critical social-ecological system studies: Integrating power and discourses to move beyond the right institutional fit. *Environmental Conservation*, *40*(01), 1–4.

Cooke, B. & Kothari, U. (2001). *Participation: The new tyranny?* Zed Books.

Culler, J. (1975). *Structuralist poetics: Structuralism, linguistics and the study of literature*. Routledge.

Culler, J. (2002). *Barthes: A very short introduction*. OUP Oxford.

Czarniawska, B. (1997). *Narrating the organization. Dramas of institutional identity*. University of Chicago Press.

Czarniawska, B. (2004). *Narratives in social science research*. Sage.

Czarniawska, B. (2014). *A theory of organizing*. Edward Elgar Publishing.

Czarniawska, B. & Joerges, B. C. (1997). *Narrating the organization: Dramas of institutional identity*. University of Chicago Press.

Czarniawska, B. & Sevón, G. (2011). *Translating organizational change*. Walter de Gruyter.

de Vries, J. & Aalvanger, A. (2015). Negotiating differences: The role of social identity in the emergence of institutions for local governance. In R. Beunen, K. Van Assche & M. Duineveld (eds.), *Evolutionary governance theory: Theory and applications* (pp. 291–304). Springer International Publishing. https://doi.org/10.1007/978-3-319-12274-8_19

de Vries, J. R., Aarts, N., Lokhorst, A. M., Beunen, R. & Munnink, J. O. (2015). Trust related dynamics in contested land use: A longitudinal study towards trust and distrust in intergroup conflicts in the Baviaanskloof, South Africa. *Forest Policy and Economics*, *50*, 302–310.

Downing, S. (2005). The social construction of entrepreneurship: Narrative and dramatic processes in the coproduction of organizations and identities. *Entrepreneurship Theory and Practice, 29*(2), 185–204.

Drazin, R. & Van de Ven, A. H. (1985). Alternative forms of fit in contingency theory. *Administrative Science Quarterly, 30*(4), 514–539. https://doi.org/10.2307/2392695

Dunsire, A. (1996). Tipping the balance: Autopoiesis and governance. *Administration and Society, 28*(2,), 299–334.

Dyrberg, T. B. (1997). *The circular structure of power: Politics, identity, community.* Verso.

Easterly, W. (2007). Inequality does cause underdevelopment: Insights from a new instrument. *Journal of Development Economics, 84*(2), 755–776.

Emihovich, C. (1995). Distancing passion: Narratives in social sceince. In J. A. Hatch & R. Wisniewski (eds.), *Life history and narrative* (p. 145). Falmer.

Esmark, A. (2009). The functional differentiation of governance: public governance beyond hierarchy, market and networks. *Public Administration, 87*(2), 351–370. https://doi.org/10.1111/j.1467-9299.2009.01759.x

Esposito, E. (2008). Social forgetting: A systems-theory approach. In *Cultural memory studies: An international and interdisciplinary handbook* (pp. 181–190). Walter de Gruyter.

Few, R. (2002). Researching actor power: Analyzing mechanisms of interaction in negotiations over space. *Area, 34*(1), 29–38. https://doi.org/doi:10.1111/1475-4762.00054

Fischer, F. (1990). *Technocracy and the politics of expertise.* Sage Publications.

Fischer, F. (2000). *Citizens, experts and the environment. The politics of local knowledge.* Duke University Press.

Flyvbjerg, B. (1998). *Rationality and power: Democracy in practice.* University of Chicago Press.

Foucault, M. (1980). *Power/knowledge: Selected interviews and other writings, 1972–1977.* Pantheon Books.

Foucault, M. (1982). The subject and power. *Critical Inquiry, 8*(4), 777–795.

Fraser, S. & Gerstle, G. (2005). *Ruling America: A history of wealth and power in a democracy.* Harvard University Press.

Friedmann, J. (1992). The past in the future: History and the politics of identity. *American Anthropologist, 94*(4), 837–859.

Fuenfschilling, L. & Truffer, B. (2016). The interplay of institutions, actors and technologies in socio-technical systems – An analysis of transformations in the Australian urban water sector. *Technological Forecasting and Social Change, 103*, 298–312.

Gabriel, Y. (2000). *Storytelling in organizations. Facts, fictions, and fantasies.* Oxford University Press.

Garud, R., Kumaraswamy, A. & Karnøe, P. (2010). Path dependence or path creation? *Journal of Management Studies, 47*(4), 760–774.

Gel'man, V. (2004). Unrule of law in the making: The politics of informal institution building in Russia. *Europe-Asia Studies, 56*(7), 1021–1040.

Golden, B. R. (1992). The past is the past – Or is it? The use of retrospective accounts as indicators of past strategy. *Academy of Management Journal, 35*(4), 848–860.

Golsorkhi, D., Rouleau, L., Seidl, D. & Vaara, E. (2010). *Cambridge handbook of strategy as practice.* Cambridge University Press.

Gomes, C. V. A., Vadjunec, J. M. & Perz, S. G. (2012). Rubber tapper identities: Political-economic dynamics, livelihood shifts, and environmental implications in a changing Amazon. *Geoforum*, *43*(2), 260–271. https://doi.org/10.1016/j.geoforum.2011.09.005

Greenwood, R. (2017). *The SAGE handbook of organizational institutionalism*, pp. 1–928.

Greif, A. (2006). *Institutions and the path to the modern economy: Lessons from medieval trade*. Cambridge University Press.

Grzymala-Busse, A. (2010). The best laid plans. The impact of informal rules on formal institutions in transitional regimes. *Studies in Comparative International Development*, *45*(3), 311–333.

Hall, P. A. & Thelen, K. (2009). Institutional change in varieties of capitalism. *Socio-Economic Review*, *7*(1), 7–34. https://doi.org/10.1093/ser/mwn020

Hammer, H. K. (2019). *Deliberation or polarisation in the Norwegian online climate change debate*. NTNU.

Haslam, S. A. (2004). *Psychology in organizations*, pp. 1–336.

Hayoz, N. & Giordano, C. (2013). *Informality in Eastern Europe*. Peter Lang.

Healey, P. (1996). Consensus-building across difficult divisions: New approaches to collaborative strategy making. *Planning Practice and Research*, *11*(2), 207–216. https://doi.org/10.1080/02697459650036350

Hillier, J. (2000). Going round the back? Complex networks and informal action in local planning processes. *Environment and Planning A*, *32*, 33–54.

Holmström, S. (2007). Niklas Luhmann: Contingency, risk, trust and reflection. *Public Relations Review*, *33*(3), 255–262. https://doi.org/10.1016/j.pubrev.2007.05.003

Hornsey, M. J. (2008). Social identity theory and self-categorization theory: A historical review. *Social and Personality Psychology Compass*, *2*(1), 204–222. https://doi.org/10.1111/j.1751-9004.2007.00066.x

Humphrey, C. (2002). *The unmaking of Soviet life*. Cornell University Press.

Igoe, J. (2006). Becoming indigenous peoples: Difference, inequality, and the globalization of East African identity politics. *African Affairs*, *105*(420), 399–420. https://doi.org/10.1093/afraf/adi127

Innes, J. E. & Booher, D. E. (2010). *Planning with complexity: An introduction to collaborative rationality for public policy*. Routledge.

Innes, J. E., Connick, S. & Booher, D. (2007). Informality as a planning strategy. Collaborative water management in the CALFED Bay-Delta Program. *Journal of the American Planning Association*, *73*(2), 195–210.

Ison, R. & Straw, E. (2020). *The hidden power of systems thinking: Governance in a climate emergency*. Routledge.

Ivory, C. (2013). The role of the imagined user in planning and design narratives. *Planning Theory*, *12*(4), 425–441. https://doi.org/10.1177/1473095212470546

Jessop, B. (2002). Governance and meta-governance in the face of complexity: On the roles of requisite variety, reflexive observation, and romantic irony in participatory governance. In H. Heinelt, P. Getimis, G. Kafkalas, R. Smith & E. Swyngedouw (eds.), *Participatory governance in multi-level context: Concepts and experience* (pp. 33–58). VS Verlag für Sozialwissenschaften. https://doi.org/10.1007/978-3-663-11005-7_2

Kanai, J. M. (2016). The pervasiveness of neoliberal territorial design: Cross-border infrastructure planning in South America since the introduction of IIRSA. *Geoforum*, *69*, 160–170.

Killeen, T. J. (2007). *A perfect storm in the Amazon wilderness: Development and conservation in the context of the Initiative for the Integration of the Regional*

Infrastructure of South America (IIRSA) (Advances in Applied Biodiversity Science, Issue 7). Conservation International.

Knorr-Cetina, K. (1999). *Epistemic cultures: How the sciences make knowledge.* Harvard University Press.

Knorr-Cetina, K. D. (2013). *The manufacture of knowledge: An essay on the constructivist and contextual nature of science.* Elsevier.

Koch, L., Gorris, P. & Pahl-Wostl, C. (2021). Narratives, narrations and social structure in environmental governance. *Global Environmental Change, 69,* 102317. https://doi.org/10.1016/j.gloenvcha.2021.102317

Kojola, E. (2020). Divergent memories and visions of the future in conflicts over mining development. *Journal of Political Ecology, 27*(1), Article 1. https://doi.org/10.2458/v27i1.23210

Latour, B. (2004). *Politics of nature: How to bring the sciences into democracy.* Harvard University Press. https://doi.org/10.4159/9780674039964

Law, J. & Mol, A. (1995). Notes on materiality and sociality. *The Sociological Review, 43*(2), 274–294.

Ledeneva, A. (2006). *How Russia really works. The informal practices that shaped post-Soviet politics and business.* Cornell University Press.

Luhmann, N. (1989). *Ecological communication.* University of Chicago Press.

Luhmann, N. (1993). Deconstruction as second-order observing. *New Literary History, 24*(1), 763–782.

Luhmann, N. (2004). *Law as a social system.* Oxford University Press.

Luhmann, N. (2006). System as difference. *Organization, 13*(1), 37–57.

Luhmann, N. (2018). *Organization and decision.* Cambridge University Press.

Masson, T. & Fritsche, I. (2021). We need climate change mitigation and climate change mitigation needs the 'We': A state-of-the-art review of social identity effects motivating climate change action. *Current Opinion in Behavioral Sciences, 42,* 89–96. https://doi.org/10.1016/j.cobeha.2021.04.006

McCoy, J., Rahman, T. & Somer, M. (2018). Polarization and the global crisis of democracy: Common patterns, dynamics, and pernicious consequences for democratic polities. *American Behavioral Scientist, 62*(1), 16–42. https://doi.org/10.1177/0002764218759576

Mielke, K. (2022). Calculated informality in governing (non)return: An evolutionary governance perspective. *Geopolitics, 0*(0), 1–24. https://doi.org/10.1080/14650045.2022.2052854

North, D. (2005). *Understanding the process of economic change.* Princeton University Press.

North, D. C. (2008). Institutions and the performance of economies over time. In C. Ménard & M. M. Shirley (eds.), *Handbook of New Institutional Economics* (pp. 21–30). Springer Berlin Heidelberg. https://doi.org/10.1007/978-3-540-69305-5_2

North, D. C., Wallis, J. J. & Weingast, B. R. (2009). *Violence and social orders: A conceptual framework for interpreting recorded human history.* Cambridge University Press.

Peck, J. & Theodore, N. (2007). Variegated capitalism. *Progress in Human Geography, 31*(6), 731–772. https://doi.org/10.1177/0309132507083505

Perez-Sindin, X. & Van Assche, K. (2020). From coal not to ashes but to what? As Pontes, social memory and the concentration problem. *The Extractive Industries and Society.* https://doi.org/10.1016/j.exis.2020.07.016

Pierre, J. & Peters, B. G. (2000). *Governance, politics, and the state.* Macmillan.

Pierson, P. (2000). Increasing returns, path dependence, and the study of politics. *American Political Science Review*, *94*(02), 251–267.

Rasche, A. (2012). Global policies and local practice: Loose and tight couplings in multi-stakeholder initiatives. *Business Ethics Quarterly*, *22*(4), 679–708. https://doi .org/10.5840/beq201222444

Renaud, F. G., Birkmann, J., Damm, M. & Gallopín, G. C. (2010). Understanding multiple thresholds of coupled social-ecological systems exposed to natural hazards as external shocks. *Natural Hazards*, *55*(3), 749–763. https://doi.org/10.1007/s11069 -010-9505-x

Scharpf, F. W. (1997). Introduction: The problem-solving capacity of multi-level governance. *Journal of European Public Policy*, *4*(4), 520–538. https://doi.org/10 .1080/135017697344046

Seidl, D. (2016). *Organizational identity and self-transformation. An autopoietic perspective*. Routledge.

Shiner, L. (1982). Reading Foucault: Anti-method and the genealogy of power-knowledge. *History and Theory*, *21*(3), 382–398.

Spicer, A., Alvesson, M. & Kärreman, D. (2009). Critical performativity: The unfinished business of critical management studies. *Human Relations*, *62*(4), 537–560.

Steffen, W., Richardson, K., Rockström, J., Cornell, S. E., Fetzer, I., Bennett, E. M., Biggs, R., Carpenter, S. R., de Vries, W., de Wit, C. A., Folke, C., Gerten, D., Heinke, J., Mace, G. M., Persson, L. M., Ramanathan, V., Reyers, B. & Sörlin, S. (2015). Planetary boundaries: Guiding human development on a changing planet. *Science*, *347*(6223), 1259855. https://doi.org/10.1126/science.1259855

Stewart Leith, M. (2010). Governance and identity in a devolved Scotland. *Parliamentary Affairs*, *63*(2), 286–301. https://doi.org/10.1093/pa/gsp032

Stryker, S. & Burke, P. J. (2000). The past, present, and future of an identity theory. *Social Psychology Quarterly*, *63*(4), 284–297. https://doi.org/10.2307/2695840

Unsworth, K. L. & Fielding, K. S. (2014). It's political: How the salience of one's political identity changes climate change beliefs and policy support. *Global Environmental Change*, *27*, 131–137. https://doi.org/10.1016/j.gloenvcha.2014.05 .002

Urry, J. (2004). The 'system' of automobility. *Theory, Culture & Society*, *21*(4–5), 25–39.

Valentinov, V. (2012). System–environment relations in the theories of open and autopoietic systems: Implications for critical systems thinking. *Systemic Practice and Action Research*, *25*(6), 537–542. https://doi.org/10.1007/s11213-012-9241-0

Van Assche, K. & Hornidge, A.-K. (2015). *Rural development; knowledge and expertise in governance*. Wageningen Academic.

Van Assche, K., Beunen, R. & Duineveld, M. (2013). *Evolutionary governance theory: An introduction*. Springer.

Van Assche, K., Beunen, R., Jacobs, J. & Teampau, P. (2011). Crossing trails in the marshes: Rigidity and flexibility in the governance of the Danube Delta. *Journal of Environmental Planning and Management*, *54*(8), 997–1018. https://doi.org/10 .1080/09640568.2010.547687

Van Assche, K., Djanibekov, N., Hornidge, A.-K., Shtaltovna, A. & Verschraegen, G. (2014). Rural development and the entwining of dependencies: Transition as evolving governance in Khorezm, Uzbekistan. *Futures*.

Van Assche, K., Duineveld, M. & Beunen, R. (2014). Power and contingency in planning. *Environment and Planning A*, *46*(10), 2385–2400.

Van Assche, K., Duineveld, M., Beunen, R. & Teampau, P. (2011). Delineating locals: Transformations of knowledge/power and the governance of the Danube Delta.

Journal of Environmental Policy & Planning, 13(1), 1–21. https://doi.org/10.1080/1523908x.2011.559087

Van Assche, K., Duineveld, M., Beunen, R., Valentinov, V. & Gruezmacher, M. (2022). Material dependencies: Hidden underpinnings of sustainability transitions. *Journal of Environmental Policy & Planning, 24*(3), 281–296. https://doi.org/10.1080/1523908X.2022.2049715

Van Assche, K., Duineveld, M., Gruezmacher, M. & Beunen, R. (2021). Steering as path creation: Leadership and the art of managing dependencies and reality effects. *Politics and Governance, 9*(2), 369–380. https://doi.org/10.17645/pag.v9i2.4027

Van Assche, K., Gruezmacher, M. & Beunen, R. (2022). Shock and conflict in social-ecological systems: Implications for environmental governance. *Sustainability, 14*(2), 610. https://doi.org/10.3390/su14020610

Van Assche, K., Gruezmacher, M. & Deacon, L. (2020). Land use tools for tempering boom and bust: Strategy and capacity building in governance. *Land Use Policy, 93,* 103994–103994. https://doi.org/10.1016/j.landusepol.2019.05.013

Van Assche, K., Gruezmacher, M. & Granzow, M. (2021). From trauma to fantasy and policy. The past in the futures of mining communities; the case of Crowsnest Pass, Alberta. *Resources Policy, 72,* 102050–102050. https://doi.org/10.1016/j.resourpol.2021.102050

Van Assche, K., Hornidge, A.-K., Schlüter, A. & Vaidianu, N. (2020). Governance and the coastal condition: Towards new modes of observation, adaptation and integration. *Marine Policy, 112.* https://doi.org/10.1016/j.marpol.2019.01.002

Van Assche, K., Teampau, P., Devlieger, P. & Suciu, C. (2008). Liquid boundaries in marginal marshes: Reconstructions of identity in the Romanian Danube Delta. *Studia Sociologia, 53*(1), 115–133.

Van Assche, K., Verschraegen, G. & Gruezmacher, M. (2021a). Strategy for collectives and common goods. Coordinating strategy, long term perspectives and policy domains in governance. *Futures, 128*(5).

Van Assche, K., Verschraegen, G. & Gruezmacher, M. (2021b). Strategy for the long term: Pressures, counter-pressures and mechanisms in governance. *Futures, 131*(2).

Van Assche, K., Verschraegen, G., Valentinov, V. & Gruezmacher, M. (2019). The social, the ecological, and the adaptive. Von Bertalanffy's general systems theory and the adaptive governance of social-ecological systems. *Systems Research and Behavioral Science, 36*(3), 308–321. https://doi.org/10.1002/sres.2587

Voß, J.-P. & Simons, A. (2014). Instrument constituencies and the supply side of policy innovation: The social life of emissions trading. *Environmental Politics, 23*(5), 735–754.

Wang, X. & Lo, K. (2021). Just transition: A conceptual review. *Energy Research & Social Science, 82,* 102291. https://doi.org/10.1016/j.erss.2021.102291

Warner, B. P. (2019). Explaining political polarization in environmental governance using narrative analysis. *Ecology and Society, 24*(3).

Weick, K. E. & Quinn, R. E. (1999). Organizational change and development. *Annual Review of Psychology, 50*(1), 361–386. https://doi.org/10.1146/annurev.psych.50.1.361

Yashar, D. J. (2007). Resistance and identity politics in an age of globalization. *The ANNALS of the American Academy of Political and Social Science, 610*(1), 160–181. https://doi.org/10.1177/0002716206297960

Zerubavel, E. (2003). *Time maps: Collective memory and the social shape of the past.* University of Chicago Press.

8. Flexibility and change: finding a balance in governance and transition

CHANGE

Governance configurations are creations and creators of contingency. They are never entirely designed, nor are they the product of chance. They are never single-mindedly aiming at collective goods, yet they cannot be reduced to the sum of actor strategies. A governance path creates its own structure, internal variation and flexibility. That flexibility has several sources and some, not all, of those sources are the same ones that create structures. In the previous chapter we ended with a discussion of roles in governance that provide an example of this principle. These roles create dependencies that stabilize governance, yet they are also a source of flexibility. Earlier, we discussed discursive dynamics. These dynamics, through their ramifications for power/knowledge, are drivers of change as well. In our previous discussion of roles, we furthermore mentioned how several drivers for change can connect, reinforce each other, and sometimes imply each other.

In this chapter we intend to map out a series of drivers and enablers of change in governance, an endeavor which will unavoidably be incomplete, where other theories certainly add variation, but which will prove useful to see how governance can be transformed and how governance can spark transformations in the community and change in its environment. We need to discern mechanisms of flexibility, which can bring about inflection points in governance, and which need to inspire our reflection in the next chapters on ways to coordinate change, to come to community strategy. Change can be intended and unintended. Change in governance can lead to significant change in outcomes, i.e. effects in and on the community, or not. Flexibility in the system can be cultivated, or not, it can be appreciated, or not at all, and it can be observed or remain opaque. Flexibility can lead to better adaptation, yet absolute adaptation does not mean there is much flexibility incorporated in the system, neither does it imply adaptive capacity – a point noted by early systems theorists (Van Assche et al., 2019; Von Bertalanffy, 1972).

Change can come about through shocks or conflicts or through other contingent events in the community or governance system. It can happen through learning, or simply through steering. It can result from actor strategy, from neglect of institutions, from shifting semantics or discourse, or through rein-terpretation of existing institutions. New institutions can trigger change, even if they were not intended to change the system (Beunen & Patterson, 2017; Mahoney & Thelen, 2010). New actors or actors redefining themselves, new roles and changing linkages between roles, actors and identity narratives all can make a difference in governance. Even if new roles or role changes seem at first insignificant, even if an identity narrative seems stable for an outsider, small differences can be amplified through the functioning of governance (Czarniawska, 2004; Koch et al., 2021). The following sections will discuss what we consider to be key mechanisms of change. We refer to the previous chapter and the two chapters on discursive dynamics for an additional discussion of some of the mechanisms already introduced, and to the strategy chapter for the implications for coordinated change.

FLEXIBILITY AND ITS SOURCES

Governance paths always retain flexibility, even in situations that seem stable and difficult to change. The inevitability of change and flexibility stem from the ongoing processes that are required to keep governance systems going and in which elements and structures are constantly created, stabilized, maintained, reproduced, disrupted, changed or eliminated. Actors need to do something to be actors, institutions need to be interpreted and applied, and discourses need ongoing communications to remain a discourse. Each of these processes comes with a certain amount of flexibility, and in their interaction the elements and structures co-evolve as we have shown in the previous chapters. Co-evolution produces both structure and flexibility. Flexibility comes with all the sources of change already mentioned. It materializes through the interplay between the dependencies (Mahoney, 2000; Van Assche, Duineveld, et al., 2021). Goals modify path dependencies and vice versa, and impossible goals introduce more unpredictability. Flexibility enters through all forms of openness, reflexivity, loose couplings, uncertainties and synergies (Borch, 2005; Mahoney & Thelen, 2010; D. North, 2005; Ostrom, 2014; Pierson, 2000; Pottage, 1998; Rhodes, 1997). Flexibility is always circumscribed, and never one-dimensional. It is always amenable to qualitative description, and will differ in a qualitative manner, and is never simply a matter of more of something or less of something else. Flexibility is present or absent in particular ways, and this presence or absence has particular effects typical for the governance system (Van Assche et al., 2011).

The interplay between complex structures (such as governance configurations) does not always produce more complicated or rigid structures. It can just as well produce unpredictability, creativity, flexibility and even simplification.

This can be associated with features of the interacting systems, their forms of flexibility and mechanisms of adaptation, and it can be the outcome of their unexpected interactions, of their partial incompatibility, or of interference in the interaction. First, one needs to understand change in a governance path, after which the capacity to change and to adapt, flexibility, can be explained. It is important to consider that flexibility or adaptive capacity cannot be summarized in one indicator. The constraints and enablers are unique and hinge on path and configuration.

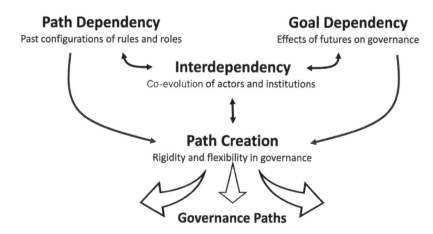

Figure 8.1   Dependencies and the flexibility and rigidity of governance paths[1]

The adaptive capacity of a governance system cannot be summarized in a set of indicators either, as all aspects that might be relevant for this capacity can be both a source of stability as well as a source of flexibility and adaptation. How things will play out will depend on the overall evolution of the configuration. Whether one feature of governance will de facto contribute to adaptation and whether it can be safely regarded as a contributing factor to adaptive capacity

---

[1]   Dependencies in governance interact with each other leading to the creation of different paths, some more rigid, others more flexible. Dependencies are both constraining and enabling. They represent rigidity but their interplay produces flexibility.

cannot always be observed, let alone predicted. In a similar way the capacity for transformative change cannot be simply grasped by a general set of indicators. That too hinges on the complex set of co-evolutions in governance, and on contingent events. Learning can be a source of adaptation and transformation, but it might just as well be used to keep everything the same and to deliberatively prevent adaptation and transformation, as argued elsewhere in this book. Processes of learning made merchants of doubt very successful in undermining effective policies to prevent a silent spring (pesticides), to prevent people getting cancer (pesticides, smoking) or to prevent the planet from warming (greenhouse gas emissions).

Rather than focusing on one measurable notion of adaptive capacity, we consider it more realistic to speak of sources of flexibility. Flexibility is not presented as unambiguously positive, as dependencies and learning processes are neither good or bad per se. Flexibility and change are related, but we can still specify sources of flexibility in slightly different terms, from a slightly different perspective.

1. For enhancing flexibility, *redundancies* in the system can help. Not focusing on the lean machine and on ultimate efficiency but accepting that things can get done through different routes, roles or procedures. Extra knowledge might be cultivated, just as institutional memory and some roles which are minimally defined or not necessary under all circumstances. Diversity of knowledge, actors and institutions can also contribute to (although is not a pre-requisite for) finding different routes, different ways of achieving the same goal and ultimately to build redundancy (Bendor, 1985; Phelps & Tewdwr-Jones, 2000). At the same time, it is important to notice that these aspects are neither a pre-requisite nor a guarantee for flexibility or adaption. Understanding their possible role in flexibility therefore does not easily translate into prescriptions for fostering flexibility and adaptation, nor in models to assess flexibility and adaptive capacity.

2. *Room for interpretation* is a *second source* of flexibility, which is always there. It can also be actively encouraged if we accept that polyvalence can be useful. It can help in connecting new master signifiers, to name one activity helpful in strategy formation. Room for *discretion* can similarly be acknowledged, and the belief in linked and integrated procedures which can solve all problems should be questioned. Tight couplings between administrative actors and between these actors and their roles in intricate procedures and routines are risky, as they might promise rationality and efficiency but de facto suppress judgment where it is needed. Looser couplings are essential to maintain flexibility, and this includes couplings between (subsets of) roles. If discretion, interpretation and redundancy

are further reduced through the coupling of administrative procedures and rigid, opaque and costly systems, flexibility is reduced, as for example digital governance promises to do through complex IT systems. The systems predefine interactions, multiply blind spots and make it harder to shift perspective and overcome obstacles (Calderaro & Blumfelde, 2022; Obendiek & Seidl, 2023).

3. As we mentioned earlier, *diversity* plays an important role in harnessing flexibility by opening the possibility for redundancies. Diversity of actors, including administrative ones, and a deliberate cultivation of truly different forms of knowledge in governance, embodies another source of flexibility. Diverse answers can be generated to questions stemming from within governance or the community, but also small adaptations needed to work in an agreed-upon direction. One can speak of adaptation for implementation, or flexibility for tactics – where strategy requires tactics to unfold (C. Ansell & Torfing, 2021; Hax & Majluf, 1988). Linking to this source of flexibility, one could list the cultivation of memory, in governance, its organization, and in the community itself. Reinserting the results of memory work in governance can enhance reflexivity and hence adaptation (Gherardi et al., 2018). If more perspectives are retained on what happened, what was tried before, on the effects of and contexts of policy tools, older strategies, big decisions, then assessment in governance of new decisions, either deliberately similar or dissimilar to what came before, takes places in a much richer and balanced frame of reference, where comparisons with the past can easily engender other learning processes (see below), including comparisons with other places (Allen, 2001; Golden, 1992). It is worth pointing out (a mantra in our story) that each governance design has a flip side, and that in this case diversity can also paralyze debate or be selectively used in processes of polarization or sabotage (see also Chapter 12).

4. An additional source of flexibility might appear counter-intuitive. *Levels of governance, differentiation of domains and arenas* which can block each other are not only a matter of checks and balances safeguarding democracy, but also a source of flexibility. This creates more sights of observation, introduces more perspectives, and the interactions between different levels, domains and arenas trigger processes of interpretation and reinterpretation. Furthermore, it allows for venue shopping, whereby changes realized at a certain level, domain or arena might trigger changes elsewhere in the governance system that otherwise would have not been easy to realize.

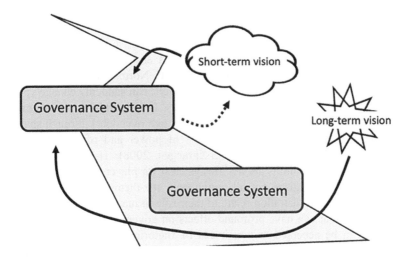

Figure 8.2   Long-term and short-term vision shape governance paths[2]

UNCERTAINTY AND PARADOX

A different angle to understand flexibility is to use a *game metaphor*, to see governance as a game, where some are strategizing beyond rules, others strategize following rules, and some just fulfill roles without much strategy going into it. The course of the game is unpredictable and it introduces uncertainties and flexible responses, yet it does not explain (beyond the strategy and opacity ideas) the sources of flexibility (Klijn & Teisman, 1997; Newig et al., 2013). If the number of actors in the game changes, coalitions might shift, and discourse coalitions and production of discourse might change. Strategizing for actors will need to adapt. Even anticipated change will necessitate strategy. Actors change, in the sense of individuals being replaced (an elected official, the mayor), or in the sense of actors redefining themselves under internal or external pressure, or even unconsciously so, through discursive dynamics and osmosis with the discursive environment (Seidl, 2007a). Rules change: new

---

[2]   Governance systems and their environments are influenced by the effects of short-term visions but also by the effects of long-term visions. Tactics enable strategy and strategy requires tactics. In other words, both long- and short-term visions shape the governance path of governance systems.

institutions, even if promoted and designed by one actor, will affect the strategizing of that actor in unpredictable ways (Golsorkhi et al., 2010; Suddaby et al., 2013; Whittington, 1996). They will be reinterpreted and used by other actors, observed and assessed by the community. As with new or redefined actors, new or redefined institutions change the game in a way that is largely independent of the intention of their creators and the process of creation (Bevir, 1999; Broto, 2013; D. North, 1990; D. C. North, 2008).

Other games, in other arenas or at other levels, can suddenly change values or positions in one arena (Swyngedouw, 2000). This could be the case because of formal couplings (at the same level or through oversight), through sharing semantics, or through informal relations of power and routine (Brans & Rossbach, 1997; Van Assche & Verschraegen, 2008). The game metaphor has limits, and these limits are not always clear for players. Not all actors see themselves as strategists, not all participants see themselves as actors, and participants in administration relate to their role in manners that are different and in ways that can have profound effects on governance. The existence of strategy can be accepted or not; it can be rhetorically opposed (professing a belief in rational decision-making, efficient decision-making as a sufficient base of governance, for example), or an opposition to strategy can be a deeply held belief (associated with an identity narrative, with ideology, with discourse on good governance and a good community). Meanwhile, power/knowledge shifts (see Chapter 6) are often hard to observe or control, and can make interpretation of what is happening difficult and strategizing based on such opacity a real challenge (Hautz et al., 2017; Kornberger, 2022).

A second metaphor that can assist in grasping the role of uncertainty and system responses to it in producing flexibility is that of *inventing roots*. While governance, from the actors' perspective, can be seen as a game, a game which creates uncertainty which is managed through the game, and its combination of rules, strategies, breaking rules, coincidence, it is also an activity that continuously needs to pretend it is certain about things it is not certain about. This need is another spring of uncertainty and of ever-changing systems responses. As with the game metaphor, and as in our discussion of roles in the previous chapter, we can see that uncertainty is created and responded to and that both structure and variation spring from the same well. Managing uncertainty is also managing the balance between rigidity and flexibility (Gunn & Hillier, 2014; Maier et al., 2016; Nair & Howlett, 2017).

As we know, several metaphors can be useful to grasp a phenomenon, and in our analysis of change and flexibility in governance this certainly is the case. The game metaphor illuminates other aspects of uncertainty driving flexibility than the metaphor of inventing roots, which derives from the Luhmannian concept of *de-paradoxification* (see also Chapter 5, The Realm of Discourse). For systems theorist Niklas Luhmann, organizations are forced to take decisions to reproduce themselves, and are obliged to find justifications for these decisions, while in the end such justification does not exist (Luhmann, 1995, 2018). In governance configurations, which are forms of complex organization, with many other organizations participating and many more linked indirectly, this process is more complex than in other organizations, yet there are also sources of simplification. This first and foremost includes the perceived mandate by 'the people' or 'the community' to do certain things.

We do, however, know that the people and the community are always abstractions that require construction, maintenance and interpretation, and that whatever is mandated requires further interpretation, and weighing against other things' mandates (Bowles & Gintis, 2002; Breede, 2017). We refer to our consideration of common goods, which rarely coalesce in a simple manner into *the* common goods. Even in places or moments where such reduction seems possible, the ways to bring this closer still require a series of contestable interpretations, and hard choices and decisions. Additional pressure in governance to de-paradoxify is the (sense of) urgency which often plagues governance: a decision has to be taken now, according to procedures; a resource has to be used or not, or alternative users show up; the weather, the enemies, our spiritual leader, tell us to do something *now*. Hence, something needs to happen, and an explanation must be produced quickly. If those selling the urgency share beliefs with those acting upon perceived urgency, this simplifies matters, as both believe in the same forms of de-paradoxification, in the same narratives which enable this operation (Copus et al., 2017; Luhmann, 2018).

Productive fictions, among which we can single out the master signifiers (Chapter 5) as highly relevant, assist in the unfolding series of de-paradoxifications that are required to keep governance going. The more uncertainty that enters the picture, the more governance will rely on de-paradoxification, and the more likely it is that new master signifiers, new meta-narratives, must be invented (Davidson, 2010; Hook & Vanheule, 2016). Political entrepreneurs and policy entrepreneurs (roles which can overlap) can seize the opportunity and create or introduce new stories, new explanations of problems and their solutions, which appear logical. This can entail a reinterpretation of the natural order, which was then supposedly misrecognized before, or, sticking to the old interpretation, but repositioning governance and good governance vis-à-vis that natural order.

Productive fictions of various sorts are thus invoked to suggest clarity, unity, causality and understanding. Together, they suggest an anchoring of a decision, a strategy, or a proposed governance reform in the nature of things, in a now finally recognized natural order. A clear example, in addition to several others briefly discussed in earlier chapters (such as 'evidence-based policy') is the fetish of efficiency (Christensen & Lægreid, 2017; Dick, 2013; Wollmann, 2003). 'We need to do this, these procedures need to be followed or these roles need to exist, certain decisions need to be taken, governance must be rearranged in this manner because it is all more efficient.' 'Something we want to achieve we should achieve faster, or cheaper, or more simply, or ... .' Says who? Who defines efficiency, its parameters, and the explicit and implicit goals? Who sees or omits the benefits of organizing things differently? Who redefined goals or reduced the identity of the organization? Who defines the risks of not changing practices towards the redefined efficiency idea? Where do we see changes in power/knowledge, in the hierarchy of values, of common goods, of time frames? Which political choices are obscured, and which identities are at play? We have to cut red tape: Is all red tape the same red? Even the interpretation of a shock, which causes, truly causes, a temporary halting of governance responses to the environment, remains an interpretation, an indirect link between system and environment (see later this chapter).

SYMBOLIC AND REPETITIVE CHANGE

Change in governance can also come about for seemingly trivial reasons. Here we briefly discuss two reasons that are often forgotten in discussions of governance, and we will call them repetitive and symbolic change. Symbolic change is change for the sake of change, change as a performance of change, while repetitive change is the change that happens just by repeated interactions in governance.

Change can indeed happen, slowly, sometimes imperceptibly, through continuing interaction in governance, between actors and institutions, between actors, between levels in governance, domains, between configuration and community. Those interactions are learning processes, but also, in each of them, interpretation takes place, and shifts elsewhere in the system can cause small differences in interpretation (Allen, 2001; Beard, 2003). Each interaction also allows for actor strategy, which can shift regularly (see the game metaphor). If actor identities or community identity narratives shift, this can lead to iterative small differences, even in routinized interactions. The community context changes continuously, and this changes the pressure on the configuration continuously, on potentially all its features.

We have already discussed how decisions are always jumps into uncertainty. They can never be derived directly from facts or values, or from situations marked by certainty (Newig et al., 2013). Otherwise, they would not be decisions. Chains of decisions therefore necessarily move governance slowly in a different direction, even if the decision is to stay the same. Each decision can bring change in two senses: by deliberately pushing for something and by reinterpreting the (never fully stable or causal) premises of decision-making.

In other words, in the seemingly repetitive interactions, apparently identical procedures, chains of seemingly similar decisions, all the sources of change (and flexibility) discussed above can creep in. Some are more obvious and visible than others, as some interactions, some differences, are more visible and some strategies more apparent. Some are less easy to grasp, as in the situation discussed earlier, where semantics on key concepts (such as democracy) slowly move. What deserves emphasis, however, is that, even without much of this occurring, without the reasons diagnosed earlier, the fact of repetition itself creates differences. Pure repetition is not possible, because of the reasons discussed; yet, even if one can imagine such pure repetition, a series of such perfectly self-similar interactions *will introduce difference* (Deleuze, 1994; Van Assche, Beunen, et al., 2022b). The reasons for this are multiple: the observations of the interactions by others, inside and outside governance, are multiple, never stable and can be incorporated in strategy. The effects of the interaction (sometimes a decision) in governance are never perfectly predictable, neither inside or outside governance, in terms of anticipated coordinative effect, and this will affect the observation of the next iteration (Harste & Laursen, 2021; Van Assche et al., 2020).

The observation of an interaction, of a decision, and the observation of results are thus connected in ways that can have implications for governance. If change is intended but not observed, this has, most likely, consequences. If change was not intended, but happens, questions will be raised. The observation of change itself thus has a value, to evaluate intentions, success and failure, competence and consistency (Brans & Rossbach, 1997). It is not illogical then that change itself can acquire a symbolic value in governance and community, compatible with dominant identities and ideologies, and that this can inspire a *performance of change* (Czarniawska-Joerges, 1989). This can be understood as exaggerating change (as intended result), pretending change, but also as achieving change more for the appearance of change than for any real rationale. This is not a matter of de-paradoxification, as there is no felt need to believe in an explanation, a real reason for change, rather an interest in a persuasive performance of change (which makes any rationale believable). Continuous administrative reform, local government reform, tinkering with participation formats, are well-known examples.

Change might have been promised in the community, or change might have a political value in a polarized environment, or, it can be in the manual of an influential faction of advisors (say, from management consultancy). Citizens might be vaguely dissatisfied, and in the absence of a real explanation a performance of change is expected to help to make the feeling just go away. Change in governance, and especially in administration, can thus have a symbolic value, and a process of eternal reform can be triggered, without ever solving any problem (Bourdieu, 1991; Christensen & Lægreid, 2003). This is not surprising, as the problem was often not the problem, yet a feeling that utopia did not arrive. Internal contradictions within the community and its expectations might have been projected on the governance system, which was supposed to act, and, if not, just to change so it could do the miracles expected.

Small government ideologies can, as we know, easily reproduce a rhetoric of efficiency at all costs and of a limited functionality of administration and governance (Centeno & Cohen, 2012). If costs creep up, if goals multiply, if policy tools start to look complicated again, if what is imagined to be simple (e.g. defining and delivering 'services') is not simple according to administration, then administration has to change, governance has to change. Yet, also in other ideologies, similar mechanisms are at work. If a greener mood captures the community and locals believe the existing configuration cannot handle a strategic shift, reform might be advocated for – in the form of a restructuring of administration, creation of new departments, mergers, a new advisory council, more links with academia. New managers or other leaders might want to assert themselves and prove their value and identity by changing things. Leaving a mark is effectuating change. That is often seen as the mark of real strategy and real leadership (Alvesson & Sveningsson, 2013).

Organization theorist Barbara Czarniawska, in an early and clear-eyed analysis of never-ending administrative reform in Sweden (1986), observes that the value of ongoing reform (beyond stated objectives) can reside (for the strategist of change) in the reshuffling of power relations, changing patterns of weak and strong ties, achieving a renewed legitimacy (where ideology can come into play) and re-socializing members of the organization (who might have lost interest because things got too boring presumably) (Blaschke et al., 2012; Czarniawska-Joerges, 1989). Indeed, a new manager, a new council, can cast a suspicious eye on a department deemed too powerful, and rewrite its role, reorganize procedures to that purpose. Or, a new manager can quickly assess which topics, which roles, which departments, which arenas are most important in public perception or closest to the interests of the governor, and can ignore those activities in administration which might be crucial, and which might be performed with greater skill. The idea of re-socialization can be used to get rid of an older generation, a faction opposing management, or can be associated with a competing ideology. The grand new challenge, the reform vision, the amazing opportunity to co-create, might be too critically observed by insiders, by old-timers, by experts, so these figures might have to be silenced, or forced to leave, and the explanation is ready at hand, as they opposed change. If the culture of leadership is to move on, and leave observable change as a sign of success, and if the community does not question these practices, a treadmill of reform can be set in motion, where purposeful reform becomes ever less likely. The difference between governance reform to enable sustainability transition and reform for other reasons becomes less and less clear, and arguments for transition strategy start to sound for the more critical observers as most likely veiling other agendas (Fischer-Kowalski & Rotmans, 2009; Gerritsen et al., 2022).

SHOCK AND CONFLICT

Governance systems can be shaken up, and shocks can come from the inside or the outside – the community, the ecosystem. We speak of a shock when no immediate response is available from the governance system to a sudden change. No response, that is, through the existing procedures, the appropriate channels. As a consequence of the shock, things cannot work the way they used to, and both routines and formalized sites of reflexivity and adaptation do not function. Governance did not see it coming and cannot coordinate. Or what was coming was observed in governance, but the situation was not assessed correctly. It is also possible that only a few saw something coming, but their observation did not carry weight (see earlier, on power/knowledge).

Collapse is not the only possible outcome of a shock, and not the most likely one. A breakdown of coordination can be temporary, local, topical, etc. Governance systems can also reconfigure, based on actors still there, institutions still functioning, and arenas able to continue (Herrfahrdt-Pähle et al., 2020; Van Assche, Gruezmacher, et al., 2022). Such reconfiguration, which can be a creative reshuffling and re-connecting of elements in governance, also depends on what is left of trust in government, in governance, and trust in narratives which were driving governance before the shock. Shocks can be productive, as they can inspire a rethinking of old procedures, patterns of rigidity, ideas, identities, therewith making governance systems more resilient (Christensen et al., 2016). What remains after a shock can be highly fragmented governance systems, or less so; multi-level governance can be shattered, or several levels survive, to an extent that re-connecting them becomes possible relatively soon (Campbell, 1997; Herrfahrdt-Pähle et al., 2020).

Shocks can easily engender conflict, and conflict tends to entangle with memory and identity. Hence, the effects of shock can be amplified, and harder to address (see below). If conflicts are latent, remaining unobserved for most actors, or are observed but not discussed and addressed in governance, they can proliferate. Once a conflict has taken hold of governance, or of the community, this can trigger hard polarizations in discourse (see earlier), and this can make the community less governable, while the opposite is needed, after a shock (Chong, 2011; Van Assche, Gruezmacher, et al., 2022).

Conflicts, like shocks, can be productive and unproductive. We know they can polarize discourse and increase rigidity. They can self-reproduce, trigger other conflicts and tend to amplify themselves, dragging in other topics, people, narratives and places (Brenneis, 1988; Drozdzewski et al., 2016). More and more things, people, places, situations become interpreted through the lens of conflict, using the categories of the topics. Not only are categories of hero and villain, right and wrong, introduced, making conciliation difficult, but also a reduction of issues to the topical structure of the conflict. This is not about topic 'A,' 'B' and 'C,' but about 'D,' which we know from the conflict; hence figuring out how A, B and C relate becomes unlikely. Discourse on homelessness, social justice and mental health can be transfigured by the other party in a governance conflict into a set of polarized positions on private property, the power of government, or religion.

Conflicts can be triggered by shock, making the effect intractable and harder to manage. Stabilizing governance after a shock becomes significantly more complicated in the presence of conflict. This largely derives from the fact that a conflict can restructure identity and memory (Bellino & Williams, 2017; Cairns et al., 2003). Past, present and future can be reinterpreted in and through the conflict. This undermines coordination mechanisms that were less than problematic before. Neither shock nor conflict are necessarily caused by resources, access to resources or resource dependencies, although it's rather clear that for the thinking on sustainability governance, resource shocks and resource conflict deserve special attention, as well as the governance of places especially dependent on one resource (Bradbury, 1978; Tunbridge & Ashworth, 1996). Yet, even where resources seem central, this is not always the case. The reason can be a power/knowledge relation which is contested, and when analysing resource conflicts it is helpful to trace if the resource, the power relation, or the narrative came first.

Reasons for conflicts are constructed and reconstructed continuously. This, too, is a form of de-paradoxification. The pressure of the conflict itself, the people it draws in, the topics, the tactics and strategies deployed, alliances made, and the counterstrategies of other parties induce these dynamics. Conflict thus hardens certain discursive features, it simplifies and polarizes, yet, in order to do so, in order to maintain a simplified reality serving the conflict, it necessitates discursive work, reinterpretation of many things, including the conflict itself (Warner, 2019). It is about 'X,' while yesterday it was 'Y'; the reason is 'A,' while yesterday it was 'B.' The conflict can be about a resource distribution, an exclusion in participation, and then turn into a conflict about factions, ideologies, individuals, or vice versa. The shifting focus of the conflict will have consequences for the balance of rigidity and flexibility, or, the selection of discursive features which will be hardened, and others which require adjustment or reinterpretation (Ampumuza et al., 2021; Van Assche, Gruezmacher, et al., 2022; Van Assche & Gruezmacher, 2023). If a conflict becomes more about a person, then all other things become more flexible; if there is a more complex analysis of a policy problem which underpins a conflict, then the elements of this analysis can remain more stable. If a conflict starts as a difference in opinion over a policy, then turns into ideological clash, the categories of the ideology can invade and restructure the conflict (Cresswell, 1996; Sanabria-Pulido & Velasquez-Ospina, 2021).

Conflict can be productive, in the sense that new discursive objects can be created, as a means of reconciliation (things to agree upon, which might have to be invented), and to perpetuate the conflict (things that will anger opponents, things that will be used in factional strategy) (Foucault, 2007; Machiavelli, 2012; Van Assche et al., 2016). New ideas, new forms of organization can be created in productive tension, out of perceived necessity, new objects and subjects can be created. New discursive configurations can form in conflict, and they can produce new shared identities, while existing identities can transform under the vicissitudes of the conflict (Beach, 2017; Drozdzewski et al., 2016). Making differences visible in governance can create conflict, but can also help preventing it. It can increase the likelihood of productive conflict, rather than conflict eroding the institutions, a distinction which was crucial for Machiavelli as well (Del Lucchese, 2009). Harnessing the power of difference, even conflict, in governance, can produce more varied solutions to problems, and can enhance flexibility (Dreu & Vliert, 1997; Tjosvold, 2008).

LEARNING AND CHANGE

Learning, in many forms, plays a crucial role in the flexibility of governance systems and has been studied intensively and from various angles (Antonacopoulou & Gabriel, 2001; Bennett & Howlett, 1992; Gerlak et al., 2018; Moyson et al., 2017; Reed et al., 2010; Van Assche, Beunen, et al., 2022b). Governance systems change because they *learn.* They can learn, and that learning is more than the sum of actor learning. Learning can lead to adaptation and other forms of change. Learning can prepare decisions, inform new institutions, enable assessment of decisions, policies and plans, and draw conclusions from experience. Learning does not have to be intentional, neither at the actor level nor at the level of the system: one can observe that something has been understood, adapted to, reorganized in a way that better fulfills a goal (Allen, 2001; Van Assche, Beunen, et al., 2022b).

It is possible that the actor or system itself is aware of learning, or becomes aware of it after the fact, but this is not necessary. Our point of view does imply that we need a point of view: an observer is needed to ascertain that something has been learned by a system. This, however, is not sufficient; an observer can be there, pay attention, observe a change which seems to embody a form of learning from an experience, but one cannot always be certain. A change might have been sparked by something unrelated, and the result might happen to solve a problem or function as a better adaptation. Such uncertainty is not a problem, however, neither for governance nor for the student of governance, because it does not stand in the way of the possibility of conscious learning, that is, the possibility to intentionally reflect on an experience and modify ideas of practices according to the conclusions. We can further speak of *unconscious learning* to distinguish unintentional learning from coincidental adaptation (Tosey, 2005; Van Assche, Beunen, et al., 2022b).

Furthermore, we can distinguish different forms of learning that are likely to co-exist in governance: learning from self-reflection (of the present and past), learning through comparison (with other places, times, systems), learning through experiment (trying something new), learning from experts, and dialectical learning (Van Assche, Beunen, et al., 2022b). Dialectical learning might sound less familiar but can be considered to be the one first theorized, as this is the learning through dialogue and discussion, where new insights emerge in the discussion. Plato and Aristotle found this essential for public discourse (Aristotle, 1954), but it has been rather neglected in modern theories of politics and administration, where experts are given either prominence or processes of participation and deliberation. Machiavelli, in early modern times, is an exception, as for him difference in perspectives makes governance productive, throws up new ideas which can inspire adaptation to ever changing environments (Machiavelli, 2004). A normative feature of our theory is that, ideally, all the forms of learning just mentioned come together in dialectical learning, before taking important decisions, and before enacting new institutions. Strategies for the longer term, integrated policies, require dialectical learning before and after adoption, as the burden of responsibility and the burden of proof are great, and the insights from diverse perspectives need to be mobilized.

Each governance path allows and disincentivizes some forms of learning, and certain relations between these forms. In each path, some forms of non-observing, non-thinking (see earlier), non-learning also exist, and some of these forms are consciously adopted and even encouraged. Mats Alvesson (see also Chapter 5, The Realm of Discourse) spoke of functional stupidity, where smart people and smart organizations dumb themselves down, simplify their images of self, organization and environment, in order to believe simple narratives and follow blind procedures which are believed to be true, or, better, recipes for success (Alvesson & Spicer, 2016). These narratives can also be associated with the identity of the organization. Functional stupidity is thus a type of non-learning, and one, alas, quite common in governance, as narrative in governance is central, and as actors and communities sometimes prefer simple narrative over complex explanation or subtle assessment. Conscious and unconscious forms of non-thinking and non-learning are unique to the governance paths, just as are the forms of learning taking place, and the way they relate in the governance process.

We cannot omit a brief mention of *dark learning* in governance, an idea elaborated by Michael Howlett, Claire Dunlop and others, to indicate processes of intentional learning, when actors use knowledge of governance to subvert governance goals and institutions, to benefit themselves (Dunlop & Radaelli, 2018; Howlett, 2000, 2020). Dark learning can lead to policy failure or it can entail a benefitting of not caring about policy failure. Elsewhere it can produce seemingly successful policies, which just do not benefit the community or the ones most deserving. Overly complex and opaque governance systems can encourage dark learning, as expertise in governance becomes valuable. Overly closed governance systems can have a similar effect, as those who can find an entrance, and are familiar with its functioning, possess a social capital which can easily be converted into economic and political capital (in the terms of sociologist Pierre Bourdieu) (Bourdieu, 1985).

An example of such a form of dark learning is the way in which Dutch government tried to circumvent and dilute European nature conservation requirements (Beunen & Kole, 2021). Over a period of 30 years, various policies, programmes and rules were introduced to ease the permitting process for activities with significant effects on protected species and habitats, many of which were later annulled in court. The result was an ever-growing web of regulation that only made the permitting process more complex, eroded trust in government, and failed to halt biodiversity loss. At the same time the government constantly developed narratives to blame conservation law, rather than to learn how the implementation of that law could be improved (Beunen et al., 2013; Ferranti et al., 2019).

Experimental learning is much touted, under various names (living labs, social innovation, institutional experimentalism, for example), but it has proven hard to implement. Organizing collective action, or a method of policy implementation or even analysis, is no mean feat, as society is no laboratory, as governance does not allow for disinterested observers. Fair comparison with other places, before and after, could prove troublesome because correcting for a myriad of other variables which can affect success and the interpretation of success and failure often prove elusive (Jost, 2004; Luhmann, 1995; Rap, 2006; Van Assche et al., 2012b). Observation of the results of the experiment rarely takes place under conditions of analytic freedom, as expectations are high and the failure of the experiment is seen as failure, not as a learning moment (Van Assche et al., 2023). Moreover, the autonomy of the organizer of the experiment to draw lessons, and the power to implement those lessons, to reform governance so the experiment can become the norm – that autonomy and those powers are usually not there.

Comparative learning and learning from experts tend to reinforce each other, as experts partly derive their expert status from the capacity to look beyond the present context, to be familiar with other geographies, eras, types of polities, and other conceptual frames which enable comparison (Jacobsen, 1966; Pierre, 1995). Comparison comes with the constraint that for a comparison to have effects in governance, the analyst needs to be familiar with both points of comparison. For comparison to work, the features and functioning of the observing system, the system trying to learn, need to be grasped as well as those of the system that could offer (positive or negative) lessons (Beyes, 2005). One traditional solution is to invite external experts, consultants or academics, who could have a healthy critical distance from both systems, a distance from ruling ideologies and master narratives; this can work yet has the drawback of limited familiarity. Similarly, expert teachers, hoped to inspire expert learning (beyond the comparative) can be invited, under the assumption that this would immunize the learning system from the blind spots caused by self-observation. This too, can work, yet comes with a drawback of limited familiarity, and, often, a return of blind spots through the selection process of experts, where those promising amazing successes and those reproducing the assumptions, culture and ideology of the employer are more likely to get hired (Stirrat, 2000).

None of these gloomy reflections should be taken to indicate that efforts to learn and to optimize learning are a waste of time. On the contrary, it means that learning processes are extraordinarily diverse, that everything that can be learned can be un-learned, ignored or abused, but also used well above expectations, through synergies with other forms of learning, and learning on unexpected learning sites, i.e. times and places, occasions, where learning tends to happen, even if this is not observed by those formally encouraging learning.

We do need to be aware that non-learning is potentially as diverse as learning, and that the incentives for non-learning and dark learning might be only very partially observed by management and by leadership (Flyvbjerg, 1996). This can be the case because leadership really wants to believe something, because it really wants to ignore something else, because it truly does not care to pay attention or, and this is not the most common situation, because the non-learning and dark learning are hidden with great skill (Howlett, 2020; Paquet, 2022). Alvesson and Spicer's functional stupidity, induced by blindly following leadership, fashions (imitation), branding efforts, organizational structures (including routines and compartmentalization) and culture (overly optimistic norms, delusional self-images, for example) might be extremely common, yet is rarely inspired by strategic teaching of nonsense and clever, secretive forms of non-learning and dark learning (Alvesson & Spicer, 2016). Avoiding headaches and hassle, navigating the system more easily, are traditional motivations to dumb down or find shortcuts.

Uncommon as these forms of non-learning might be, we do need to acknowledge the existence of *strategic stupidity*. We refer here to deliberate forms of non-learning, of not responding, not analysing, not picking up signals, not fixing, or not listening (Schoenmakers & Duysters, 2006; Van Assche, Beunen, et al., 2022b). A charitable interpretation of one version is a sincere desire to not change, to keep things exactly as they are, whereby any opening up to an outside world or seemingly calling for change all the time, apparently aching for more complexity, is seen as a threat, as an invitation of signals which will inevitably lead to unwanted change. This version of strategic non-learning, in its sheer stubbornness, can still have positive intentions, and can be linked to conservative identity narratives, narratives of community identity and ideologies of governance (which is supposed to be simple, unchanging, cheap). A different version, where a sympathetic interpretation is more difficult, is strategic non-learning that amplifies non-response and blindness to run an organization or a governance system into the ground, bring a disaster closer, smoke out actors or whole communities (Van Assche, Beunen, et al., 2022a; Voß & Freeman, 2016).

The previous paragraphs, including the more pessimistic reflections, underline the importance of reflexive learning in governance. Indeed, if reflexivity can be enhanced, if sites of reflexivity can multiply, if practices can be routinized, then the understanding of the system in the system can be dramatically improved (Feindt & Weiland, 2018; Voß et al., 2006). People can see beyond their immediate task, role, moment, fashion, or worry, and understand their systemic context, the relations of the system which make it function and constrain it, the modes of self-transformation which give an indication about future change, power relations which could be problematic, forgotten forms of expertise, or unused institutions. Jan-Peter Voß et al. (2006) cogently pointed out that reflexivity is no panacea, that it has no natural limit, and can trigger an infinite regression (observation of observation, etc.), and for Luhmann (2018) the risk of rampant reflexivity would be double, as introducing a threat of de-differentiation (see earlier) and as overburdening the system with its internal complexity. Alvesson and Spicer (2016) would also agree that not everyone in an organization can be hypercritical or else things would not be able to move forward. We agree, yet this does not contradict the need, in most systems and for most practical purposes, to incentivize reflexive learning, as much more is possible before the traps revealed by Voß and Luhmann would become real.

Furthermore, reflexive learning improves the other forms of learning and their productive coupling. We mentioned that comparative learning and expert learning benefit from a deeper understanding of the system that is asking questions, which is willing to learn. Reflexive learning can make such knowledge more readily available, in a diversity stemming from different perspectives and sites of reflection (Schön, 1983). Experimental learning arguably places the highest demands on reflexivity in the system, the highest capacity for reflexive learning, as continuous self-observation is required, as is deep understanding of the limitations of the previous way of organizing (pre-experiment), as well as flexibility in observation, and an ability to redefine success (Seidl, 2007b).

Reflexive learning also come to bear on dialectical learning, as a discussion between several parties representing several forms of reflexivity is likely to be much more productive, and lead to an innovative yet context-specific outcome, than a confrontation between non-reflexive actors, repeating positions based on stable and non-scrutinized understandings of self, system and community (Voß et al., 2006; Voß & Bornemann, 2011). Also, recognizing dark learning and non-learning will be easier when reflexivity from different viewpoints is common. (Hence, Chapter 10 on strategy will lean heavily on the fostering of reflexivity, as the basis for a self-analysis which can inspire strategy.)

Rhythms and Cycles and Learning

The structuring of time chosen in a governance path affects its possibilities to learn and to change. The multiplication of governance elements in config-urations that tend to become more elaborate over time, and the multiplication therefore of different temporalities (associated with actors, institutions, nar-ratives and conceptual frames), enables a multiplication of observations and learning options, yet also makes coordination harder (see earlier, on good governance) (Beyes, 2005; Harste & Laursen, 2021). A coordinated response to a signal coming from the environment thus becomes more difficult, while the belief tends to take hold that a specialized response, taken care of by a spe-cialized actor, is sufficient.

Rhythms in governance can inspire cyclical patterns of cognitive openness and closure, of changing focus on topics where learning might be important (Boston, 2021; Chaffin & Gunderson, 2016). Elections, in democracies, create both cognitive openness and closure, as something needs to be picked up from the environment, about the environment and about governance itself, and as hardening positions to clarify identity and embrace ideology might be expected by voters. Rhythms in the community, shifting moods, patterns of activity and rhythms in the social-ecological system (ecological processes, linked processes of extraction and use) can affect change in governance as well as what can be changed in governance (Bornemann et al., 2022). Seasons cannot be changed, and if important activities are tied to them, those activities will not be restructured in a temporal sense, or subjected to new regulations which hamper their seasonal patterning. Activities that change quickly, depending on unpredictable ecological or economic processes, do not neces-sarily require change in governance, nor new regulation, as the temporality, the regular switching can be internalized in the designated institution; procedures can include either/or switches and determining variables.

Multiplication of temporalities, or increased awareness in governance of a multiplicity of temporalities, complicates synthesis into visions and their implementation and therewith coordination and strategic change (Bain &

Landau, 2019; Hillier, 2011; Luhmann, 1995). We discussed earlier the benefits of differentiation in society and governance, and the associated problems of re-synthesizing specialized perspectives into comprehensive visions. Now we can add that temporalities aggravate this issue. If, moreover, temporalities differ much in character, coming to a synthesis – which means coming to a narrative and a credible form of coordination – looks more daunting. One reason for this is the methodological preference in most governance systems for that which is clear, predictable and certain (Miller, 2012). What is clear, what can be measured, what can be acted upon more easily, creeps into the ontological domain of 'more real' and tends to be acted upon more quickly (see our discussion on quantification in governance) (Hacking, 1990; Luuk & Gert, 2016; Rotmans & Kemp, 2003). Hence, coordination of a more predictable, observable or cyclical activity or parameter is preferred over the coordination of a less predictable one. Or the coordination can be structured around that which is closer to the activities and the worldview of an actor. This means that those temporalities that are less known, less observed and less represented by an actor tend to be ignored, even if they could undermine the social-ecological system. The sea is not at the table, nor the birds nor the seagrass. The few scientists paying attention to their temporalities are rarely actors in governance. Coordination giving equal weight requires more regular observation, fair representation and dropping methodological biases. In addition, it requires practice in coordination, as binding time in governance is an art in itself that can be learned (Jordana & Levi-Faur, 2004; Kornberger, 2012; Rhodes, 2016).

STABILIZATION

Stabilization can mean the maintenance of a steady state or working towards a steady state, with less dramatic changes in governance and reproduction based on existing routines. Stabilization does not entail or enable a return to the past and stabilization cannot be permanent, as the interactions in and between the configurations, and between governance and community, continue. Stabilization can occur when interdependencies are created, restored or reinforced, or, when a discursive coalition or configuration is created or invoked. Restoration of trust or legitimacy can stabilize governance, and so can the sharing of futures and other narratives.

Stabilization can be encouraged when ad hoc responses or decision-making styles are turned into routines governed by institutions, with meta-institutions regulating the creation and functioning of other institutions, and couplings between actors becoming codified, and roles crystallize (see earlier on role formation). It happens when environments stabilize themselves (floods recede) or are stabilized by means of previous decisions and interventions (wildfires extinguished through collaboration with neighbors). Stabilization can come from many sides, therefore, and can be the result of strategy and collaboration, or new forms of participation (calming down sentiment, finding new solutions), or not. Stabilization comes with drawbacks, as a solution to a present problem can be turned into a rigid feature of governance (Duit et al., 2010; Thelen, 2009; Uzunca et al., 2022).

Stabilization can further occur when new topics or domains emerge within the purview of governance. New problems, topics, opportunities, environments that become observable enough, demands for governance accrue, and the belief that something is and should be governable starts to grow (C. K. Ansell et al., 2017; Teisman et al., 2009). The addition of new topics, domains, etc., can stabilize governance if the absence of the topic or domain caused instability before. This could have been the result of disturbances (for Luhmann, 'irritations') from the environment that were not adequately conceptualized in governance, or it could have been instability caused by internal inabilities to coordinate – which might require the definition of a new topic, a new narrative, and new institutions to make expectations compatible (Mölders, 2021).

Another governance mechanism favoring stabilization is the *internalization of conflict and disagreement* (Held, 2013). We do not refer only to the existence of conflict management mechanisms, applicable inside and outside governance, but also to the creation of sites, arenas, topics, institutions and even actors that trigger the appearance of conflict in governance. This makes conflict more visible, more manageable and more amenable to resolution or at least stabilization through application of the tools of governance. A delineated space inside governance is created for airing grievances (an important topic in Machiavelli's tightly woven city-states), a committee is established to focus on a controversial topic, or a specially crafted participation process is set in motion (Del Lucchese, 2009; O'Riordan et al., 2015).

If people feel something should be regulated and if that something becomes more knowable, then a pressure towards the formation of actor-institution configurations will build up. If governance remains absent, then new aspiring actors will present themselves at some point as a problem is perceived in the community. Processes of expansion of the governable are not without controversy, as ideologies in governance tend to have ideas on the limits of governance. Conflicts about the limits of governance can easily become intractable, if competing ideologies are around the table, if common ground on similar issues is not found. Arguments might simply not be compatible, and thus power relations may not be won easily. Checks and balances, including institutions anchoring other institutions, making them harder to change, come in and can keep situations ungovernable (Bevir, 1999; Mahoney & Thelen, 2010).

The formation of *roles*, we know, also helps to stabilize governance, while it also introduces a productive instability, which contributes to adaptive capacity. Roles are connectors and catalysts in governance, and, crucial for our present discussion, changing roles can be easier than changing actors (Agrawal et al., 2008; Jessop, 1999). It can take place, often, with fewer challenges to the legitimacy of the change. Once roles are re-delineated, their catalytic function can come into play and effectuate further change in governance and in the community. Once roles are codified, coordination towards change can speed up, or, conversely, coordination towards stabilization can occur (Koliba et al., 2017). The structure of roles can create identities and incentives for actors to work towards coordination in one direction, whereby both change or stabilization are possible (Ben-Amos & Weissberg, 1999; Cohen, 1975). Arenas can assume a catalytic function, if they become the site of debate and ensuing role creation. Conversely, roles can be brought together not only in new structures of administration, but also in new arenas. One such arena could deliberate long-term futures and strategic change.

SELF-TRANSFORMATION

In order to understand change in governance, and the possibilities and limits of steering change, in and through governance, we need to talk about both rigidity and flexibility, both stability and change, and we need to discuss mechanisms of change which take place more or less automatically, through ongoing interactions and streams of signals from the environment, and deliberate, intentional and coordinated change. It is imperative to discern what can be steered, with what degree of predictability, what feedback mechanisms, and with what costs and risks. The next few chapters will develop such analysis further, but in this chapter and in the previous one, on dependencies, we have laid the groundwork.

Each governance path is marked by a unique combination of rigidity and flexibility; whereby stability, longer-term certainty about coordination, and flexibility or adaptive capacity are required for each system. Flexibility and rigidity each have their benefits, and in co-evolution produce their unique form of contingency, where both structure and variation are the input and output of governance (Brans & Rossbach, 1997). The concept of the dependencies, developed by evolutionary governance theory (Beunen et al., 2014; Van Assche et al., 2013), building on systems theory (Luhmann, 1990, 1995; Von Bertalanffy, 1969), institutional economics and anthropology (Acemoglu & Robinson, 2013; D. North, 1990), is one way of analysing the interplay between rigidity and flexibility, and the concepts of roles and identities, which lean on sociology and management, offer a compatible and complementary perspective (Seidl, 2016; Van Assche et al., 2012a).

Some mechanisms in governance favor change more than stability, while others, such as role formation, can catalyze both. Conflict tends to destabilize and can do this in productive and unproductive ways (see earlier discussion).

Strategy for sustainability transitions

Learning can enable change as well as stabilization. Stability is not a given, but it has to be conquered and redefined continuously. Learning, moreover, exists in a precarious balance with non-learning and dark learning, a relation which is shaped by the path and its dependencies, and by strategies of actors pursuing public and private goals. Non-learning might envision stability, but rarely ends up achieving this because it can undermine adaptation, render coordination brittle, and because it takes place in a governance environment where learning and non-learning combine to create opacity and uncertainty (Dunlop & Radaelli, 2018; Nair & Howlett, 2017).

Knowing and organizing, in their complex entanglement, introduce both stability and instability in governance and community. Stability is a precondition for coordination, hence coordinated change, while change can produce new forms of stability, new system-environment relations which might manage turbulence better. Managing change is still managing, hence some form of stability will be needed, such as anchoring institutions, meta-narratives, checks and balances, grounding decisions, or longer-term perspectives which are less questioned than others (Armitage & Plummer, 2010; D. North, 1990). Stability becomes dangerous if it denies the co-evolving nature of governance, the instabilities introduced by environmental interactions, human desire, discursive dynamics and cognitive limitations. It becomes a threat when the irrationality and opacity of individuals and communities are not considered, turning stability into a fetish, or a safeguard of identities presumed to be stable or believed to be superior. Stability, considered as a transient state, which always remains subjected to the powers of co-evolution, is an essential enabler of change, and a necessary state by itself (if temporary and selective). Strategy for the long term, however adaptive, will remain elusive if instability in governance is too great, if all productive fictions are questioned continuously, and if anchoring institutions are uprooted too easily (Ospina & Marks, 2014; Stetter, 2007).

Coordinated change is not always possible, and one reason for this can be irresolvable disagreement on the nature and the limits of governance (Brandtner & Bromley, 2022; Stavrakakis, 2018). Another one is disagreement on knowledge, its relevance for governance, and its limits. Biding time in governance, organizing for the long run, proves hard indeed if the nature and limits of both knowing and organizing are disputed, and no tools remain to resolve the dispute, while a middle ground might not be there. Climate change is either accepted or denied, and a role for national governments or international agreements to govern climate change can be seen as legitimate or not. We know by now that even such conundrums can be dislodged, as people can be convinced, as identities and ideologies do get reshuffled. What can be planned or steered in the process is context-specific, and discerning limits in this regard will be part of any attempt at transition strategy (Fischer-Kowalski & Rotmans, 2009; Voß & Bornemann, 2011).

A CONCLUDING NOTE: UNDERSTANDING CHANGE AND THE POTENTIAL FOR STEERING

We return thus to the importance of reflexivity and reflexive learning, which also brings us to the next chapter, in which the importance of memory will be treated in more detail. Memory enables all functionalities in governance, improves reflexivity, and shapes the options for thinking about and organizing for the future.

In this chapter on change in governance, a crucial chapter to understand options for strategic change, we had to cover much ground. Transitions towards sustainability require adaptation, yet not only that kind change, and at the same time not all change is adaptation, and not all adaptation is positive. Following the resilience literature, we recognized that for those reasons a shift of attention towards adaptive capacity makes more sense, in practical and analytic terms, yet adaptive capacity cannot be summarized into one or a set of indicators, and an adaptive capacity is always the capacity to adapt to a range of conditions, where developing capacity in one range will have trade-offs for limitations somewhere else. We discussed shock and conflict to illustrate that the understanding of this range of situations to envision building adaptive capacity is always imperfect, that internal and external environments can always come up with unpleasant surprises. Externally and internally induced instability and uncertainty can reinforce each other in a way that cannot be designed away.

Similar to the conceptual move from adaptation to adaptive capacity, yet more general, is the proposal to look at both mechanisms of change and sources of flexibility. Flexibility in governance systems is the condition for change and adaptation – cultivating and first understanding sources of flexibility is essential when mapping modes and drivers of change in governance – and the potential for strategy. The previous chapters already intimated that, just as with adaptive capacity, flexibility is neither good nor bad, and that each system requires a unique balancing of flexibility and rigidity. Our co-evolutionary perspective proved helpful in identifying change as potentially stemming from interactions between all elements in governance, interactions which sometimes entail intentionality, sometimes not.

We can safely assume that transition strategies will do more than enhance adaptation to changing environments. They will have to engender transformations in society and in governance itself. As it is abundantly clear that a template for transition strategy does not exist, one must keep open the possibility that *everything* needs to be changed, and that the relation between social and ecological systems will need to be re-examined and redefined on a regular basis. This means that new knowledge must be used and produced, that new

narratives might be needed as well as new perspectives on sustainability problems, but also on community and environment, on identity, past and future, and
on governance itself. Many such processes have been captured under the label
of 'learning' – organizational learning, social learning, sustainability learning.

Learning is not the answer to all questions of steering and change, as not
all forms of change can be associated with learning, as not all learning is
intentional. Learning can be dark learning, eying individual or group interests,
potentially undermining common goods and the quality of governance, while
(perceived) self-interest can just as well inspire non-learning, including what
we call strategic stupidity. Learning, however, does deserve our attention, as
learning can be fostered, as deliberately linking sites and forms of learning
can increase the capacity to observe and solve problems, and as it can help
to find or build common ground for strategy. In governance, individuals,
organizations and the governance system itself can learn, which can lead to
modifications in the inclusion of expertise. It can also lead to new patterns of
inclusion and participation, to new policies and plans, to new narratives and
possibly strategies, and to a form of institutional redesign which can work
because it starts from the actual potential for self-transformation.

REFERENCES

Acemoglu, D. & Robinson, J. A. (2013). *Why nations fail: The origins of power, pros-
perity, and poverty*. Profile Books.
Agrawal, A., Chhatre, A. & Hardin, R. (2008). Changing governance of the world's
forests. *Science, 320*(5882), 1460–1462. https://doi.org/10.1126/science.1155369
Allen, P. M. (2001). A complex systems approach to learning in adaptive networks.
International Journal of Innovation Management, 5(02), 149–180.
Alvesson, M. & Spicer, A. (2016). *The stupidity paradox: The power and pitfalls of
functional stupidity at work*. Profile Books.
Alvesson, M., & Sveningsson, S. (2013). Essay: Authentic leadership critically
reviewed. In *Authentic Leadership*. Edward Elgar Publishing.
Ampumuza, C., Duineveld, M. & van der Duim, R. (2021). Material pacification: How
a conflict over paving Uganda's tourism road got accidentally resolved. *Tourism
Planning & Development*, 1–16. https://doi.org/10.1080/21568316.2021.1988693
Ansell, C. & Torfing, J. (2021, May). *Public governance as co-creation: A strategy
for revitalizing the public sector and rejuvenating democracy*. Cambridge Core;
Cambridge University Press. https://doi.org/10.1017/9781108765381
Ansell, C. K., Trondal, J. & Øgård, M. (2017). *Governance in turbulent times*. Oxford
University Press.
Antonacopoulou, E. P. & Gabriel, Y. (2001). Emotion, learning and organizational
change: Towards an integration of psychoanalytic and other perspectives. *Journal
of Organizational Change Management, 14*(5), 435–451. https://doi.org/10.1108/
EUM0000000005874
Aristotle. (1954). *Aristotle: Rhetoric*. Random House.
Armitage, D. & Plummer, R. (2010). *Adapting and transforming: Governance for
navigating change*. In D. Armitage & R. Plummer (eds.), *Adaptive capacity and*

environmental governance (pp. 287–302). Springer Berlin Heidelberg. https://doi .org/10.1007/978-3-642-12194-4_14

Bain, A. L. & Landau, F. (2019). Artists, temporality, and the governance of collaborative place-making. *Urban Affairs Review, 55*(2), 405–427. https://doi.org/10.1177/1078087417711044

Beach, A. I. (2017). *The trauma of monastic reform: Community and conflict in twelfth-century Germany*. Cambridge University Press. https://doi .org/10.1017/9781108277341

Beard, V. A. (2003). Learning radical planning: The power of collective action. *Planning Theory, 2*(1), 13–35. https://doi.org/10.1177/1473095203002001004

Bellino, M. J. & Williams, J. H. (2017). *(Re)constructing memory: Education, identity, and conflict.* Sense Publishers.

Ben-Amos, D. & Weissberg, L. (eds.) (1999). *Cultural memory and the construction of identity*. Wayne State University Press.

Bendor, J. (1985). *Parallel systems: Redundancy in government.* University of California Press.

Bennett, C. J. & Howlett, M. (1992). The lessons of learning: Reconciling theories of policy learning and policy change. *Policy Sciences, 25*(3), 275–294.

Beunen, R. & Kole, S. (2021). Institutional innovation in conservation law: Experiences from the implementation of the Birds and Habitats Directives in the Netherlands. *Land Use Policy, 108*, 105566.

Beunen, R. & Patterson, J. J. (2017). Analysing institutional change in environmental governance: Exploring the concept of 'institutional work'. *Journal of Environmental Planning and Management*, 1–18.

Beunen, R., Van Assche, K. & Duineveld, M. (2013). Performing failure in conservation policy: The implementation of European Union directives in the Netherlands. *Land Use Policy, 31*, 280–288. https://doi.org/10.1016/j.landusepol.2012.07.009

Beunen, R., Van Assche, K. & Duineveld, M. (2014). *Evolutionary governance theory.* Springer.

Bevir, M. (1999). Foucault, power, and institutions. *Political Studies, 47*(2), 345–359. https://doi.org/10.1111/1467-9248.00204

Beyes, T. P. (2005). Observing observers. Von Foerster, Luhmann, and management thinking. *Kybernetes, 34*(3/4), 448–459. https:// doi .org/ 10 .1108/03684920510581639

Bisschops, S., Beunen, R. & Hollemans, D. (2023). Institutionalizing ideas about citizens' initiatives in planning: Emerging discrepancies between rhetoric and assurance. *Land Use Policy, 124*, 106425. https://doi.org/10.1016/j.landusepol.2022 .106425

Blaschke, S., Schoeneborn, D. & Seidl, D. (2012). Organizations as networks of communication episodes: Turning the network perspective inside out. *Organization Studies, 33*(7), 879–906. https://doi.org/10.1177/0170840612443459

Borch, C. (2005). Systemic power: Luhmann, Foucault, and analytics of power. *Acta Sociologica, 48*(2), 155–167. https://doi.org/10.1177/0001699305053769

Bornemann, B., Knappe, H. & Nanz, P. (2022). *The Routledge handbook of democracy and sustainability.* Routledge.

Boston, J. (2021). Assessing the options for combatting democratic myopia and safeguarding long-term interests. *Futures, 125*, 102668–102668. https://doi.org/10 .1016/j.futures.2020.102668

Bourdieu, P. (1985). The social space and the genesis of groups. *Social Science Information, 24*(2), 195–220. https://doi.org/10.1177/053901885024002001

Bourdieu, P. (1991). *Language and symbolic power.* Harvard University Press.
Bowles, S. & Gintis, H. (2002). Social capital and community governance. *The Economic Journal, 112*(483), F419–F436. https://doi.org/10.1111/1468-0297.00077
Bradbury, J. H. (1978). Class structures and class conflicts in 'instant' resource towns in British Columbia – 1965 to 1972. *BC Studies: The British Columbian Quarterly, 37,* 3–18.
Brandtner, C. & Bromley, P. (2022). Neoliberal governance, evaluations, and the rise of win-win ideology in corporate responsibility discourse, 1960–2010. *Socio-Economic Review, 20*(4), 1933–1960. https://doi.org/10.1093/ser/mwab001
Brans, M. & Rossbach, S. (1997). The autopoiesis of administrative systems: Niklas Luhmann on public administration and public policy. *Public Administration, 75*(3), 417–439.
Breede, H. C. (2017). *The idea of failed states: Community, society, nation, and patterns of cohesion.* Routledge.
Brenneis, D. (1988). Telling troubles: Narrative, conflict and experience. *Anthropological Linguistics, 30*(3/4), 279–291.
Broto, V. C. (2013). Review: Adapting institutions: Governance, complexity and socio-ecological resilience. *Environment and Planning C: Government and Policy, 31*(1), 182–183. https://doi.org/10.1068/c460wr1
Cairns, E. A., Roe, M. D. & Cairns, E. (eds.) (2003). *The role of memory in ethnic conflict* (1st edn.). Palgrave Macmillan.
Calderaro, A. & Blumfelde, S. (2022). Artificial intelligence and EU security: The false promise of digital sovereignty. *European Security, 31*(3), 415–434. https://doi.org/ 10.1080/09662839.2022.2101885
Campbell, J. L. (1997). Mechanisms of evolutionary change in economic governance: interaction, interpretation and bricolage. In *Evolutionary economics and path dependence* (pp. 10–32). Edward Elgar Publishing. https://www.elgaronline.com/ display/book/9781035303281/book-part-9781035303281-7.xml
Centeno, M. A. & Cohen, J. N. (2012). The arc of neoliberalism. *Annual Review of Sociology, 38*(1), 317–340. https://doi.org/10.1146/annurev-soc-081309-150235
Chaffin, B. C. & Gunderson, L. H. (2016). Emergence, institutionalization and renewal: Rhythms of adaptive governance in complex social-ecological systems. *Journal of Environmental Management, 165,* 81–87. https://doi.org/10.1016/j.jenvman.2015 .09.003
Chong, D. (2011). Coordination and conflict. In *Rational lives: Norms and values in politics and society* (pp. 76–115). University of Chicago Press. https://doi.org/10 .7208/9780226104379-006
Christensen, T. & Lægreid, P. (2003). Administrative reform policy: The challenges of turning symbols into practice. *Public Organization Review, 3*(1), 3–27. https://doi .org/10.1023/A:1023002810428
Christensen, T. & Lægreid, P. (eds.) (2017). *Transcending new public management: The transformation of public sector reforms.* Routledge.
Christensen, T., Lægreid, P. & Rykkja, L. H. (2016). Organizing for crisis management: Building governance capacity and legitimacy. *Public Administration Review, 76*(6), 887–897. https://doi.org/10.1111/puar.12558
Cohen, A. P. (1975). The definition of public identity: Managing marginality in outport Newfoundland following Confederation. *The Sociological Review, 23*(1), 93–119.
Copus, C., Roberts, M. & Wall, R. (2017). Policy narratives in local and national government. In *Local Government in England* (pp. 37–55). Springer.

Cresswell, T. (1996). *In place/out of place: Geography, ideology, and transgression.* University of Minnesota Press.

Czarniawska, B. (2004). *Narratives in social science research.* Sage.

Czarniawska-Joerges, B. (1989). The wonderland of public administration reforms. *Organization Studies, 10*(4), 531–548. https://doi.org/10.1177/017084068901000404

Davidson, M. (2010). Sustainability as ideological praxis: The acting out of planning's master-signifier. *City, 14*(4), 390–405. https:// doi .org/ 10 .1080/ 13604813 .2010.492603

Del Lucchese, F. (2009). Crisis and power: Economics, politics and conflict in Machiavelli's political thought. *History of Political Thought, 30*(1), 75–96.

Deleuze, G. (1994). *Difference and repetition.* Athlone Press.

Dick, D. L. (2013). The chapter 11 efficiency fallacy. *BYU Law Review*, 759.

Dreu, C. K. W. D. & Vliert, E. V. de. (1997). *Using conflict in organizations.* SAGE.

Drozdzewski, D., De Nardi, S. & Waterton, E. (2016). Geographies of memory, place and identity: Intersections in remembering war and conflict: Geographies of memory, place and identity. *Geography Compass, 10*(11), 447–456. https://doi.org/ 10.1111/gec3.12296

Duit, A., Galaz, V., Eckerberg, K. & Ebbesson, J. (2010). *Governance, complexity, and resilience.* Elsevier.

Dunlop, C. A. & Radaelli, C. M. (2018). The lessons of policy learning: Types, triggers, hindrances and pathologies. *Policy & Politics, 46*(2), 255–272. https:// doi .org/ 10 .1332/030557318X15230059735521

Feindt, P. H. & Weiland, S. (2018). Reflexive governance: Exploring the concept and assessing its critical potential for sustainable development. Introduction to the special issue. *Journal of Environmental Policy & Planning, 20*(6), 661–674. https:// doi.org/10.1080/1523908X.2018.1532562

Ferranti, F., Beunen, R., Vericat, P. & Geitzenauer, M. (2019). The fitness check of the Birds and Habitats Directives: A discourse analysis of stakeholders' perspectives. *Journal for Nature Conservation, 47*, 103–109. https://doi.org/10.1016/j.jnc.2018 .11.004

Fischer-Kowalski, M. & Rotmans, J. (2009). Conceptualizing, observing, and influencing social-ecological transitions. *Ecology and Society, 14*(2).

Flyvbjerg, B. (1996). *The dark side of planning: Rationality and 'realrationalität'* (SSRN Scholarly Paper 2278431). https://papers.ssrn.com/abstract=2278431

Foucault, M. (2007). *Security, territory, population: Lectures at the Collège De France, 1977–78.* Palgrave Macmillan UK.

Gerlak, A. K., Heikkila, T., Smolinski, S. L., Huitema, D. & Armitage, D. (2018). Learning our way out of environmental policy problems: A review of the scholarship. *Policy Sciences, 51*(3), 335–371.

Gerritsen, M., Kooij, H.-J., Groenleer, M. & van der Krabben, E. (2022). To see, or not to see, that is the question: Studying Dutch experimentalist energy transition governance through an evolutionary lens. *Sustainability, 14*(3), 1540. https://doi.org/ 10.3390/su14031540

Gherardi, S., Cozza, M. & Poggio, B. (2018). Organizational members as storywriters: On organizing practices of reflexivity. *The Learning Organization, 25*(1), 51–62.

Golden, B. R. (1992). The past is the past – Or is it? The use of retrospective accounts as indicators of past strategy. *Academy of Management Journal, 35*(4), 848–860.

Golsorkhi, D., Rouleau, L., Seidl, D. & Vaara, E. (2010). *Cambridge handbook of strategy as practice.* Cambridge University Press.

Gunn, S. & Hillier, J. (2014). When uncertainty is interpreted as risk: An analysis of tensions relating to spatial planning reform in England. *Planning Practice & Research, 29*(1), 56–74. https://doi.org/10.1080/02697459.2013.848530

Hacking, I. (1990). *The taming of chance* (vol. 17). Cambridge University Press.

Harste, G. & Laursen, K. B. (2021). Niklas Luhmann's anti-totalitarian observation of systems. *Kybernetes, 51*(5), 1710–1723. https://doi.org/10.1108/K-04-2021-0328

Hautz, J., Seidl, D. & Whittington, R. (2017). Open strategy: Dimensions, dilemmas, dynamics. *Long Range Planning, 50*(3), 298–309. https://doi.org/10.1016/j.lrp.2016.12.001

Hax, A. C. & Majluf, N. S. (1988). The concept of strategy and the strategy formation process. *Interfaces, 18*(3), 99–109. https://doi.org/10.1287/inte.18.3.99

Held, D. (2013). *Political theory and the modern state*. John Wiley & Sons.

Herrfahrdt-Pähle, E., Schlüter, M., Olsson, P., Folke, C., Gelcich, S. & Pahl-Wostl, C. (2020). Sustainability transformations: Socio-political shocks as opportunities for governance transitions. *Global Environmental Change, 63*, 102097. https://doi.org/10.1016/j.gloenvcha.2020.102097

Hillier, J. (2011). Strategic navigation across multiple planes: Towards a Deleuzean-inspired methodology for strategic spatial planning. *Town Planning Review, 82*(5), 503–528.

Hook, D. & Vanheule, S. (2016). Revisiting the master-signifier, or, Mandela and repression. *Frontiers in Psychology, 6*. https://www.frontiersin.org/articles/10.3389/fpsyg.2015.02028

Howlett, M. (2000). Managing the 'hollow state': Procedural policy instruments and modern governance. *Canadian Public Administration/Administration Publique Du Canada, 43*(4), 412–431. https://doi.org/10.1111/j.1754-7121.2000.tb01152.x

Howlett, M. (2020). Dealing with the dark side of policy-making: Managing behavioural risk and volatility in policy designs. *Journal of Comparative Policy Analysis: Research and Practice, 22*(6), 612–625. https://doi.org/10.1080/13876988.2020.1788942

Jacobsen, K. D. (1966). Public administration under pressure: The role of the expert in the modernization of traditional agriculture. *Scandinavian Political Studies, 1*(A1), 59–93. https://doi.org/10.1111/j.1467-9477.1966.tb00509.x

Jessop, B. (1999). The changing governance of welfare: Recent trends in its primary functions, scale, and modes of coordination. *Social Policy & Administration, 33*(4), 348–359. https://doi.org/10.1111/1467-9515.00157

Jordana, J. & Levi-Faur, D. (2004). *The politics of regulation: Institutions and regulatory reforms for the age of governance*. Edward Elgar Publishing.

Jost, J. (2004). External and internal complexity of complex adaptive systems. *Theory in Biosciences, 123*(1), 69–88.

Klijn, E. H. & Teisman, G. R. (1997). Strategies and games in networks. In W. Kickert, E. H. Klijn & J. F. M. Koppenjan (eds.), *Managing complex networks. Strategies for the public sector* (pp. 98–118). Sage.

Koch, L., Gorris, P. & Pahl-Wostl, C. (2021). Narratives, narrations and social structure in environmental governance. *Global Environmental Change, 69*, 102317. https://doi.org/10.1016/j.gloenvcha.2021.102317

Koliba, C., Meek, J. W., Zia, A. & Mills, R. W. (2017). *Governance networks in public administration and public policy*. Routledge. https://doi.org/10.4324/9781315093451

Kornberger, M. (2012). Governing the city: From planning to urban strategy. *Theory, Culture & Society, 29*(2), 84–106. https://doi.org/10.1177/0263276411426158

Kornberger, M. (2022). *Strategies for distributed and collective action connecting the dots.* Oxford University Press USA – OSO. http://public.eblib.com/choice/PublicFullRecord.aspx?p=6836917

Luhmann, N. (1990). *Political theory in the welfare state.* De Gruyter.

Luhmann, N. (1995). *Social systems.* Stanford University Press.

Luhmann, N. (2018). *Organization and decision.* Cambridge University Press.

Luuk, B. & Gert, de R. (2016). *Spatial planning in a complex unpredictable world of change.* InPlanning. https://doi.org/10.17418/B.2016.9789491937279

Machiavelli, N. (2004). *The prince & the art of war.* Collector's Library.

Machiavelli, N. (2012). *Discourses on the first decade of Titus Levius.* Hardpress Publishing.

Mahoney, J. (2000). Path dependence in historical sociology. *Theory and Society VO, 29*(4), 507–507.

Mahoney, J. & Thelen, K. (eds.) (2010). *Explaining Institutional change: Ambiguity, agency, and power.* Cambridge University Press. https://doi.org/10.1017/CBO9780511806414.001

Maier, H. R., Guillaume, J. H., van Delden, H., Riddell, G. A., Haasnoot, M. & Kwakkel, J. H. (2016). An uncertain future, deep uncertainty, scenarios, robustness and adaptation: How do they fit together? *Environmental Modelling & Software, 81,* 154–164.

Miller, H. T. (2012). *Governing narratives: Symbolic politics and policy change.* University of Alabama Press.

Mölders, M. (2021). Irritation design: Updating steering theory in the age of governance. *Politics and Governance, 9*(2), 393–402. https://doi.org/10.17645/pag.v9i2.4075

Moyson, S., Scholten, P. & Weible, C. M. (2017). Policy learning and policy change: Theorizing their relations from different perspectives. *Policy and Society, 36*(2), 161–177. https://doi.org/10.1080/14494035.2017.1331879

Nair, S. & Howlett, M. (2017). Policy myopia as a source of policy failure: Adaptation and policy learning under deep uncertainty. *Policy & Politics, 45*(1), 103–118. https://doi.org/10.1332/030557316X14788776017743

Newig, J., Voß, J.-P. & Monstadt, J. (2013). *Governance for sustainable development: Coping with ambivalence, uncertainty and distributed power.* Routledge.

North, D. (1990). *Institutions, institutional change and economic performance.* Cambridge University Press.

North, D. (2005). *Understanding the process of economic change.* Princeton University Press.

North, D. C. (2008). Institutions and the performance of economies over time. In C. Ménard & M. M. Shirley (eds.), *Handbook of new institutional economics* (pp. 21–30). Springer Berlin Heidelberg. https://doi.org/10.1007/978-3-540-69305-5_2

Obendiek, A. S. & Seidl, T. (2023). The (false) promise of solutionism: Ideational business power and the construction of epistemic authority in digital security governance. *Journal of European Public Policy, 30*(7), 1305–1329. https://doi.org/10.1080/13501763.2023.2172060

O'Riordan, M., Mahon, M. & McDonagh, J. (2015). Power, discourse and participation in nature conflicts: The case of turf cutters in the governance of Ireland's raised bog designations. *Journal of Environmental Policy & Planning, 17*(1), 127–145.

Ospina, C. & Marks, T. A. (2014). Colombia: Changing strategy amidst the struggle. *Small Wars & Insurgencies*, *25*(2), 354–371. https://doi.org/10.1080/09592318.2014.903641

Ostrom, E. (2014). Do institutions for collective action evolve? *Journal of Bioeconomics*, *16*(1), 3–30.

Paquet, G. (2022). *Scheming virtuously: The road to collaborative governance*. University of Ottawa Press.

Phelps, N. A. & Tewdwr-Jones, M. (2000). Scratching the surface of collaborative and associative governance: Identifying the diversity of social action in institutional capacity building. *Environment and Planning A*, *32*(1), 111–130.

Pierre, J. (1995). *Bureaucracy in the modern state: An introduction to comparative public administration*. Edward Elgar Publishing.

Pierson, P. (2000). Increasing returns, path dependence, and the study of politics. *American Political Science Review*, *94*(02), 251–267.

Pottage, A. (1998). Power as an art of contingency: Luhmann, Deleuze, Foucault. *Economy and Society*, *27*(1), 1–27.

Rap, E. (2006). The success of a policy model: Irrigation management transfer in Mexico. *Journal of Development Studies*, *42*(8), 1301–1324.

Reed, M., Evely, A. C., Cundill, G., Fazey, I. R. A., Glass, J., Laing, A., Newig, J., Parrish, B., Prell, C. & Raymond, C. (2010). What is social learning? *Ecology and Society*, *15*(4).

Rhodes, R. A. W. (1997). *Understanding governance: Policy networks, governance, reflexivity, and accountability*. Open University Press.

Rhodes, R. A. W. (2016). Recovering the craft of public administration. *Public Administration Review*, *76*(4), 638–647. https://doi.org/10.1111/puar.12504

Rotmans, J. & Kemp, R. (2003). *Managing societal transitions: Dilemmas and uncertainties: The Dutch energy case-study*.

Sanabria-Pulido, P. & Velasquez-Ospina, M. (2021). Public administration, institutional capacity and internal conflict in Colombia: An Intertwined relationship. In J. Nemec & P. S. Reddy (eds.), *Public Administration in Conflict Affected Countries* (pp. 347–368). Springer International Publishing. https://doi.org/10.1007/978-3-030-74966-8_16

Schoenmakers, W. & Duysters, G. (2006). Learning in strategic technology alliances. *Technology Analysis & Strategic Management*, *18*(2), 245–264. https://doi.org/10.1080/09537320600624162

Schön, D. A. (1983). *The reflective practitioner: How professionals think in action*. Basic Books.

Seidl, D. (2007a). General strategy concepts and the ecology of strategy discourses: A systemic-discursive perspective. *Organization Studies*, *28*(2), 197–218.

Seidl, D. (2007b). Standard setting and following in corporate governance: An observation-theoretical study of the effectiveness of governance codes. *Organization*, *14*(5), 705–727. https://doi.org/10.1177/1350508407080316

Seidl, D. (2016). *Organisational identity and self-transformation: An autopoietic perspective*. Routledge.

Stavrakakis, Y. (2018). Paradoxes of polarization: Democracy's inherent division and the (anti-) populist challenge. *American Behavioral Scientist*, *62*(1), 43–58. https://doi.org/10.1177/0002764218756924

Stetter, S. (ed.) (2007). *Territorial conflicts in world society: Modern systems theory, international relations and conflict studies*. Routledge.

Stirrat, R. L. (2000). Cultures of consultancy. *Critique of Anthropology, 20*(1), 31–46. https://doi.org/10.1177/0308275x0002000103

Suddaby, R., Seidl, D. & Lê, J. K. (2013). Strategy-as-practice meets neo-institutional theory. *Strategic Organization, 11*(3).

Swyngedouw, E. (2000). Authoritarian governance, power, and the politics of rescaling. *Environment and Planning D: Society and Space, 18*(1), 63–76. https://doi.org/ 10.1068/d9s

Teisman, G., Buuren, A. van & Gerrits, L. M. (2009). *Managing complex governance systems.* Routledge.

Thelen, K. (2009). Institutional change in advanced political economies. *British Journal of Industrial Relations, 47*(3), 471–498. https://doi.org/10.1111/j.1467-8543 .2009.00746.x

Tjosvold, D. (2008). The conflict-positive organization: It depends upon us. *Journal of Organizational Behavior, 29*(1), 19–28. https://doi.org/10.1002/job.473

Tosey, P. (2005). The hunting of the learning organization: A paradoxical journey. *Management Learning, 36*(3), 335–352. https://doi.org/10.1177/1350507605055350

Tunbridge, J. E. & Ashworth, G. J. (1996). *Dissonant heritage: The management of the past as a resource in conflict.* Wiley.

Uzunca, B., Sharapov, D. & Tee, R. (2022). Governance rigidity, industry evolution, and value capture in platform ecosystems. *Research Policy, 51*(7), 104560. https:// doi.org/10.1016/j.respol.2022.104560

Van Assche, K. & Gruezmacher, M. (2023). Remembering Ypres. Post-war reconstruction, land and the legacies of shock and conflict. *Land, 12*(1). https://doi.org/10 .3390/land12010021

Van Assche, K. & Verschraegen, G. (2008). The limits of planning: Niklas Luhmann's systems theory and the analysis of planning and planning ambitions. *Planning Theory, 7*(3), 263–283.

Van Assche, K., Beunen, R. & Duineveld, M. (2012a). Formal/informal dialectics and the self-transformation of spatial planning systems: An exploration. *Administration & Society, 46*(6), 654–683.

Van Assche, K., Beunen, R. & Duineveld, M. (2012b). Performing success and failure in governance: Dutch planning experiences. *Public Administration, 90*(3), 567–581. https://doi.org/10.1111/j.1467-9299.2011.01972.x

Van Assche, K., Beunen, R. & Duineveld, M. (2013). *Evolutionary governance theory: An introduction.* Springer.

Van Assche, K., Beunen, R. & Duineveld, M. (2016). Citizens, leaders and the common good in a world of necessity and scarcity: Machiavelli's lessons for community-based natural resource management. *Ethics, Policy & Environment, 19*(1), 19–36.

Van Assche, K., Beunen, R., Jacobs, J. & Teampau, P. (2011). Crossing trails in the marshes: Rigidity and flexibility in the governance of the Danube Delta. *Journal of Environmental Planning and Management, 54*(8), 997–1018.

Van Assche, K., Beunen, R., Verweij, S., Evans, J. & Gruezmacher, M. (2022a). 'No time for nonsense!': The organization of learning and its limits in evolving governance. *Administration & Society, 54*(7), 1211–1225. https://doi.org/10.1177/ 00953997221093695

Van Assche, K., Beunen, R., Verweij, S., Evans, J. & Gruezmacher, M. (2022b). Policy learning and adaptation in governance; a co-evolutionary perspective. *Administration & Society, 54*(7), 1226–1254. https://doi.org/10.1177/00953997211059165

Van Assche, K., Duineveld, M., Gruezmacher, M. & Beunen, R. (2021). Steering as path creation: Leadership and the art of managing dependencies and reality effects. *Politics and Governance*, *9*(2), 369–380. https://doi.org/10.17645/pag.v9i2.4027

Van Assche, K., Gruezmacher, M. & Beunen, R. (2022). Shock and conflict in social-ecological systems: implications for environmental governance. *Sustainability*, *14*(2), 610. https://doi.org/10.3390/su14020610

Van Assche, K., Hornidge, A.-K., Schlüter, A. & Vaidianu, N. (2020). Governance and the coastal condition: Towards new modes of observation, adaptation and integration. *Marine Policy*, *112*, 103413. https://doi.org/10.1016/j.marpol.2019.01.002

Van Assche, K., Verschraegen, G., Valentinov, V. & Gruezmacher, M. (2019). The social, the ecological, and the adaptive. Von Bertalanffy's general systems theory and the adaptive governance of social-ecological systems. *Systems Research and Behavioral Science*, *36*(3), 308–321. https://doi.org/10.1002/sres.2587

Van Assche, K., Verschraegen, G., Beunen, R., Gruezmacher, M. & Duineveld, M. (2023). Combining research methods in policy and governance: Taking account of bricolage and discerning limits of modelling and simulation. *Futures*, *145*, 103074. https://doi.org/10.1016/j.futures.2022.103074

Von Bertalanffy, L. (1969). *General system theory; foundations, development, applications* (revised edition, issue 1968, p. 40). George Braziller.

Von Bertalanffy, L. (1972). The history and status of general systems theory. *Academy of Management Journal*, *15*(4), 407–426.

Voß, J.-P. & Bornemann, B. (2011). The politics of reflexive governance: Challenges for designing adaptive management and transition management. *Ecology and Society*, *16*(2). https://www.jstor.org/stable/26268901

Voß, J.-P. & Freeman, R. (2016). *Knowing governance: The epistemic construction of political order*. Springer.

Voß, J.-P., Bauknecht, D. & Kemp, R. (2006). *Reflexive governance for sustainable development*. Edward Elgar Publishing.

Warner, B. P. (2019). Explaining political polarization in environmental governance using narrative analysis. *Ecology and Society*, *24*(3). https://www.jstor.org/stable/26796972

Whittington, R. (1996). Strategy as practice. *Long Range Planning*, *29*(5), 731–735. https://doi.org/10.1016/0024-6301(96)00068-4

Wollmann, H. (2003). *Evaluation in public-sector reform: Concepts and practice in international perspective*. Edward Elgar Publishing.

9. Looking forward and back: building futures and encoding pasts in governance

REMEMBERING AND FORGETTING

Phenomenology taught us that, for humans, past, present and future are *always* co-constitutive (Gallagher, 2010, 2013). They shape each other continuously, and they require each other to function, and to make humans function. People without a past cannot imagine a future; people without an image of the future have difficulties in grasping a past. Construction of pasts and futures happens in the present, and intentionality is possible in the present, yet both pasts and futures exert their own effects, on the formation of personalities, identities and, at community level, on the functioning of governance (Butters et al., 2018; Friedmann, 1992; Van Assche et al., 2009).

Each unique entangling of a past, a present and a future can be called a temporality, and such temporality can be tied to an identity or subjectivity. Identities are possible when they construct a past which gives meaning to their present and possible if they envision a future which gives orientation to the present (Ashworth et al., 2007; Liu & Hilton, 2005). Pasts can give direction without being actively remembered, and this adds complexity to analytic efforts, to attempts to understand and map out a temporality or a set of temporalities in governance. We know, moreover, that governance coordinates existing temporalities and creates new ones, as human temporalities, and as in more elementary structuring of time (Bain & Landau, 2019; Clancy, 2014).

In governance systems, temporalities co-exist, coordinated and uncoordinated, knowingly and unknowingly. This includes entangled pasts/futures of diverse actors and the temporalities induced by the need for organization. Some pasts and futures are institutionalized, others not. Some are deliberately reflected upon, others less so. Some are mangled or reshaped by others: futures can be pre-coded by cycles of organizing in governance, pasts can be reinterpreted in terms of the cycles of governance (Boston, 2021; Van Assche, Verschraegen, et al., 2021a). Consider a previously elected head of government who brought in a suite of institutional changes that defined what most

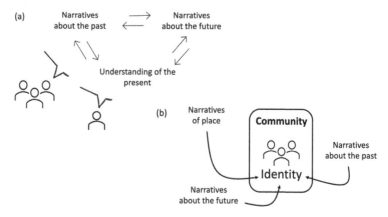

Figure 9.1   *Narratives, identity and interpretations of the past and the future*[1]

people would say is nowadays part of national identity; a national healthcare system, a national anthem, a national flag or national festivities. Competition between pasts, and between futures occurs, but so does formation of new shared pasts and futures, and formation of coalitions around them. Discussion and debate around the 'lessons' to be drawn from the past, about reflexive learning, are part and parcel of governance. Such discussions are never comprehensive, or entirely strategic, as the past is never entirely transparent, as it is continuously reconstructed, and as the workings of the past in the present are not fully observable.

As memory, for individuals, groups, organizations, governance systems, is always selective, and always constructed, *forgetting* is as important as retaining information (Esposito, 2008; Van Assche et al., 2009). The processes of forgetting and retaining also construct the information and what counts as facts. Information and facts never exist in isolation but are constructed on the basis of their distinction from other things, and they make sense because of their figuration in narratives. Narratives and discourses change and affect what

---

[1]   (a) The way individuals and groups understand the present is a result of the way narratives about the past and the future are interpreted or reinterpreted. The same applies to the understanding of past and future. This simultaneous production of past, present and future is the production of one temporality, and this enables human positionality and identity. (b) Community identity and group identity is by a selective entangling of narratives of self, past, future and place. Here, the process is not always simultaneous, and a collective can be marked more strongly by a narrative about the past than by shared imagined futures, more by an activity than a place, more by a home in the past than the current home.

is remembered and what is worth remembering. In the writing of *histories*, these narratives come to the foreground, and facts can become codified and sanctioned as facts, by the power of an academic, administrative, political authority. Memory thus feeds into history and history gives shape to the process of remembering and forgetting (Legg, 2007; J. Moran, 2004).

The process of remembering is structured by the pattern of actors, their perspectives, discourses and preoccupations. It is influenced by the need for convergence in governance regarding memory, identity and future (Ben-Amos & Weissberg, 1999; Kleinherenbrink, 2015). The expectations regarding cohesion of memory (and future) again differ per governance path and are regulated informally by community identity and other influential narratives, and formally by institutions which codify what counts as relevant pasts and how these are used for future coordination. Yet, the needs of the moment can reshuffle the past and break the routine construction and use of pasts. A conflict, a shock, new topics felt to be imposed by the environment can cause forgetting, reinterpretation of the past, or new paths of remembering. New explanations might be needed on the spot, and infrastructures of memory (see earlier) can be fragmented or lost.

Forgetting thus happens all the time and is needed for the functioning of memory. Some forms of forgetting are problematic, however. Deeper forms of forgetting can make it difficult to understand past conditions and experiments, and lead to repetitions of mistakes, or to the construction of futures which stray far from realistic options. This can happen when the conditions for remembering are gone, when new institutions and narrative make recall impossible, destroy infrastructures of memory, or make some versions of history illegal (Bellino & Williams, 2017). Such deep forgetting can also assert itself when perspectives are gone. Take for example an Eastern European town where there are no Armenians left to reconstruct an Armenian perspective or no Habsburg Empire to remember the Habsburg Empire. A town might be standing, but those living there now belong to very different cultural groups (Graham, 1998). Deep forgetting tends to happen when communities have undergone dramatic changes, so new discourses become largely disconnected from old ones, where new actors and old actors differ greatly, and when this happened by shocks rather than gradual self-transformation. Authoritarian regimes can encourage forgetting of this sort, disrupt self-transformation, weed out narratives through coercion, move people, and burn archives (Ledeneva, 2006). Cooking the books, censorship, propaganda and politicized education are methods that tend to help.

When forgetting and reorganization in governance render it hard to bring in alternative memories and restrict the collective reflection on what counts as memory and history, then the democratic transformation of memory in governance comes to a halt. This means that the inclusion and exclusion of narratives is cemented into a rigid pattern, where adaptation to changes in society and environment cannot happen. This will cause a deep disconnect with sections of the population, a gradual alienation, and it will cause a deep forgetting that closes off alternative pasts, as it raises obstacles to a reinterpretation of the present.

MEMORY, LEGACIES AND ORGANIZATION

Memory and legacy are quite different things, and they must be carefully distinguished, just as with memory and history. Legacies are a broader, more encompassing category of traces of the past. In governance, we spoke of path dependencies of different sorts. Some legacies are opaque because of the functioning of memory: not all that shaped us is remembered (Assmann & Czaplicka, 1995; Van Assche & Gruezmacher, 2023). Some are opaque because of the functioning of governance. The autopoiesis, hence the evolution of governance, is not fully transparent from within. Legacies can be encoded old narratives, or roles of actors reflecting old hierarchies, vanished environments, or otherwise forgotten problems. As memory is selective, the awareness of legacies is selective, and as observation of the present is selective, this selectivity is further sharpened. Reconstruction of legacies can be possible, however. Second-order observation (see Chapter 5) can be helpful, as can more elaborate forms of self-analysis (see Chapter 10 on strategy).

Legacies will evolve in their effects. A legacy can suddenly become clear in a new situation, which offers an opportunity for reassessment, after which the legacy can disappear or be reinforced, in a more deliberate and conscious manner. A legacy can become more relevant to a new situation, after which it becomes enshrined in new institutions (Chayinska & McGarty, 2021; Žižek, 2002). Or a new vision for the future can encounter legacies, in a negative way as a previously unobserved obstacle, or in a positive way as an asset or a catalyst (Van Assche et al., 2023). Legacies can include the construction of a discursive coalition, still in place, or of a memory infrastructure which shapes the evolution of memory – a network of local museums, a group of historians talking to schools, a habit of meticulous archiving of dissenting opinions. Collective memory can then shape orientation towards the future.

The processes described for the system can also apply to individual actors. Organizations need memories, identities and narratives about past and future to guide their behavior (see the earlier discussion of power/knowledge). The entire governance configuration can serve as a support or infrastructure for organizational memory and vice versa. Gaps can be filled thanks to other organizations, or through the infrastructures of arenas. The structure of domains and themes can also help organizations to remember and navigate governance and the world. Organizational memory and institutional memory

Figure 9.2   Memory and governance[2]

can thus support each other (Luhmann, 2018; Rhodes, 1997). We can remind ourselves that arenas are both sites and organizations, though with a specific function and an aspiration for stability benefitting the community, an aspiration which can be buttressed by mythologies – not dissimilar to the situation of grounding institutions, a constitution, or a declaration of independence.

If we speak of collective and institutional memory, we need to bring *affect* into the discussion (see earlier, on discourse). Groups can feel things, which are expressed in discourse, and they can feel things *because* of discourse, including narratives of identity, history and others (Brown & Augusta-Scott, 2006; Hinchman & Hinchman, 1997). Affects can be spontaneous, and they can be manipulated. In governance, affect is central as identities, their hopes, aspirations and anxieties are at play, making the decision-making about more than resources, services and taxes. Governance can cause conflicts and solve conflicts because affects are at stake. Interactions in governance can transform affects, reduce suspicion and lead the way to new shared values and common grounds. Futures are invested with affect because memories and identities are invested with it (see earlier, cathexis in governance paths). Memories constitute identity (Assmann & Czaplicka, 1995; Ben-Amos & Weissberg, 1999).

---

[2]   The past is remembered through different mechanisms and infrastructures. Each actor in governance brings to the configuration its own interpretation, its own selective memories and awareness of legacies. Governance itself can contribute to infrastructures of memory and can retain diversity in memory. Even where assembling narratives of a shared sustainable future is the goal, maintaining diverse perspectives on the pasts is essential.

Affect is not to be understood as separate from other discursive and organizational processes. It arises in governance, accompanies each move, is sometimes conceptualized, sometimes not, and can be of strategic importance, yet not all the time. One can interpret bureaucratization, the slowing down of governance, the increasing reliance on routines, not only as ways to manage complexity, but also as a mechanism to *disinvest* affect in governance (Styhre, 2008). De-personalization in governance (and certainly within its administrative actors) can be persuasively linked to distancing from affect (Moran, 2003). This is supposed to calm down administrative interactions, arenas and processes of participation, which is then supposed to benefit more cool and rational decision-making, which in turn is expected to materialize the common good. Although these linked assumptions are too simple and often incorrect, they are built into many governance systems.

Complex technological systems aggravate the situation, by reducing space for discretion and interpretation and minimizing real interactions. As a consequence, essential affects can be missed in the process, and negative affects can be created (as people feel locked out of real communication with systems which are supposed to listen and represent them) (Jasanoff, 2015; Lascoumes & Le Gales, 2007). Many organizations now have automated systems to diffuse complaints by sending them through a virtual assistant or helper, or through a long list of frequently asked questions or automated tutorials, which in turn aggravates the feeling of frustration and exasperation of many consumers. In governance, such procedural and de-personalized approaches can frustrate and alienate people, while real and created feelings of alienation can in return be used to criticize the procedures and the systems of which these are part.

MEMORY AND SUMMARY

Memory can be a problem for governance, for strategic governance, especially when they keep communities locked into an imagined past, or when competing memories cannot be reconciled with the tools of governance (Cairns et al., 2003; Van Assche, Gruezmacher, et al., 2021). When politics becomes identity politics, governance becomes rigid and blind, as we know. Yet memory is a necessity, to maintain the identities of actors, of the system as a whole, and of the community, to keep governance going and to give it direction. Shifting selections of remembering and forgetting and a continuous reconstruction of memory is part and parcel of the dynamics of governance; these mnemonic dynamics contribute to the adaptive construction of futures and to the rebalancing of stability and change in governance. Memories stabilize but can also give inspiration for a new direction; memories can instill nostalgia, but also desire for change (Cairns et al., 2003; Smith & Campbell, 2017). Their reinterpretation, under pressures of evolving governance and shifting semantics in the community, opens new perspectives on the future (Blokland, 2001).

Memory can be a resource in solving conflicts by invoking other places and times, shared values, roots, similar experiences, and it is a resource in finding answers to new questions. Memory thus helps in the orientation in governance and the world at large (Borer, 2010). It underpins learning of the different sorts discussed in the previous chapter. It can also assist in the discovery of new solutions, the construction of new objects (which must be new yet recognizable) and subjects (which need to relate and be based on something), and paths to innovation.

Space

History is expressed in space, and governance is expressed in space. Layers of history can be present in a landscape (Hague & Jenkins, 2004). These layers can be erased over time or can be preserved incompletely (Claeys, 2017). If old layers can be recognized or reconstructed, with some effort, one can speak of a palimpsest (Van Assche & Teampau, 2009). Memory and expertise can help in the reading of spaces, of landscapes and cityscapes, and, by remembering more about place and people, the interplay of space and memory, or the spatial amplification of memory, can make past governance and past decisions clearer and more understandable. The rhetoric of governance, which cannot be erased from the archives, can be punctured by reading in space what actually happened (Leta et al., 2019; J. Moran, 2004).

Space can thus serve as an expression but also as an infrastructure of memory. This can happen with or without intention by those governing in the past, and with or without any intention to organize space. Yet spatial planning and design can increase this function of memory space, of space expressing and supporting narratives and identities (Legg, 2007; Neill, 2001; Van Assche et al., 2020). Special places can also be singled out, to memorialize, to express an identity, hope and aspiration. Steering the interpretation of place, however, is not a simple matter. People assign new meanings to place, ignore official meanings, and minute details, or barely perceptible changes (paint peeling off, new shades of grey creeping in) can suddenly shift experience. Even silence, both empty and full of meaning, can invite reinterpretations of spaces way beyond what could be imagined or intended by those shaping the place (Van Assche & Costaglioli, 2011).

FUTURES

Futures are stories about the long term or about long-term perspectives (Ahvenharju et al., 2018; Allmendinger & Tewdwr-Jones, 2002; Hoch, 2016;

Sardar, 2010; Van Assche, Verschraegen, et al., 2021b). They are produced in the now, partly inherited, and partly derived from older ideas about the future. Past, present and future entangle in each attempt to make sense of the world and ourselves. Futures build on an idea of what is real right now, and consider what might become real in the future, with and without our intervention. Which implies an assessment of what is not only real now, but also relevant for processes which will not stop and are likely to shape the future. Futures embody ideas of what is hoped for and what is feared and must be avoided. Those affects pervade the construction of futures; they can drive the construction of futures and they can be invested in constructed futures afterwards, often by osmosis with other narratives. Affect can come first, then stories, or the other way around. Fear and hope can be inspired by what is observed now, or by stories circulating about the future (Van Assche, Verschraegen, et al., 2021a).

Hopes and fears are not always translated into collective goals and futures are not always important and explicitly present in governance. Some are present, but without a deliberate attempt at broadening or connecting into a shared future, a vision which can buttress a collective strategy (Millett, 2006). Futures might be important for some actors, less so for others. Some collective futures might appear truly collective, but without becoming an object of governance. They might be more relevant to some domains than others, or at some levels. Comprehensive visioning might work locally, while at national level the only strategy at work is military strategy.

The attachment to particular futures and the affective investment cannot always be understood by outsiders. Insiders might not always be aware of this investment either. Psychoanalytic perspectives can be helpful, in second-order observation (Bailly, 2012; Luhmann, 1993). This means that a therapeutic investigation, with involvement from outsiders, but driven by insiders, can be effective in disentangling the silent expectations, identifications and ambivalences with regards to a desired future and the governance tools to bring it closer (Fotaki, 2010; Gunder & Hillier, 2009). In such an analytic process, forgotten formative events and other legacies can be unearthed, as well as problematic borrowings and identifications with ideologies and other master-narratives or signifiers. We know that some ideologies cast doubt on the possibility and desirability of constructing and pursuing futures in governance, while communities subsumed in them might still have such desires and could in practical terms use integrated policies for the long term (Ferguson, 2010; Van Assche, Verschraegen, et al., 2021a).

What is at stake in governance is the future of the community. This can be shaped by the futures in governance to very different degrees. The interplay between futures can be seen and structured as powerplay, as deliberation, as picking and choosing from the wish lists of actors and their futures, and as deliberate construction of a new, shared and cohesive future. For some, continuation of the present into the future should be the focus of collective efforts, and this is more likely if there is a belief that the current system reflects a universal truth about the need for limited government and governance. What is simple should stay simple, and should not stray from a focus on individual rights, property or, locally, services.

If futures enter governance, the point of entrance and the site of construction can differ, as well as its transformation through governance. Governance assembles futures, which can alter the path of a community, and vice versa. The process is different in each model of democracy, and in other types of polity (Flyvbjerg, 1998; Held, 1996). It hinges on contingent events. Observations change, as do moods, identities and values, first in the environment, later in governance. To what extent the futures in governance can shape the futures in the community depends on the power of governance in the community, the persuasive power of entrepreneurial or charismatic actors, and the lure of the proposed future. As mentioned, among the first things needed to persuade people of a future is the reality of what is assumed as present and real in that future. Futures in governance can resist thematization yet remain active; they can linger on in institutions, identities, in unarticulated fears or hopes (Van Assche et al., 2022; Voß & Freeman, 2016).

RELATING PASTS AND FUTURES

Understanding the functioning of memories and the relations with affect and identity helps to constructively use memory towards shared futures. Understanding the forms and functions of forgetting helps in such an effort. Understanding the differentiation *and* synthesis of memories and futures in governance helps in the re-assemblage of shared futures (Esmark, 2009; Luhmann, 2006). This always takes place in a structure, a contingent pattern of arenas, domains, actors, institutions and levels of governance that is inherited from the past. The relation between pasts and memories is thus rather complex and makes the relation between pasts and futures inherently ambiguous (Smith & Campbell, 2017; Teampau & Van Assche, 2007).

Also, the concepts, tools and forces that mediate between past and future will differ per community and governance path. Who defines and codifies memory and history, who is aware of which legacies, and who shares this awareness? Who is able to manage legacies and manage identification and distancing from them, in order to produce futures which do not imagine repeating the past, and who is able to bring together groups with diverging hopes and fears, and project a new shared future? Which old plan failed miserably yet still captures a real desire? How can reflexive learning be encouraged, and how can reinterpretation of the past be linked more systematically to enhanced observation of new challenges and opportunities in the environment? How can this happen in a way that is neither too slow nor too fast, that preserves what is valued and functional, and adapts potentially everything else? It is clear by now that universal answers do not exist, that no institutional design, no form of a governance system, can guarantee all this. We do know that awareness of remembering and forgetting, of legacies and histories, and of the way the past comes into play in the construction of futures, is extremely helpful when there is a desire to construct a shared future and to map out collectively a path in that direction.

Some histories leave legacies that are more opaque and harder to manage. They can leave unobserved traces that make it harder to break an unsustainable path, to disrupt problematic repetitive patterns in governance, and to distinguish a vision from a fantasy. Trauma, exclusion, marginality and alienation can foster forgetting, and can render their own legacies invisible (Drozdzewski et al., 2016; Erikson, 1994; Van Assche, Gruezmacher, et al., 2021). Trauma in a community can mark governance in profound manners. Repetition of moves, even when they do not make sense for outside observers, and, on reflection, also look like failure for insiders, is common. Hopes for the future can be repetitions of a glorified past, while the problems of that past are not remembered (Van Assche et al., 2023). What remains out of scope is also the way that past has structured governance, the limited toolset, the narrow perspective on the future, and the dominant narratives and identifications. In extreme cases, looking forward at all is difficult, and what is repeated symptomatically is not the production of policies trying to achieve something impossible or irrelevant, but, more elementary, the routines that enable functioning at a low level, that avoid thinking and looking forward. A low level for us is not a primitive level, a sign of inferiority, but a level of functioning in which the community does not reach its potential, is not fully aware of the tools it has to shape its own future, and is not aware that it can alter the distance to the identity narratives and development scenarios it has relied upon yet never scrutinized (Dollery & Robotti, 2008; Hope, 2009).

Trauma in governance can be trauma with a group, a segment of the population, which suffered from a history of marginalization and abuse. When identity narratives in the community, and dominant in governance, are tied up with a latent event or history, one can speak of community trauma (Freire, 2018; van der Watt, 2018). On such occasions, futures are more likely to take the character of fantasies, loosely coupled to reality, tightly coupled to what is forgotten. Such fantasies have to be deconstructed, or traversed (in psychoanalytical parlance), in order to find alternative futures that have a chance of guiding a community to real change (Eyers, 2012).

Memory is always there, but cultivating it makes a difference. Practices of memory, of community memory, are valuable for reasons discussed earlier. Analysing memory, the functioning of memory and of legacies, is valuable as well. Since, as we know, some patterns in forgetting and remembering and some legacies of undigested pasts are a real problem that cannot be displaced just by finding new facts, or by telling new stories (Perez-Sindin & Van Assche, 2020; Van Assche, Gruezmacher, et al., 2021). Old stories, old patterns of remembering and forgetting must be dislodged before new futures become realistic ones. *Redundancy of memory* can be just as useful as the streamlining and modification of futures (Jessop, 2020; Van Assche & Duineveld, 2013). Institutional memory cannot be treated as waste nor as an obstacle for change. Archives and libraries can be kept as local as possible, and as accessible as possible, stories about the past can be allowed to diffuse and multiply even where they are not the focus of work, and context-specific expertise can be defined more generously, cultivated and supported beyond what is immediately applicable.

Cultivation of something is creation of memory and infrastructure of memory, and cultivation of locally relevant knowledge in governance is creation of redundant memories and mnemonic infrastructures which embody a diversity of possible connections in the past and in the social-ecological environment at the same time. Mnemonic redundancy is mnemonic diversity, a diversity of paths to establish what happened, an intensification of awareness of couplings to the environment. The accessibility of many different connections to an archived past, to different versions of that past, can therefore be of use in contrasting those versions, of gradually deconstructing dominant versions, of slowly dismantling neurotic attachments to unquestioned futures and linking them to unobserved pasts. Redundant memories then can be therapeutic, in dissolving blind spots, and in dislodging a past and an imagined future which made it hard for a community to chart its own course.

REFERENCES

Ahvenharju, S., Minkkinen, M. & Lalot, F. (2018). The five dimensions of Futures Consciousness. *Futures, 104*, 1–13. https://doi.org/10.1016/j.futures.2018.06.010
Allmendinger, P. & Tewdwr-Jones, M. (2002). *Planning futures: New directions for planning theory*. Routledge.
Ashworth, G. J., Graham, B. & Tunbridge, J. (2007). *Pluralising pasts: Heritage, identity and place in multicultural societies*. Pluto Press.
Assmann, J. & Czaplicka, J. (1995). Collective memory and cultural identity. *New German Critique, 65*, 125. https://doi.org/10.2307/488538
Bailly, L. (2012). *Lacan: A beginner's guide*. Simon and Schuster.
Bain, A. L. & Landau, F. (2019). Artists, temporality, and the governance of collaborative place-making. *Urban Affairs Review, 55*(2), 405–427. https://doi.org/10.1177/1078087417711044
Bellino, M. J. & Williams, J. H. (2017). *(Re)constructing memory: Education, identity, and conflict*. Sense publishers.

Ben-Amos, D. & Weissberg, L. (eds.) (1999). *Cultural memory and the construction of identity*. Wayne State University Press.

Blokland, T. (2001). Bricks, mortar, memories: Neighbourhood and networks in collective acts of remembering. *International Journal of Urban and Regional Research*, 25(2), 268–283. https://doi.org/10.1111/1468-2427.00311

Borer, M. I. (2010). From collective memory to collective imagination: Time, place, and urban redevelopment. *Symbolic Interaction*, 33(1), 96–114. https://doi.org/10.1525/si.2010.33.1.96

Boston, J. (2021). Assessing the options for combatting democratic myopia and safeguarding long-term interests. *Futures*, 125, 102668. https://doi.org/10.1016/j.futures.2020.102668

Brown, C. & Augusta-Scott, T. (2006). *Narrative therapy: Making meaning, making lives*. SAGE Publications.

Butters, L., Okusipe, O. M., Eledi, S. B. & Vodden, K. (2018). Engaging the past to create a new future: A comparative study of heritage-driven community development initiatives in the Great Northern Peninsula. *Journal of Rural and Community Development*, 12(2–3).

Cairns, E. A., Roe, M. D. & Cairns, E. (eds.) (2003). *The role of memory in ethnic conflict* (1st edn.). Palgrave Macmillan.

Chayinska, M. & McGarty, C. (2021). The power of political déjà vu: When collective action becomes an effort to change the future by preventing the return of the past. *Political Psychology*, 42(2), 201–217. https://doi.org/10.1111/pops.12695

Claeys, D. (2017). World War I and the reconstruction of rural landscapes in Belgium and France: A historiographical essay. *Agricultural History Review*, 65(1), 108–129.

Clancy, C. A. (2014). The politics of temporality: Autonomy, temporal spaces and resoluteness. *Time & Society*, 23(1), 28–48. https://doi.org/10.1177/0961463X11425224

Dollery, B. & Robotti, L. (2008). *The theory and practice of local government reform*. Edward Elgar Publishing. https://econpapers.repec.org/bookchap/elgeebook/12719.htm

Drozdzewski, D., De Nardi, S. & Waterton, E. (2016). Geographies of memory, place and identity: Intersections in remembering war and conflict: Geographies of memory, place and identity. *Geography Compass*, 10(11), 447–456. https://doi.org/10.1111/gec3.12296

Erikson, K. (1994). *A new species of trouble: Explorations in disaster, trauma, and community*. Norton.

Esmark, A. (2009). The functional differentiation of governance: Public governance beyond hierarchy, market and networks. *Public Administration*, 87(2), 351–370. https://doi.org/10.1111/j.1467-9299.2009.01759.x

Esposito, E. (2008). Social forgetting: A systems-theory approach. In *Cultural memory studies: An international and interdisciplinary handbook* (pp. 181–190). Walter de Gruyter.

Eyers, T. (2012). *Lacan and the concept of the 'real'*. Palgrave Macmillan.

Ferguson, J. (2010). The uses of neoliberalism. *Antipode*, 41(s1), 166–184. https://doi.org/10.1111/j.1467-8330.2009.00721.x

Flyvbjerg, B. (1998). *Rationality and power: Democracy in practice*. University of Chicago press.

Fotaki, M. (2010). Why do public policies fail so often? Exploring health policy-making as an imaginary and symbolic construction. *Organization*, 17(6), 703–720.

Freire, P. (2018). *Pedagogy of the oppressed: 50th anniversary edition*. Bloomsbury Academic.

Friedmann, J. (1992). The past in the future: History and the politics of identity. *American Anthropologist, 94*(4), 837–859.

Gallagher, S. (2010). Merleau-Ponty's Phenomenology of perception. *Topoi, 29*(2), 183–185. https://doi.org/10.1007/s11245-010-9079-y

Gallagher, S. (2013). Husserl and the phenomenology of temporality. In *A companion to the Philosophy of Time* (pp. 135–150). John Wiley & Sons, Ltd. https://doi.org/10.1002/9781118522097.ch9

Graham, B. J. (1998). The past in Europe's present: Diversity, identity and the construction of place. In B. J. Graham (ed.), *Modern Europe: Place, culture and identity* (pp. 19–49). Arnold.

Gunder, M. & Hillier, J. (2009). *Planning in ten words or less: A Lacanian entanglement with spatial planning.* Ashgate Publishing, Ltd.

Hague, C. & Jenkins, P. (eds.) (2004). *Place identity, participation and planning.* Routledge. https://doi.org/10.4324/9780203646755

Held, D. (1996). *Models of democracy.* Stanford University Press.

Hinchman, L. P. & Hinchman, S. (1997). *Memory, identity, community: The idea of narrative in the human sciences.* SUNY Press.

Hoch, C. (2016). Utopia, scenario and plan: A pragmatic integration. *Planning Theory, 15*(1), 6–22.

Hope, K. R. (2009). Capacity development for good governance in developing societies: Lessons from the field. *Development in Practice, 19*(1), 79–86. https://doi.org/10.1080/09614520802576401

Jasanoff, S. (2015). Future imperfect: Science, technology, and the imaginations of modernity. In *Dreamscapes of modernity: Sociotechnical imaginaries and the fabrication of power*, 1–47.

Jessop, B. (2020). The governance of complexity and the complexity of governance. In B. Jessop (ed.), *Putting civil society in its place: Governance, metagovernance and subjectivity.* Policy Press. https://doi.org/10.1332/policypress/9781447354956.003.0002

Kleinherenbrink, A. (2015). Territory and Ritornello: Deleuze and Guattari on thinking living beings. *Deleuze Studies, 9*(2), 208–230. https://doi.org/10.3366/dls.2015.0183

Lascoumes, P. & Le Gales, P. (2007). Introduction: Understanding public policy through its instruments – from the nature of instruments to the sociology of public policy instrumentation. *Governance, 20*(1), 1–21. https://doi.org/10.1111/j.1468-0491.2007.00342.x

Ledeneva, A. (2006). *How Russia really works. The informal practices that shaped post-Soviet politics and business.* Cornell University Press.

Legg, S. (2007). Reviewing geographies of memory/forgetting. *Environment and Planning A: Economy and Space, 39*(2), 456–466. https://doi.org/10.1068/a38170

Leta, G., Kelboro, G., Van Assche, K., Stellmacher, T. & Hornidge, A.-K. (2019). Rhetorics and realities of participation: The Ethiopian agricultural extension system and its participatory turns. In *Critical Policy Studies*, 1–20.

Liu, J. H. & Hilton, D. J. (2005). How the past weighs on the present: Social representations of history and their role in identity politics. *British Journal of Social Psychology, 44*(4), 537–556. https://doi.org/10.1348/014466605X27162

Luhmann, N. (1993). Deconstruction as second-order observing. *New Literary History, 24*(1), 763–782.

Luhmann, N. (2006). System as difference. *Organization, 13*(1), 37–57.

Luhmann, N. (2018). *Organization and decision.* Cambridge University Press.

Millett, S. M. (2006). Futuring and visioning: Complementary approaches to strategic decision making. *Strategy & Leadership*, *34*(3), 43–50.

Moran, J. (2004). History, memory and the everyday. *Rethinking History*, *8*(1), 51–68. https://doi.org/10.1080/13642520410001649723

Moran, M. (2003). *The British regulatory state: High modernism and hyper-innovation*. Oxford University Press.

Neill, W. (2001). Memory, spatial planning and the construction of cultural identity in Belfast and Berlin – An overview. In H.-U. Schwedler (ed.), *Urban planning and cultural inclusion: Lessons from Belfast and Berlin* (pp. 3–23). Palgrave Macmillan UK. https://doi.org/10.1057/9780230524064_1

Perez-Sindin, X. & Van Assche, K. (2020). From coal not to ashes but to what? As Pontes, social memory and the concentration problem. *The Extractive Industries and Society*. https://doi.org/10.1016/j.exis.2020.07.016

Rhodes, R. A. W. (1997). *Understanding governance: Policy networks, governance, reflexivity, and accountability*. Open University Press.

Sardar, Z. (2010). The namesake: Futures; futures studies; futurology; futuristic; foresight – What's in a name? *Futures*, *42*(3), 177–184. https://doi.org/10.1016/j.futures.2009.11.001

Smith, L. & Campbell, G. (2017). 'Nostalgia for the future': Memory, nostalgia and the politics of class. *International Journal of Heritage Studies*, *23*(7), 612–627. https://doi.org/10.1080/13527258.2017.1321034

Styhre, A. (2008). Management control in bureaucratic and postbureaucratic organizations: A Lacanian perspective. *Group & Organization Management*, *33*(6), 635–656. https://doi.org/10.1177/1059601108325697

Teampau, P. & Van Assche, K. (2007). Sulina, the dying city in a vital region. Social memory and nostalgia for the European future. *Ethnologia Balkanica*, *11*(1), 257–278.

Van Assche, K. & Costaglioli, F. (2011). Silent places, silent plans: Silent signification and the study of place transformation. *Planning Theory*, *11*(2), 128–147. https://doi.org/10.1177/1473095211421086

Van Assche, K. & Duineveld, M. (2013). The good, the bad and the self-referential: Heritage planning and the productivity of difference. *International Journal of Heritage Studies*, *19*(1), 1–15. https://doi.org/10.1080/13527258.2011.632639

Van Assche, K. & Gruezmacher, M. (2023). Remembering Ypres. Post-war reconstruction, land and the legacies of shock and conflict. *Land*, *12*(1). https://doi.org/10.3390/land12010021

Van Assche, K. & Teampau, P. (2009). Layered encounters. Performing multiculturalism and the urban palimpsest at the gateway of Europe. *Anthropology of East Europe Review*, *27*(1), 7–19.

Van Assche, K., Beunen, R. & Oliveira, E. (2020). Spatial planning and place branding: Rethinking relations and synergies. *European Planning Studies*, *28*(7), 1274–1290.

Van Assche, K., Beunen, R., Verweij, S., Evans, J. & Gruezmacher, M. (2022). 'No time for nonsense!': The organization of learning and its limits in evolving governance. *Administration & Society*, *54*(7), 1211–1225. https://doi.org/10.1177/00953997221093695

Van Assche, K., Devlieger, P., Teampau, P. & Verschraegen, G. (2009). Remembering and forgetting in the margin: Constructing past and future in the Romanian Danube Delta. *Memory Studies*, *2*(2), 211–234.

Van Assche, K., Gruezmacher, M. & Granzow, M. (2021). From trauma to fantasy and policy. The past in the futures of mining communities; the case of Crowsnest Pass,

Alberta. *Resources Policy*, *72*, 102050–102050. https://doi.org/10.1016/j.resourpol
.2021.102050

Van Assche, K., Gruezmacher, M., Lochner, M. & Perez-Sindin, X. (2023). *Resource
communities: Past legacies and future pathways* (1st edn.). Routledge. https://
www.routledge.com/Resource-Communities-Past-Legacies-and-Future-Pathways/
Assche-Gruezmacher-Marais-Sindin/p/book/9781032364728

Van Assche, K., Verschraegen, G. & Gruezmacher, M. (2021a). Strategy for collectives and common goods: Coordinating strategy, long-term perspectives and policy
domains in governance. *Futures*, *128*, 102716–102716. https://doi.org/10.1016/j
.futures.2021.102716

Van Assche, K., Verschraegen, G. & Gruezmacher, M. (2021b). Strategy for the
long term: Pressures, counter-pressures and mechanisms in governance. *Futures*,
131(102758).

van der Watt, P. (2018). Community development in wounded communities: Seductive
schemes or un-veiling and healing? *Community Development Journal*, *53*(4),
714–731. https://doi.org/10.1093/cdj/bsx017

Voß, J.-P. & Freeman, R. (2016). *Knowing governance: The epistemic construction of
political order*. Springer.

Žižek, S. (2002). *Did somebody say totalitarianism?: Five interventions in the (mis)use
of a notion*. Verso.

10. Strategy in governance: communities and their futures reimagined and reconstructed

INTRODUCTION: UNDERSTANDING STRATEGY

Thinking about strategy is as old as writing about politics and military affairs and practicing strategy as old as humanity. The theme was especially important in military writings, but it developed into a separate field of inquiry in 20th-century business schools. Strategy has therefore been defined in a variety of ways, but for us it is an idea of a desired future coupled with a structured idea on how to get there (Van Assche, Gruezmacher, et al., 2019; Van Assche, Verschraegen, et al., 2021). In the management literature, this is often the future of an organization in a context of competition or conflict. Strategy in business was often tied to high-level management, to executive leadership, and was distinguished from operational work, from short-term concerns. Links with organizational identity, and positioning in specific markets, were accepted as relevant factors for defining strategy. Some authors emphasized the internal ecology of the organizations, others the importance of society, or of a landscape of competing organizations (see Kornberger (2017, 2022) for an overview).

The Canadian management scholar Henry Mintzberg already knew in the 1970s that strategy could not be productively understood as a product that could be finished in the halls of higher management and then dropped in the organization and unleashed on the world (Mintzberg, 1978, 1987). Strategy, in most cases, was *emerging*, and looking at the process of strategizing is more productive than seeing strategy as a product. He distinguished these *emergent* strategies from *deliberate* strategies that concern the realization of previously existing intentions. With that, he brought attention to patterns of behavior that can become seen as strategy, even if intentions are lacking, or if these are not realized. Observation and interpretation of intentions, actions, behavior and effects, and labelling something as strategy, are thus important processes in Mintzberg's understanding of strategy. Strategizing is not always possible, from any point in time and from any position in the organization (even if this is the highest one). It can become possible and can be made possible. Strategy can emerge when a set of existing conditions and virtual possibilities are matched, and when someone is in a position to recognize this match and communicate it to the rest of the organization. Strategy thus adapts to reality and vice versa, in a step-wise process in which continuous observation of this matching is necessary – as environments are never stable or predictable (Carter et al., 2008; Golsorkhi et al., 2010; Kornberger & Engberg-Pedersen, 2019).

From this starting point, David Seidl and colleagues developed the idea of *strategy as practice*: strategizing is doing things, not only articulating a vision and implementing it. The activities of thinking about coordination and altering coordination so future coordination becomes possible (organizing for organizational capacity and direction) are twinned (Golsorkhi et al., 2010; Seidl, 2007, 2019). Moreover, contributions to this process can come from different sites in the organization. This is rather natural as observations of internal and external environments differ according to the position in the organization, and new observations can contribute to a new understanding of strategic options. Workers are allowed to have ideas, and the human resources department can spot problems that are not on the horizon for others.

Seidl and colleagues, inspired by systems theory, drew further reaching conclusions from the idea that emergence, practice and observation are essential for strategy (Becker, 2012; Hendry, 1995; Jarzabkowski, 2004; Rasche & Seidl, 2020; Seidl, 2016). They realized that strategy could be recognized a posteriori, after the facts. Courses of action could be presented as coordination afterwards, or suddenly understood as such. Such recognition of nascent or latent strategy can then become the basis for more deliberate steering. A recognition of a direction is not always a projection, as not all coordination mechanisms and not all aspects of the autopoiesis of the organization are understood internally, let alone are visible to higher management (Seidl & Becker, 2006). The direction can even represent an intentionality that was not recognized higher up the ladder, as strategizing (by individuals or departments) might have avoided the gaze of management, and as old intentionality might have been forgotten. Thus, not only patterns but also direction and even intention can become recognized later.

Strategies are tools to bind time and to make a new world at the same time (Carter et al., 2008). They become possible when ideas about the future and current circumstances come together in a felicitous way, or when new ideas about the future crystallize from observation of changing situations, after which these ideas require fine-tuning, linking to others, in order to arrive at a grander strategy. Goals can be new, emerging themselves in the process of strategizing, or they can pre-exist the strategy but acquire a new pregnancy due to changes in the present, or when parallel lines of events, seemingly disconnected developments, can be understood as amenable to synergy or coordination later. In this sense, strategy is always adaptive, but not necessarily aiming at the adaptive capacity of the organization (Jarzabkowski, 2004).

Strategy transforms the linkages between past, present and future in the organization. It can only function as strategy if a future becomes persuasive, and this is likely to require an adjustment of futures, but also a reinterpretation of the past, its legacies, and of the power and tools in the present to move in a clear direction. A reinterpretation of legacies, a restructuring of memory might thus be at work. A growing or changing awareness of the past, and the grip of the past, can open the door to alternative futures. Previously silent connections between past and future might be revealed.

Binding time thus reveals itself as a more complicated process than we could sketch in Chapter 3 (Basic Concepts for Transition Mapping: Institutions). Its enabling factors and supportive processes are a multiplicity, and the processes it triggers are numerous, with some of the engendered processes further supporting the structuring of time itself, in governance and in the community. The co-production of past, present and future in organizations, the stabilizing and destabilizing roles of identities and roles, the unceasing dynamics of power-knowledge and the unknowability of environments and environmental couplings conspire to make the binding of time through strategy a Herculean task, yet, at the same time multiply the opportunities to strategize, to stabilize expectations, and to bind time.

We know from our earlier discussions (Chapter 3 and later scattered passages) that binding time requires internal coordination and external coordination. A future needs to become knowable, imaginable and imbued with shared values, and it has to coalesce into a narrative which can persuade internal stakeholders, and which can engender coordination between existing coordination tools and institutions (Copus et al., 2017; Czarniawska & Gagliardi, 2003). The temporalities of actors, procedures and other institutions, dominant narratives, and of processes to be coordinated or initiated in society and in the physical environment cannot be perfectly harmonized (see Chapters 4 and 10). Making the coordinating institution, the strategy, itself more complex, with procedures and sub-procedures, and identification of moments where cycles can be linked, is a solution with severe limitations, as it tends to trip over its own complexity and trigger a backlash (Luhmann, 2018; Schoemaker, 1990). Imposing a unified temporality on governance and environment has similarly crippling shortcomings, as in the USSR where the winter had to start the same day for everyone.

What remains then, is the possibility of a strategy that selectively observes temporalities, selectively accepts existing couplings, carefully constructs new couplings and cautiously imposes new temporalities. What remains is an idea of productive fiction that can be highly productive, that can change the world, in steps, but does not force all thinking and all action into those steps. If the world has to serve the strategy rather than the other way around, this is likely to cause disruption, resistance and inefficiency, and it almost certainly favors new and creative forms of functional stupidity (Alvesson & Spicer, 2012; Kornberger, 2017).

STRATEGY AND COMMUNITY

In our perspective, strategy at community level is possible and useful. It can help to articulate and pursue public goods. Such a pursuit can be ambitious or modest and can range from slight improvements in the coordination of decision-making and provision of services to wholesale reinvention of the community. For EGT, community strategy must pass through governance. Even if the core ideas do not originate in the governance system, it should pass the configuration because of the need for collective-binding decision-making. One can also simply invoke democratic principles. Ideally, a strategy emerges in governance, is developed in governance and finds implementation in governance. We insist on such embedding of strategy in governance because we insist on democracy.

The embedding endows the strategy with legitimacy, as the accepted procedures to come to and implement collectively binding decisions are followed and there is the promise of practicality, as a range of policy tools become available and can be considered at each stage of the process. This makes strategy in governance different from a situation in which either consultants or managers create strategy (Fincham, 1999; Stirrat, 2000; Sturdy, 2011). Strategy for public goods intends to integrate institutions and coordinate collective action. Not locating such a form of strategy in governance would risk the silent establishment of parallel coordination mechanisms and sites.

At community level, strategy aims at coordination and a strategy can therefore be considered as an institution, but also as something that produces and changes institutions. Strategy intends to coordinate action, and in many cases this happens via existing institutions, which are brought into contact and into coordination. This could lead to integration of institutions, where strategy replaces myriad old institutions, but more commonly existing institutions and other policy tools remain in place and take a place in the new strategy framework (Smink et al., 2015; Suddaby et al., 2013). This framework will also show blank spots, ideas still to be found and institutions to be created. A community strategy is therefore both an institution and a collection of other institutions; it only has value when the strategy produces an emergent order, becomes more than the sum of the coupled institutions. Even then, it will likely not be persuasive, and will probably be seen as a technocratic construct. The more precise is the bureaucratic fine-tuning and creative internal coordination, the less attractive the strategy can become for everybody not involved, which can include citizens but also their elected representatives.

In the end, we are talking about community futures, and this places strategy immediately in the realm of narrative. In order to be persuasive, and link to imagined futures and all associated affects in the community, the strategy ought to be a narrative itself (Czarniawska, 1997; Van Assche, Verschraegen, et al., 2021). The narrative dimension can lend a persuasive character to the institutional construction, but can also give direction to the process of internal coordination. Without narrative, finding cohesion among more and more specialized institutions and organizations is an improbable event. Strategy, as a process of coordination between other coordinative tools can be greatly aided by a unifying narrative that turns a set of tools into a new institution which has a better chance to remain cohesive and to be persuasive. Not all strategy documents function therefore as strategy. Some are more likely to end up as dead institutions than others. In order to work, community strategies, both narrative and institutional dimensions, need to function as one institution, giving direction to coordination in a variety of terrains (Beunen et al., 2022; Kornberger & Engberg-Pedersen, 2019). This does not always work, and it might work only for some topics and situations. One can draw a parallel with arenas, which can (and should) function as actors only sometimes.

STRATEGY AND SEMIOTICS

To function, a strategy is expected to coalesce into one thing, a thing that must be observed and accepted inside and outside governance. That thing – the strategy – needs to do something to represent value, and that something must be observed as well. For the strategy process to work, the thing must be trusted and along the way it has to be connected to other narratives, issues, expectations and affects (Botan & Soto, 1998; Hiedanpaa & Bromley, 2012). It will become a sign of other things. For it to work, it should connect to or incorporate stories that are circulating in the community (Czarniawska & Gagliardi, 2003; Hinchman & Hinchman, 1997). At the very least, it needs to start from an idea of reality that is more widely shared (see the previous two chapters), and define problems, qualities, assets, values in the community in a way that is understandable for those who believe they will be affected by the strategy.

We refer again to the idea of complex institutions (Chapter 3), which unfold over time, function as text and context at the same time, and touch upon a variety of topics, affects and stories. This also implies that the careful selection of institutions to be coordinated in the strategy is a must, as not only institutional but also narrative associations need to be grasped. Affective and ideological connections might alter the interpretation and functioning of the overarching narrative (Bateman, 2018; Clark & Newman, 1997).

Think of a predominantly right-leaning municipality, with a recently elected left-leaning national government proposing a new economic and social development strategy. It would not be surprising to hear remarks along the lines of 'My God, what did these crazy people come up with now?'

A strategy, in the terms of a semiotician, or interpretation theorist C. S. Peirce, is an *argument, a legisign and a symbol.* It intends to translate vague ideas about qualities, problems or values (what he calls *firstness*) into action (*second*) through the development of rules (*legisigns*). For the special type of complex institutions we label as strategies, those rules (*institutions*) *are also narratives (arguments)* (Eco, 1976a; Liszka, 1996). This opens the interpretation and use of strategies to whatever can happen to narratives (see earlier, discursive dynamics). A strategy intends to engender and manage a process of meaning-making in which problems, qualities or assets are further codified in the community, and in governance, and where they are more systematically connected to understanding and feeling, ideally leading to action. This chain of 'hoped-for' events can be analysed as a process of sign development. For Peirce signs, and especially complex and layered signs, *unfold over time.*

A novel, as a complex sign, an argument, is interpreted slowly through reading, reflection, discussion, slow and fast establishing links with ideas, feelings and with other novels, with other stories in real life, present and past (Short, 1982). A municipal development plan can be derailed because most of it is being ignored while a polarizing discussion evolves around one sketch design on a specific page. An example can be found in the Netherlands where the discussions about a policy aiming to address various environmental issues in a comprehensive and integrated way primarily focused on an indicative map showing required emissions reductions in different regions and zones. The indicative nature of the map was largely ignored, and the map became a sign of a heavily contested strategy and a government that according to some interest groups could not be trusted. This sign further polarized the debate, and was strategically used by politicians who didn't like the strategy and made it difficult to actually move forward.

Still adopting Peircean language, one can say that a strategy aims to produce its own *final interpretant.* While the final interpretant of a piece of travel advice is the actual form of travel, a strategy is self-consciously aiming to push us in a certain direction, as individuals and as a community (Eco, 1976b; Van Assche, 2015). Possibly, the final interpretant of the most ambitious strategy is therefore a new world. To function, a strategy has to balance carefully between self-reflection (admitting that one cannot be certain about anything here) and hardening the productive fiction (we're sure we can do this), because self-reflection can undermine the persuasive character (see later in this chapter, reality effects) while lack of awareness will lead to disappointing fantasies (Glynos, 2011; Glynos & Stavrakakis, 2008; Mintzberg & Lampel, 1999).

In the community, and in governance, the strategy as narrative and as a tool of organization is making new *publics*, and remaking actors. If the strategy underpins beliefs, deeper agreement on reality, on an interpretation, or a direction, then the strategy creates its own support. It is entirely possible that the public does not stop there, take things into their own hands, and further developing the narrative. They might elaborate creatively on the aims espoused by the narrative, and invent new tools, or develop new branches and transmutations of the story (Eeten, 2007; Hinchman & Hinchman, 1997). In the Canadian province of Quebec, rural planners tried to impose a rural development process but decided to withdraw before it was really established. The locals were already on board, disagreed with the withdrawal and therefore decided to reintroduce and reinvent the rural development process on their own. Strategies, therefore, can touch identity narratives, but they can also alter identities – which then happily modify the governance path beyond any intentions of the earlier strategists (Czarniawska & Gagliardi, 2003; Neill, 2003).

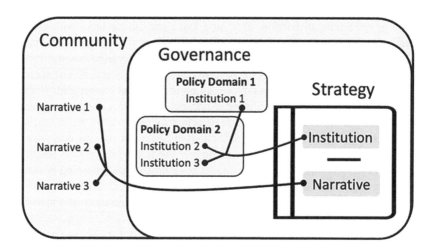

Figure 10.1   Strategy as a function coordinating institutions and narratives[1]

---

[1]   Understanding strategy as narrative and institution enables us to see how it can link to other institutions and to different narratives existing in the community. Strategy thus is more than 'a thing'; it becomes a function – a coordinating function within the community. Strategy can transcend the coordination of what exists, as it can be driven by a new narrative, and can lead to the creation of new institutions.

FUTURES AND VISIONS

Long-term perspectives, or futures, always exist in the community and in governance (see also the previous chapter). Whether governance is the place to articulate or enact long-term perspectives is a more contentious question. We are all aware that not all ideologies and systems believe that governance systems are allowed and equipped to do this. The multiplicity of futures in the community, their diversity and compatibility, make a difference for governance capacity and the capacity to strategize. Futures can hamper strategizing, as when people believe no change is needed, that strategy was never at work, and that even calamitous change is the hand of fate. Conversely, a strategy can transform and synthesize existing long-term perspectives. If the community is homogeneous in a cultural, religious or ideological sense, if many narratives and futures are shared, it is easier to strategize – and easier to believe one is good at strategizing (Bell & York, 2010; Kiernan, 1983; Metzger et al., 2021).

If futures are tied to identities, and strategy can build on that, it might smoothen implementation. Ease of implementation does not prove, however, that the best strategy was chosen. The flipside of relying on existing identities is that identity narratives can make transformative change exceedingly difficult, either through the power of sheer difference (the threat of the new and unexpected versus the lure of the familiar) or through the power of polarization if more than one identity is involved.

Identities, in strategy formation, can thus be primary, with futures springing from identity narratives, which then lead to easily agreed upon strategy. Or one might build on existing futures that are loosely coupled to identities. However, futures that at first appear neutral to identity narratives (or ideologies) can be discovered or colonized by those master narratives, which then hardens politics, and crystallizes positions vis-à-vis possible strategies. In other situations, strategy might exist already, yet without a clear link to a well-defined long-term perspective, which can lead to the failure of strategy but also to the formation of new narratives which can propel the further development of strategy. Identities can form in the process of strategizing, or in the process of implementation, either in line with the intention of the strategists, or as an unanticipated effect, possibly opposing the strategy, its underlying or assumed ideology, or the whole system producing it (Assmann & Czaplicka, 1995; de Vries & Aalvanger, 2015). Strategy can bring futures together, but implementation can therefore also spark new divisions.

Tactics, as short-term or ad hoc responses, are needed for strategy implementation, yet a proliferation of tactics can engender a new phase of strategy formation, while some tactics which at first seem to fit an unfolding strategy can also be kernels of alternative strategies. The same can be said about policy tools, which can be chosen to fit a strategic frame and can open the eyes of participants in governance for the potential of that tool, and for its fit in alternative strategies (Beunen & Van Assche, 2021; Carter, 2010). Some tools are already linked to budding strategies in the margin of governance, or hoped-for strategies in the community. Discovery of those buds can make them sprout, move to the center of attention, and spark discussions on different paths and tools. Some tactics, and some tools, tend to create their own path and their own dependencies, unbeknownst to their early users, and repeated use of some has long-term consequences that were not anticipated first. Thus, tactics and strategy imply each other, but, as some say, short-term solutions do not exist (Van Assche et al., 2017).

A vision is something we understand to be an intermediary between the multiplicity of future narratives and a strategy. For us, a vision is not a strategy but an important stepping stone, especially in the context of governance. Visioning can be a managed process, participatory and intense, whereby a vision is forged that can serve as the basis of strategy (Elkins et al., 2009; Gruezmacher & Van Assche, 2022). The vision can become the narrative aspect of strategy, or a precursor when direct translation (vision into narrative) is not possible. Visions require coupling to institutions for their translation into strategies, and knowledge of those institutions and their couplings and (in-)compatibilities is hence valuable. Knowledge of institutions, of the governance system, of partial goals and means, can serve as input for both visioning and later phases of strategizing (Griffiths et al., 1998; Millett, 2006).

Visioning driven by experts or strategy directly devised by experts, or by politicians and their favorite administrative advisors, is very common and is sometimes required. Yet, if a vision is intended to pave the way for strategy, and if divisions in the community do not allow for an easy translation into strategy, then participatory visioning, and ideally participatory strategizing, are commendable. Here we take a normative stance: visioning is useful when the current procedures of governance do not enable the kind of change felt as necessary, and visioning can enable strategy driving such change. Visioning can increase the support for a resulting strategy, but the presence of visioning by itself does not guarantee such outcome (Gruezmacher & Van Assche, 2022).

Decision support systems and other expert driven systems, or expertly pre-structured deliberation procedures, tend to produce shallow visions, because creative possibilities to come to new narratives are not explored (Easterly, 2013; Fischer, 1990). Often, mapping problems, listing wishes, measuring resources are presented as objective inputs for rational decision procedures. Yet, neither the inputs nor the procedures are objective, as assumptions always exist, and the potential for dialectical and reflexive learning is rarely acknowledged and used (Mintzberg, 1994). Learning in visioning ought to extend to the exploration of more diverse and truly new futures. This also makes it a process of persuasion, self-reflection and creation (Throgmorton, 1996). We refer to our earlier discussions of evidence-based policy, where the limits and pitfalls of such an approach are amplified in the case of strategy.

REALITY EFFECTS AND STRATEGY

A strategy will engender goal dependencies in governance. Those will interact with the other dependencies (see earlier, dependencies) and ideally move the community in the desired direction. The strategizing actors thus need to be aware of the pattern of dependencies marking the governance path. The interplay between dependencies cannot be predicted with great certainty, but familiarity with the system and path will highlight key effects of and on the dependencies relevant for the strategist. The remaining uncertainty is one reason why continuous observation and adaptation of strategy and tactics are needed.

Steering in and through governance will thus depend on the quality of self-analysis and self-awareness with the actors in governance. New actors, perhaps in new participatory settings, must be honestly informed about the functioning of governance, a presentation which should include formal/informal interactions, past failures, present imperfections, tensions and internal cleavages, as well as limits in cognitive and organizational capacities (Hughes et al., 2021; Roberts, 2009). We define steering as deliberate *path creation*, and the intentionality at work can be visible in the form of a strategy. Path creation in a managed fashion thus depends on the understanding of the dependencies and their interplay. Other learning processes will be at play, but the self-analysis, reflection on previous steering attempts and entwining of dependencies in those past episodes will be especially relevant (Dunlop & Radaelli, 2018; Van Assche, Gruezmacher, et al., 2019).

If strategy is not only governance reform, but also aims to change something in the community, then managing goal dependencies is not sufficient. The strategy will want to maximize and manage *reality effects*. Goal dependencies, as we know, are effects of institutions (for us, strategy) in governance, while reality effects are those effects outside governance which transform reality (Van Assche, Duineveld, et al., 2021). This can be a matter of discursive change (new stories creating new realities) and of material change (the physical, observable reality is changed). The effects can also be material and discursive, and one sort of change can support the other; new stories making small interventions in space look significant, maybe. Discursive effects can precede and trigger material effects, or vice versa, while discursive changes in society (see earlier Chapter 5 The Realm of Discourse and Chapter 9 Looking Forward and Back) can inform strategy and enhance their discursive effects.

A downtown revitalization strategy leads to renovations and new construction. However, critical press finds out that all projects are carried out by friends of the governing party, at the same time the quality of the work raised questions with the advocates for the downtown. As a result, public discourse on the ruling party and the downtown revitalization initiative shifted to the effect that a new coalition was elected and the strategy was abandoned.

In both material and discursive domains, *thresholds* are present. Incremental changes might not be perceived at first. A series of small, even minute, changes can result in a tipping point in the ecological system, which will be observed in the social system (Cote & Nightingale, 2012; de Molina & Toledo, 2014). But they can also bring about a growing awareness and a sudden shift in discourse, in sentiment, a breakout resistance. A difference might suddenly be noticed, a problem assembled. This, in our interpretation, is what Alain Badiou calls *the event*, where something new breaks through and, afterward, it cannot be undone (Badiou, 2013).

Figure 10.2   Discursive and material environments and governance[2]

---

[2]   A community's discursive and material environments are shaped by and influence the community's governance system. Strategies enacted in the governance system cannot escape such external influences, while potentially reshaping both environments and influences. Discursive effects of strategy can precede and trigger material effects, or

Material changes might be natural, artificial or hybrid, and the difference might be subtle. Unobserved material changes might cause material dependencies, without triggering reality effects. Material events (see earlier, dependencies) can be unobserved, even if those events are the result of strategy. As always, the impacts of a new institution, the reverberations through the governance configuration and through the discursive divisions and connections in society, cannot be entirely observed. Hence, not all reality effects will be recognized as results of strategy.

SPEED OF REFORM AND STABILITY

Strategies are aiming at the long-term but must deal with short- and long-term futures and issues with myriad temporalities (see earlier in the chapter). Some problems and opportunities appear quickly, others more slowly. Temporalities within and outside governance can resist observation and coordination. Also, solutions can be fast or slow in appearing and in implementation; they can be tied to new chance observations, occurrences, to only partly understood temporalities now revealing themselves. Strategies can be tied to such solutions and problems, but also, as we know, introduce their own temporalities in a way not entirely of their choosing.

The choice of policy tools affects the functioning of synchronization in the process of strategizing and implementation. Adopting laws takes time, changing a constitution takes more time and introduces more uncertainty, while the implementation of a measure based on an existing law can be fast – if seen to emanate from a strict rule. Speedy reform associated with new strategy comes with risks, can disrupt coordination, and can reduce the chances that any later strategy effort will lead to much (Brouwer & Huitema, 2017). Ongoing reform, and getting used to reform, can help, can enable self-transformation through strategy, without too many of the disruptive effects of change, but as we noted earlier (following Czarniawska), in never-ending reform each iteration tends to make the next one less persuasive, appearing more as a vehicle to put up a show and further careers (Czarniawska-Joerges & Wolff, 1991). Slowing down a hasty strategist can buttress checks and balances and improve the quality of coordination in and through the strategy. Slowing down can be a self-centered tactic by actors with the intention to undermine strategy or the public good envisioned, but this is not always the case. Collective strategy can be oppressive, serving elites, or can simply be foolhardy, a testament to

vice versa, while discursive changes in society can inform strategy and enhance their discursive effects.

imperfect institutions, and, hence, democratic principles would dictate that space for actor strategies and for counterstrategy must be safeguarded (Van Assche, Verschraegen, et al., 2021). Slowing down reform helps to preserve such spaces.

The presence or absence of counterstrategy (see also Chapter 12) can further be related to the stability or instability of governance and community. The capacity to strategize, which we now know as an important aspect of governance capacity, relies on stability (see earlier, on change and stability) (Jarzabkowski & Paul Spee, 2009; Mintzberg & McHugh, 1985). Polarization, dramatic inequality and incompatible ideologies might be a problem, but in general both calm and tumultuous governance bases have pros and cons in terms of strategic capacity (Pejovic, 1999). Tumult can undo problematic routines, and resolve blind spots, while reshuffling expectations and casting ideologies in a new light. Questionable path dependencies and interdependencies can become more visible after a shock or less damaging instability, new questions can be asked (Herrfahrdt-Pähle et al., 2020; Van Assche & Gruezmacher, 2023). While, on the other side, stability can mean reliable forms of coordination, recognized and legitimized power relations, predictable streams of resources.

If the mechanisms of participation and representation still work, if checks and balances are still there, then alternative strategies can come through resistance, actor strategies, counterstrategy. Tumult, either after a shock or because of the absence of good governance, because of policy failures, or changing expectations, can be the yeast in the fermentation of new futures and strategies, the incentive to resist existing strategies or the system itself. For EGT, new legitimacy quickly associates with changes stemming from the accepted modes of self-transformation; if those modes are preserved, then instability can more likely be productive of corrective strategy.

ADAPTATION AND LEARNING

Governance is always adapted to an environment and is always equipped with a form of adaptive capacity. Those adaptations and capacities might have to be retooled and revised, and new forms of observation and coordination might have to be favored, to rejuvenate governance, enhance legitimacy, and to rethink the embeddings in community and ecology (Berkes & Folke, 1998; Chaffin & Gunderson, 2016). Perfect adaptation, as we know, is risky, as it tends to suppress observation of self and environment, ignoring the importance of loose couplings, redundancy in coordination forms and diversity in perspectives.

Strategy, in many cases, is not adaptive, although it ought to be. New observations, during implementation, should trigger new episodes of self-analysis, which can deliver new insights on the interplay between dependencies, on the management of goal dependencies. Dependencies can enable and hamper adaptation and flexibility. Strategy can slowly transform these dependencies, as a goal or as a side effect of other substantive goals. Maximizing adaptive capacity should not be a tenet of good governance, nor a goal of all reform strategies (strategies focusing on changing governance itself). Strategy might have to diminish or downplay a particular adaption, or even reduce adaptive capacity in one sense, and introduce new rigidities to force or strongly encourage coordination and integration of policy in strategy. All policy tools can be considered, ranging from strong incentives and disincentives for citizens, to align with strategy, to new laws which could enshrine values, goals and concepts central to the strategy. Discretion by civil servants and politicians when dealing with requests might have to be reduced to steer the course. Not all such actions increase rigidity, as not all change the rules of the game.

Good governance hence entails workable adaptation, but best governance is not a matter of the best adaptation. Slow adaptation cannot be equated to a slow survival of the fittest, a weeding out of alternative policies or configurations. Systems survive, learning and collaboration happens, and selection can happen through shocks and chance events as much as through adaptation and competition (Koontz et al., 2015; Nooteboom & Marks, 2010). Experiments are possible, to test alternative policy solutions, to adapt governance to find and test strategy. However, just as Darwinian metaphors are misleading, comparison with natural science experiments is deceiving (see earlier, learning).

We argue for adaptive strategy (not strategy for perfect adaptation), by which we mean that, in most situations, a strategy which can be adapted is preferable over one that seems perfect but reveals itself as brittle and must be abandoned when obstacles occur. In general, finding and combining a new narrative, new actor and discursive coalitions, a new selection of institutions which can perform a wholly new form of coordination, is more difficult than modifying an existing strategy, as long as a basic agreement on direction and values remains.

Adaptation (and implementation) comes in through changing patterns of tactics, yet it cannot be reduced to this mechanism (Brown, 2011; Folke et al., 2005). Adaptive governance requires that self-analysis, implementation and strategy adjust to each other in an iterative process, through self-transformation. What drives the self-transformation is continuous observation of both governance and environment, to establish both goal dependencies and reality effects. This adaptive process can lead to regular adjustments to governance itself (in its institutional and organizational dimension) and changes to the environment (Koontz et al., 2015; Van Assche, Verschraegen, et al., 2019). Changes to the environment are not only adaptations to ecological systems in trouble or causing us trouble. Many other reasons can be imagined. As always, quality of observation determines quality of (self-) analysis (Jessop, 2002).

For adaptive strategy, learning in all the modes discussed earlier can be helpful; not only learning through self-observation and experiment, but also through comparison (did it work elsewhere), from experts (observing implementation, assessing efficiency, cognitive limitations), and, last but not least, dialectical learning. Dialectical learning is often ignored, as adaptations are easily considered technicalities, yet if what requires adaptation is a community strategy, adaptation might involve the search for a revised narrative and alternative ways of binding institutions and goals to that narrative (Vaara, 2002; Van Assche, Verschraegen, et al., 2021). Democratic deliberation might be in place, then, as what appears as a technical adjustment to some looks like a deviation or even a betrayal of the 'true' spirit of the strategy to others.

The coordination or integration of institutions, through narrative coupling, can always happen in different ways, so where a revised narrative is unnecessary, maintaining the narrative might not be difficult, even if one path of integration did not work out. The overarching narrative can assist in defining goals, topics, times and places to focus on, sometimes in selecting policy tools. Constructing procedures helps to separate and relate topics, sub-goals, and incorporate other institutions (step 5: take old heritage plan into account). As the architecture beneath the roof of the narrative is always intricate, there are

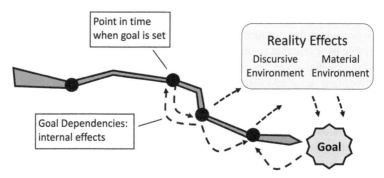

Figure 10.3   Goal dependencies and reality effects in governance[3]

---

[3]   Strategies trigger goal dependencies and reality effects. The set goal triggers goal dependencies in governance and a strategy informed by self-analysis will make sure those dependencies are predictable enough to maintain the course. Reality effects or the effects of governance on the material and/or discursive environment are hoped to align, so what one can see as changed and what one can hear about the changes makes sense and resembles what was promised in the strategy.

many ways to hold up the roof. Adaptive strategy is often about rethinking the couplings between elements still preserved. Elsewhere, of course, it might be necessary to bring in new topics, add sites of participation, or alter the narrative (Sandercock, 2003; Throgmorton, 2003; Van Assche, 2004).

Whether one remains a 'gateway to the Cordillera,' if other cities positioned themselves as such, and when the mountains increasingly became marginal for the economy and the identity narratives in a community, remains to be seen. At the same time, an older tourism strategy, focused on mountain connections, can stay relevant and can be incorporated into a new strategy revolving around a leading role in energy transition, with mountain tourism taking a back seat to the attraction of highly skilled workers, who happen to enjoy an attractive natural environment.

LEADERSHIP AND STRATEGIC CAPACITY

Strategy is not always present in communities, even when strategic documents exist. We mentioned earlier that they can easily end up as dead institutions. It might indicate that the capacity to strategize and to implement is not there, that there was never a real intention to strategize or implement, or that the capacities are lost. The diagnosis could also be that the strategy was serious and functional, yet lost support, and that its demise prefigured the demise of all future strategies because trust in strategizing was lost.

The capacity to strategize is one of the capacities that can be labeled as 'governance capacity,' but the problem is that to achieve an effect and preserve its position, its legitimacy, its functionality and the other capacities must be there as well. If implementation fails, strategic capacity will wither and implementation of a community strategy only works if all other aspects of governance work (Beunen et al., 2013; Wargent, 2020). As we discussed, adaptive capacity is not a matter of increasing or decreasing but of qualitatively different capacities to perform certain adaptations to certain environments, strategic capacity must be tailored to specific conditions and understood as such (Armitage, 2005; Jarzabkowski & Fenton, 2006; Van Assche, Verschraegen, et al., 2019). One can observe after the fact that strategic capacity is there, as a strategy was articulated to great effect. One can further observe that memory, diversity in perspectives, a combination of participation and representation, of flexibility and rigidity, expert and local knowledge are useful, as are the cultivation of reflexivity, dialectical learning and the existence of specialized roles, arenas, forms of expertise, policy tools and available resources (Gherardi et al., 2018). Some ideologies and narratives favor community strategy more than others. Yet such lists, never exhaustive, are not all that helpful in outlining strategic capacity, as they indicate that virtually any feature of governance can be beneficial for strategizing.

The absence of strategic capacity can be more easily noted and can often be associated with the absence of aspects of good governance, and the overall weakness of governance capacity. If it is hard to organize anything, if coordination in and through governance rarely happens and often breaks down, if legitimacy of governance and institutions is low, if administrative capacity and institutional memory are not there, if open discussion is not possible and many feel marginalized, then collective strategy is unlikely to appear or to have real effects (Campbell et al., 2000; Chong, 2011).

One can also reorganize the discussion on good governance from the perspective of what is needed for community strategy, as such effort, as we know, will require all aspects of governance to work in unison. One can distinguish then between the capacities to observe, to respond, to remember, to process, to coordinate, and to assess. If we understand the capacity to strategize, to move the community in a different direction as the culmination of good governance, all these capacities must be listed as contributing to good governance (Diduck, 2010; Waters & Adger, 2017). Observation then includes observation of internal and external environments, through a variety of perspectives, response is response to those observations, through discussion, learning, decision-making, formation of new institutions, interventions in the environment (Jessop, 2002; Paul Beyes, 2005). Processing comes in-between observation and response, and involves cognitive and organizational processing, through the development of procedures which manage complexity, the linking to other knowledges, narratives, institutions, resources, arenas. None of it works without memory, as discussed in Chapter 9 (Looking Forward and Back), and all of it receives orientation through narratives, identities, roles and, in fact, by virtue of the existence of the configurations.

What is still missing from this understanding of strategic capacity and governance capacity is leadership. Leadership in democratic governance is typically distributed, with ideas, initiatives, inspiration and impetus coming from many sides (Alvesson & Sveningsson, 2013; Young, 1991). Most often, the routines of governance, even in the most admired systems, do not produce strategy. And if they do, if strategy is a normalized product of the procedures of governance, such strategy is unlikely to capture fully the portent of trends in the environment, the mood swings in the population, the potential for new goals, for reinvention, and for shifting patterns of inclusion and exclusion. Leadership, then, is not about pushing the buttons of the political-bureaucratic machine (Alvesson & Sveningsson, 2013; Van Assche et al., 2016).

In terms of the previous passages, leadership requires insight and judgment, to assess and manage reality effects and dependencies. Expertise in governance is required, and access to more of it, yet the best leader is not the best technocrat, not even in technocratic systems (Fischer, 1990). Deep familiarity with the community, with the effects of and perception of governance in the community, as well as thorough knowledge of the formal and informal aspects of governance are a sine qua non for strategic leadership. Glorification of individual leader figures tends to obscure the naturally distributed character of leadership in governance.

Leadership must be aware of the interplay between dependencies, between formal and informal institutions, and must be willing and capable to use informality to move things forward (Czarniawska-Joerges & Wolff, 1991; Mielke, 2022; Mukhija & Loukaitou-Sideris, 2015). This requires a broad scope and large diversity of observations and depth of analysis that goes beyond what an individual can handle. One could even say that the work of Machiavelli could be interpreted in such a way; the notorious Prince is not necessarily an individual, but rather a group of people, an organization, or a system that needs to sustain governance, 'Mantenere lo stato,' as Quentin Skinner has argued.

Leadership cannot be missed in the aligning of goal dependencies, by which we mean the observation and transformation of goal dependencies to optimize and align reality effects in the community. Aligning in this second sense is the modification of interventions (and coordination mechanisms underlying intervention and changing behavior) to bring reality effects more in line with the intentions of the strategy (Berger & Luckmann, 1967; Van Assche, Duineveld, et al., 2021). Without leadership, it is all too easy to hide behind specialized roles and to not connect the dots, the steps and insights from numerous procedures. Without leadership, anything that is not formal in terms of actors, institutions, effects and dependencies, is likely to escape observation, processing, assessment and action (Fischer-Kowalski & Rotmans, 2009; Paul Beyes, 2005). Adaptation and adaptive strategy, then, requires leadership also because of the always incomplete self-understandings and self-descriptions of governance systems.

REFERENCES

Alvesson, M. & Spicer, A. (2012). A stupidity-based theory of organizations. *Journal of Management Studies, 49*(7), 1194–1220.

Alvesson, M. & Sveningsson, S. (2013). Essay: Authentic leadership critically reviewed. In *Authentic leadership*. Edward Elgar Publishing.

Armitage, D. (2005). Adaptive capacity and community-based natural resource management. *Environmental Management, 35*(6), 703–715. https:// doi .org/ 10 .1007/ s00267-004-0076-z

Assmann, J. & Czaplicka, J. (1995). Collective memory and cultural identity. *New German Critique, 65*, 125. https://doi.org/10.2307/488538

Badiou, A. (2013). *Philosophy and the event*. Polity.

Bateman, J. A. (2018). Peircean semiotics and multimodality: Towards a new synthesis. *Multimodal Communication, 7*(1). https://doi.org/10.1515/mc-2017-0021

Becker, E. (2012). Social-ecological systems as epistemic objects. In *Human-nature interactions in the Anthropocene* (pp. 55–77). Routledge.

Bell, S. E. & York, R. (2010). Community economic identity: The coal industry and ideology construction in West Virginia. *Rural Sociology*, *75*(1), 111–143. https://doi .org/10.1111/j.1549-0831.2009.00004.x

Berger, P. L. & Luckmann, T. (1967). *The social construction of reality: A treatise in the sociology of knowledge*. Anchor.

Berkes, F. & Folke, C. (1998). Linking social and ecological systems for resilience and sustainability. In F. Berkes & C. Folke (eds.), *Linking social and ecological systems: Management practices and social mechanisms for building resilience* (pp. 1–25). Cambridge University Press.

Beunen, R. & Van Assche, K. (2021). Steering in governance: Evolutionary perspectives. *Politics and Governance*, *9*(2), 365–368. https://doi.org/10.17645/pag.v9i2 .4489

Beunen, R., Van Assche, K. & Duineveld, M. (2013). Performing failure in conservation policy: The implementation of European Union directives in the Netherlands. *Land Use Policy*, *31*, 280–288. https://doi.org/10.1016/j.landusepol.2012.07.009

Beunen, R., Van Assche, K. & Gruezmacher, M. (2022). Evolutionary perspectives on environmental governance: Strategy and the co-construction of governance, community, and environment. *Sustainability*, *14*(16), article 16. https://doi.org/10 .3390/su14169912

Botan, C. H. & Soto, F. (1998). A semiotic approach to the internal functioning of publics: Implications for strategic communication and public relations. *Public Relations Review*, *24*(1), 21–44. https://doi.org/10.1016/S0363-8111(98)80018-0

Brouwer, S. & Huitema, D. (2017). Policy entrepreneurs and strategies for change. *Regional Environmental Change*, 1–14. https://doi.org/doi:10.1007/s10113-017 -1139-z

Brown, K. (2011). Sustainable adaptation: An oxymoron? *Climate and Development*, *3*(January 2013), 21–31. https://doi.org/10.3763/cdev.2010.0062

Campbell, D. J., Gichohi, H., Mwangi, A. & Chege, L. (2000). Land use conflict in Kajiado District, Kenya. *Land Use Policy*, *17*(4), 337–348.

Carter, C. (2010). *Re-framing strategy: Power, politics and accounting*. Emerald Group Publishing Limited.

Carter, C., Clegg, S. R. & Kornberger, M. (2008). *A very short, fairly interesting and reasonably cheap book about studying strategy*. SAGE.

Chaffin, B. C. & Gunderson, L. H. (2016). Emergence, institutionalization and renewal: Rhythms of adaptive governance in complex social-ecological systems. *Journal of Environmental Management*, *165*, 81–87. https://doi.org/10.1016/j.jenvman.2015 .09.003

Chong, D. (2011). Coordination and conflict. In *Rational lives: Norms and values in politics and society* (pp. 76–115). University of Chicago Press. https://doi.org/10 .7208/9780226104379-006

Clark, J. & Newman, J. (1997). *The managerial state: Power, politics and ideology in the remaking of social welfare*. Sage.

Copus, C., Roberts, M. & Wall, R. (2017). Policy narratives in local and national government. In *Local Government in England* (pp. 37–55). Springer.

Cote, M. & Nightingale, A. J. (2012). Resilience thinking meets social theory: Situating social change in socio-ecological systems (SES) research. *Progress in Human Geography*, *36*(4), 475–489.

Czarniawska, B. (1997). *A narrative approach to organization studies*. SAGE Publications.

Czarniawska, B. & Gagliardi, P. (2003). *Narratives we organize by* (vol. 11). John Benjamins Publishing.

Czarniawska-Joerges, B. & Wolff, R. (1991). Leaders, managers, entrepreneurs on and off the organizational stage. *Organization Studies, 12*(4), 529–546.

de Molina, M. G. & Toledo, V. M. (2014). *The social metabolism: A socio-ecological theory of historical change* (vol. 3). Springer.

de Vries, J. & Aalvanger, A. (2015). Negotiating differences: The role of social identity in the emergence of institutions for local governance. In R. Beunen, K. Van Assche & M. Duineveld (eds.), *Evolutionary governance theory: Theory and applications* (pp. 291–304). Springer International Publishing. https://doi.org/10.1007/978-3-319 -12274-8_19

Diduck, A. (2010). The learning dimension of adaptive capacity: Untangling the multi-level connections. In D. Armitage & R. Plummer (eds.), *Adaptive capacity and environmental governance* (pp. 199–221). Springer. https://doi.org/10.1007/978 -3-642-12194-4_10

Dunlop, C. A. & Radaelli, C. M. (2018). The lessons of policy learning: Types, triggers, hindrances and pathologies. *Policy & Politics, 46*(2), 255–272. https://doi.org/10 .1332/030557318X15230059735521

Easterly, W. (2013). *The tyranny of experts: Economists, dictators, and the forgotten rights of the poor*. Basic Books.

Eco, U. (1976a). *A theory of semiotics*. Indiana University Press.

Eco, U. (1976b). Peirce's notion of interpretant. *MLN, 91*(6), 1457–1472. https://doi .org/10.2307/2907146

Eeten, M. M. J. van. (2007). Narrative policy analysis. In *Handbook of public policy analysis*. Routledge.

Elkins, L. A., Bivins, D. & Holbrook, L. (2009). Community visioning process: a tool for successful planning. *Journal of Higher Education Outreach and Engagement, 13*(4), 75–84.

Fincham, R. (1999). The consultant–client relationship: Critical perspectives on the management of organizational change. *Journal of Management Studies, 36*(3), 335–351.

Fischer, F. (1990). *Technocracy and the politics of expertise*. Sage Publications.

Fischer-Kowalski, M. & Rotmans, J. (2009). Conceptualizing, observing, and influenc- ing social-ecological transitions. *Ecology and Society, 14*(2).

Folke, C., Hahn, T., Olsson, P. & Norberg, J. (2005). Adaptative governance of social-ecological systems. *Annual Review of Environment and Resources, 30*(1), 441–473. https://doi.org/10.1146/annurev.energy.30.050504.144511

Gherardi, S., Cozza, M. & Poggio, B. (2018). Organizational members as storywriters: On organizing practices of reflexivity. *The Learning Organization, 25*(1), 51–62.

Glynos, J. (2011). On the ideological and political significance of fantasy in the organ- ization of work. *Psychoanalysis, Culture & Society, 16*(4), 373–393. https://doi.org/ 10.1057/pcs.2010.34

Glynos, J. & Stavrakakis, Y. (2008). Lacan and Political subjectivity: Fantasy and enjoyment in psychoanalysis and political theory. *Subjectivity, 24*(1), 256–274. https://doi.org/10.1057/sub.2008.23

Golsorkhi, D., Rouleau, L., Seidl, D. & Vaara, E. (2010). *Cambridge handbook of strategy as practice*. Cambridge University Press.

Griffiths, D., Boisot, M. & Mole, V. (1998). Strategies for managing knowledge assets: A tale of two companies. *Technovation, 18*(8–9), 529–588.

Gruezmacher, M. & Van Assche, K. (2022). *Crafting strategies for sustainable local development*. InPlanning.

Hendry, J. (1995). Strategy formation and the policy context. *Journal of General Management, 20*(4), 54–64. https://doi.org/10.1177/030630709502000404

Herrfahrdt-Pähle, E., Schlüter, M., Olsson, P., Folke, C., Gelcich, S. & Pahl-Wostl, C. (2020). Sustainability transformations: Socio-political shocks as opportunities for governance transitions. *Global Environmental Change, 63*, 102097.

Hiedanpaa, J. & Bromley, D. W. (2012). Contestations over biodiversity protection: Considering Peircean semiosis. *Environmental Values, 21*(3), 357–378. https://doi.org/10.3197/096327112X13400390126091

Hinchman, L. P. & Hinchman, S. (1997). *Memory, identity, community: The idea of narrative in the human sciences.* SUNY Press.

Hughes, J., Kornberger, M., MacKay, B., O'Brien, P. & Reddy, S. (2021). Organizational strategy and its implications for strategic studies: A review essay. *Journal of Strategic Studies, 46*(2), 427–450. https://doi.org/10.1080/01402390.2021.1994950

Jarzabkowski, P. (2004). Strategy as practice: Recursiveness, adaptation, and practices-in-use. *Organization Studies, 25*(4), 529–560.

Jarzabkowski, P. & Fenton, E. (2006). Strategizing and organizing in pluralistic contexts. *Long Range Planning, 39*(6), 631–648. https://doi.org/10.1016/j.lrp.2006.11.002

Jarzabkowski, P. & Paul Spee, A. (2009). Strategy-as-practice: A review and future directions for the field. *International Journal of Management Reviews, 11*(1), 69–95.

Jessop, B. (2002). Governance and meta-governance in the face of complexity: On the roles of requisite variety, reflexive observation, and romantic irony in participatory governance. In H. Heinelt, P. Getimis, G. Kafkalas, R. Smith & E. Swyngedouw (eds.), *Participatory governance in multi-level context: concepts and experience* (pp. 33–58). VS Verlag für Sozialwissenschaften. https://doi.org/10.1007/978-3-663-11005-7_2

Kiernan, M. J. (1983). Ideology, politics, and planning: Reflections on the theory and practice of urban planning. *Environment and Planning B: Planning and Design, 10*(1), 71–87.

Koontz, T. M., Gupta, D., Mudliar, P. & Ranjan, P. (2015). Adaptive institutions in social-ecological systems governance: A synthesis framework. *Environmental Science & Policy, 53*, 139–151.

Kornberger, M. (2017). The values of strategy: Valuation practices, rivalry and strategic agency. *Organization Studies, 38*(12), 1753–1773. https://doi.org/10.1177/0170840616685365

Kornberger, M. (2022). *Strategies for distributed and collective action: Connecting the dots.* Oxford University Press USA – OSO. http://public.eblib.com/choice/PublicFullRecord.aspx?p=6836917

Kornberger, M. & Engberg-Pedersen, A. (2019). Reading Clausewitz, reimagining the practice of strategy. Strategic Organization, 1476127019854963–1476127019854963. https://doi.org/10.1177/1476127019854963

Liszka, J. J. (1996). *A general introduction to the semiotics of Charles Sanders Peirce.* Indiana University Press.

Luhmann, Ni. (2018). *Organization and decision* (D. Baecker, trans.). Cambridge University Press.

Metzger, J., Allmendinger, P. & Kornberger, M. (2021). Ideology in practice: The career of sustainability as an ideological concept in strategic urban planning. *International Planning Studies, 26*(3), 302–320. https://doi.org/10.1080/13563475.2020.1839390

Mielke, K. (2022). Calculated informality in governing (non)return: An evolutionary governance perspective. *Geopolitics, 28*(3), 1106–1129. https://doi.org/10.1080/14650045.2022.2052854

Millett, S. M. (2006). Futuring and visioning: Complementary approaches to strategic decision making. *Strategy & Leadership 34*(3), 43–50.

Mintzberg, H. (1978). Patterns in strategy formation. *Management Science, 24*(9), 934–948. https://doi.org/10.1287/mnsc.24.9.934

Mintzberg, H. (1987). *Crafting strategy*. Harvard Business Publishing.

Mintzberg, H. (1994). Rethinking strategic planning part I: Pitfalls and fallacies. *Long Range Planning, 27*(3), 12–21. https://doi.org/10.1016/0024-6301(94)90185-6

Mintzberg, H. & Lampel, J. B. (1999). Reflecting on the strategy process. *MIT Sloan Management Review*.

Mintzberg, H. & McHugh, A. (1985). Strategy formation in an adhocracy. *Administrative Science Quarterly, 30*(2), 160–197. https://doi.org/10.2307/2393104

Mukhija, V. & Loukaitou-Sideris, A. (2015). Reading the informal city: Why and how to deepen planners' understanding of informality. *Journal of Planning Education and Research, 35*(4), 444–454. https://doi.org/10.1177/0739456X15591586

Neill, W. (2003). *Urban planning and cultural identity*. Routledge.

Nooteboom, S. & Marks, P. (2010). Adaptive networks as second order governance systems. *Systems Research and Behavioral Science, 27*(1), 61–69. https://doi.org/10.1002/sres.985

Paul Beyes, T. (2005). Observing observers. Von Foerster, Luhmann, and management thinking. *Kybernetes, 34*(3/4), 448–459. https://doi.org/10.1108/03684920510581639

Pejovic, S. (1999). The effects of the interaction between formal and informal institutions on social stability and development. *Journal of Markets and Morality, 2*(2), 164–181.

Rasche, A. & Seidl, D. (2020). A Luhmannian perspective on strategy: Strategy as paradox and meta-communication. *Critical Perspectives on Accounting, 73*, 101984–101984. https://doi.org/10.1016/j.cpa.2017.03.004

Roberts, J. (2009). No one is perfect: The limits of transparency and an ethic for 'intelligent' accountability. *Accounting, Organizations and Society, 34*(8), 957–970. https://doi.org/10.1016/j.aos.2009.04.005

Sandercock, L. (2003). Out of the closet: The importance of stories and storytelling in planning practice. *Planning Theory & Practice, 4*(1), 11–28. https://doi.org/10.1080/1464935032000057209

Schoemaker, P. J. H. (1990). Strategy, complexity, and economic rent. *Management Science, 36*(10), 1178–1192. https://doi.org/10.1287/mnsc.36.10.1178

Seidl, D. (2007). General strategy concepts and the ecology of strategy discourses: A systemic-discursive perspective. *Organization Studies, 28*(2), 197–218.

Seidl, D. (2016). *Organisational identity and self-transformation: An autopoietic perspective*. Routledge.

Seidl, D. (2019). *Organisational identity and self-transformation: An autopoietic perspective*. Taylor & Francis Group.

Seidl, D. & Becker, K. H. (2006). Organizations as distinction generating and processing systems: Niklas Luhmann's contribution to organization studies. *Organization, 13*(1), 9–35. https://doi.org/10.1177/1350508406059635

Short, T. L. (1982). Life among the Legisigns. *Transactions of the Charles S. Peirce Society, 18*(4), 285–310.

Smink, M. M., Hekkert, M. P. & Negro, S. O. (2015). Keeping sustainable innovation on a leash? Exploring incumbents' institutional strategies. *Business Strategy and the Environment, 24*(2), 86–101.

Stirrat, R. L. (2000). Cultures of consultancy. *Critique of Anthropology, 20*(1), 31–46. https://doi.org/10.1177/0308275X0002000103

Sturdy, A. (2011). Consultancy's consequences? A critical assessment of management consultancy's impact on management. *British Journal of Management, 22*(3), 517–530. https://doi.org/10.1111/j.1467-8551.2011.00750.x

Suddaby, R., Seidl, D. & Lê, J. K. (2013). Strategy-as-practice meets neo-institutional theory. *Strategic Organization*, *11*(3), 329–344. https:// doi .org/ 10 .1177/ 1476127013497618

Throgmorton, J. A. (1996). *Planning as persuasive storytelling: The rhetorical construction of Chicago's electric future.* University of Chicago Press.

Throgmorton, J. A. (2003). Planning as persuasive storytelling in a global-scale web of relationships. *Planning Theory*, *2*(2), 125–151.

Vaara, E. (2002). On the discursive construction of success/failure in narratives of post-merger integration. *Organization Studies*, *23*(2), 211–248. https:// doi .org/ 10 .1177/0170840602232003

Van Assche, K. (2004). Signs in time: An interpretive account of urban planning and design, the people and their history. *Wageningen: Wageningen University*.

Van Assche, K. (2015). Semiotics of silent lakes. Sigurd Olson and the interlacing of writing, policy and planning. *Journal of Environmental Policy & Planning*, *17*(2), 262–276. https://doi.org/10.1080/1523908X.2014.941460

Van Assche, K. & Gruezmacher, M. (2023). Remembering Ypres. Post-war reconstruction, land and the legacies of shock and conflict. *Land*, *12*(1). https://doi.org/10 .3390/land12010021

Van Assche, K., Beunen, R. & Duineveld, M. (2016). Citizens, leaders and the common good in a world of necessity and scarcity: Machiavelli's lessons for community-based natural resource management. *Ethics, Policy & Environment*, *19*(1), 19–36.

Van Assche, K., Deacon, L., Gruezmacher, M., Summers, R., Lavoie, S., Jones, K., Granzow, M., Hallstrom, L. & Parkins, J. (2017). *Boom & bust. Local strategy for big events. A community survival guide to turbulent times.* Groningen/Edmonton, Alberta: InPlanning and University of Alberta, Faculty of Extension.

Van Assche, K., Duineveld, M., Gruezmacher, M. & Beunen, R. (2021). Steering as path creation The art of managing dependencies and reality effects. *Politics and Governance 9*(2), 369–380.

Van Assche, K., Gruezmacher, M. & Deacon, L. (2019). Mapping institutional work as a method for local strategy; learning from boom/bust dynamics in the Canadian west. *Journal of Environmental Planning and Management*, *62*(1), 51–71.

Van Assche, K., Verschraegen, G. & Gruezmacher, M. (2021). Strategy for collectives and common goods: Coordinating strategy, long-term perspectives and policy domains in governance. *Futures*, *128*, 102716. https:// doi .org/ 10 .1016/ j .futures .2021.102716

Van Assche, K., Verschraegen, G., Valentinov, V. & Gruezmacher, M. (2019). The social, the ecological, and the adaptive. Von Bertalanffy's general systems theory and the adaptive governance of social-ecological systems. *Systems Research and Behavioral Science*, *36*(3), 308–321.

Wargent, M. (2020). Localism, governmentality and failing technologies: The case of neighbourhood planning in England. *Territory, Politics, Governance*, *9*(2), 1–21.

Waters, J. & Adger, W. N. (2017). Spatial, network and temporal dimensions of the determinants of adaptive capacity in poor urban areas. *Global Environmental Change*, *46*, 42–49. https://doi.org/10.1016/j.gloenvcha.2017.06.011

Young, O. R. (1991). Political leadership and regime formation: On the development of institutions in international society. *International Organization*, *45*(3), 281–308.

11. Transitions reconsidered: navigating dilemmas, negotiating futures, affecting identities

INTRODUCTION: TRANSITIONS WHERE?

Transitions are processes of change, change already occurring or often aspired change, towards a goal that looks essential but that is not easy to reach (Grin et al., 2010; Johnstone & Newell, 2018; Köhler et al., 2019; Markard et al., 2012; Rauschmayer et al., 2015). Transitions are needed when change is expected to be transformative (Avelino & Rotmans, 2009; Scheffer et al., 2009, 2012). Transition and transformation are also open concepts, whereby much depends on the labeling of something as a transition or transformation and whereby that labeling can take place upfront or a posteriori. Structural changes that at some point get the label transition often only become observable and acknowledgeable over time, and in most cases the changes that become labeled as a transition are not the result of a deliberate attempt to achieve exactly those changes. Furthermore, the concept transition is often used to refer to desired change.

Acknowledging the openness of the concept is important in the context of strategy and governance because it allows reflection on the different understandings of transition, the rhetoric value of the concept, its performative power, as well as perspective that goes beyond transition as something that can be designed and steered towards in a mechanistic matter. The concept has gained popularity because of its promise for more profound changes deemed necessary to solve contemporary issues that go beyond minor adaptations, and because it links desired changes in the social-ecological system to necessary changes in the governance system. Transitions require coordination, they place a higher demand on coordination than other goals, and the strategies aiming at transition are saddled with a coordination task greater than usual. In addition, uncertainty around precise goals and paths is often high (Grunwald, 2007; Rotmans & Kemp, 2003). Some transitions require global coordination, others can be local. All transitions take place in multi-level governance settings and ought to take account of this, whether several levels are mobilized or not (Armitage, 2008; Brondizio et al., 2009; Di Gregorio et al., 2019).

Many literatures have evolved focusing on one type of transition (see also the Introduction) and many develop prescriptions. One can find prescriptions for sustainability transitions (Köhler et al., 2019), for energy transition (Cheung & Oßenbrügge, 2020), for a more innovative society (During et al., 2009), for resilient social-ecological systems (Rauschmayer et al., 2015), for deliberative or participatory democracy (Anderson, 1999), for social innovation and social justice (Kornai & Rose-Ackerman, 2004), for efficient public management, good governance, inclusive development, transformative governance (Loorbach, 2007), for just and fair transitions (Wang & Lo, 2021), and so forth. The language of transition is not always used, but the belief in prescription is high and the connectivity with the breadth of theories in social science and humanities is often limited. Some of the approaches are focused on content, on goals in the world, others on procedure, or on transforming governance as a goal in and by itself; a transformation which will then, it is expected, naturally produce better decisions and strategies and a more sustainable world (Chaffin et al., 2016; Cotilla-Sanchez et al., 2012; Loorbach, 2009; Scheffer et al., 2009, 2012; Visseren-Hamakers et al., 2021).

The previous chapters have elaborated on the functioning of governance, the difficulties of strategizing for collective goods, and the difficulties of coordinating and steering change. This implies that understanding transition in the context of governance, without a theory of governance, of organization, of the social, of knowledge, and of discourse, limits itself analytically in such a way that many relevant drivers and obstacles for transition remain invisible. Ideas of transition and transformation then remain aspirational, stating goals and means without grasping the dynamics of the systems that are supposed to be changed. For that reason, one can for example observe that the socio-technical transitions literature, formerly more technical, prescriptive and focused on innovation goals, has transformed itself into a perspective on sustainability transitions, open for social innovation and the shifting meanings and power relations in society and governance.

This book builds on these notions, explicitly intending to present something new, a new perspective on transition, where transitions must be envisioned in governance, and transitions require collective strategy. Within this context a transition strategy will have to be a governance strategy. It will require a reconfiguration of governance to achieve the ambitious goals for the social-ecological system.

What transpires, from the vantage point of this chapter, is that defining transitions in a narrow or technical sense makes little sense. Transitions thinking needs to be big thinking, generous thinking, allowing for variation in the nature and pathways of transitions, and the tools deployed. Put simply: some big problems do call for big strategy, for a coordinated societal change on a large scale, and this we can call transition. Several transitions might be going on at the same time, and this multiplicity of developments might be associated with recognized governance domains, or not (Andersen et al., 2020; Artioli et al., 2017; Sýkora & Bouzarovski, 2012; Teschner et al., 2012). If transitions are not linked to recognized governance domains, the steering of transitions, let alone the coordination of several transitions, increases in difficulty. Some of the already occurring, possibly observed, transitions will be more coordinated than others. Top-down, bottom-up, same-level and mixed initiatives combine.

Transition can lead to reinvention, but not necessarily so. It can enhance resilience, but this is not always the case, as it can introduce new rigidities, can be limited to one domain, and can envision a rebuilding of systems rather than enhancing adaptive capacity (Fischer-Kowalski & Rotmans, 2009). Transitions can focus on sustainability, but not always do so. We would argue that transitions, in the context of contemporary society, *should* consider sustainability, in a social and ecological sense. Transitions come with major risks. The limits of strategy, of coordination, of learning and adaptation, and of democracy, are regularly tested. Not everything can be understood, forecasted and integrated, and communities are not easily persuaded if identity narratives, central values, or livelihoods are affected (Meyer & Geschiere, 1999). Each recipe and each choice of focus and tools carries such risks, and knowledge of the governance system supposed to carry out the transition, the dependencies, blind spots, instabilities and tensions in governance are key. Transition naturally engenders the risk to simplify governance and society in the name of urgency, speed, efficiency, or moral superiority. This, however, can undermine differentiation in governance and community and might put pressure on checks and balances (Roth & Valentinov, 2020; Scholz, 2017; Valentinov, 2014).

Despite such risks, there is agreement in the literatures that transitions are needed, that the current governance systems are not equipped to deal with the problems of our time (Fischer-Kowalski & Rotmans, 2009; Loorbach, 2009; Schaffartzik et al., 2014; Van Assche, Beunen, et al., 2020; Voß & Bornemann, 2011). Tough situations call for transitions. The risks of doing nothing, or continuing business as usual, are greater than the risks of transition, of pushing the boundaries of governance and stepping on toes in society. Of course, those boundaries might be tested, but the depth of understanding of boundaries, and the location and sensitivity of whose toes are where, make a difference. Many expertly crafted sustainability strategies, however, end up on a shelf, or bring about their own demise, by not grasping informality, affect, identity, values and power/knowledge relations. Lastly, a transition is likely to face critiques, resistance and backlash, topics we discuss separately in the following chapter.

Whatever is endeavored, basic questions need to be asked. Who decides that a transition is needed? Who chooses the nature and direction of the transition? Who can deliberate what kind of problem or opportunity warrants a transition? We argue that there is no objective neutral description available of a problem imposing itself as a reason for transition. Problems are always defined in the social part of social-ecological systems. People recognize things as problems or opportunities, and they are the ones who are convinced change of a more radical nature is needed. This can be based on felt scarcities, scarcity of things valued, of things deemed hard to replace, a collective assessment which can be based on changing values and narratives, on routines or lifestyles finding resistance, running into trouble. New ideologies can cast a new light on old lifestyles and forms of organization. A new metaphor might gain traction, diffuse itself into all more areas of thinking and later decision-making. Old habits might spark new affects in polarized ways: new narratives reinterpreted them as terrible, old identities are hardened by this new opposition and the often-implied moral judgments (Penz & Sauer, 2019).

The direction of the transition (towards a specific goal) might be clear, or less so. A direction might be seemingly clear, but continuing debate leads to the unraveling of master signifiers and productive fictions (Newman, 2004). Agreement dissolves into disagreement over facts, values, priorities and definitions when details and decisions come closer. Or, a direction might be clear, but consensus starts to weaken when the realization dawns what the costs of transition might be, the risks, the required change in governance, the burdensome reconstruction of governance. Deep forgetting (see Chapter 9, Looking Forward and Back), marginality, trauma and inequality can contribute to a multiplication of blind spots in governance, so the need for transition remains invisible (Esposito, 2008; Feischmidt, 2020; Legg, 2007).

Transition can be a rhetorical tool and ploy. The need for change, and change itself, can be amped up rhetorically, to gain power, or to maintain power. Even if the intention is the pursuit of a public good, such rhetorical tactics are risky and irresponsible. When a more sincere attempt at transition announces itself, public trust might be missing. The lack of support for climate policy that can be observed in many places shows that tackling environmental problems and realizing transitions is anything but self-evident (Drews & van den Bergh, 2016; Geels, 2013; Kulin et al., 2021). Moreover, the rhetoric is likely to increase polarization, which renders any form of future coordination more difficult (see earlier) (Dear, 1989; Throgmorton, 1996).

Beyond superficiality, transition can be embraced in contradictory ways, and the contradiction can be conscious or not. People inside and outside governance tend to gloss over contradictions, if it suits them or if it fits their values, ideologies and interests (Antonacopoulou & Gabriel, 2001; Lapping, 2020). Contradictions can be accepted when the promise is great, when the problem is urgent, when it allows the combination of values or activities which are truly incompatible, when it enables the formation of coalitions and compromises which cannot really cohere. Everything is local, yet global; all decision-making will be participatory, yet expert-driven; we pursue sustainability but build pipelines; we empathize with indigenous people, but not when they're on the street and called homeless.

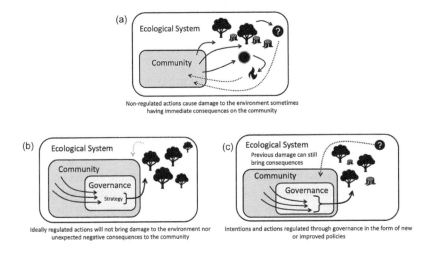

Figure 11.1   A transition strategy will need to be a governance strategy[1]

Governance Gaps?

Strategy for transition can be associated with perceived governance gaps. Gaps might have been discovered through self-analysis, through external critique or

---

[1]   (a) With weak or non-existent coordination of actions towards the environment the environmental outcomes of our actions will be more difficult to trace. Non-coordinated or non-regulated actions can have a series of effects that directly affect the community or that affect other elements in the ecological system which in turn indirectly affect the community. (b) Ideally all actions towards the ecological system can be observed in their effects and regulated through governance and there would be little or no negative consequences for ecosystem and community. (c) Realistically, not all actions and effects of human action on the ecosystem are visible and understandable, and the effects of environmental damage on the community are logically even less perfectly visible. Moreover, previous damage to the environment can remain unobserved and contribute to cumulative effects which become visible only when a threshold is crossed, and a material event occurs.

through confrontation with new problems. Those gaps can be spatial (an area that is weakly governed; the ocean, a war zone, for example). Gaps can also be conceptual or thematic (think of artificial intelligence or genetic engineering). Gaps can appear as a result of increasing awareness that coordination at new scales is needed (higher/lower level, a missing regional middle). It is also possible that a new mapping of the governance domains, a redrawing of boundaries, is needed in such a way that some topics that are as yet poorly governed can be clearly located on the map. New goals might appear (achieving sustainable futures), new forms of coordination might be aspired to, and all these create gaps.

Yet, as with the recognition of need and urgency and direction of transition, the governance gaps remain a matter of interpretation, an interplay of interpretations where democratic principles and other societal values cannot be thrown overboard without reflection. Urgencies are very real *and* very constructed. Their urgent nature does not constitute an argument for abandoning all principles of good governance, but a stringent application of them. Construction of urgency, of needs for rapid and systemic transition are modes of (often necessary) de-paradoxification (see Chapters 6 and 9). Governance gaps do not exist objectively. Gaps become gaps in a web of interpretations that reflect changing values, needs, anxieties and desires in society. The interpretation of something as a gap that requires filling is of course connected to narratives, values, ideologies (Hinchman & Hinchman, 1997; Žižek, 1989).

What existed before, the old configuration, might not be assessed fairly and perceived accurately. The fact that new stories and semantics and shifting affects are at play might not be observed at all. Merely stating that gaps exist, that nothing existed there before, that a value was simply trampled before, but is now enshrined in the community of a new domain, arena or policy, tends to gloss over the complexity of the old system state, and the complexity of the actual transformation (as opposed to aspired or stated). What existed before might also be exaggerated, perceived as functional when it actually wasn't, presented as inclusive while it wasn't, defended as rational and expert-driven while there were few experts and of the wrong sort. Taking the self-description of governance systems at face value is an additional problem, as it means that the desired transformation, the filling in of a gap, might not start from the base it is to start from. Political and academic rhetoric can start from idealized understandings of the governance system, mixing wish and reality, or of unjust vilifying of configurations, which then creates unrealistic images of governance gaps and of transitions as possible and desirable.

NAVIGATING DILEMMAS

Transitions almost certainly require structural change in governance (Chaffin et al., 2016; Köhler et al., 2019; Meadowcroft, 2011; Patterson et al., 2017). What needs to be changed in governance will depend both on the problem, the ambitions and the goal definitions as well as on the state of the governance system, its modes of learning, roles, institutions, etc. From the perspective of an aspired transition, all features of the social-material configuration, including its governance system, can potentially be changed and adapted. Strategy for transition therefore will have to pursue both internal and external goals, goals pertaining to governance change, which then facilitates social and environmental change. Design choices for institutional structures are on the table, as well as substantive priorities. Trade-offs always occur. Key substantive choices have implications for other decisions, and if governance structures are altered, power/knowledge relations will shift, which means that certain course corrections become harder. We refer to our discussion on adaptive capacity as just one example of such a trade-off. Indeed, adaptive capacity cannot exist as a universal capacity for adaptation, and must be qualitatively defined, as the potential to adapt to one range or matrix of possible situations (Cundill & Fabricius, 2009; Jarzabkowski, 2004). Tinkering with governance is retooling adaptive capacity, even if this was not the intention.

Focusing governance more on a limited set of goals will shift the pattern of policy coordination and integration, role formation and observation of environments, with increased coordination towards one goal necessarily leading to blind spots, and fewer resources elsewhere. Trade-offs, in other words, go beyond increased rigidity (Brans & Rossbach, 1997; Christensen et al., 2016). Choices for one mode of organization create downsides elsewhere, as one structure of the governance configuration, and strong preferences for certain policy tools, or homogenization of explanatory narratives will reduce attention to other functions of the system and responsivity to other signals (Chisholm, 1995; Vermeule, 2007). When transitions are taking place, and governance becomes aware in the middle, conscious and careful choices are not always made, yet even then there is space for deliberation and strategy, for reflexivity and carefully assessing the tightening of focus or change in organization. Patterns of policy integration and dependencies in the governance deserve close scrutiny.

The previous paragraphs indicated that no transition can be perfect. This is not a surprise given the previous chapters and our unfolding argument that perfection and universality in governance, good governance and reform governance cannot exist, as things change all the time, as coordination is never perfect, and as optimization of a system design for function or goal 'A'

Strategy for sustainability transitions

comes with drawbacks elsewhere. We now identify a set of dilemmas that cannot be eliminated, but can be navigated in a transition, with each dilemma representing a point of choice or evolution where trade-offs occur (Elster et al., 1998; Vermeule, 2007). Looking at the whole set of dilemmas can then help to clarify, for actors designing a transition trajectory, and for others in the middle of an unplanned transition, which choices and distinctions are key in system and path, for the understanding of a certain transition in a certain context, its chances of success, and the trade-offs implied.

Path Dependence Versus Path Creation

A transition can count on more radical path creation, breaking of path dependencies, or it can accept path dependencies which can also represent assets, shared values, proven forms of coordination (Ampe et al., 2021; Duineveld et al., 2007; Köhler et al., 2019; Martin & Sunley, 2006). Awareness of the path dependencies, in the pattern of other dependencies, is helpful in this later version. In the first option, the risk is that not all dependencies are considered and that too radical governance transformation is assumed as a starting point for achieving the substantive transition goals. Further, path creation comes with the risk that a radically novel system of governance triggers unanticipated effects inside and outside governance, which can interfere with the transition goals (Mascio et al., 2020; Van Assche, Duineveld, et al., 2020). It is also possible that resistance and backlash will appear in the process of path creation (see Chapter 12). Conversely, accepting too many path dependencies, for pragmatic reasons (Haikola & Anshelm, 2022) or because of limited reflexivity, can mean that no real transition takes place.

Long Term Versus Short Term

Even for transition paths where one could assume a longer time horizon, the short-term versus long-term distinction remains relevant, not only because strategy needs tactics, as discussed earlier, but also because even a strong embrace of a long-term perspective can still see this parceled up in governance practice, in small tasks with short time horizons (MacKenzie, 2021; Van Dijk, 2006). In differentiated systems, this can be expected, but what can happen, or can be designed, is the practical disappearance of the long term in daily compartmentalized decision-making, driven by sub-goals and sub-topics, short-term targets and highly selective monitoring and assessment. Just as reflexivity can make the most difference when it is widespread and active, long-term perspectives can only make a difference when they are understood and considered widely (reducing the risks of functional stupidity). Where a transition is already under way, without much strategy, introducing long-term

Different transition paths in the community

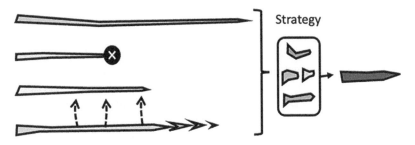

Figure 11.2   Strategy coordinating transitions[2]

perspectives and policy tools in its favor can enable more future steering of transition (Beunen & Barba Lata, 2021; Boston, 2021). Over-reliance on long-term perspectives is real too, as (and we know this) what is possible in terms of organizing and thinking for the long term in the system is limited, unique, and these limits must be grasped before establishing new expectations for the performance of new long-term perspectives.

Flexibility Versus Rigidity

This dilemma we discussed at length elsewhere, yet it bears repetition in the context of transition design and transition awareness. Transition goals and strategies quickly introduce new rigidities, through advanced policy integration and narrowing of focus of governance (Andersen et al., 2020; Persson et al., 2016; Scholz, 2017). Power/knowledge configurations will alter as actors

---

[2]   In any given place, a number of transitions might be in progress at the same time. Some might continue their path uninterrupted, others can be halted or terminated, yet others might interfere with each other. This can result in mutual support, modification, or in one of them being canceled out. Others might peter out, slowly lose traction, or fade under backlash and disappear. Transition strategies ought to be informed by such patterns of simultaneous partial transitions. Ideally, they revive what was lost but valuable, in terms of transition goals and tools, and combine partial transitions into an overarching perspective. In this effort, assessment of what was intended as strategy, what could be amenable to steering, and what was simply labeled strategy, deserves attention.

associated with the transition will move to the center, limiting the importance of other perspectives, other forms of knowledge, and other actors (Murdoch & Clark, 1994). Old departments or ministries must reinvent themselves and adjust to new roles, or new organizations can monopolize discourse on transition, and become the center of coordination.

We know that flexibility and rigidity co-exist, that neither is good or bad per se, and that each combination of rigidity and flexibility represents a different set of pros and cons for a governance system; while a pro or con will work out as such only in a particular situation. Ambitious transition strategies, however, driven by a sense of urgency, often emphasize tight and novel forms of policy integration, fixed targets, goals, time frames and other new rigidities. Easily overlooked is the reshuffling of the government environment resulting from the strategy, the goal dependencies which in turn can affect rigidity and reality effects. Broadening reflexivity, diversifying learning and widening the range of adaptive capacity embodies a different strategic choice.

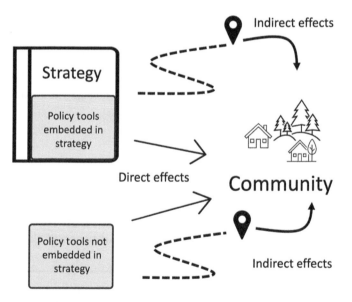

Figure 11.3   Strategy coordinating policy tools[3]

---

[3]   Policy tools can have direct or indirect effects in the community. Indirect effects can appear through interaction with other policies, other tools, and resonances in the social and ecological environment. They can be or not be embedded in strategy. Strategy will serve a coordinating function, coordinating other policies, coordinating the narrative and institutions, with the aim of coordinating action in the community. Strategy itself can also have direct or indirect effects in the community.

Fast Response Versus Slow Response (to Change)

Adaptive capacity is qualitatively different in each situation, not only in terms of the kinds of signals implied, the types of changes recognized, and the variation of answers provided, but also in terms of the speed of response. The capacity to respond quickly to certain things, not others, and the choice for routine fast versus slow response for some issues and topics, makes a difference in defining adaptive capacity (Hobbs, 2020; Mascio et al., 2020). The flexibility in navigating a transition path comes from observational capacity and adaptive capacity, which includes a selectivity in fast and slow responses. If the terrain navigated is rugged, if the system governing the transition needs to be aware of continuously changing findings in the environment and rapid responses to interventions emanating from the strategy, then fast responses can be favored. Policy tools with short procedures, scarce input, assessment, deliberation and simple coordination can be utilized for rapid response to changes that come fast but are not perceived to be qualitatively very different. If a new type of change occurs, then more elaborate and slow system responses can be prepared.

We discussed earlier the benefits of slowness, of anchoring institutions and the impossibility of defining a perfect balance between fast and slow, and, similar to the remarks above about rigidity, we have to say that transition strategies can be such anchoring institutions, of great value for steering the course, and at great risk since the pattern of fast and slow response tends to become ossified.

Differentiation Versus De-differentiation

The previous dilemmas can be linked to the sometimes-tragic choice between differentiation and de-differentiation, where de-differentiation is often an alluring path for those wanting to get things done faster, to steer more firmly, and for those who believe in rational systems of knowledge integration underpinning rational comprehensive policy integration (Esmark, 2009). Differentiation, in other words, is problematic for all those who see the need to change, the direction and the tools required, and who have difficulties convincing others, in complex, slow, plodding, democratic complex systems full of strife and quarrel. Differentiation is a major headache for designers, proponents and managers of transitions, yet it is also their greatest asset, as differentiation allows for more specialized observations, and more intricate coordination of organizations with specialized skills, irreplaceable for any attempt to move a community or society through a self-transformation while rebuilding its steering mechanisms (Luhmann, 2006).

Centralized Versus Decentralized

Centralized steering, and centrally planned and managed transition strategies, can be combined with decentralized steering, as with rigidity and flexibility, and fast and slow, but, as with the other distinctions, there are choices to be made (Englebert & Mungongo, 2016; Kvalsund, 2009). At system level, centralization and decentralization are even likely to be combined, as not everything can be centralized, and as the myth of the pyramidal government is indeed a myth. Saying that governance always existed and that power works at and across all levels is saying that pure centralization is a fiction. This being said, at subsystem level, for certain domains, arenas, topics, departments and policy tools, things have to be either centralized or decentralized. Modifiers might exist, as when a central administration or government establishes local offices, yet the balance between participation and representation, between local and higher levels, will still be different from truly localized systems. A transition strategy might be centralized itself, but still must operate in a governance environment which it cannot transform completely; hence, the pattern of centralization and decentralization of the governance system will constrain the strategy options.

Formal Versus Informal

We know that formal and informal institutions co-exist, shape each other, and can relate in various ways. We also reiterate that what needs to be assessed is not informality, but the configuration of formal and informal institutions. Transition strategy, in other words, cannot ignore informality, and ought to be informed by the interplay between formal and informal. This means that the strategy itself can have informal aspects, can rely on or attempt to create new informal institutions or actors, or it can carefully craft new formality, less affected by informal actors and institutions.

Transition leadership familiar with formal-informal relations must guide the process, and unanticipated interplay with informal institutions might require adaptation. An intervention aiming to support transition might be perceived as about something else, or might confirm a negative judgment about administration, and activate informal institutions coordinating the topic not intended by the strategist. Dilemmas will occur, as formality might appear as the easier route, or the more rational or certain path, especially when many experts and administrations are involved, who tend to take the formal self-description of the system for granted. Conversely, arranging interests informally might look more attractive, or old-fashioned bullying, yet if formality is too sparsely used, or lost legitimacy because of its informal emergence, this can weaken the strategy.

Expert Knowledge Versus Local Knowledge

Transitions tend to be technically complex, drawing in a variety of experts. Competition between experts and their organizations can ensue, inside governance and towards governance, for a role in defining the focus, direction and means of the transition (Van Assche & Hornidge, 2015). Unobserved goal dependencies are common in such a process, as the promise of power and resources is considerable. Governance shifts will occur that are not intended by strategy, not resulting from deliberate decisions at governance reform for enabling the transition. Meanwhile, local knowledge is easily marginalized where it had a position, and new local knowledge enters the system only, if at all, through the narrow selectivity of transition topics (Herbert-Cheshire & Higgins, 2004). Marginalizing local knowledge comes with the usual drawbacks of downgrading local implementation, adaptation and correction, while undermining local support and reducing connectivity with helpful informal institutions (Teampau & Van Assche, 2009). Relying largely on local knowledge to garner support, to connect to existing problem definitions in the community, will prove tricky as well, as the relevance of larger scales, technical issues and their relations, as well as the steering limitations in governance, might not be immediately apparent. As with the other dilemmas, the two sides of the distinction are routinely combined, but a perfect balance does not exist, is not even knowable for one situation, and as soon as one aspect of governance is organized according to one side of the distinction, the other side becomes invisible, and inaccessible in organizational terms (Ponte & Cheyns, 2013).

LEARNING AND ASSETS

Navigating transitions puts pressure on learning in governance. As ambitions are high, learning for adaptive strategy is at a premium, while maintaining the course is simultaneously emphasized, both inside and outside the system. There are no easy solutions, as can be expected. Transition strategists and public proponents must tread carefully, in not overpromising, not rendering the productive fiction unbelievable, not combining opposites for the sake of rhetoric and coalition building. One can argue that routines, maybe unquestioned for a long time, might have to become more open to scrutiny, that cultivation of reflexivity comes at a premium. Possibly, transitional forms of governance (see below) might be warranted, including temporarily intensified and diversified participation. This does not eliminate the problem, as increased reflexivity and participation can also create more pressure towards continuous adaptation and towards a rethinking of basic choices and assumptions. As often, enhancing observation and encouraging questioning leads to more answers, but also to new questions. Finding the balance between adaptation and staying the course does not come easily; learning modes will have to be finely crafted to contribute to this endeavor.

If efficiency or austerity discourse takes over ('enough experiment – now let's get serious') or a backlash against transition appears ('enough of this nonsense'), or if a very singular focus on one form of policy integration is maintained, shifting the balance between rigidity and flexibility will prove harder, and adjusting learning processes to that end even more so. This meta-dilemma of transition makes *redundancy* even more important. It requires cognitive and organizational resources that can be accessed at short notice in order to manage the uncertainty accompanying transitions (Bendor, 1985; Felsenthal, 1980; Hobbs, 2020; Miranda & Lerner, 2001).

A tolerance of redundancy, of expertise and of learning sites and modes is a great virtue in articulating and navigating transition paths. Redundancy, possibly increased temporarily through more intense local and expert participation, is just like adaptive capacity and reflexivity, qualitatively different in each system (Bendor, 1985; Duit & Galaz, 2008; Low et al., 2003). It is to a degree amenable to institutional design, which means that it can be pre-structured to support an envisioned transition process. In small government ideologies, this will not be popular. Redundancies in memory infrastructure, expertise and policy tools can serve as a catalyst for diversifying learning processes and for finding new connectivity between them (Gable & Meier, 2013). Meanwhile, demand for learning in transitions can vary dramatically, and the required or invoked forms of governance learning can switch swiftly. Comparative learning, expert learning, reflexive learning, experimental learning and dialectical learning can all be mobilized in transition strategies, in their preparation and implementation. While key decisions in the articulation phase might be more easily recognized as requiring dialectical learning, this form of learning cannot be omitted later, as transition strategies cannot be routinized or left to administration. We are dealing with a dramatic change in course, affecting many aspects of life, requiring collective effort and investment, hence building insight, and creating solutions through discussion and debate cannot be relegated to the margins.

Reflexivity, expertise and comparisons can be mobilized and intensified in the process of continuous assessment and adaptation during implementation. Not all expertise has to be present in governance, nor in administration at all times, and not all expertise has to be designated as 'transition expertise' (Bendor, 1985; van Mierlo & Beers, 2020). Universities, businesses, citizen scientists or specialized NGOs can contribute more easily if connected to the transition process, either throughout, with clear roles in the process design, or through a multiplicity of participation events. Uncertainty and a desire to increase participation might make experimental learning attractive, but it is worth noticing that the transition itself cannot be treated as an experiment. One cannot wait, see what happens, and try something else. If this is the attitude, there is no serious transition attempt. Transition strategies might enhance their own adaptivity *and* steering capacity (for adaptation and maintaining a course) by explicitly embedding their governance reform agenda to rethink the learning potential of the governance system. This means that whatever change to the system is considered, the implications for learning capacity are considered. It is also possible to reconfigure learning modes by changing the way each learning mode is situated in processes and organizational structures, in arenas and domains, considering how they can be more productively connected (towards dialectical learning), and then contemplating the implications for governance reform (always with the intended transition in mind).

We do encounter a weakness of the transition concept itself. A transition is not a thing with one aim, one shape, one procedure and temporality. Nevertheless, the previous paragraphs did make the case that the transition concept does have an analytic as well as a rhetorical and political value. Transition might always be a multiplicity of processes, in governance and society, some more tightly coupled than others, and a multiplicity with such staggering diversity of manifestations that the unity of the concept can be questioned (Feola & Jaworska, 2019; Hodson et al., 2017; Lawhon & Murphy, 2012; Loewen, 2022). Yet in our current era, a consensus did emerge that major overhauls of governance and society, a rethinking of livelihoods and lifestyles, of our connection to each other and the planet is in order, and a belief that, despite all our limitations, we can imagine and organize alternatives, a process we call transition strategy.

The current consensus on transitions, in its diversity, is that our economies and lifestyles cannot continue to rely on non-renewable natural resources, and that the other resources need to be used and produced in much more sustainable manners. Governance needs assets and resources, and it impacts the creation, use and distribution of assets and resources in the community. Assets and resources do not exist in the abstract, however. They become this in the context of social-ecological systems that assign value and meaning and organize extraction, production and use (Berkes et al., 2002; Underwood & Friesner, 2017). Assets are further shaped by producing futures, by their position in a story about the future. Something becomes an asset in a perspective, and that perspective can be created, altered or undermined. What counted as normal, as of little value, or as highly valuable will shift in a de-carbonized perspective. A transition strategy, in other words, will erode and undermine, yet also create assets. This process of asset creation through future creation can be explored more productively if more different perspectives are around the table (Haikola & Anshelm, 2022; Hermans et al., 2016; Turnheim & Geels, 2012).

Dependence on resources and their economies makes transition both necessary and difficult. Transition of this sort needs to focus on breaking path dependencies and interdependencies, yet this must start from a recognition of such dependencies in governance. The dependencies shape the learning modes of the system, and the modes of self-transformation (Lawrie et al., 2011; Marquardt & Nasiritousi, 2022; Van Assche et al., 2014). A key question is how to use some dependencies to change others, as leverage points. Inspiration in answering this question can come from careful analysis of the governance path. One value, one narrative, one trusted coordination mechanism, one functional arena can be used to question false certainties, bring in new problem definitions and deconstruct habits, lifestyles and other values (Van Assche & Hornidge, 2015). Management of this sort is not technical management, but, especially in democratic settings, an art of the possible, of respecting roles, narratives and identities and acknowledging affect, while pushing against them when the collective good is clear and demands it. One narrative can be used to cast a new light on another one, and new narratives can be forged, other affects invoked, to bring home the seriousness of the situation and the reality of alternatives.

As a means to finding sources of income, some indigenous communities in the Amazon region have established tourism operations. For many it has been a successful venture; for others a big disappointment. They are challenged with connectivity issues (no internet or cell phone networks) and also lack of technological expertise (setting up a website or an e-mail account). Perhaps more significant is the difference between indigenous and non-indigenous ways of organizing, of collectively deciding and assigning tasks, distribution of benefits, etc. Although many local and higher-level governments are on board with tourism development in the region as an alternative to other less environmentally friendly economic activities such as cattle ranching or agriculture expansion, they are blind to the context of many indigenous communities in the region, to their way of self-organizing and understanding organization. We can add to this the differences between indigenous and non-indigenous narratives in relation to the environment which are, for indigenous people, tightly coupled to their identity.

Documents with an expected strategic function

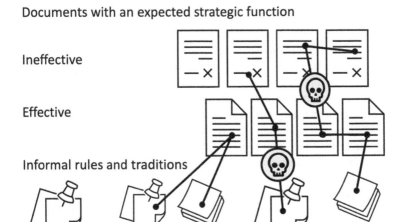

Ineffective

Effective

Informal rules and traditions

Figure 11.4   Connections between ineffective and effective strategic documents and informal rules and traditions[4]

TECHNICALITIES

Fragmentation

Transition strategy will most likely be toned to overcome fragmentation in governance (see Chapter 4, Governance Paths as History and Infrastructure for Transition), and in order to utilize the coordinative capacity of governance it will have to improve cohesion. If the parts of the machine that are supposed to engage each other are disconnected, its full power cannot be accessed. The spatial/temporal shard structure of governance represents a form of fragmentation which cannot, per definition, be overcome. The structure can only be reshuffled, as shards will always be there. The selectivities of knowledge and organizing do not allow for a complete coverage of the world by governance, and prevent us from realistically seeing the world as a puzzle and governance as a way to see and finish the puzzle (Gruezmacher & Van Assche, 2022; Van Assche, Gruezmacher, et al., 2022; Van Assche, Gruezmacher, et al., 2020).

---

[4]   Documents that are expected to have a strategic function may be ineffective, might be left on the shelf, but might still have connections to other strategic documents that are actually effective. In some cases, strategic documents can be supported by informal institutions enhancing their effectiveness. Elsewhere, strategic documents can conflict with other formal institutions, and with informalities which can restrict or modify their effects (represented here by a skull).

A second form of fragmentation, discussed earlier, is the lack of cohesion between existing governance tools, which can aggravate if this loose coupling allows tools to follow their own evolutionary path when they shouldn't. This form of fragmentation can be largely remedied, as we know, and the appearance of a transition strategy itself can help in this remedy of improved coordination and partial retooling. Fragmentation is an obstacle for strategy, yet strategy can help to overcome fragmentation.

Fixing fragmentation, improving cohesion towards improved coordination, can slide into simplification of governance under the banner of efficiency. Rendering governance more cohesive does not need to imply such simplification. The temptation might be there, as what is unified is more cohesive and integrated, and what is abolished cannot stand in the way of coordination. Such a path, we know, leads to de-differentiation and will see redundancy as wasteful complexity. A more helpful approach, maintaining differentiation and flexibility, is to understand the effort as we did in Chapter 4, as a systematic tracing of obstacles for strategy which stem from overly loose couplings between institutions, between topics, between domains. Too loose has a technical meaning, as the lack of reference, coordination or integration where other institutions and implied functionality require so.

Integration

Formation of strategy is per definition policy integration, as a new institution emerges which coordinates others (Baker Associates & O'Rourke, 2008). Here we do not speak of promoting the integration of one topic (say, environmental impact) in all topics, sites, arenas, domains, but of finding new forms of coordination between them (Candel & Biesbroek, 2016; Van Assche, Hornidge, et al., 2020). Potentially anything can be harnessed towards transition strategy. This means that transition strategies will have to deal with, or alter, existing patterns of policy integration and coordination. This further means that some organizational structures might have to be rethought, as they embody and further a pattern of knowledge integration and policy integration which might stand in the way of the envisioned transition (engineers and accountants in charge of all city departments, public works in charge of environmental planning). As always, an organizational structure has pros and cons, makes it harder to see and organize alternatives, and can create problems for transition (Jordan & Lenschow, 2010).

Transition strategies are ambitious in terms of policy integration, as otherwise they will not work. If transition remains a separate domain of governance, an institutional experiment in the margin, it has little value. Yet, as we know, the ambition comes with risks, and here the technicalities of policy integration, of transition overriding existing patterns of integration, of an overall furthering of policy integration towards a goal so important that it binds everything and everyone, are important (Biesbroek, 2021). If transition strategies do not take into consideration the existing (formal and informal) pattern of policy integration, its functionalities and benefits, and if they do not recognize the effort it took to come to some of the existing integration modes, then one cannot assess the investment needed to come to a new form of integration, nor the risks this process of breaking and rebuilding integration will carry (Peters, 2018). Once again, reflexive and dialectical learning can minimize such risks, with input from internal and external experts (Lockhart, 1982; Voß & Bornemann, 2011).

In order to make sense, policies (and other institutions) that are tightly integrated (maybe because of transition strategy) require an ordering principle. This can be a rule, a theme, a concept which can then generate a first ordering *structure*, which can be conceptual, organizational, spatial or temporal, and most likely a combination of those. One type of structure often engenders a different type – conceptual structure triggers emergence of spatial structure and temporal order. If several ordering principles are at work, one can speak of a first ordering principle when this provides the first level of order, of organization, after which and around which the other principles generate structure (Van Assche et al., 2014).

A first ordering principle can be deliberately chosen, and it can emerge from the functioning of governance. Transition strategy will want to champion a first ordering principle and persuade governance and community of the need to rethink old orders and hierarchies, whether they were products of accident, of actors' strategies or of communal deliberation (Rode, 2019). Such promoted choice can be climate change, overriding all other concerns, or providing a first goal, and a first conceptual order to develop other policies and coordinate them. If climate change is the focus of transition, a first ordering structure can be inspired by the conceptual hierarchies in climate science, where other forms of knowledge need to be translated into climate adaptation terms, and linked to those concerns, or become relegated to a less structured margin of governance. Other forms of knowledge can remain outside the strategy, be under less pressure, but also receive less attention and impact. A different situation can reveal that water management provides the first ordering principle, that water flows and bodies come first, while climate change, spatial planning and economic development must be coordinated according to the logic of water management. This, then, could lead to a spatial structure of water that determines which activity comes where.

WHERE IS TRANSITION STRATEGY LOCATED?

For administrations, for governance systems generally, it is tempting to make big pronouncements and then tweak them a little. Such can be expected, as the logic of politics favors big stories and sweeping statements (whether they are conservative or advocate change), while the logic of administration dictates gentle reform, self-transformation which does not disrupt the gradually evolved modes of coordination and evolution which we can call highly improbable (following Luhmann, 1995). A painfully fought victory of order over the forces of dissipation (King & Thornhill, 2006; Luhmann, 1993, 2018). As governance is both politics and administration, this contradiction becomes an internal tension, which cannot be structurally resolved. Governance will continue to produce narratives and promises that cannot be achieved through the current configuration, and stories about governance reform which underestimate the difficulties, overestimate the benefits of the reform (Christensen & Lægreid, 2003; Christensen & Lwogreid, 1998).

One cannot resolve this tension and simplify the explanation by distinguishing between 'politics' before governance and then governance itself, as the process of decision-making. Similarly, referring to the decision process as executive, legislative, or both, does not solve much. The roles of executive, legislative and judicial differ per polity, and, more fundamentally, the process of decision-making which we call governance, *always* blends politics in the narrow sense and administration (Van Assche, Beunen, et al., 2022; Van Assche et al., 2013, 2021). We speak of governance as politics in the broad sense, as it is in and through the configurations that communities can see themselves as unity (and diversity) and shape their future. Our understanding of the co-evolving configurations highlights that governance is per definition dealing with irresolvable tensions, which become visible in always unstable role patterns, imperfect institutions and unpredictable discursive dynamics (Peters et al., 2022; Solomon, 2010).

Ultimately, the different logics of politics and administration, the inconsistency and opacity of thinking, and the imperfect matching of thinking and organizing make governance both unstable and productive. Governance is *forced* to incorporate these tensions, as it is obliged to come up with big stories (not only before elections, not only outside the sphere of governance) that can persuade and drive new forms of coordination, and is obliged to make it work, to make it fit into slowly evolved patterns of coordination.

Where does that leave us with regards to the location of transition strategy? Transitions and their strategies test the limits of governance, and the mechanisms to reconcile its inherent contradictions. This is a different way of revealing the risks coming with transition. Transition strategies must be big and bold in order to convince enough people that change is necessary yet possible. They must reshape imaginaries, forge new coalitions, step on toes (see following chapter), manage uncertainty in a manner that is technically impossible, yet they are expected to reshuffle governance in such a way that adaptive strategy becomes possible, that the imaginary keeps its attraction.

This, in our view, means that the formulation, implementation and assessment of transition strategy cannot be in the same hands everywhere, and that they cannot be outsourced or relegated to specialized administrative departments. Relegation in administration can take a few forms and all are problematic. One is relying on consultants, who are not familiar enough with the community and its governance system and do not have enough time to remedy this (Fincham, 1999). Another one is relying on academics, who might have more time but are similarly unfamiliar with the intricacies of local governance and community sentiment (Lockhart, 1982). Both options rely on comparative learning and expert learning by outsiders and from outsiders, without enhancing reflexive and dialectical learning much. A third and fourth form of relegation are delegation to administration, either for the strategy as whole (articulation and/or implementation), or leaning more directly on differentiation, politicians and other non-administrative actors sending projects and themes framed by the strategy directly to specialized departments. All four options de-politicize transition strategy.

Because of the complexities and risks of transition, because of the time frames and investments involved, because of the tinkering with identities that is implied, de-politicization is not a good idea (Meadowcroft, 2011). It appears to reduce risks, as it looks like rational decision-making, staying the course, and leaving complexity to the experts. However, for transitions it will increase risks, as what is moving behind the scenes is too important and potentially too aggravating for the community; hence, our proposal not only to keep political what is political now, but also to *re-politicize* what has been relegated to administrative experts and procedures. A new look at the whole system is in place, and everybody should be invited to look (Scoones et al., 2015). Articulation, implementation and assessment of the strategy ought to be integrated into politics, become the object of governance, the object of decision-making (and not merely preparation or implementation). Thus, governance does become messier, as what was not expected to be discussed now requires discussion, and as what was formerly left to representation now requires participation.

Re-politization can take diverse forms, and the options will, as usual, be shaped by the range of possible adaptations and modes of self-transformation of the governance system. An elected council can focus on the transition strategy, more local committees can provide input to politicians and administration, participation opportunities can grow in number, scope and intensity, experts can be brought into discussions in participatory settings, as well as in elected arenas. One can note here that expertise does not need to be downplayed under re-politization. As Machiavelli pointed out, it is entirely possible to have strong and active citizens in a strong and active state (Machiavelli, 2012; Van Assche et al., 2016).

The learning capacities of the system will have to be increased and reflected upon (see earlier, on memory and on learning). This can then can assist in guiding the system through a phase in which it is forced to confront its external complexity, and likely increase that complexity, to address major challenges and invent new modes of coordination to that aim (Van Assche, Beunen, et al., 2022). As governance transformation most likely accompanies and reinforces transition strategy, the exercise of goal-setting is double: we are inventing a future desired state of society (sometimes reduced to negative goals of reducing a problem, sometimes combining positive and negative goals in more detail) and a new governance configuration which is hoped to bring us there.

TRANSITIONAL GOVERNANCE AND INCREASED PARTICIPATION

Honesty requires us to say that the options described above are not realistic for each and every polity; hence, the utility of what we call *transitional governance*. Transitional governance is not the governance of transitions, but a temporary form of governance, for situations in which a grand strategy is needed but the direction is less clear (Gruezmacher & Van Assche, 2022; Van Assche et al., 2017; Van Assche, Duineveld, et al., 2020). It might be clear that the community is not sustainable, but 'sustainability transition' does not mean much, or does not provide direction or suggest content. In such cases, when routines do not work, and there is an awareness that radical change is needed, it might be useful to consider a temporary form of governance. Defining and presenting it transparently and unambiguously as temporary is of the essence, as confusion can undermine the legitimacy of the effort from the start (González Ocantos, 2014; Lockwood et al., 2017).

Increased participation can be part of it, intense, broad and deep self-reflection and self-analysis in governance and community can be the face of transitional governance. Sometimes, this can take the character of community therapy, as when trauma and histories of marginalization, of dependence on one authority, on one resource, have blinded communities to the reality of their own situation (see earlier). The scale of the community makes a difference, the complexity of administration and governance, the depth of forgetting and the scope of blind spots.

One could interject that, if the future deemed desirable and realistic cannot be imagined yet, then the desirable state of the governance system might not be within grasp (Lockwood, 2018). This cannot be denied, but it does not render the idea of transitional governance impossible. In concrete situations, not everything is and can be questioned with regards to governance and the community future; partial agreement does exist and can be the basis of further learning and transformation. If transitional governance configurations are, in essence, platforms that enable a community to see and organize more, to increase its governance capacity in its different dimensions (see earlier), they still must enable self-transformation towards the desired state of governance and they have to emerge from the present and limited state of the configuration. Working with what we have then means both working with the areas of agreement, regarding future and governance, and working with the governance capacities of the current system.

In one place, the agreement can be on a negative (reduce a risk, clean up something, transform a dependency), while elsewhere it is a positive. The positive can be a seemingly objective quantitative goal, but, as with the negatives, is most likely hiding suppressed master-signifiers, which inspire narratives of fear, hope or resignation. Even where internal divisions are fierce and stubborn, common ground for a rebuilding towards transition can be found, even when this is a piece of infrastructure, missing according to all, a basic service restored, an amenity sorely missing, or a form of expertise acknowledged as relevant. It can be a role, now unfulfilled, yet existing before or observed elsewhere: Why don't we have an economic development specialist? Why not an economic development department?

REFERENCES

Ampe, K., Paredis, E., Asveld, L., Osseweijer, P. & Block, T. (2021). Power struggles in policy feedback processes: Incremental steps towards a circular economy within Dutch wastewater policy. *Policy Sciences*, *54*(3), 579–607. https://doi.org/10.1007/s11077-021-09430-6

Andersen, A. D., Steen, M., Mäkitie, T., Hanson, J., Thune, T. M. & Soppe, B. (2020). The role of inter-sectoral dynamics in sustainability transitions: A comment on the transitions research agenda. *Environmental Innovation and Societal Transitions*, *34*, 348–351. https://doi.org/10.1016/j.eist.2019.11.009

Anderson, L. (1999). *Transitions to democracy.* Columbia University Press.

Antonacopoulou, E. P. & Gabriel, Y. (2001). Emotion, learning and organizational change: Towards an integration of psychoanalytic and other perspectives. *Journal of Organizational Change Management*, *14*(5), 435–451. https://doi.org/10.1108/EUM0000000005874

Armitage, D. (2008). Governance and the commons in a multi-level world. *International Journal of the Commons*, *2*(1), 7–32.

Artioli, F., Acuto, M. & McArthur, J. (2017). The water-energy-food nexus: An integration agenda and implications for urban governance. *Political Geography*, *61*, 215–223. https://doi.org/10.1016/j.polgeo.2017.08.009

Avelino, F. & Rotmans, J. (2009). Power in transition: An interdisciplinary framework to study power in relation to structural change. *European Journal of Social Theory*, *12*(4), 543–569. https://doi.org/10.1177/1368431009349830

Baker Associates & O'Rourke, T. (2008). *Participation and policy integration in spatial planning. Spatial plans in practice: Supporting the reform of local planning.* Department for Communities and Local Development.

Bendor, J. (1985). *Parallel systems: Redundancy in government*. University of California Press.

Berkes, F., Colding, J. & Folke, C. (eds.) (2002). *Navigating social-ecological systems: Building resilience for complexity and change*. Cambridge University Press. https://doi.org/10.1017/CBO9780511541957

Beunen, R. & Barba Lata, I. (2021). What makes long-term perspectives endure? Lessons from Dutch nature conservation. *Futures*, *126*, 102679. https://doi.org/10.1016/j.futures.2020.102679

Biesbroek, R. (2021). Policy integration and climate change adaptation. *Current Opinion in Environmental Sustainability*, *52*, 75–81. https://doi.org/10.1016/j.cosust.2021.07.003

Boston, J. (2021). Assessing the options for combatting democratic myopia and safeguarding long-term interests. *Futures*, *125*, 102668. https://doi.org/10.1016/j.futures.2020.102668

Brans, M. & Rossbach, S. (1997). The autopoiesis of administrative systems: Niklas Luhmann on public administration and public policy. *Public Administration*, *75*(3), 417–439.

Brondizio, E. S., Ostrom, E. & Young, O. R. (2009). Connectivity and the governance of multilevel social-ecological systems: The role of social capital. *Annual Review of Environment and Resources*, *34*.

Candel, J. J. L. & Biesbroek, R. (2016). Toward a processual understanding of policy integration. *Policy Sciences*, *49*(3), 211–231. https://doi.org/10.1007/s11077-016-9248-y

Chaffin, B. C., Garmestani, A. S., Gunderson, L. H., Benson, M. H., Angeler, D. G., Arnold, C. A. (Tony), Cosens, B., Craig, R. K., Ruhl, J. B. & Allen, C. R. (2016). Transformative environmental governance. *Annual Review of Environment and Resources*, *41*(1), 399–423. https://doi.org/10.1146/annurev-environ-110615-085817

Cheung, T. T. T. & Oßenbrügge, J. (2020). Governing urban energy transitions and climate change: Actions, relations and local dependencies in Germany. *Energy Research & Social Science*, *69*, 101728. https://doi.org/10.1016/j.erss.2020.101728

Chisholm, D. (1995). Problem solving and institutional design. *Journal of Public Administration Research and Theory*, *5*(4), 451–492. https://doi.org/10.1093/oxfordjournals.jpart.a037259

Christensen, T. & Lægreid, P. (2003). Administrative reform policy: The challenges of turning symbols into practice. *Public Organization Review*, *3*(1), 3–27. https://doi.org/10.1023/A:1023002810428

Christensen, T. & Lwogreid, P. (1998). Administrative reform policy: The case of Norway. *International Review of Administrative Sciences*, *64*(3), 457–475. https://doi.org/10.1177/002085239806400308

Christensen, T., Lægreid, P. & Rykkja, L. H. (2016). Organizing for crisis management: Building governance capacity and legitimacy. *Public Administration Review*, *76*(6), 887–897. https://doi.org/10.1111/puar.12558

Cotilla-Sanchez, E., Hines, P. D. H. & Danforth, C. M. (2012). Predicting critical transitions from time series synchrophasor data. *IEEE Transactions on Smart Grid*, *3*(4), 1832–1840. https://doi.org/10.1109/TSG.2012.2213848

Cundill, G. & Fabricius, C. (2009). Monitoring in adaptive co-management: Toward a learning based approach. *Journal of Environmental Management*, *90*(11), 3205–3211.

Deacon, L., Candlish, J. & Jamwal, A. (2022). Land use policy and community strategy. Factors enabling and hampering integrated local strategy in Alberta, Canada. *Land Use Policy, 118*, 106101. https://doi.org/10.1016/j.landusepol.2022.106101

Dear, M. (1989). Survey 16; Privatization and the rhetoric of planning practice. *Environment and Planning D: Society and Space, 7*(4), 449–462.

Di Gregorio, M., Fatorelli, L., Paavola, J., Locatelli, B., Pramova, E., Nurrochmat, D. R., May, P. H., Brockhaus, M., Sari, I. M. & Kusumadewi, S. D. (2019). Multi-level governance and power in climate change policy networks. *Global Environmental Change, 54*, 64–77. https://doi.org/10.1016/j.gloenvcha.2018.10.003

Drews, S. & van den Bergh, J. C. J. M. (2016). What explains public support for climate policies? A review of empirical and experimental studies. *Climate Policy, 16*(7), 855–876. https://doi.org/10.1080/14693062.2015.1058240

Duineveld, M., Beunen, R., Ark, R. & Assche, K. (2007). *The difference between knowing the path and walking the path. Over het steeds terugkerend maakbaarheidsdenken in beleidsonderzoek.* Wageningen Universiteit.

Duit, A. & Galaz, V. (2008). Governance and complexity – Emerging issues for governance theory. *Governance, 21*(3), 311–335.

During, R., Van Assche, K. A. M. & Zande, A. N. van der. (2009). Culture, innovation and governance in Europe; Systems theories and the analysis of innovation in INTERREG programs. In K. J. Poppe & K. Termeer (eds.), *Transitions towards sustainable agriculture, food chains in peri-urban areas* (pp. 127–146). Wageningen Academic Publishers.

Elster, J., Offe, C. & Preuss, U. K. (1998). *Institutional design in post-communist societies: Rebuilding the ship at sea.* Cambridge University Press.

Englebert, P. & Mungongo, E. K. (2016). Misguided and misdiagnosed: The failure of decentralization reforms in the DR Congo. *African Studies Review, 59*(1), 5–32. https://doi.org/10.1017/asr.2016.5

Esmark, A. (2009). The functional differentiation of governance: Public governance beyond hierarchy, market and networks. *Public Administration, 87*(2), 351–370. https://doi.org/10.1111/j.1467-9299.2009.01759.x

Esposito, E. (2008). Social forgetting: A systems-theory approach. In *Cultural memory studies: An international and interdisciplinary handbook* (pp. 181–190). Walter de Gruyter.

Feischmidt, M. (2020). Memory-politics and neonationalism: Trianon as Mythomoteur. *Nationalities Papers, 48*(1), 130–143. https://doi.org/10.1017/nps.2018.72

Felsenthal, D. S. (1980). Applying the redundancy concept to administrative organizations. *Public Administration Review, 40*(3), 247–252. https://doi.org/10.2307/975378

Feola, G. & Jaworska, S. (2019). One transition, many transitions? A corpus-based study of societal sustainability transition discourses in four civil society's proposals. *Sustainability Science, 14*(6), 1643–1656. https://doi.org/10.1007/s11625-018-0631-9

Fincham, R. (1999). The consultant–client relationship: Critical perspectives on the management of organizational change. *Journal of Management Studies, 36*(3), 335–351.

Fischer-Kowalski, M. & Rotmans, J. (2009). Conceptualizing, observing, and influencing social-ecological transitions. *Ecology and Society, 14*(2).

Gable, L. & Meier, B. M. (2013). Complementarity in public health systems: Using redundancy as a tool of public health governance. *Annals of Health Law, 22*(2), 224–245.

Geels, F. W. (2013). The impact of the financial-economic crisis on sustainability transitions: Financial investment, governance and public discourse. *Environmental Innovation and Societal Transitions*, 6, 67–95. https://doi.org/10.1016/j.eist.2012.11.004

González Ocantos, E. (2014). Persuade them or oust them: Crafting judicial change and transitional justice in Argentina. *Comparative Politics*, 46(4), 479–498. https://doi.org/10.5129/001041514812522725

Grin, J., Rotmans, J. & Schot, J. (2010). *Transitions to Sustainable development: New directions in the study of long term transformative change*. Routledge.

Gruezmacher, M. & Van Assche, K. (2022). *Crafting strategies for sustainable local development*. InPlanning.

Grunwald, A. (2007). Working towards sustainable development in the face of uncertainty and incomplete knowledge. *Journal of Environmental Policy & Planning*, 9(3–4), 245–262.

Haikola, S. & Anshelm, J. (2022). The modern railway and the Swedish state – Competing storylines about state capacity, modernisation and material dependencies in the Swedish high-speed rail discourse, 1995–2020. *Journal of Environmental Policy & Planning*, 24(3), 325–342. https://doi.org/10.1080/1523908X.2022.2038104

Herbert-Cheshire, L. & Higgins, V. (2004). From risky to responsible: Expert knowledge and the governing of community-led rural development. *Journal of Rural Studies*, 20(3), 289–302. https://doi.org/10.1016/j.jrurstud.2003.10.006

Hermans, F., Roep, D. & Klerkx, L. (2016). Scale dynamics of grassroots innovations through parallel pathways of transformative change. *Ecological Economics*, 130, 285–295. https://doi.org/10.1016/j.ecolecon.2016.07.011

Hinchman, L. P. & Hinchman, S. (1997). *Memory, identity, community: The idea of narrative in the human sciences*. SUNY Press.

Hobbs, J. E. (2020). Food supply chains during the COVID-19 pandemic. *Canadian Journal of Agricultural Economics/Revue Canadienne d'agroeconomie*, 68(2), 171–176. https://doi.org/10.1111/cjag.12237

Hodson, M., Geels, F. W. & McMeekin, A. (2017). Reconfiguring urban sustainability transitions, analysing multiplicity. *Sustainability*, 9(2), article 2. https://doi.org/10.3390/su9020299

Jarzabkowski, P. (2004). Strategy as practice: Recursiveness, adaptation, and practices-in-use. *Organization Studies*, 25(4), 529–560.

Johnstone, P. & Newell, P. (2018). Sustainability transitions and the state. *Environmental Innovation and Societal Transitions*, 27, 72–82. https://doi.org/10.1016/j.eist.2017.10.006

Jordan, A. & Lenschow, A. (2010). Environmental policy integration: A state of the art review. *Environmental Policy and Governance*, 20(3), 147–158.

King, M. & Thornhill, C. (2006). *Luhmann on law and politics: Critical appraisals and applications*. Bloomsbury Publishing.

Köhler, J., Geels, F. W., Kern, F., Markard, J., Onsongo, E., Wieczorek, A., Alkemade, F., Avelino, F., Bergek, A., Boons, F., Fünfschilling, L., Hess, D., Holtz, G., Hyysalo, S., Jenkins, K., Kivimaa, P., Martiskainen, M., McMeekin, A., Mühlemeier, M. S., … Wells, P. (2019). An agenda for sustainability transitions research: State of the art and future directions. *Environmental Innovation and Societal Transitions*, 31, 1–32. https://doi.org/10.1016/j.eist.2019.01.004

Kornai, J. & Rose-Ackerman, S. (2004). *Building a trustworthy state in post-socialist transition*. Palgrave.

Kulin, J., Johansson Sevä, I. & Dunlap, R. E. (2021). Nationalist ideology, rightwing populism, and public views about climate change in Europe. *Environmental Politics*, *30*(7), 1111–1134. https://doi.org/10.1080/09644016.2021.1898879

Kvalsund, R. (2009). Centralized decentralization or decentralized centralization? A review of newer Norwegian research on schools and their communities. *International Journal of Educational Research*, *48*(2), 89–99. https://doi.org/10.1016/j.ijer.2009.02.006

Lapping, C. (2020). *Freud, Lacan, Zizek and education: Exploring unconscious investments in policy and practice*. Routledge.

Lawhon, M. & Murphy, J. T. (2012). Socio-technical regimes and sustainability transitions: Insights from political ecology. *Progress in Human Geography*, *36*(3), 354–378. https://doi.org/10.1177/0309132511427960

Lawrie, M., Tonts, M. & Plummer, P. (2011). Boomtowns, resource dependence and socio-economic well-being. *Australian Geographer*, *42*(2), 139–164.

Legg, S. (2007). Reviewing geographies of memory/forgetting. *Environment and Planning A: Economy and Space*, *39*(2), 456–466. https://doi.org/10.1068/a38170

Lockhart, A. (1982). The insider-outsider dialectic in native socio-economic development: A case study in process understanding. *Canadian Journal of Native Studies*, *2*(1), 159–168.

Lockwood, M. (2018). Right-wing populism and the climate change agenda: Exploring the linkages. *Environmental Politics*, *27*(4), 712–732. https://doi.org/10.1080/09644016.2018.1458411

Lockwood, M., Kuzemko, C., Mitchell, C. & Hoggett, R. (2017). Historical institutionalism and the politics of sustainable energy transitions: A research agenda. *Environment and Planning C: Politics and Space*, *35*(2), 312–333. https://doi.org/10.1177/0263774X16660561

Loewen, B. (2022). Revitalizing varieties of capitalism for sustainability transitions research: Review, critique and way forward. *Renewable and Sustainable Energy Reviews*, *162*, 112432. https://doi.org/10.1016/j.rser.2022.112432

Loorbach, D. (2007). *Transition management: New mode of governance for sustainable development*. International Books. https://books.google.ca/books?id=toAYPQAACAAJ

Loorbach, D. (2009). Transition management for sustainable development: A prescriptive, complexity-based governance framework. *Governance*, *23*(1), 161–183. https://doi.org/10.1111/j.1468-0491.2009.01471.x

Low, B., Ostrom, E., Simon, C. & Wilson, J. (2003). Redundancy and diversity: Do they influence optimal management? In *Navigating Social-Ecological Systems: Building Resilience for Complexity and Change*, pp. 83–114.

Luhmann, N. (1993). Deconstruction as second-order observing. *New Literary History*, *24*(4), 763. https://doi.org/10.2307/469391

Luhmann, N. (1995). *Social systems* (vol. 1). Stanford University Press.

Luhmann, N. (2006). System as difference. *Organization*, *13*(1), 37–57.

Luhmann, N. (2018). *Organization and decision*. Cambridge University Press.

Machiavelli, N. (2012). *Discourses on the first decade of Titus Levius*. Hardpress Publishing.

MacKenzie, M. K. (2021). There is no such thing as a short-term issue. *Futures*, *125*, 102652–102652. https://doi.org/10.1016/j.futures.2020.102652

Markard, J., Raven, R. & Truffer, B. (2012). Sustainability transitions: An emerging field of research and its prospects. *Research Policy*, *41*(6), 955–967. https://doi.org/10.1016/j.respol.2012.02.013

Marquardt, J. & Nasiritousi, N. (2022). Imaginary lock-ins in climate change politics: The challenge to envision a fossil-free future. *Environmental Politics, 31*(4), 621–642. https://doi.org/10.1080/09644016.2021.1951479

Martin, R. & Sunley, P. (2006). Path dependence and regional economic evolution. *Journal of Economic Geography, 6*(4), 395–437.

Mascio, F. D., Natalini, A. & Cacciatore, F. (2020). Public administration and creeping crises: Insights from COVID-19 pandemic in Italy. *The American Review of Public Administration, 50*(6–7), 621–627. https://doi.org/10.1177/0275074020941735

Meadowcroft, J. (2011). Engaging with the politics of sustainability transitions. *Environmental Innovation and Societal Transitions, 1*(1), 70–75. https://doi.org/10.1016/j.eist.2011.02.003

Meyer, B. & Geschiere, P. (eds.) (1999). *Globalization and identity: Dialectics of flow and closure.* Blackwell Publishers.

Miranda, R. & Lerner, A. (2001). Bureaucracy, organizational redundancy, and the privatization of public services. In *Performance Based Budgeting.* Routledge.

Murdoch, J. & Clark, J. (1994). Sustainable knowledge. *Geoforum, 25*(2), 115–132. https://doi.org/10.1016/0016-7185(94)90010-8

Newman, S. (2004). Interrogating the master: Lacan and radical politics. *Psychoanalysis, Culture & Society, 9*(3), 298–314. https://doi.org/10.1057/palgrave.pcs.2100021

Patterson, J., Schulz, K., Vervoort, J., Van Der Hel, S., Widerberg, O., Adler, C., Hurlbert, M., Anderton, K., Sethi, M. & Barau, A. (2017). Exploring the governance and politics of transformations towards sustainability. *Environmental Innovation and Societal Transitions, 24*, 1–16.

Penz, O. & Sauer, B. (2019). *Governing affects: Neoliberalism, neo-bureaucracies, and service work.* Routledge.

Persson, Å., Eckerberg, K. & Nilsson, M. (2016). Institutionalization or wither away? Twenty-five years of environmental policy integration under shifting governance models in Sweden. *Environment and Planning C: Government and Policy, 34*(3), 478–495. https://doi.org/10.1177/0263774X15614726

Peters, B. G. (2018). The challenge of policy coordination. *Policy Design and Practice, 1*(1), 1–11. https://doi.org/10.1080/25741292.2018.1437946

Peters, B. G., Pierre, J., Sørensen, E. & Torfing, J. (2022). Bringing political science back into public administration research. *Governance, 35*(4), 962–982. https://doi.org/10.1111/gove.12705

Ponte, S. & Cheyns, E. (2013). Voluntary standards, expert knowledge and the governance of sustainability networks. *Global Networks, 13*(4), 459–477. https://doi.org/10.1111/glob.12011

Rauschmayer, F., Bauler, T. & Schäpke, N. (2015). Towards a thick understanding of sustainability transitions – Linking transition management, capabilities and social practices. *Ecological Economics, 109*, 211–221. https://doi.org/10.1016/j.ecolecon.2014.11.018

Rode, P. (2019). Urban planning and transport policy integration: The role of governance hierarchies and networks in London and Berlin. *Journal of Urban Affairs, 41*(1), 39–63. https://doi.org/10.1080/07352166.2016.1271663

Roth, S. & Valentinov, V. (2020). East of nature. Accounting for the environments of social sciences. *Ecological Economics, 176*, 106734. https://doi.org/10.1016/j.ecolecon.2020.106734

Rotmans, J. & Kemp, R. (2003). *Managing societal transitions: Dilemmas and uncertainties: The Dutch energy case-study.* OECD.

Schaffartzik, A., Mayer, A., Gingrich, S., Eisenmenger, N., Loy, C. & Krausmann, F. (2014). The global metabolic transition: Regional patterns and trends of global material flows, 1950–2010. *Global Environmental Change, 26*, 87–97. https://doi.org/10.1016/j.gloenvcha.2014.03.013

Scheffer, M., Bascompte, J., Brock, W. A., Brovkin, V., Carpenter, S. R., Dakos, V., Held, H., van Nes, E. H., Rietkerk, M. & Sugihara, G. (2009). Early-warning signals for critical transitions. *Nature, 461*(7260), 53–59.

Scheffer, M., Carpenter, S. R., Lenton, T. M., Bascompte, J., Brock, W., Dakos, V., van de Koppel, J., van de Leemput, I. A., Levin, S. A., van Nes, E. H., Pascual, M. & Vandermeer, J. (2012). Anticipating critical transitions. *Science, 338*(6105), 344–348. https://doi.org/10.1126/science.1225244

Scholz, R. W. (2017). The normative dimension in transdisciplinarity, transition management, and transformation sciences: New roles of science and universities in sustainable transitioning. *Sustainability, 9*(6), article 6. https://doi.org/10.3390/su9060991

Scoones, I., Leach, M. & Newell, P. (eds.) (2015). *The politics of green transformations*. Taylor & Francis. https://doi.org/10.4324/9781315747378

Solomon, J. M. (2010). New governance, preemptive self-regulation, and the blurring of boundaries in regulatory theory and practice symposium: New governance and the transformation of law. *Wisconsin Law Review, 2010*(2), 591–626.

Sýkora, L. & Bouzarovski, S. (2012). Multiple transformations: Conceptualising the post-communist urban transition. *Urban Studies, 49*(1), 43–60. https://doi.org/10.1177/0042098010397402

Teampau, P. & Van Assche, K. (2009). Migratory marginalities: Making sense of home, self and mobility. *Ethnologia Balkanica, 13*, 147–163.

Teschner, N., McDonald, A., Foxon, T. J. & Paavola, J. (2012). Integrated transitions toward sustainability: The case of water and energy policies in Israel. *Technological Forecasting and Social Change, 79*(3), 457–468. https://doi.org/10.1016/j.techfore.2011.08.013

Throgmorton, J. A. (1996). *Planning as persuasive storytelling: The rhetorical construction of Chicago's electric future*. University of Chicago Press.

Turnheim, B. & Geels, F. W. (2012). Regime destabilisation as the flipside of energy transitions: Lessons from the history of the British coal industry (1913–1997). *Energy Policy, 50*, 35–49. https://doi.org/10.1016/j.enpol.2012.04.060

Underwood, D. A. & Friesner, D. (2017). Asset mapping, the social fabric matrix, economic impact analysis, and criteria for sustainability and justice: Operational elements for holistic policy planning. *Journal of Economic Issues, 51*(3), 813–827. https://doi.org/10.1080/00213624.2017.1359051

Valentinov, V. (2014). The complexity–sustainability trade-off in Niklas Luhmann's social systems theory. *Systems Research and Behavioral Science, 31*(1), 14–22.

Van Assche, K. & Hornidge, A.-K. (2015). *Rural development: Knowledge and expertise in governance*. Wageningen Academic.

Van Assche, K., Beunen, R. & Duineveld, M. (2013). *Evolutionary governance theory: An introduction*. Springer.

Van Assche, K., Beunen, R. & Duineveld, M. (2016). Citizens, leaders and the common good in a world of necessity and scarcity: Machiavelli's lessons for community-based natural resource management. *Ethics, Policy & Environment, 19*(1), 19–36.

Van Assche, K., Beunen, R., Gruezmacher, M. & Duineveld, M. (2020). Rethinking strategy in environmental governance. *Journal of Environmental Policy & Planning, 22*(5), 695–708. https://doi.org/10.1080/1523908X.2020.1768834

Van Assche, K., Beunen, R., Verweij, S., Evans, J. & Gruezmacher, M. (2022). 'No time for nonsense!': The organization of learning and its limits in evolving governance. *Administration & Society, 54*(7), 1211–1225. https://doi.org/10.1177/00953997221093695

Van Assche, K., Deacon, L., Gruezmacher, M., Summers, R., Lavoie, S., Jones, K., Granzow, M., Hallstrom, L. & Parkins, J. (2017). *Boom & bust. Local strategy for big events. A community survival guide to turbulent times.* Groningen/Edmonton, Alberta: InPlanning and University of Alberta, Faculty of Extension.

Van Assche, K., Djanibekov, N., Hornidge, A.-K., Shtaltovna, A. & Verschraegen, G. (2014). Rural development and the entwining of dependencies: Transition as evolving governance in Khorezm, Uzbekistan. *Futures, 63*, 75–85. https://doi.org/10.1016/j.futures.2014.08.006

Van Assche, K., Duineveld, M., Gruezmacher, M. & Beunen, R. (2021). Steering as path creation: The art of managing dependencies and reality effects. *Politics and Governance 9*(2), 369–380.

Van Assche, K., Duineveld, M., Birchall, S. J., Deacon, L., Beunen, R., Gruezmacher, M. & Boezeman, D. (2020). Resilience, reinvention and transition during and after quarantine. *Space and Culture, 23*(3), 230–236. https:// doi .org/ 10 .1177/ 1206331220938628

Van Assche, K., Gruezmacher, M. & Deacon, L. (2020). Taming the boom and the bust? Land use tools for mitigating ups and downs in communities. *Land Use Policy, 93*, 104058–104058. https://doi.org/10.1016/j.landusepol.2019.104058

Van Assche, K., Hornidge, A.-K., Schlüter, A. & Vaidianu, N. (2020). Governance and the coastal condition: Towards new modes of observation, adaptation and integration. *Marine Policy, 112.* https://doi.org/10.1016/j.marpol.2019.01.002

Van Assche, K., Gruezmacher, M., Summers, B., Culling, J., Gajjar, S., Granzow, M., Lowerre, A.,

Van Dijk, T. (2006). How the hands of time mould planning instruments: Iterative adaptation pushing limits in rural areas. *European Planning Studies, 14*(10), 1449–1471. https://doi.org/10.1080/09654310600852621

van Mierlo, B. & Beers, P. J. (2020). Understanding and governing learning in sustainability transitions: A review. *Environmental Innovation and Societal Transitions, 34*, 255–269. https://doi.org/10.1016/j.eist.2018.08.002

Vermeule, A. (2007). *Mechanisms of democracy: Institutional design writ small.* Oxford University Press.

Visseren-Hamakers, I. J., Razzaque, J., McElwee, P., Turnhout, E., Kelemen, E., Rusch, G. M., Fernández-Llamazares, Á., Chan, I., Lim, M., Islar, M., Gautam, A. P., Williams, M., Mungatana, E., Karim, M. S., Muradian, R., Gerber, L. R., Lui, G., Liu, J., Spangenberg, J. H. & Zaleski, D. (2021). Transformative governance of biodiversity: Insights for sustainable development. *Current Opinion in Environmental Sustainability, 53*, 20–28. https://doi.org/10.1016/j.cosust.2021.06.002

Voß, J.-P. & Bornemann, B. (2011). The politics of reflexive governance: Challenges for designing adaptive management and transition management. *Ecology and Society, 16*(2), 9. [online] URL: http:// www. ecologyandsociety.org-9. [online] URL: http://www. ecologyandsociety.org.

Wang, X. & Lo, K. (2021). Just transition: A conceptual review. *Energy Research & Social Science, 82*, 102291. https://doi.org/10.1016/j.erss.2021.102291

Žižek, S. (1989). *The sublime object of ideology.* Verso.

12. If people don't like it: resistance, backlash and counterstrategy

SO MANY REASONS TO BE UPSET

Transition strategies, by any name, are a tricky business. Not only are the ambitions and stakes high, but there are also plenty of ways they can get derailed. The previous chapters have extensively elaborated on the difficulties of change and strategy in governance and all these are likely to be more profound in transition strategies. This is the case because transition requires a radical deviation from familiar ways of organizing, because the risks and uncertainties increase during transformation. Ideas, visions and interests are likely to diverge when transition strategies are detailed and implemented. People can get upset for many reasons, and at all phases of the process, and the irritation can grow into anger, resistance, backlash and counterstrategy. In the previous chapters, these phenomena were encountered a few times, but they deserve a closer look. It is not wise, in our view, to see them as marginal, simply deplorable, or avoidable. They need to be well understood to address them, and they must be tied to the understanding of transition itself, which is bound to upset people (and their toes).

Resistance, backlash and counterstrategy can occur during early discussion, during articulation of a strategy, or during implementation and assessment (Rupnik, 2007; Stokes, 2016; Vaughn, 1997). The powerful opposition that even minor changes in governance face, polarizing debates on the issues that trigger calls for transition, and the prevalence of regulatory or state capture, show that steering towards collective goods and more sustainable ways of working and living is indeed very challenging (Oreskes & Conway, 2010; Scoones et al., 2015; Seto et al., 2016; Stoddard et al., 2021). The long time frames and (hopefully) open character of strategizing enable the appearance of counterforce, which can come from many different angles, and take many different forms. Questioning the identity of a community, a region, a country, and its governance tradition, is bound to provoke questions and affects (Cooke & Kothari, 2001; Gupta & Ferguson, 1997; Van Assche et al., 2021). In some ideologies, the very idea of transition strategy will be felt as overreach. New expert groups amassing power and garnering media attention can quickly be perceived as arrogant, and hence vilified by those already feeling excluded or targeted. Governmental experts and departments that are not close to the new center of steering power, politicians looking for wedge issues, industries not able to transform themselves to benefit from the transition, groups who feel nothing was explained or asked, civil society organizations interested in things other than the transition focus, and many others, can have good reasons to detest what is felt to be unleashed on them (de Gooyert et al., 2016; Gonzalez-Arcos et al., 2021; Steg & Gifford, 2005). Nobody knows exactly what transition path will work where, and in all existing transition attempts resistance, backlash and counterstrategy were very real.

If social memory and institutional memory recall previous ambitious strategies, maybe under different names, which proved grandiose failures, or symptoms of grandiose ambitions of key actors, this will make communities less receptive (Corbett et al., 2020; Howlett, 2012; Van Assche et al., 2022). If trust in government is low, if self-interest and corruption are rampant, if no connections were meaningfully made between the transition narrative and the narrative configurations, identities and affects in the community, then one can expect problems (Drozdzewski et al., 2016; Friedmann, 1992). If existing conflict, marginality, trauma or exclusion are not observed by the strategists, nor too the potential effects of the strategy, then anxiety and anger will loom large (Erikson, 1994; Loney, 1995; van der Watt, 2018). New subjects can be made in response and in resistance to the strategy. New discourses can be created, then mobilized, and can alter power relations in governance (Buschmann & Oels, 2019; Kooij, 2014; Rosenbloom, 2018; Szabo, 2022).

Once new identities, discourses or actors are created that identify with resistance against transition and the ideology projected behind it, these are not easy to erase, and they are likely to move governance in a different direction. Examples include the narratives in which current resources, such as gas, are relabeled as green or necessary for the transition (Bosman et al., 2014; Janzwood & Millar, 2022), or in which polluting industries are presented as key actors for successful transitions, therewith softening transition narratives and limiting institutional change (Tilsted et al., 2022). If transition is associated with a return of socialism or a corporate takeover that too will structure the resistance and trigger counterstrategy.

Resistance can thus occur within and outside governance, and inside resistance can trigger community resistance and vice versa. Resistance can lead to public backlash or to quieter counterstrategy, both in governance and outside (Broz et al., 2021; Pel, 2021). Counterstrategy will first be actor strategy or factional strategy, yet once enough support is gathered within governance this can lead to the emergence of more collective strategies, true alternatives in governance. This was the case in the Netherlands, where ambitious policy to halt biodiversity decline was diluted, withdrawn and replaced by much less ambitious policies lacking implementation tools, a shift that largely emerged from counterstrategies from the agribusiness sector (Beunen & Kole, 2021; Buijs et al., 2014; van der Ploeg, 2020). Counterstrategies can exist as opposition strategy first, then merge with the dominant one in a compromise formation, or replace the transition strategy with another strategy, which might or might not be an actual strategy. When the counter-formation attacks the idea of transition or the idea of strategy itself, when values, problem definitions and identity narratives are so diverging, then an alternative strategy will not be a transition strategy. However, one can also imagine, and observe empirically, many cases where a basic consensus exists regarding problem definitions and transition goals but not, or not at all, regarding the path and the tools deployed (Gonzalez-Arcos et al., 2021).

PATHS AND CONVERSIONS

Resistance can lead to backlash, which then produces counterstrategy, but the order can be reversed or varied. Backlash, as in public outcry against the strategy, possibly against the system and ideology associated with it, can be purely negative, or it can lead to new positions (Howlett, 2020; Pløger, 2017; Tryggvason, 2017). Existing alternatives might be embraced, in terms of ideology, identity or governance reform, or new alternatives might emerge in the process of opposition. Backlash is an event, or a relatively brief process, yet it can stabilize itself when new identities or organizations are formed, or other ones empowered, and when new actors in governance appear. Backlash can move into counterstrategy through such a path, and if the new elite is vindictive the core of the strategy can simply be the undoing of all traces of transition (Buijs et al., 2014; Wedel, 2003). This can be accompanied by a fantasy of returning to a purer, more prosperous, more moral, less complicated, less scary, or less uncertain past (McCormick, 2011; Stokes & Breetz, 2018).

Resistance can remain stuck in the stage of resistance as can be expected for various reasons. Maybe loud protest, taking radical positions, or even disagreeing with administration is not part of tradition. Maybe the interest in the matter is not great enough. Possibly there is still a limited understanding of the stakes and of the transition pain still to come (Cai, 2010; Colomb & Novy, 2016). Possibly the tools to organize resistance are not there, not even the minimum tools to translate resistance into collective noise. Or resistance might be widespread, but strong enough to overcome factional, ideological or cultural divisions in the community. Resistance might represent an initial reflex of those who will soon understand the necessity of transition or become able to shift their calculations. And, in a most positive interpretation, resistance can be a symptom of a healthy critical attitude in the community, a community which however trusts its governance system completely, so once any questions are answered governance is allowed to resume its course, its transition path (Scoones et al., 2015; Voß et al., 2006).

Counterstrategy can be an evolved response to transition, which started from vaguely articulated resistance, which crystallized into arguments, discourse, narrative and activism, yet counterstrategy can also be the starting point (Switzer, 1997). Either inside or outside governance, people can plot to amplify resistance in the community, hoping for repercussions in governance (Wedel, 2003). Such a strategy can aim at stirring protest, triggering, and possibly organizing, backlash, even conflict, or it can intend to shift the mood about transition more subtly by creating confusion, peddling incoherent or inconclusive stories, and spreading dissatisfaction (Haikola & Anshelm, 2022; Marquardt & Nasiritousi, 2022). As mentioned, a new collective strategy might already be in the minds of the counterstrategists, yet the goal for the moment can also be destabilizing or even destroying the existing order (Turnheim & Geels, 2012). What is knowns as authoritarian backsliding, and some versions of populism, can fit here (Bermeo, 2016).

Public backlash can, in another variation, turn into more quiet dissatisfaction, which can later turn again into more active resistance and counterstrategy. If protest was quelled, even in seemingly deliberative and participatory ways, large groups of the population can still be dissatisfied, yet nothing happens until entrepreneurial and creative leader figures appear to capitalize on that discontent (Bache & Taylor, 2003; Scott, 1985; van der Ploeg, 2020). Or something happens, maybe a missed transition goal, a new conflict, an emerging narrative on a related topic or in a neighboring polity, which gives the old affect a new meaning, and a new narrative and organizational life. As Machiavelli noted, old griefs and injustices long forgotten can easily be brought back to life (Bock et al., 1990; Machiavelli et al., 1997; McCormick, 2011). Social memory, indeed, is more than a technical recall, and never unambiguously a positive contributor to good governance, stability or sustainability.

BELIEVING AND NOT BELIEVING

In previous chapters we asserted repeatedly that something must look and sound real to be accepted as the basis for governance. For transition strategies, that means that the starting point, the definition of problems, of governance capacity, of duty and responsibility, and the idea of the goal must seem achievable, while the need and urgency to move in that direction ought to look real as well. If trust in science is low, trust in the possibility of dialectical learning, trust in the current governance system or in governance as such, this can represent a formidable obstacle to transition strategy. Even if such basic trust is there, hence the potential to agree on a reality, the value of the transition might not be agreed upon. Or the transition itself, already under way, might not be observed.

Some common features, habits (and ills) of governance systems make it harder for citizens (and many actors in governance) to believe proponents of transition strategy and ambitious policy generally. First of all, if the system has systematically lied to its citizens, cultivated non-learning, marginalized local forms of knowing, downplayed some problems and exaggerated others, this will not stimulate much rational conversation leading to shared beliefs on transition goals and paths (Tryggvason, 2017). Rebuilding trust and the capacity to believe is not a luxury but a necessity under such circumstances. In former colonies or settler states, indigenous peoples or former colonial subjects have reason to doubt what comes at them from governmental experts and politicians, however well-meaning they might be (Bernauer, 2019). They operate in a system that was oppressive and that is in all likelihood still oppressive, robbing indigenous (and probably other) groups of their voice. In less-than-democratic settings, when minorities were poorly treated, coerced or criminalized, new and creative forms of participation, part of an unfolding transition strategy, will be met with resistance, or instrumentalized when possible (Escobar, 2009, 2011).

A *second common ill* is that of de-politization by means of science. This can mean a few different things which are not always distinguished in the literature, but each version is problematic for trust in science, in government and in governance. One version is that politics refuses to take decisions and take responsibility, and delegates this to the experts (Ferguson, 1994; Fischer, 1990). This is a classic trope of modernism, which can be driven by weak politicians or by a real belief in the power of unity to see and solve everything (as in the post-war reconstruction in many European countries). Elsewhere, expert groups are more interested in power than in the real contribution of their expertise, while other situations will reveal political and economic actors, or, more likely, coalitions of experts, politicians and industries constructing facades of seemingly hard truths legitimizing their own play for power and resources. Strategies to weaken science and undermine trust in experts can have an impact, and can affect trust in the governance system and the problem definitions and forms of expertise circulating there.

Third, traditions of overpromising, or of false promises, might pose challenges; a habit that might stem from a naïve over-enthusiasm and unbridled confidence, from deliberate populist calculation or from a genuine belief in what overpromising experts tell politicians (Centeno & Silva, 2016). The experts themselves, in administration and academia, tend to be overpromising in a gambit for resources and influence, invoking the master trope of societal relevance. This reduces the importance of analysis, favoring normative statements, policy advice, consultancy. The lure of becoming an expert-actor can extract many promises of relevance, prospects of problems solved, of clarity finally provided. The risk of overpromising is real and common, especially where ambitions are high. Various authors observed that the successes of the welfare state led to unrealistic expectations which in the long run eroded trust that government would live up to these expectations (Kaufmann, 2012; Verschraegen, 2015).

The fourth common ill is that forgotten and ignored conflicts can simmer for a long time, and trip up any policy (O'Riordan et al., 2015; Whitson, 2007). For transition strategies, there are per definition many places to trip, and if conflicts are not observed or become part of the deliberations this will lead to obstacles much beyond the non-cooperation of some segments of the population. It will most likely lead to a polarized interpretation of the strategy process and of every document, every study, every narrative and every fact presented there as real and relevant. Even if trust in the system is still there, a new and ambitious initiative, affecting the future of the community more than usual, and potentially reshuffling power and prosperity, can reactivate dormant conflicts. Avoiding not-so-simmering conflict in governance might become impossible, as the transition strategy will touch many people, places and topics.

A fifth ill is that the dominant character in governance or the community of certain master signifiers, meta-narratives and ideologies, and the way narratives in and outside governance relate, can enable or disable transition strategy by naturalizing discourse that is compatible or incompatible (Davidson, 2010; Hook & Vanheule, 2016). If, for example, the free market is seen as a solution to all problems, if the government is the problem, it is very unlikely that people will accept a transition strategy from that government. Along the same line of thought, if one believes that power corrupts, and strategy is evil, then nobody should believe any transition theory inspired by the work of Machiavelli.

Agreeing on the reality of something as the cornerstone of transition processes assumes sincerity. The complexity, duration and pressures of transition can easily engender dark learning; that is learning to abuse the system and its rhetoric, as well as the associated resources and promises (Dunlop & Radaelli, 2020; Howlett, 2020). *Willingness to observe and to learn* equally determines the quality of agreement on reality and unreality and relevance and irrelevance in transition processes. While transitions require more than usual in terms of individual, organizational and systems learning, they provide perfect environments for non-learning as well. If too many things become too different, too many stories are involved, with too many people, goals and organizations, the task of observing environments and steering in and through governance becomes too complex – hence the temptation to generate new and ever-simpler simplifications. Yet such a process ropes in new master signifiers, inserts new types of uncertainty and ambiguity, and conjures up new problems in assessment.

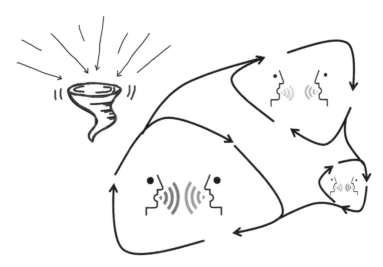

Figure 12.1   Amplification of conflicts[1]

FEELING AND NOT FEELING

Something can look real because it feels real, and it can feel real because it looks real or sounds real. Affect, as we know, does not have to come first, but it can. Expert opinions can be read, understood, yet not feel real. Nonsensical stories might be analysed as nonsense, yet still feel real. Desire can trigger affect and create arguments, while desire can drive fantasy which then perpetuates desire, and gives an impetus to rationalize, to argue, to naturalize or to reify (Brent, 2004; Saari, 2022).

Transition strategies are about communities, their identities and their futures. They show up when things are *not good.* Yet not everybody will feel bad, not everyone will see the problem nor agree on the solution. Those who

---

[1]   Conflict changes the perception of what the other party says, and what the other party says can create conflict. In governance, where individuals are usually not individuals, but representatives of actors, and where interests and values create pressure to disagree and misinterpret, the tendency for conflict to perpetuate itself is amplified. As in governance, wherein many topics can be decided upon, and many things happening in the community are discussed, the tendency for conflict to colonize more and more topics, and to polarize along factional lines, is aggravated.

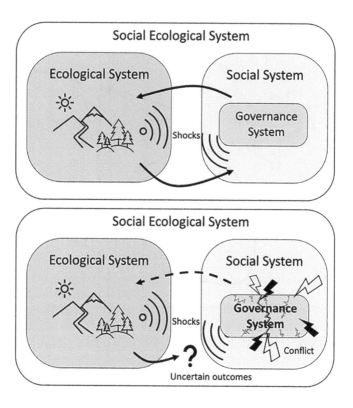

Figure 12.2   Shocks and conflict and their effects in social ecological systems[2]

do feel bad, or terrible, might find many different explanations, and many different encounters with the problem. The problem can be couched in moral, religious, cultural, economic, ecological or other terms, and can be framed in

---

²   (a) Both social and ecological systems can experience shocks, and so can the encompassing social-ecological system. Shocks do not necessarily cause collapse, but on the social side they do entail that an immediate response through governance is not possible using the existing conceptual and institutional apparatus. (b) When shocks cause conflict in governance and in the community, this can significantly aggravate the effects and it can make it harder to respond to those effects through coordinated action. As conflict has the tendency to reinforce itself and absorb and polarize ever more concepts and narratives, it introduces additional uncertainty. The always unpredictable

ideologies, in narratives of time, place and group identity (Ashworth et al., 2007; Drozdzewski et al., 2016). Some will swing back to old identities, which might be hardened or reinvented in the process, and choose denial; others will acknowledge the problem and acquiesce, and, elsewhere, communities might coalesce around solutions which perpetuate social bonds and ritualize participation, yet solve nothing.

Transition might be alienating, and transition strategies even more so. Being forced to agree on a problem definition, on a set of entangled narratives and forms of knowledge that are not ascribed to, or on policy measures felt as draconic, can clash with a whole set of master signifiers, structuring personal identity and belonging (Blaikie, 2006; Taylor, 2014). Tropes of freedom, individualism, participation, consensus, localism, efficiency and critical thinking might be mobilized against the strategy, which is felt to deform the society one belonged to. Many governance systems cannot reject those signifiers, as they are also woven into their self-understanding, rhetoric and institutional structures (Kellert et al., 2000; Potter, 1996). Yet the new initiative can expose the internal contradictions that were always there and can lead to an imagined shattering of society, to severe disappointment, non-belonging, and formation of counter-identities where feelings can find a new place in a new narrative and group. Alternatively, feelings of suspicion, of alienation and marginalization might have been there (see earlier in this chapter), feelings that were confirmed and reinforced by the strategy. Transition processes can then offer a (negative) narrative mold, to project those feelings, and create a group around them. The felt revelation, in transition, of government as inadequate, as hostile, as disrespectful, is also a confrontation with the fantasy of harmony, symbiosis and unity in society. That imaginary home can be shattered, and accepting that it never existed is not an easy task. Productive fiction can turn destructive.

Sigmund Freud, in *Civilization and its Discontents*, did not pretend to offer much consolation to those hoping to hear a story about relentless and irreversible progress towards ever more civilized and stable societies (Freud, 2015). Nothing is irreversible; atrocities and primitive drives can return at any moment. Aggressive instincts are still there, yet so is the drive to (re-) find unity, belonging and, of course, love. Aggression became internalized through the super-ego, an authority which is feared by the ego, an authority which trans-mutated aggression into an injunction to behave, to fit into society, to love others. The imagined smooth fit in a world where everything fits smoothly, a productive fiction trademark *eros*, can be imposed aggressively by the super-ego of government. The aggression can be veiled and accepted as

---

course of conflict makes it harder to predict the effects of shock, and harder to grasp which policy tools might be available to deal with the effects of shock and conflict.

part of the responsibility of government, or it can be emphasized and detested, as abuse of power and destructive of the imagined unity (Escobar, 2011).

For Freud, the process of civilization, which altered communities and individuals, in a long evolutionary process, is marked by repression. It is a process that offers stability and reduces friction in psyche and community by introducing new frictions and new tensions, for which a price must be paid (Freud, 2015; Freud et al., 2005). The price is the feeling of unease in the world, of an always imperfect fit in society, and an imperfect fit between society and its natural environment. The price is guilt; feeling guilty as the super-ego knows that we are inadequate and not well-behaved and well-intentioned enough. For some, transition strategy can come to represent a double threat, as the certainty of the world is shaken up and the imagined home broken up (why a transition?), and as the super-ego of government revealed itself in its true aggressive nature. For others, trusting in government, in science, and in the need for transition, transition strategies can be the consolation hoped for, allaying anxieties, restoring order in the imagined home.

Both positions, the common polarization in transition discourse under different guises, come with problems (Wildavsky, 1979). Both rely on fantasies that make it harder to see problems or to see problems with the solutions. Both are unable to manage adequately the anxieties about one's place in the community, and the place of the community in nature. Following Freud, one can say that transition strategy is prone to translate anxiety into impossible desires, which then generate narratives and rationalizations. 'Value inspired by anxiety,' in Freudian language, an outright rejection or overly tight embrace and fetishization of a policy tool and approach which can only exist on the edge of the possible.

REFERENCES

Ashworth, G., Graham, B. & Tunbridge, J. (2007). *Pluralising pasts: Heritage, identity and place in multicultural societies*. Pluto Press.
Bache, I. & Taylor, A. (2003). The politics of policy resistance: Reconstructing higher education in Kosovo. *Journal of Public Policy*, *23*(3), 279–300. https://doi.org/10.1017/S0143814X03003131
Bermeo, N. (2016). On democratic backsliding. *Journal of Democracy*, *27*(1), 5–19.
Bernauer, W. (2019). The limits to extraction: Mining and colonialism in Nunavut. *Canadian Journal of Development Studies/Revue Canadienne d'études Du Développement*, *40*(3), 404–422.
Beunen, R. & Kole, S. (2021). Institutional innovation in conservation law: Experiences from the implementation of the Birds and Habitats Directives in the Netherlands. *Land Use Policy*, *108*, 105566.
Blaikie, P. (2006). Is small really beautiful? Community-based natural resource management in Malawi and Botswana. *World Development*, *34*(11), 1942–1957. https://doi.org/10.1016/j.worlddev.2005.11.023

Bock, G., Skinner, Q., Viroli, M. & European University Institute. European Culture Research Centre. Conference on Machiavelli and Republicanism (1990). *Machiavelli and republicanism.* Cambridge University Press.

Bosman, R., Loorbach, D., Frantzeskaki, N. & Pistorius, T. (2014). Discursive regime dynamics in the Dutch energy transition. *Environmental Innovation and Societal Transitions, 13,* 45–59. https://doi.org/10.1016/j.eist.2014.07.003

Brent, J. (2004). The desire for community: Illusion, confusion and paradox. *Community Development Journal, 39*(3), 213–223.

Broz, J. L., Frieden, J. & Weymouth, S. (2021). Populism in place: The economic geography of the globalization backlash. *International Organization, 75*(2), 464–494. https://doi.org/10.1017/S0020818320000314

Buijs, A., Mattijssen, T. & Arts, B. (2014). 'The man, the administration and the counter-discourse': An analysis of the sudden turn in Dutch nature conservation policy. *Land Use Policy, 38,* 676–684.

Buschmann, P. & Oels, A. (2019). The overlooked role of discourse in breaking carbon lock-in: The case of the German energy transition. *WIREs Climate Change, 10*(3), e574. https://doi.org/10.1002/wcc.574

Cai, Y. (2010). Collective resistance in China: Why popular protests succeed or fail. In *Collective Resistance in China.* Stanford University Press. https://doi.org/10.1515/9780804773737

Centeno, M. A. & Silva, P. (2016). *The politics of expertise in Latin America.* Springer.

Colomb, C. & Novy, J. (2016). *Protest and resistance in the tourist city.* Routledge.

Cooke, B. & Kothari, U. (2001). *Participation: The new tyranny?* Zed Books.

Corbett, J., Grube, D. C., Lovell, H. C. & Scott, R. J. (2020). Institutional memory as storytelling: How networked government remembers. *Elements in Public and Nonprofit Administration.* https://doi.org/10.1017/9781108780001

Davidson, M. (2010). Sustainability as ideological praxis: The acting out of planning's master-signifier. *City, 14*(4), 390–405. https:// doi .org/ 10 .1080/ 13604813 .2010.492603

de Gooyert, V., Rouwette, E., van Kranenburg, H., Freeman, E. & van Breen, H. (2016). Sustainability transition dynamics: Towards overcoming policy resistance. *Technological Forecasting and Social Change, 111,* 135–145. https:// doi .org/ 10 .1016/j.techfore.2016.06.019

Drozdzewski, D., De Nardi, S. & Waterton, E. (2016). Geographies of memory, place and identity: Intersections in remembering war and conflict. *Geography Compass, 10*(11), 447–456. https://doi.org/10.1111/gec3.12296

Dunlop, C. & Radaelli, C. (2020). The lessons of policy learning: Types, triggers, hindrances and pathologies. In G. Capano & M. Howlett, *A modern guide to public policy* (pp. 222–241). Edward Elgar Publishing. https:// doi .org/ 10 .4337/ 9781789904987.00024

Erikson, K. (1994). *A new species of trouble: Explorations in disaster, trauma, and community.* Norton.

Escobar, A. (2009). *Beyond the Third World: Imperial globality, global coloniality and anti-globalisation social movements.* Routledge.

Escobar, A. (2011). *Encountering development: The making and unmaking of the Third World.* Princeton University Press.

Ferguson, J. (1994). *The anti-politics machine: 'Development', depolicization, and bureaucratic power in Lesotho.* University of Minnesota Press.

Fischer, F. (1990). *Technocracy and the politics of expertise.* Sage Publications.

Freud, S. (2015). *Civilization and its discontents.* Broadview Press.

Freud, S., Ellman, M. & Whiteside, S. (2005). *On murder, mourning and melancholia.* Penguin UK. https://books.google.ca/books?id=r9UnxaOj83oC

Friedmann, J. (1992). The past in the future: History and the politics of identity. *American Anthropologist, 94*(4), 837–859.

Gonzalez-Arcos, C., Joubert, A. M., Scaraboto, D., Guesalaga, R. & Sandberg, J. (2021). 'How do I carry all this now?' Understanding consumer resistance to sustainability interventions. *Journal of Marketing, 85*(3), 44–61. https://doi.org/10.1177/0022242921992052

Gupta, A. & Ferguson, J. (eds.) (1997). *Culture, power, place: Explorations in critical anthropology.* Duke University Press.

Haikola, S. & Anshelm, J. (2022). The modern railway and the Swedish state – Competing storylines about state capacity, modernisation and material dependencies in the Swedish high-speed rail discourse, 1995–2020. *Journal of Environmental Policy & Planning, 24*(3), 325–342. https:// doi .org/ 10 .1080/ 1523908X .2022 .2038104

Hook, D. & Vanheule, S. (2016). Revisiting the master-signifier, or, Mandela and repression. *Frontiers in Psychology, 6.* https://www.frontiersin.org/articles/10.3389/fpsyg.2015.02028

Howlett, M. (2012). The lessons of failure: Learning and blame avoidance in public policy-making. *International Political Science Review, 33*(5), 539–555. https://doi.org/10.1177/0192512112453603

Howlett, M. (2020). Dealing with the dark side of policy-making: Managing behavioural risk and volatility in policy designs. *Journal of Comparative Policy Analysis: Research and Practice, 22*(6), 612–625. https:// doi .org/ 10 .1080/ 13876988 .2020 .1788942

Janzwood, A. & Millar, H. (2022). Bridge fuel feuds: The competing interpretive politics of natural gas in Canada. *Energy Research & Social Science, 88,* 102526. https://doi.org/10.1016/j.erss.2022.102526

Kaufmann, F.-X. (2012). European foundations of the welfare state. In *European Foundations of the Welfare State.* Berghahn Books. https:// doi .org/ 10 .1515/ 9780857454775

Kellert, S. R., Mehta, J. N., Ebbin, S. A. & Lichtenfeld, L. L. (2000). Community natural resource management: Promise, rhetoric, and reality. *Society & Natural Resources, 13*(8), 705–715.

Kooij, H.-J. (2014). Object formation and subject formation: The innovation campus in the Netherlands. *Planning Theory,* 1473095214527278.

Loney, M. (1995). Social problems, community trauma and hydro project impacts. *Canadian Journal of Native Studies, 15*(2), 231–254.

Machiavelli, N., Bondanella, J. C. & Bondanella, P. E. (1997). *Discourses on Livy.* Oxford University Press.

Marquardt, J. & Nasiritousi, N. (2022). Imaginary lock-ins in climate change politics: The challenge to envision a fossil-free future. *Environmental Politics, 31*(4), 621–642. https://doi.org/10.1080/09644016.2021.1951479

McCormick, J. P. (2011). *Machiavellian democracy.* Cambridge University Press.

Oreskes, N. & Conway, E. M. (2010). *Merchants of doubt: How a handful of scientists obscured the truth on issues from tobacco smoke to global warming.* https:// philpapers.org/rec/OREMOD

O'Riordan, M., Mahon, M. & McDonagh, J. (2015). Power, discourse and participation in nature conflicts: The case of turf cutters in the governance of Ireland's raised bog designations. *Journal of Environmental Policy & Planning, 17*(1), 127–145.

Pel, B. (2021). Transition 'backlash': Towards explanation, governance and critical understanding. *Environmental Innovation and Societal Transitions*, *41*, 32–34. https://doi.org/10.1016/j.eist.2021.10.016

Pløger, J. (2017). Conflict and agonism. In *The Routledge Handbook of Planning Theory*. Routledge.

Potter, J. (1996). *Representing reality: Discourse, rhetoric and social construction*. Sage.

Rosenbloom, D. (2018). Framing low-carbon pathways: A discursive analysis of contending storylines surrounding the phase-out of coal-fired power in Ontario. *Environmental Innovation and Societal Transitions*, *27*, 129–145. https://doi.org/10.1016/j.eist.2017.11.003

Rupnik, J. (2007). From democracy fatigue to populist backlash: Is East-Central Europe backsliding? *Journal of Democracy*, *18*(4), 17–25.

Saari, A. (2022). Topologies of desire: Fantasies and their symptoms in educational policy futures. *European Educational Research Journal*, *21*(6), 883–899. https://doi.org/10.1177/1474904120988389

Scoones, I., Leach, M. & Newell, P. (eds.) (2015). *The politics of green transformations*. Taylor & Francis. https://doi.org/10.4324/9781315747378

Scott, J. C. (1985). *Weapons of the weak: Everyday forms of peasant resistance*. Yale University Press.

Seto, K. C., Davis, S. J., Mitchell, R. B., Stokes, E. C., Unruh, G. & Ürge-Vorsatz, D. (2016). Carbon lock-in: Types, causes, and policy implications. *Annual Review of Environment and Resources*, *41*, 425–452.

Steg, L. & Gifford, R. (2005). Sustainable transportation and quality of life. *Journal of Transport Geography*, *13*(1), 59–69. https://doi.org/10.1016/j.jtrangeo.2004.11.003

Stoddard, I., Anderson, K., Capstick, S., Carton, W., Depledge, J., Facer, K., Gough, C., Hache, F., Hoolohan, C., Hultman, M., Hällström, N., Kartha, S., Klinsky, S., Kuchler, M., Lövbrand, E., Nasiritousi, N., Newell, P., Peters, G. P., Sokona, Y., … Williams, M. (2021). Three decades of climate mitigation: Why haven't we bent the global emissions curve? *Annual Review of Environment and Resources*, *46*(1), 653–689. https://doi.org/10.1146/annurev-environ-012220-011104

Stokes, L. C. (2016). Electoral backlash against climate policy: A natural experiment on retrospective voting and local resistance to public policy. *American Journal of Political Science*, *60*(4), 958–974. https://doi.org/10.1111/ajps.12220

Stokes, L. C. & Breetz, H. L. (2018). Politics in the U.S. energy transition: Case studies of solar, wind, biofuels and electric vehicles policy. *Energy Policy*, *113*, 76–86. https://doi.org/10.1016/j.enpol.2017.10.057

Switzer, L. (1997). *South Africa's alternative press: Voices of protest and resistance, 1880–1960*. Cambridge University Press.

Szabo, J. (2022). Energy transition or transformation? Power and politics in the European natural gas industry's trasformismo. *Energy Research & Social Science*, *84*, 102391. https://doi.org/10.1016/j.erss.2021.102391

Taylor, M. (2014). *The political ecology of climate change adaptation: Livelihoods, agrarian change and the conflicts of development*. Routledge.

Tilsted, J. P., Mah, A., Nielsen, T. D., Finkill, G. & Bauer, F. (2022). Petrochemical transition narratives: Selling fossil fuel solutions in a decarbonizing world. *Energy Research & Social Science*, *94*, 102880. https://doi.org/10.1016/j.erss.2022.102880

Tryggvason, Á. (2017). The political as presence: On agonism in citizenship education. *Philosophical Inquiry in Education*, *24*(3), 252–265. https://doi.org/10.7202/1070610ar

Turnheim, B. & Geels, F. W. (2012). Regime destabilisation as the flipside of energy transitions: Lessons from the history of the British coal industry (1913–1997). *Energy Policy, 50*, 35–49. https://doi.org/10.1016/j.enpol.2012.04.060

Van Assche, K., Greenwood, R. & Gruezmacher, M. (2022). The local paradox in grand policy schemes. Lessons from Newfoundland and Labrador. *Scandinavian Journal of Management, 38*(3), 101212. https://doi.org/10.1016/j.scaman.2022.101212

Van Assche, K., Gruezmacher, M., Vodden, K., Gibson, R. & Deacon, L. (2021). Reinvention paths and reinvention paradox: Strategic change in Western Newfoundland communities. *Futures, 128*, 102713–102713. https:// doi .org/ 10 .1016/j.futures.2021.102713

van der Ploeg, J. D. (2020). Farmers' upheaval, climate crisis and populism. *The Journal of Peasant Studies, 47*(3), 589–605.

van der Watt, P. (2018). Community development in wounded communities: Seductive schemes or un-veiling and healing? *Community Development Journal, 53*(4), 714–731. https://doi.org/10.1093/cdj/bsx017

Vaughn, J. (1997). *Green backlash: The history and politics of the environmental opposition in the U.S.* Lynne Rienner Publishers.

Verschraegen, G. (2015). The evolution of welfare state governance. In R. Beunen, K. Van Assche & M. Duineveld (eds.), *Evolutionary governance theory: Theory and applications* (pp. 57–71). Springer International Publishing. https://doi.org/10.1007/978-3-319-12274-8_4

Voß, J.-P., Bauknecht, D. & Kemp, R. (2006). *Reflexive governance for sustainable development.* Edward Elgar Publishing.

Wedel, J. R. (2003). Clans, cliques and captured states: Rethinking 'transition' in Central and Eastern Europe and the former Soviet Union. *Journal of International Development, 15*(4), 427–440. https://doi.org/10.1002/jid.994

Whitson, R. (2007). Hidden struggles: Spaces of power and resistance in informal work in urban Argentina. *Environment and Planning A, 39*, 2916–2934.

Wildavsky, A. (1979). *Speaking truth to power: The art and craft of policy analysis.* Little, Brown and Co.

13. Good governance as a precondition and goal in sustainability transitions

GOOD GOVERNANCE GOOD GRIEF?

Now that we have reached the final chapters of this book we consider it useful to explicitly reflect on the various ways in which normativity plays a role in governance. As we have shown, knowing and organizing are strongly intertwined, and any desire for governance, for steering, for strategy and for transition rests on implicit or explicit ideas and ideals about governance, society and the world at large. Many of these ideas and ideals come together in the discussions about good governance. Also, in the context of transitions good governance is an important topic, but since good governance is an open concept par excellence, we consider it useful to unpack this concept into more detail and explore how it relates to strategy and transition in governance. This allows for more profound insight into transformations in governance as well as useful reflections on the way in which normative ideas, ideals and models do play a role in governance, in strategy and in transitions. This role is often overlooked, partly because of the openness of many models of good governance, and partly because of the underlying ideologies that are widely shared among those writing about good governance. Thinking about good governance helps us to consider both the conditions before and during transition, but also the desired end situation, which has to be more than sustainable. It has to be a society which is still governed according to principles embraced by the population.

The notion of good governance is in various ways linked to the history of modernistic approaches to governance, policy, planning and development (Fischer, 2009; Flyvbjerg, 1998b; Foucault, 2003; Latour, 2004; Lushaba, 2009; Mosse, 2005; Van Assche et al., 2014a). In modernist versions of development studies, community development, and planning, in engineering-oriented versions of development, and in economics, the decades after the Second World War, roughly up to the 1980s, saw a dominance of blueprint approaches to development, in the sense of technical interventions, recipes for economic growth (supposed to solve all problems), or, for modern and functional communities, in their spatial form and socio-economic organization. The more rash and radical impositions of simplistic versions of such blueprints could be found in colonial or neo-colonial relations, but also in the west the high modernist state and its handmaiden disciplines were eager to provide for clear and simple reasons to bring about progress, a more rational organization of society and space, and increased prosperity. James Scott's book *Seeing Like a State* (Scott, 1998) and Jane Jacobs' work *The Death and Life of Great American Cities* (Jacobs, 1961) are well-known examples in which the impact of modernistic approaches on governance and planning is scrutinized and criticized. Later, other goals and values were added to the agenda, such as environmental quality, heritage values or participation, but were still subjected to the blueprint approach. We refer to previous chapters for the finer points. Simplicity here is used because the problems and failures of (modernist) formulaic approaches to planning, policy and development tend to be forgotten when new problems arise, leading to new calls for big and simple solutions.

When 'governance' entered academic and policy discourses in the 1990s (Bevir, 2010; Pierre & Peters, 2000; Rhodes, 1997; Stoker, 1998) it came with a twin discourse on 'good governance,' and both governance and good governance were captured in, indeed, modernist recipes (Addink, 2019; Doornbos, 2001; Nanda, 2006). Governance was supposed to be new, and ideally taking on one form, while good governance was supposed to be not new, rather an abstraction and idealization of western (Anglo) democratic-capitalist practices. Both were supposed to be amenable to capture in a perfect recipe, but as soon as the rabbit came out of the hat, the recipes proliferated, leaving one to question the whole idea of a perfect recipe.

For achieving 'good governance,' a list of criteria had to be checked. Such lists included various features of governance, together making it 'good.' Recurring features of good governance, in academic and policy declarations, include rule of law, participation, accountability, responsibility, responsiveness, efficiency, effectiveness, inclusivity, consensus focus, sustainable, equitability, justice and transparency (Addink, 2019; Doornbos, 2001; Güney, 2017; Omri & Ben Mabrouk, 2020; Van Doeveren, 2011).

Many lists with criteria and indicators for good governance exist, but the idea of a list itself is problematic. Given our previous remarks on assessing governance configurations, this might come as no surprise. Maintenance of differentiation, of mechanisms of self-preservation and delivery of public goods, however defined, are for us the key criteria to assess governance configurations (Van Assche et al., 2014a). What communities see as the good community, the good life, a good environment and as good governance can differ widely. As we have shown in Chapters 6 and 7, these perspectives are part of power/knowledge configurations, embedded in discourses and linked to identities of communities, places and organizations. The presence of different perspectives and the uniqueness of each community implies that many different criteria of good governance will exist and be deemed useful for a certain situation. Second, what can be grasped and what can be organized and reorganized will differ per governance system. Assessing and comparing the 'goodness' of governance systems based on one version of good governance and the criteria that come with it is therefore problematic. Third, and most importantly, each of the criteria appearing in the lists can be interpreted in various ways, has darker sides and limitations, and is bound to come into conflict with other criteria. We develop this argument in more detail for a few of the commonly listed criteria later in this chapter and show that much depends on ideal models of the polity, or, in narrower scope, ideal models of democracy, which are embraced in the community, and which structured the governance system.

The Role of Formal Politics and Administration

Formal politics and administrative actors are important in most governance systems, although this is not always fully recognized in the governance literature (Bell & Hindmoor, 2009; Van Assche et al., 2014a). Just as formal and informal institutions imply each other and rely on each other, state actors (political and administrative) and non-state actors (commercial and otherwise) de facto rely on each other, and so do participation and representation. No system of governance can work on the basis of formality alone, through state actors alone, or by representation alone. Conversely, no form of governance is likely to be stable, comprehensive and inclusive if state actors are weak or absent, or if political actors miss administrative capacity. Looking at variations in democracies alone, one can observe many locally acceptable relations between political, administrative, non-governmental and commercial actors, embodying quite different bases for 'good governance' (Coetzee, 2018; Coleman, 2000; Luhmann, 2004).

For these reasons, we presented governance not as an alternative to formal politics, nor as a radically participatory alternative to representation, but as a system that includes a multitude of different forms of organization of collective-binding decision-making (Pierre & Peters, 2000). What is labeled as politics, and accepted as formal procedures and actors, confers a different status on certain parts of the actual political system, i.e. the governance configuration (Pusca, 2009; Teitel, 2000). The actual functioning of governance and the potential for change towards more open participation hinges on the functioning of formal politics and its arenas. If these do not work, or if people are dissatisfied, informality will proliferate, and shadow governance might emerge (see previous chapters).

Similarly important are relations between politics and administration (Luhmann, 1990). These are part and parcel of governance, unique for each community and governance configuration, and always evolving. As noted earlier, some administrative organizations function as actors; this can be acceptable, desirable, deemed natural, but it needs to be observed and understood. To assess a governance configuration, it helps to see how that configuration works: Where are actual decisions taken (not just stamped)? Who is really pushing? Are the actual powers the agreed-upon power? All this must be observed and assessed. A set of relations presumed to be ideal cannot be imposed a priori on the analysis.

Independent of the desired role of administrative actors in governance, one can spell out potential benefits of their presence in general, some of which were mentioned before. Administrative organizations perform many functions and some of these functions can be described as being an actor in governance (Beunen & Patterson, 2016; Brouwer & Huitema, 2017; Ewalt & Jennings Jr., 2004; Mintrom & Norman, 2009). Benefits of blurring some lines between politics and administration, between policy and (formal) politics, as governance perspectives recognize to be common, are that weaknesses in politics and civil society can be compensated for or improved (Coetzee, 2018; Sørensen & Torfing, 2016).

Memory, subject expertise and expertise in governance itself, both locally and at other levels, stability of coordination, all help not just in advising elected politicians and implementing what they decide, but in the processes of governance, steering and coordination itself. We also know that such 'influence,' turning something or someone into an actor, can take many forms, and might be subtle. People and organizations in administration can introduce ideas, suggest solutions for recognized problems, create recognition for new problems, select policy tools, raise awareness of the need for strategy or the failure of a previous strategy, establish new connections, lobby, find resources that open new policy options, create new narratives, form discursive coalitions, or mobilize citizens or civil society organizations. All these activities can be labeled as part of governance and that can be 'good governance.'

A priori, it is not possible to declare which role administration *should* play, and which role would amount to good governance. This, again, depends on local ideals of democracy, ideas of the good community, evolved roles and responsibilities, as well as volatility, strengths and weaknesses in formal politics, civil society, and administration itself.

The Role of Law and the Rule of Law

The above observations can be useful to understand the role of law in establishing or recognizing good governance. Especially in economics (and of course among legal scholars and juridically inspired development scholars) one can recognize a centrality of 'rule of law' ideas in perspectives on good governance (Bingham, 2011; Stein, 2009; Tamanaha, 2004). It is assumed that as long as 'the rule of law' exists, politics will be inclusive and fair, economic development is possible, and conflict will be minimized. Rule of law then becomes shorthand for 'good governance,' a synonym for whatever is needed in terms of rules and regulations to stabilize society and make things predictable enough for everybody. In our perspective, things are much more complicated, whereby rule of law can mean many different things, some of which might not be beneficial for the quality of governance. Situations in which 'the rule of law' is applied to benefit a few at the cost of many others and in ways that undermine public goods include, for example, forms of legal and state capture (Harris, 2001; Wedel, 2003) or certain forms of land or water grabbing (Dell'Angelo et al., 2016; Rulli et al., 2013).

Laws in our perspective are one among other types of institution in governance, not ideas or objects that exist outside the realm of governance, nor policy tools or frames that can be studied only from one perspective or discipline. They do perform specific functions and have special features, some of which we have already come across – such as the deliberate slowing down of decision-making and the anchoring of values and other institutions. A general function of laws is linking the political to the legal system (Luhmann, 2004; Teubner, 1988). This linking imposes different modes of formation and transformation on both sides of the coupling: law cannot ignore politics as it can revoke and create laws, and politics cannot ignore laws, as these limit which policies, plans and new laws can be produced, and how (King & Thornhill, 2003; Luhmann, 1995). The cohesion and internal logic of the legal system make it powerful, yet still unpredictable, as different relations will still evolve around law. Not only politics but also the economy will reconfigure vis-à-vis law in manners unique to the governance path.

The function systems of law, politics and the economy are key to the evolution of governance (King & Thornhill, 2003; Luhmann, 1995). The set of relations between the three systems shapes what is possible in terms of governance, but, conversely, the evolution of governance, where law, politics and economy are continuously recoupled in different ways, has an effect on the way these three different systems relate and can relate (cf. Zumbansen, 2013). We have to remind ourselves that *governance is politics in the broad sense*, which means the actual sense, beyond formal political organizations, beyond what the law and what politics itself define as politics and its tools, since, as we know, these formalities are never able to capture, understand and mold exactly how collective decision-making and its implementation takes place. What can count as good governance, as a frame in which transition strategies can crystallize, and as a set of qualities which needs to be preserved, is therefore real, but it is a reality created in a contingent manner in governance, and that contingency extends to the desirable and possible relations between politics, administration, law and the economy. Which means that transition strategy cannot ignore good governance yet needs to observe carefully which relations between the function systems support what counts as good governance locally and can simultaneously support the strategy. Internal contradictions can occur, which have to be acknowledged, and serve as input for ensuing discourse in governance (we refer to the passages on transition dilemmas).

Enforcement and Reliance on Law

A transition strategy can take the form of a policy, a plan, a law and even an informal institution. The effect of the strategy should extend beyond the production of the document itself, and must include reality effects and goal dependencies, as argued earlier. The question of implementation and the issue of 'enforcement' (enforcing implementation) immediately come to the fore. Laws, again, take a special place as they trigger different enforcement mechanisms and actors than policies and plans. Yet, flexibility and contingency remain. Laws need to be interpreted and applied in specific situations and, as the sociology of law has shown, this implies that the meaning and effect of law will start to diverge as soon as the law is put into practice (Gregg, 1999; Griffiths, 2003). We can refer to the already mentioned interplay between formal and informal institutions that plays a role in the interpretation and application of legal rules (Van Assche et al., 2014b).

This interplay between institutions is important because laws are not the only policy tool that can be enforced. A bias towards using laws as the main tool for enforcing collective-binding decisions can make actors blind to the potential benefits of other tools for coordination and implementation, such as economic incentives, plans or voluntary agreements, and for alternative ways of working towards public goods or goals, such as participatory processes. Enforcement in practice can mean many things and can be carried out in various ways. For laws, as for the other types of institutions, this suggests that the most effective rules are those that people unconsciously follow and have been normalized and naturalized (Griffiths, 2003), a point already made by Plato who understood that 'good people do not need laws to tell them to act responsibly, while bad people will find a way around the laws.' Enforcement can range from subtle hints to legal procedures and the use of fines, force and violence. Each of these types of enforcement might be needed on certain occasions, and each comes with its own benefits and pitfalls. Calls for more enforcement, less rigid interpretations of laws, deregulation and more empathy in the enforcement of laws co-exist in societies, showing that the how and why of enforcement is anything but straightforward.

Reflections on enforcement cannot ignore the underlying ambitions of laws and their actual effects in governance. Laws can unintentionally or purposely be designed in such a way that their actual enforcement undermines public goods and goals. The extensive discussions about tax avoidance for example, show very clearly how the legal system can be used to create and aggravate inequalities in society. Those responsible for writing laws and those in charge of enforcement might ignore their responsibilities or apply laws very selectively, in very flexible or rigid ways, or de facto circumventing other legal requirements (Acemoglu, 2005; Collins, 2006; Pusca, 2009). All these actions have implications, not just for the implied or envisioned public goals or goods, but also for the functioning of law and governance, and for public trust in politics and law (Franz, 2019; Mazzarella, 2019). Here we can again highlight the importance of narratives through which people make sense of law and its enforcement. These can include narratives of success or failure that drive societal discussions and the evolution of governance, as well as narratives of fairness, good governance and the good life (see earlier).

Speaking of the 'rule of law' as a synonym of 'good governance' signifies an over-reliance on legal tools in governance. It is a symptom of a legalism that fetishizes one governance tool over others, and rather unthinkingly ignores the centrality of governance and its diversity of tools in shaping what is possible in a community. The extremely diverging definitions of 'rule of law' illustrate easily how very different possible relations between function systems, and different ideologies and understandings of the good community and the good life, lead to different meanings of the 'rule of law.'

We can distinguish between minimalist and maximalist understanding of the rule of law, whereby minimalist ideas focus on establishing a limited set of preconditions, after which, in a process of adaptation, experimentation and exercise of freedoms, the best possible quality of life will emerge (Van Assche & Hornidge, 2015). Rule of law can then easily mean a retreat of government, a reduction of policy tools, a reliance on private investment and a focus on attracting such investment. Or, in an alternative version, still minimalist, the emphasis can come to lie on establishing procedures of participation, arenas, and enhancing anti-corruption legislation. Maximalist views of the 'rule of law' could include many policy goals if they are associated with perceived basic rights (housing, education, health and others).

The good governance of transition strategies therefore cannot be reduced to one possible relation between the function systems of law, politics and the economy, nor to the presence or dominance of one type of governance tool. We do know that a diversity of tools at the disposal of actors is helpful, and that implementation and enforcement tools cannot be omitted from the toolbox, while we underline that both tools and their enforcement mechanisms can be captured by factional interests at any stage. The following paragraphs examine key features of governance that are prevalent in the literature, and that hold the promise to pinpoint quality of governance more clearly – participation, checks and balances, transparency and absence of corruption. After discussing their value and limitations as litmus tests, we inquire into the value of simply resorting to quality of democracy as a measure of good governance.

PARTICIPATION, TRANSPARENCY AND CORRUPTION

Participation

One of the most common requirements listed for good governance is public participation. Participation is expected to make governance more inclusive, more adaptive and more sensitive to local knowledge, which could be beneficial in these efforts. The calls for more participation and more inclusive forms of decision-making were an answer to emerging critiques on technocratic and expert-driven forms of governance that showed how these approaches marginalized and excluded certain actors and stakeholders, as well as their perspectives, opinions, knowledge or interests (Fischer, 1990; Goodin, 2008; Mosse, 2001; Reed, 2008). The calls have in many places stimulated an evolution from involving stakeholders in the implementation of policies, to involvement in policy formulation, to involving people in all phases and aspects of governance as well as in research on governance. It is now widely recognized that participatory and inclusive forms of governance are important. But over time, the theories and practices of participation have also become an object of critiques (Arnstein, 1969; Mosse, 2001; Turnhout et al., 2010), partly because the practical realities of participation often do not live up to expectations. Some expectations turn out to be rather naïve or even incorrect.

In our view some form of participation is always present in governance (Van Assche et al., 2014a). At the same time more participation is not a panacea for the issues that are brought to the fore in society. Increasing participation without considering the functioning of both participation and representation and the selection of domains, topics and actors who can participate, can in fact undermine democracy. Increasing participation without reflecting on its effects on representation and on participation elsewhere in the system can shift selectivities away from what the community would recognize as fair representation and inclusion. It can create new shadow networks, empower existing ones, make it possible for illicit networks to show an acceptable face. It can make existing forms of coordination difficult by introducing unpredictability, bias, ignorance, short-termism, factionalism and simplification to the extent that complex institutions aiming at long-term change become impossible to enact.

Calls for participation, and images of participation as new and good, often arise when people are not happy with the existing forms of participation and representation, with the way these lines of power are connected, with the role of experts or higher-level governments, or when they dislike the perceived rigidity of policies and plans (Norris, 2011). And indeed, more radical, reconfigured, comprehensive and intense participation processes might be necessary when the routines of governance do not work anymore, when societal issues remain unaddressed, questions go unanswered and fears are not allayed. When topics that are felt as key to the experience of community life are seen to be marginal to the activity of governance, when no experts and resources are assigned, when the topic does not show up on council meetings, does not have administrative champions nor a recognizable position in the organization, and the system is seen to simply reproduce itself and slowly move in a direction not asked for by citizens, then calls for participation should certainly be taken seriously (see our reflections on transitional governance in previous chapters).

Polarized situations (see earlier chapters) remind us that more radical change always involves risk, whether the main route is participation or representation, a more intense use of existing instruments and procedures (more meetings, discussions, elections), or the elaboration of new procedures, structures and sites (a crisis management committee, a special parliamentary committee, a transition council, or new 'engagement' efforts by previously invisible administrations) (Coetzee, 2018; Kuiper, 2000; Urbinati & Warren, 2008). Early elections can lead to a populist or authoritarian takeover, myriad new participation sites can do the same, yet early elections and new participation sites can also calm down public sentiment, or lead to intense self-reflection and a situation where more people recognize themselves again in the governance system that is supposed to represent them, while more state actors become aware that certain procedures, rhetoric, jargon, infighting and unexplained long-term goals have alienated part of the population.

When considering the pros and cons of participation and representation, it is important not only to consider that their precise forms and functions make all the difference and that the devil is in the detail, but also that they co-evolve in complex patterns (Birch, 1993; Luhmann, 1990). This means that forms of participation and representation implicate each other, form the condition for each other's use, can transform into each other, and have to be combined in many different ways. Participation can still accommodate expert advice and expert roles. If people who participate are representative of organizations, there was likely internally a combination of participation and representation preceding the participation in the governance arena (see earlier). Similarly, if a participatory arena comes to a decision, but this decision takes on the character of a proposal in a higher-level or more comprehensive arena, the participatory process will have to send someone to represent itself. Participatory arenas and procedures can be designed by an administration that is associated with the system of representation, or by their experts. Representative arenas can just as well be designed in a participatory fashion, although likely requiring a lengthy and complex participation process (as public consultation) that requires some form of administration in its structuring.

Transparency

Transparency is another recurring feature of 'good governance' discourse. Transparency is appreciated for its own sake, in the tradition of Enlightenment thinking, which was supposed to make things, indeed, transparent, as in understandable and clear. Rationality and clear thinking was supposed to make things visible, to create transparency where opacity existed. Within this Enlightenment thinking, science could assist politics and administration in making things visible in society, both qualities and problems, and the governance system itself was expected to be transparent to itself and to the members of the community. Making things visible could make community and governance more comprehensible for each other, although modernist perspectives came to dominate the thinking on governance in the long term, implying an emphasis on state actors observing and mapping out the territory and the community – what Foucault called the *mathesis* (Foucault, 1970).

Transparency is expected to increase efficiency and trust in governance, to decrease corruption, and to reveal hidden powers of administrative, political and economic actors (Capano & Howlett, 2020; Johnston, 2006; Valentinov et al., 2019). Recent discourses on open data and smart cities capitalize on the same symbolism, while many corruption fighters (see below) invoke transparency as the way to diagnose and resolve corruption issues. The strong associations between transparency, honesty, virtue, efficiency, public-mindedness and rationality became so strong because several discourses co-evolved and became entrenched in academia, education, media and, over time, in institutional structures themselves. Modernist ideology, which refuses to die and reappears on a regular basis under different names, is part of the reason why these conceptual linkages around transparency became so deeply engrained in public and academic discourse on good governance. This ideology blends many such connections into its narrative of efficient, evidence-based and honest governance. The modernist-backed transparency ideal is attractive for both left and right-wing ideologies, and for technocratic approaches aspiring to be neutral or evidence-based.

Transparency is always selective. The drive to increase transparency requires distinctions in the observation of governance systems (King & Thornhill, 2003). In this case it means privileging the distinction transparent/ opaque over other possible distinctions. The internal hierarchy of values and distinctions, which might reflect what society wanted it to do, is thereby easily ignored. The internal distinction transparency/opacity can easily be ignored or overridden, if, as usual, outsiders impose parameters to improve transparency. This is supposed to lead to more objectivity, a safeguard against internal actors gaming the system, against resistance to change. This is understandable, but also blind to the fact that a neutral distinction does not exist. It is always contingent, and what is understood as transparent, and as the most relevant aspects of transparency (to create a fair picture of the organization) always rests on a *decision* to make the distinction in one way and not another (Luhmann, 2004). In Foucaultian terms, one can say that each discourse, including a discourse on transparency, creates its own combination of transparency and opacity, its own blind spots, foreground and background, hierarchies of relevance, and preferential connections.

In mainstream discussions of transparency, the need for opacity is rarely grasped. Machiavelli, who hammered on transparency, did notice that it is not always possible or desirable. Leadership cannot always reveal what is necessary to achieve a goal supported by the public. This can be for strategic or tactical reasons, as being open or open too soon can influence the moves of other actors, and it can be a matter of complexity, where things need to happen and often happen fast, which cannot be explained without boring and annoying citizens with excruciating detail, or without causing suspicion, as not everything that leadership or the administration does seems immediately useful (Valentinov et al., 2019). Not all prerequisite activities, conceptual connections and involved networks can be grasped by the community. Machiavelli would speak of the necessities that leadership (including distributed leadership in governance) has to discern and act upon, even if the community does not see the same things (Mansfield, 1996). This can be a matter of alternative paths to the same outcome, of unexpected problems arising, of new opportunities, of internal contradictions in public discourse that cannot be resolved in the open. Exposing military strategy early and widely is probably the worst strategy, and an observer of strategy would interpret such early revelation as clever deceit. Large projects rarely work if all internal complexity, all uncertainties, all necessary tactics, are exposed (Flyvbjerg, 1998a).

Another reason why radical transparency is not achievable or desirable is that the interplay between the formal and informal institutions upon which governance rests is always partly opaque (see earlier). Often, actors in governance are not even aware of all informal institutions that make a policy work or fail, nor the world of informality which is accountable for their current form and functioning, for internal hierarchies and the positioning of expertise in decision-making. We argue that *managing the balance between transparency and opacity* in governance is essential in order to speak of good governance (Van Assche et al., 2014b).

Corruption

Corruption can be systemic, as in state capture, and it can be small scale. It can be restricted to certain governance domains or sites, to certain actors, to certain occasions, or it can be anywhere. If it is prevalent, resources are distributed in

Strategy for sustainability transitions

a way so different from formal intentions that nothing in governance, nothing in delivery of services, in basic administration, will function as it should. Not only will organizations and individuals lack the resources, motivation and permission to do their job, but almost certainly those organizations and individuals will have to do something else, and that other thing might be just a distraction for those expecting good governance, or it might be an obstacle, even a threat (Rose-Ackerman & Palifka, 2016). The lines between politics, administration, economic actors and criminal actors tend to blur when corruption is widespread, and governmental actors can use their connections to grab resources, or run a business.

Local or regional clans can be economic, political, criminal and administrative actors. Criminals can use their assets to become politicians and vice versa, while businesspeople might use the services of criminals to pressure politicians. The blurring of these lines is less remarkable when one considers it as a symptom of dysfunctional institutions. Differentiation processes can collapse or be reversed, just as coordination can collapse, or form around informal institutions which do not envision public goods or a long term (Acemoglu, 2005; Franz, 2019). Shadow governance, clan governance and largely informal governance easily foster corruption. Or, more subtly: when corruption takes hold, self-correction is more difficult. Visibility, a public sphere, an accepted combination of formal and informal institutions, of participation and representation, do offer advantages for the preservation of public goods. Corruption then entails the ignoring or forgetting of agreed upon public goods, for private or group interests. When such rules were clearly existing before, and were ascribed legitimacy in the community, it was easier to agree that corruption exists.

Clientelism is a more subtle and often less visible version of corruption that clearly plays a role in environmental and sustainability issues. Public goods and goals and laws are ignored or overridden to favor certain business, and funds for sustainability transition are captured by companies that de facto obstruct these transitions. Examples include subsidies and tax relief for oil and gas companies, for airline companies, for livestock farming. Clientelism can be reinforced by forms of social organization and cultural features, which can be used as an explanation or excuse for practices otherwise labeled as corruption. Politics can thus generate into clan politics, and the resources of nature and the state can be divvied up in a game of clan competition and clientelism (Collins, 2006).

Corruption, in any form, tends to aggravate inequality, foster conflict and undermine the rule of law (Johnson, 2006). It can lead to economic decline and human rights abuses, as well as environmental degradation. It will most certainly undermine trust in government, in institutions, in public goods as such, and in the possibility of strategy for the long term. Government starts to look like a threat, a nuisance, or a milking cow, but not as something representing citizens and helping the community to pursue collective goals. Governance appears then as a description of the current situation, rife with corruption, and if the mess ever gets cleaned up, trust will remain low that anything beyond formal representation and the guaranteeing of rights and freedoms could be positive features of governance (Pusca, 2018). Governance returns to an ideal of government, even if this is impossible, and good governance starts to look like mere absence of corruption.

Culture and contingent paths do make a difference though, and while corruption might be universally reviled, defining and observing corruption are still context-dependent (Rose-Ackerman & Palifka, 2016). Accepting a present (or a cup of coffee) can represent a minor form of corruption, or it can be seen as a gesture of cultural sensitivity, or simply a way to open up the conversation. Accepting twelve shots of vodka can be seen as submitting to a corrupting system, as a necessary evil to make connections, enter the governance configuration, learn something, or simply as a health risk. A lobby activity can be seen as corrupt or as part of the system of governance (see below, models of democracy). Simply focusing on forced and unseeming transactions, on bribes, does not clarify much, as what counts as a bribe or illegally extracted taxes or fines by outsiders could be seen as a way to make an organization function by locals, in an environment in which they have to be creative to fulfill their actual role – public good remaining public good (Mungiu-Pippidi, 2020; Wayne Taylor, 2000). Conversely the most undermining forms of what could be labeled corruption are those whereby practices that undermine public goods are institutionalized in formal rules. Laws can selectively favor tax avoidance, carefully designed loopholes can legalize pollution and oppression, administrative hurdles can favor large companies and polluters, and land and water grabbing can be encoded in law and policy, couched in benevolent rhetoric.

Checks and Balances

Too much power in the hands of a person or a faction fosters corruption and is likely to undermine the public interest. A separation of powers, in any form, is therefore often promoted. This idea, in the Anglo-Saxon sphere known as checks and balances, is as old as political theory, although it was not dominant until the 19th century. Many 18th-century Enlightenment thinkers were on the side of the enlightened despot, an autocrat who knew what was good for the people, and was able to take rational decisions and unpopular yet necessary ones. Plato favored such a person, while Aristotle's ideal state included different groups and perspectives on leadership. Machiavelli, in the 16th century, represents both positions, advocating (not entirely sincerely) for an authoritarian Prince, and later, in the *Discourses*, for a republic where internal dissensus would be a virtue and a source of continuous innovation and adaptation (Coleman, 2000; Pasquino, 2009).

Checks and balances can be exemplified in various ways. One can focus on institutional structures, by imposing term limits, limiting the power of the executive branch and buttressing judicial autonomy, defining roles for individuals and organizations, for sites and topics, which limit the scope of discussion, the amount of power, or the time in power. Differentiation and the formation of departments and specialties can function as a form of checks, as this will imply that there will also be different voices of administration (Luhmann, 1990; Wayne Taylor, 2000). Multi-level governance can be understood as a check and balance, as the existence of levels delimits the power of each level and forces governments to – at least – take into account perspectives and decisions made at another level. A relatively autonomous administration, able to criticize politicians keen to abuse power, to take ignorant decisions, to favor the short term and their home base, or to ignore institutions and previous decisions, must be understood as a check (Barrett, 2013; Gupta, 2012; Howlett & Rayner, 2007).

Another path towards checks and balances, straddling the discursive-institutional divide, is the one leading towards a guaranteed diversity of perspectives, interests, voices, and forms of knowledge in governance (see previous chapters). This requires space for disagreement, testing to what extent conflict can be productive, and support for the development of truly different points of view. Without such support, some actors and some segments of the population would always remain under-represented, and less informed, as access to expertise and to knowledge of political and administrative procedures, of governance broadly, is not spread equally. To engender truly productive discussions in the arenas of governance, access to the arena, and to the arguments, needs to be there.

The interventions to reinforce checks and balances, or more broadly the features of governance systems that can be interpreted as contributing to checks and balances, can have drawbacks. The previous chapter revealed that ambitious transition strategies easily erode checks and balances, yet strong checks and balances can complicate or prevent the formation of any transition strategy. Checks and balances render policy integration and knowledge integration more difficult, as well as defining a long-term future which can drive such integration. Furthermore, strong checks and balances can foster the evolution of factional identities that polarize and hence jeopardize the possibility to come to agreement, find common ground, or define common goods which can form the basis for long-term strategies (Mazzarella, 2019). Strong checks and balances can thus contribute to the evolution of less adaptive systems, and to factional identities that forget the idea behind the initial governance design (cf. Vermeule, 2019). As another paradox that marks governance, strong checks and balances can, under certain conditions, produce that which will destroy them. Irresponsible leadership is one of those conditions, and no institutional design can exclude this.

Good governance, in other words, cannot be reduced to the presence of one of the qualities of governance discussed in previous paragraphs and in much of the (good) governance literature. Combining the features into a list supposedly embodying good governance does not resolve the situation, as they contradict and undermine each other and themselves, depending on the emphasis placed on them, the creation of new blind spots elsewhere in the system, and, depending on the topics, the arenas and procedures chosen to represent and implement the desired quality of governance (what counts as transparent, how it is observed, performed, narrated). Democracies are expected to resolve such problems by continuous self-observation and self-transformation, leading to an appropriate choice of governance tools, and a context-sensitive understanding of what transparency, participation, etc., can mean, and how they can relate to each other in a system which, as a whole, embodies good governance for the community.

DEMOCRACY

Democracy as a Source of Universal Design?

The discussions on good governance are strongly related to those on democracy. In a certain perspective one could argue that good governance is the application of democratic principles in governance. In our view, things are not that simple, as democratic government is easier to define than democratic governance, and because democracy is a word that describes a widely varying set of practices and a series of divergent ideas on what a real democracy is, what the community is, who should be involved in governing, what that governing actually is, how participation and representation are combined, how governance is scaled, and what public goods are (Carnoy, 2014, p. 201; Norris, 2011; Urbinati & Warren, 2008). In the realm of ideas on democracy, partly inspired by and inspiring practices, one can distinguish several models of democracy, even if we restrict ourselves to the western tradition. In practice, we find many different paths leading to different relations between the systems of law, politics, economy and others (we refer to earlier passages on differentiation and on governance dimensions).

Certain narratives of good governance land better in some versions of democracy than in others. Some versions are directly derived from a particular model of democracy and some versions are clearly more practical than others. Imposing one idea of democracy without being aware of the diversity that is possible and existing (Held, 1996; Young, 2000), and without being aware of the unique governance configuration in place (democratic or otherwise), will not only lead to a situation far removed from the imposed ideal, but also one far different from what the community is interested in. Existing forms of coordination will be disrupted, new types of uncertainty will be introduced, new openings for corruption created (Acemoglu, 2005; Alexander, 2002). In other words, a reference to 'democracy' cannot suffice to quell discussions of good governance.

Models of Democracy

In the western tradition one can distinguish several models of democracy (Held, 1996; Van Assche et al., 2014a; Young, 2000). An actual existing polity will be marked by a combination of features of different models. This is the case because virtually no community designs itself from scratch and only based on a theoretical model, because the theoretical models are never an abstraction of just one existing polity, and because, over time, difference is introduced, with political and cultural shifts modifying democracy yet leaving traces of the models previously dominant. Each configuration is thus a unique hybrid of the different theoretical models, and it embodies a unique set of relations between politic, law and other function systems (Birch, 1993; Carnoy, 2014; King & Thornhill, 2003; Zumbansen, 2013). Distinguishing the theoretical models of democracy is useful for analytical reasons, as this helps to bring attention to the different features of governance and their actual or desired coupling to versions of democracy. The models help to understand the various ways in which diverse stories of the real democratic society are coupled to (positions on) specific governance dimensions. We briefly elaborate on five main models – liberal democracy, civil society, social democracy, communitarianism, and civic republicanism – to illustrate ideological differences and how these can play out in governance.

Liberal democracy is a small-government model, where the community is the collection of individuals, and the role of government is restricted to the protection of individual rights and freedoms and the prevention and management of conflict. Natural rights are considered to be easily recognizable and universal. Participation is weak, and elections are the main way to signal intentions and to structure representation. Collective goods are hard to define, and the role of government is not to do this. Governance for the long term, and choosing a direction, an idea of what the community could be in the future, are unlikely to materialize. Capitalism and liberal democracy blend well, as the emphasis on individual freedoms (to make, to sell, to buy, to move, to self-define) is shared.

Civil society models are similarly small-government ideas, but this time depicting society as a collection of organizations. Elections take place, in a system of representation, but citizens are expected to be more active, with a strong participatory line in governance through membership in organizations. People can be members of several organizations, and each organization can have a system of internal participation and representation. Organizations lobby government informally or participate visibly in formal sites of participation. Both for-profit and not-for-profit organizations participate, trying to shape the agenda of governmental actors, political and administrative, and the outcome is hoped to be the best possible reflection of the desires of the community. Collective goods are partial goods, as proposed by organizations, except when these proposals can coalesce into ideals which work for the community as a whole. If business picks up social or environmental practices promoted by NGOs and by a major political party, this could translate into a policy embodying a collective good.

Socialism and social democracy do believe that the community is more than a sum of individuals of organizations, and that governmental actors play an active role in the recognition, formulation and pursuit of collective goods. Long-term strategy is deemed possible and desirable, as government is felt to be responsible to move society to a course which enables it to fulfill its collective aspirations. Under socialism, government owns resources, and highly integrated policy and planning is undertaken, while social democracy allows for private property and a form of capitalism with less absolute property rights compared to liberal democracies. Government bureaucracies are replete with expertise identifying problems and opportunities and enabling the polity to move in the desired direction. Socialist states tended to be modernist, aiming for progress and a perfect communist society through science, engineering and collectivization. Participation was possible but within the frames of the vision defined by party leaders and bureaucrats. Recent forms of social democracy rhetorically embrace participation and localism, while holding on to steering power at higher levels. This is not necessarily empty rhetoric, as it does not necessarily veil a contradiction.

Communitarianism is localism in pure form, an old ideal revived in recent decades, where local communities govern themselves, either emphasizing formal or informal coordination tools. Collective interests and identity prevail over individual interests, social networks are dense and strong, active participation in community life is expected. This participation is broader than what we would call participation in governance, as many activities are not involved, even indirectly, in coming to collectively binding decisions. People thus play several roles in this community, which increases the interdependence and shared identity and multiplies the mechanisms of mutual assistance. Individual autonomy, choosing one's own identity, can be difficult, and functioning in multi-level systems or simply dealing with neighboring communities can be difficult and prone to conflict.

Civic republicanism is the model vigorously defended by Machiavelli, less localist than communitarianism but more so than the other models. The individual and the community are expected to be strong and active, both participating in the formulation and pursuit of public goods. This creates tensions, possibly conflicts, but that is seen as positive. Long-term perspectives are needed, as well as adaptive governance. Adaptive strategies are quite a different beast from absent strategies. Perfect communities and governance configurations do not exist, as they are the product of contingency and necessity, of historical identities and environmental adaptation.

Policy Tools, Models and Paths

Lists of policy tools can be presented as neutral pallets of options, yet more commonly they are associated with implicit ideas on good governance and with ideologies, which implies a preference for certain tools (Carnoy, 2014; Scott, 1998). Some policy tools are therefore recommended, and others are discouraged, depending on underlying ideas and ideologies. While a comprehensive plan might look rational and necessary in a social-democratic polity, it can be experienced as wasteful, undemocratic or authoritarian in neo-liberal systems. The different models of democracy sketched above come with their own preferences for policy tools, for combinations of formal and informal institutions, participation and representation, and they have their own ideas on the desirability and possibility of long-term strategy (Van Assche et al., 2014b, 2022).

Certainly, the existence and utility of certain instruments or tools will be universally recognized: few would claim that taxes can be abolished, as infrastructures are needed and not everything can be privatized easily. Norms and standards are near-universally accepted as ways to enable coordination, while reporting and accounting makes society more transparent, and thus easier to coordinate. Assessment of proposals reduces their risk and social and environmental impact, while subsidies, lowering taxes, grants and awards are incentives to make things happen. Penalties are negative incentives, and so are court cases and whatever might come from them. Information might improve the quality of public consultation and other forms of public engagement (Howlett, 2019).

Competition *might* spark innovation and enhance the quality of public projects and policy initiatives. Public private partnerships *might* bring down costs and speed things up. Bringing in consultants *might* share responsibility and divert attention. Working with brokers can ease pain in participation sites, working groups or project organizations. Temporary committees can be temporary and advisory, while standing committees can remain standing but at a distance. Guidelines can detail visions, but without punishing or forcing sensitive groups or powerful stakeholders. Strategies can be spatial, sectoral, topical or tied to an arena; they can be preceded by draft strategies, pre-assessment, pre-studies, or public consultation reports, and can be followed by assessments, modifications, economic impact studies, internal protest notes, engineering studies, calls for proposals, grant regulations, or new bylaws, *etcetera ad infinitum.*

The 'ad infinitum' hints at the simple observation that potentially *anything* can be a policy tool (Fischhoff, 1990), and the slightly mocking tone of the previous paragraph indicates that the choice of policy tool has something to do with fashions, learning processes in governance, governance traditions, and harder path dependencies in governance (see earlier chapters). The choice of tools is certainly connected to the dominant model of democracy; social democracies are less likely to embrace public private partnerships unless that's the only way to finance a project. Different governance paths entail experience with different sets of tools, acceptance in the community of some but not others. The fashions just mentioned can be ideological, cultural or academic, and fashions in the world of governance itself. Tools can travel, can be learned and can be modified to circumstances and governance paths. Tools develop preferential linkages, meaning that some combinations of tools are more likely to occur than others, and that experience with some tools will quickly spur demand for certain others (Anand, 2017; Capano & Howlett, 2020; Hull, 2012). Consultation sessions are a prelude to visions that produce designs that are not implemented yet trigger the production of design guidelines that are suggested, after which a grant system might encourage one to follow the guidelines.

The creation of a new organization can be the creation of a tool, yet that tool can evolve into an actor. It is also possible that the new organization can be envisioned from the start as the creation of a new actor, which is then expected to do something (at arms-length) that cannot be achieved by the current set of actors (and their resources, roles and scrutiny). Tools can be invented on the spot or thoughtlessly copied. Their existence in a context does not show that they are adapted to the context, nor that they are used or used well (Creutzig et al., 2022; Gupta, 2012). Some tools are institutions, in our terms, while others are organizations, arenas, procedures or simply decisions. The language of policy tools can be helpful but can also obscure these distinctions.

The presence of certain tools is therefore not equivalent to a *governance quality*, to a form of good governance (Howlett & Rayner, 2007). Nor can such presence be understood as a certain *governance capacity*. Possibly, things would be difficult to achieve without the tool, but the presence of a certain tool by itself does not show much in terms of use or effects. It is also possible that the system has the capacity to create a new tool quickly, after which it can be used to increase the capacity to do certain things. The absence of the tool can then be interpreted as a deliberate choice not to create it yet, or the absence of the right opportunity to choose a course and create the appropriate tools. For such a positive interpretation of governance capacity, in the *absence* of tools, we do need to assume learning capacity, and the easy familiarity with many different ideas on policy tools, as well as well-known and shared processes of tool creation. Thus, the absence can be seen as a cost saving, as healthy simplicity and finely attuned adaptive capacity, but this can only work when there are other forms of redundancy, as in distributed leadership with a rich and diverse experience, administrative experts aware of many other communities and their policy tools, and a strong institutional memory (Acemoglu, 2005; Hull, 2012; Sørensen & Torfing, 2016).

Democracy, in other words, cannot be taken as a simple synonym for good governance. Even if we subscribe to the general idea of democracy as self-determination by the people, and as maintaining the options for self-transformation, we know that democracy can take many forms, which associate with different sets of narratives, ideologies, organizational struc- tures and sets of actors, with preferences for certain policy tools and, most profoundly, with a particular pattern of differentiation between the function systems. Each concrete example of a democracy embodies a different ideal of democracy, a unique understanding of good governance and a specific set of possibilities to come closer to that ideal, based on existing conditions. Each system will value and define participation and the other classic features of good governance (literatures) in a unique manner. This book, in its concern for sustainability transitions, and in its building on the insights of EGT and its con- tributing and related literatures, was able to refine the idea of good governance in its application to the question of transition strategy. In the final paragraphs of this chapter, we start by invoking the required capacity of a system to strategize, and from there bring back the insights on good governance which emerged slowly in previous chapters.

STRATEGY AND GOOD GOVERNANCE

Good governance, in its various manifestations, *has* to enable the production of long-term perspectives on the community, and strategies to move in that direction. However, good governance also *has* to keep the option open to limit, modify or contest strategy processes in the community. This could undermine the strategy, revamp it or revoke it, yet it would maintain the legitimacy of a subsequent strategy and the legitimacy and functionality of governance itself.

As stated earlier, good governance is not only a precondition for the emer- gence of viable strategies; it has to be preserved in the process of strategy formulation and implementation. Where it does not exist yet, it needs to be constructed, as a new context in which sustainability can be observed and appreciated. Most likely, a strategy for sustainability transition will imply a transformation of governance, as it is unlikely that the current configuration, underpinning an unsustainable social-ecological system, can trigger the transition towards a more sustainable state. Such a common situation retains the basic requirement of good governance during and after transition: the goal of sustainability cannot be separated from other social goals and goods, and quality of governance cannot be sacrificed.

Good governance, therefore, asserts itself as critical for any serious reflection on transition strategy. Yet, it cannot be reduced to a recipe or a set of fixed indicators. What we retained as criteria previously, i.e. delivering the goods, maintaining differentiation and stable self-transformation, is entirely compatible with the need for transition strategy, as current conditions unquestionably demand a transition and transition strategies can be devised that maintain differentiation. None of the criteria identified earlier can be sustainably met, anywhere, without drastic change. Our unsustainable economic and political systems reveal the need to add a fourth criterion, i.e. sustainability itself. One can see this is a basic version of the demand to satisfy public needs, and provide public goods, yet morally it makes sense to present the need for survival as a feature of good governance. While the previous chapters strongly indicated that sustainability transitions require strategy, such strategy cannot squander whatever degree of good governance might already exist.

A vision for a sustainable future can stem from a largely participatory process, as a creative reconciliation of many long-term perspectives. Even so, a coupling with the system of administration, and of representative democracy, can link this more easily to policy tools that are likely to work in the existing governance system, turning the vision into a strategy (Gruezmacher & Van Assche, 2022). Expertise in and memory of governance itself serve to use existing governance capacity in the production and implementation of the strategy, and in the use of the strategy for enhancing that capacity. If strategies are dominated by one expert group, a limited coalition of actors, checks and balances comes into play. If it looks like the strategy is the product of corruption or a tool to ease corruption, then it must be revoked, and transparency has to be increased in the next iteration. If a strategy is imposed by a higher-level actor or arena, and legitimate arenas for participation, locally and nationally, were sidelined, this undermines the legitimate patterns of differentiation and self-transformation.

It is imaginable, and entirely possible, that the process of strategizing for and reflecting on sustainable community futures causes a collective rethinking of quality of life, of community identity, and hence of good governance. If common goods are redefined in the harsh light of a possible social-ecological collapse, if rivalries and factionalism are reconsidered, what appears as good governance, supporting a redefined community and a reinterpreted quality of life, can entail a productive shift in the relation between participation and representation, between politics and administration, between levels of governance, between topics and arenas, yet nothing of this can be predicted. The pressures of naked survival can just as well expose the brittle character of the configuration, internal fissures in the community, and a deeply anchored unwillingness to learn and adapt. Which tendency will dominate hinges on all the factors identified in earlier chapters. In terms of this chapter, we can say that an ongoing care for the quality and capacity of governance and a cultivation of memory, reflexivity, learning and diversity will be worthwhile as they create conditions for the emergence of realistic images of the social-ecological system, of societal problems, of governance itself and, from there, the creation of adequate transition strategies.

REFERENCES

Acemoglu, D. (2005). Politics and economics in weak and strong states. *Journal of Monetary Economics*, *52*(7), 1199–1226. https://doi.org/10.1016/j.jmoneco.2005.05.001

Addink, H. (2019). *Good governance: Concept and context*. Oxford University Press.

Alexander, G. (2002). Institutionalized uncertainty, the rule of law, and the sources of democratic stability. *Comparative Political Studies*, *35*(10), 1145–1170. https://doi.org/10.1177/001041402237946

Anand, N. (2017). *Hydraulic city: Water and the infrastructures of citizenship in Mumbai*. Duke University Press. https://doi.org/10.1215/9780822373599

Arnstein, S. R. (1969). A ladder of citizen participation. *Journal of the American Institute of Planners*, *35*(4), 216–224.

Barrett, S. (2013). The necessity of a multiscalar analysis of climate justice. *Progress in Human Geography*, *37*(2), 215–233. https://doi.org/10.1177/0309132512448270

Bell, S. & Hindmoor, A. (2009). *Rethinking governance: The centrality of the state in modern society*. Cambridge University Press.

Beunen, R. & Patterson, J. (2016). Analysing institutional change in environmental governance: Exploring the concept of 'institutional work'. *Journal of Environmental Planning and Management*, *62*(1), 12–29.

Bevir, M. (2010). *Democratic governance*. Princeton University Press.

Bingham, T. (2011). *The rule of law*. Penguin UK.

Birch, A. H. (1993). *Concepts and theories of modern democracy*. Routledge. https://doi.org/10.4324/9780203187647

Brouwer, S. & Huitema, D. (2017). Policy entrepreneurs and strategies for change. *Regional Environmental Change*, *18*, 1259–1272. https://doi.org/doi:10.1007/s10113-017-1139-z

Capano, G. & Howlett, M. (2020). The knowns and unknowns of policy instrument analysis: Policy tools and the current research agenda on policy mixes. *SAGE Open*, *10*(1), 2158244019900568. https://doi.org/10.1177/2158244019900568

Carnoy, M. (2014). *The state and political theory*. Princeton University Press.

Coetzee, T. (2018). The contribution of governance towards political science. *Journal of Public Administration*, *53*(1), 24–38. https://doi.org/10.10520/EJC-114f820908

Coleman, J. (2000). *A history of political thought* (vol. 1). Blackwell Oxford.

Collins, K. (2006). *Clan politics and regime transition in Central Asia.* Cambridge: University Press.

Creutzig, F., Acemoglu, D., Bai, X., Edwards, P. N., Hintz, M. J., Kaack, L. H., Kilkis, S., Kunkel, S., Luers, A., Milojevic-Dupont, N., Rejeski, D., Renn, J., Rolnick, D., Rosol, C., Russ, D., Turnbull, T., Verdolini, E., Wagner, F., Wilson, C., ... Zumwald, M. (2022). Digitalization and the Anthropocene. *Annual Review of Environment and Resources, 47*(1), 479–509. https://doi.org/10.1146/annurev-environ-120920-100056

Dell'Angelo, J., D'Odorico, P., Rulli, M. C. & Marchand, P. (2016). The tragedy of the grabbed commons: Coercion and dispossession in the global land rush. *World Development, 92*, 1–12.

Doornbos, M. (2001). 'Good governance': The rise and decline of a policy metaphor? In *Changing the Conditions for Development Aid.* Routledge.

Ewalt, J. A. G. & Jennings Jr., E. T. (2004). Administration, governance, and policy tools in welfare policy implementation. *Public Administration Review, 64*(4), 449–462. https://doi.org/10.1111/j.1540-6210.2004.00391.x

Fischer, F. (1990). *Technocracy and the politics of expertise.* Sage Publications.

Fischer, F. (2009). *Democracy and expertise: Reorienting policy inquiry.* Oxford University Press.

Fischhoff, B. (1990). Psychology and public policy: Tool or toolmaker? *American Psychologist, 45*(5), 647–653. https://doi.org/10.1037/h0091626

Flyvbjerg, B. (1998a). Habermas and Foucault: Thinkers for civil society. *British Journal of Sociology, 49*(2), 210–233.

Flyvbjerg, B. (1998b). *Rationality and power: Democracy in practice.* University of Chicago Press.

Foucault, M. (1970). *The order of things.* Pantheon Books.

Foucault, M. (2003). *Society must be defended: Lectures at the Collège de France, 1975–76.* Allen Lane/The Penguin Press.

Franz, T. (2019). Why 'good governance' fails: Lessons from regional economic development in Colombia. *International Journal of Urban and Regional Research, 43*(4), 776–785. https://doi.org/10.1111/1468-2427.12742

Goodin, R. (2008). *Innovating democracy: Democratic theory and practice after the deliberative turn.* Oxford University Press.

Gregg, B. (1999). Using legal rules in an indeterminate world, overcoming the limitations of jurisprudence. *Political Theory, 27*(3), 357–378.

Griffiths, J. (2003). The social working of legal rules. *Journal of Legal Pluralism, 48*(1), 1–84.

Gruezmacher, M. & Van Assche, K. (2022). *Crafting strategies for sustainable local development.* InPlanning.

Güney, T. (2017). Governance and sustainable development: How effective is governance? *The Journal of International Trade & Economic Development, 26*(3), 316–335. https://doi.org/10.1080/09638199.2016.1249391

Gupta, A. (2012). *Red tape: Bureaucracy, structural violence, and poverty in India.* Duke University Press.

Harris, D. C. (2001). *Fish, law, and colonialism: The legal capture of salmon in British Columbia.* University of Toronto Press.

Held, D. (1996). *Models of democracy* (2nd edn.). Polity.

Howlett, M. (2019). Procedural policy tools and the temporal dimensions of policy design. *International Review of Public Policy, 1*(1), article 1. https://doi.org/10.4000/irpp.310

Howlett, M. & Rayner, J. (2007). Design principles for policy mixes: Cohesion and coherence in 'new governance arrangements'. *Policy and Society, 26*(4), 1–18. https://doi.org/10.1016/S1449-4035(07)70118-2

Hull, M. S. (2012). Documents and bureaucracy. *Annual Review of Anthropology, 41*(1), 251–267. https://doi.org/10.1146/annurev.anthro.012809.104453

Jacobs, J. (1961). *Death and life of great American cities.* Penguin.

Johnson, D. S. (2006). Category, narrative, and value in the governance of small-scale fisheries. *Marine Policy, 30*(6), 747–756.

Johnston, M. (2006). Good governance: Rule of law, transparency, and accountability. *New York: United Nations Public Administration Network,* 1–32.

King, M. & Thornhill, E. (2003). *Niklas Luhmann's theory of politics and law.* Palgrave Macmillan.

Kuiper, J. (2000). A checklist approach to evaluate the contribution of organic farms to landscape quality. *Agriculture, Ecosystems & Environment, 77*(1–2), 143–156.

Latour, B. (2004). *Politics of nature. How to bring the sciences into democracy.* Harvard University Press.

Luhmann, N. (1990). *Political theory in the welfare state.* Mouton de Gruyter.

Luhmann, N. (1995). *Social systems.* Stanford University Press.

Luhmann, N. (2004). *Law as a social system.* Oxford University Press.

Lushaba, L. (2009). *Development as modernity, modernity as development.* African Books Collective.

Mansfield, H. C. (1996). *Machiavelli's virtue.* University of Chicago Press.

Mazzarella, W. (2019). The anthropology of populism: Beyond the liberal settlement. *Annual Review of Anthropology, 48*(1), 45–60. https://doi.org/10.1146/annurev-anthro-102218-011412

Mintrom, M. & Norman, P. (2009). Policy entrepreneurship and policy change. *Policy Studies Journal, 37*(4), 649–667. https://doi.org/10.1111/j.1541-0072.2009.00329.x

Mosse, D. (2001). 'People's knowledge', participation and patronage: Operations and representations in rural development. In B. Cooke & U. Kothari (eds.), *Participation: The new tyranny?* Zed Books.

Mosse, D. (2005). *Cultivating development: An ethnography of aid policy and practice.* Pluto Press.

Mungiu-Pippidi, A. (2020). The rise and fall of good-governance promotion. *Journal of Democracy, 31*(1), 88–102. https://doi.org/10.1353/jod.2020.0007

Nanda, V. P. (2006). The 'good governance' concept revisited. *The ANNALS of the American Academy of Political and Social Science, 603*(1), 269–283. https://doi.org/10.1177/0002716205282847

Norris, P. (2011). *Democratic deficit: Critical citizens revisited.* Cambridge University Press.

Omri, A. & Ben Mabrouk, N. (2020). Good governance for sustainable development goals: Getting ahead of the pack or falling behind? *Environmental Impact Assessment Review, 83,* 106388. https://doi.org/10.1016/j.eiar.2020.106388

Pasquino, P. (2009). Machiavelli and Aristotle: The anatomies of the city. *History of European Ideas, 35*(4), 397–407. https://doi.org/10.1016/j.histeuroideas.2009.05.002

Pierre, J. & Peters, B. G. (2000). *Governance, politics, and the state.* Macmillan.

Pusca, A. (2009). *Revolutions, democratic transition and disillusionment. The case of Romania.* Manchester University Press.

Pusca, A. (2018). *Revolution, democratic transition and disillusionment: The case of Romania.* Manchester University Press. https://doi.org/10.7765/9781526135292

Reed, M. (2008). Stakeholder participation for environmental management: A literature review. *Biological Conservation, 141*(10), 2417–2431. https://doi.org/10.1016/j.biocon.2008.07.014

Rhodes, R. A. W. (1997). *Understanding governance. Policy networks, governance, reflexivity and accountability*. Open University Press.

Rose-Ackerman, S. & Palifka, B. J. (2016). *Corruption and government: Causes, consequences, and reform*. Cambridge University Press.

Rulli, M. C., Saviori, A. & D'Odorico, P. (2013). Global land and water grabbing. *Proceedings of the National Academy of Sciences, 110*(3), 892–897. https://doi.org/10.1073/pnas.1213163110

Scott, J. C. (1998). *Seeing like a state: How certain schemes to improve the human condition have failed*. Yale University Press.

Sørensen, E. & Torfing, J. (2016). *Theories of democratic network governance*. Springer.

Stein, R. (2009). Rule of law: What does it mean? *Minnesota Journal of International Law, 18*, 293.

Stoker, G. (1998). Governance as theory: Five propositions. *International Social Science Journal, 50*(155), 17–28.

Tamanaha, B. Z. (2004). *On the rule of law: History, politics, theory*. Cambridge University Press.

Teitel, R. G. (2000). *Transitional justice*. Oxford University Press.

Teubner, G. (1988). *Autopoietic law: A new approach to law and society*. Walter de Gruyter.

Turnhout, E., Bommel, S. & Aarts, N. (2010). How participation creates citizens: Participatory governance as performative practice. *Ecology and Society, 15*(4), 26.

Urbinati, N. & Warren, M. E. (2008). The concept of representation in contemporary democratic theory. *Annual Review of Political Science, 11*(1), 387–412. https://doi.org/10.1146/annurev.polisci.11.053006.190533

Valentinov, V., Verschraegen, G. & Van Assche, K. (2019). The limits of transparency: A systems theory view. *Systems Research and Behavioral Science, 36*(3), 289–300. https://doi.org/10.1002/sres.2591

Van Assche, K. & Hornidge, A.-K. (2015). *Rural development: Knowledge and expertise in governance*. Wageningen Press.

Van Assche, K., Beunen, R. & Duineveld, M. (2014a). *Evolutionary governance theory: An introduction*. Springer.

Van Assche, K., Beunen, R. & Duineveld, M. (2014b). Formal/informal dialectics and the self-transformation of spatial planning systems: An exploration. *Administration & Society, 46*(6), 654–683. https://doi.org/10.1177/0095399712469194

Van Assche, K., Gruezmacher, M., Summers, B., Culling, J., Gajjar, S., Granzow, M., Lowerre, A., Deacon, L., Candlish, J. & Jamwal, A. (2022). Land use policy and community strategy. Factors enabling and hampering integrated local strategy in Alberta, Canada. *Land Use Policy, 118*, 106101. https://doi.org/10.1016/j.landusepol.2022.106101

Van Doeveren, V. (2011). Rethinking good governance. *Public Integrity, 13*(4), 301–318. https://doi.org/10.2753/PIN1099-9922130401

Vermeule, A. (2019). The Publius Paradox. *The Modern Law Review, 82*(1), 1–16. https://doi.org/10.1111/1468-2230.12386

Wayne Taylor, D. (2000). Facts, myths and monsters: Understanding the principles of good governance. *International Journal of Public Sector Management, 13*(2), 108–124. https://doi.org/10.1108/09513550010338755

Wedel, J. R. (2003). Clans, cliques and captured states: Rethinking 'transition' in Central and Eastern Europe and the former Soviet Union. *Journal of International Development, 15*(4), 427–440. https://doi.org/10.1002/jid.994

Young, I. M. (2000). *Inclusion and democracy*. Oxford University Press.

Zumbansen, P. (2013). Transnational private regulatory governance: Ambiguities of public authority and private power. *Law and Contemporary Problems, 76*, 117.

14. Conclusion: strategy in governance for transition

PERFECTION AND STABILITY

Niccolò Machiavelli pointed out that no society is perfect, eternal and entirely stable. Perfect laws are perfectly adaptable laws, but perfect adaptation is impossible since laws can only function if their adaptation is slowed down. Perfect adaptation undermines adaptive capacity (Mansfield, 1979; 1996). We know, after navigating the chapters of this book, that governance is full of such paradoxes. Stability is necessary, but instability is endemic and productive as well. Strong leadership requires speed and strategic insight, the power to break some rules and evade checks and balances, but in the long run all this proves problematic (Alvesson & Kärreman, 2016; Van Assche et al., 2016). Given these insights, it is amazing that many theories of policy, politics, administration, environmental change, or planning either embrace an idea of perfectibility and steering or an idea that what remains is only damage control.

This book, inspired by evolutionary governance theory (EGT), critical management studies, strategy as practice thinking, and a series of thinkers mentioned throughout, aimed to find a middle ground between the opposing perspectives of social (and environmental) engineering and neo-liberalism. It shows how governance works, how attempts for coordination and steering work, how strategy works, and how transitions work, while acknowledging the uncertainties and contingencies that in the end mark the evolution of governance paths. For us, transition in and through governance is possible, despite the map of limitations and instabilities outlined in this book. Steering as path creation is a reality, but a reality which can only become such via productive fictions. Steering for transitions requires one to understand society and its form of governance to be able to distinguish between possible paths and dead-end streets, to recognize and anticipate opportunities and threats, and to prepare for resistance and backslash.

In this book we have explored the various mechanisms and processes that shape governance systems and governance paths and the way in which seemingly similar interventions might create contrasting outcomes at different places and times. Governance paths are contingent upon many different

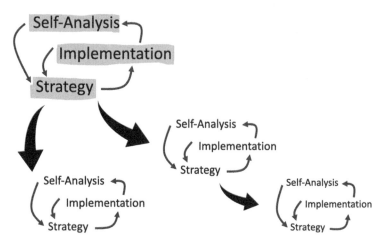

Figure 14.1   Adaptive strategy in governance[1]

processes, many of which are beyond control and some of which are out of sight, and any decision sooner or later comes with trade-offs as there is no perfect or eternal fit. We have also shown how awareness about the various paradoxes that mark governance systems and their role in steering, strategy and transition can help in strategizing for and in transition. Co-evolution in governance accounts not only for steering limits, but also for steering options. The dependencies we distinguished can imply obstacles for steering and strategy, yet at the same time they also represent assets and leverage points, as well as proven strengths and identity orientations that can prove valuable. The elusive character of power/knowledge (P/K) configurations makes it difficult to predict interpretations of the world, of self, governance and environment which could appear and overturn everything supporting the strategy. Yet these interpretations can also mobilize new and unexpected forms of support. The nature of P/K configurations also allows for the functioning of productive fictions, and for managing of goal dependencies and reality effects.

Much hinges on the quality of reflexivity and of learning more generally, and of the diversity of perspectives present in the governance system. Strategy for transition is subjected to all ambiguities, tensions, instabilities and inter-

---

[1]   Adaptive strategy is quite different from having no strategy. Adaptive transition strategies can help to navigate the waters of transition, the inherent dilemmas, in an iterative process. The process is driven by a continuing, and ideally institutionalized, process of self-analysis that makes it possible to respond to implementation challenges and new opportunities in a way that links to the self-understanding of the community.

nal contradictions mentioned and explored in the previous chapters. It must balance the felt and real need for focus, speed and policy integration with the need to cultivate diverse observations, reflexivity, redundancy and adaptive capacity. Contingency, evolution and paradox mark governance, with the major implication that any design of a governance configuration, and any strategy for change, comes with imperfections and trade-offs. Those trade-offs are not entirely stable, visible, predictable from the position of the strategist, in the system of governance and in time. In order to make path creation more likely, to improve the possibility of success, understanding governance, its continuous self-transformation driven by competing and impossible goals, its selective observation and creation of reality, ought to be at the center of transition strategy.

Actors and institutions, power and knowledge going into a transition, are likely to be transformed in the process (Pel, 2021; Turnheim & Geels, 2012). Transitions can start from the margins, from niches, and they can start from the center, but if the transition works, the chances are slim that key players and institutions remain unchanged, that the forms of knowledge at work in governance are not transformed. The resistance and backlash to and reinterpretations of the transition strategy and its proponents that can be expected in democratic societies, as well as the processes of object and subject formation inside and outside governance which will be triggered by ambitious transitions, make this very likely (Rupnik, 2007; Vaughn, 1997). Redundancy, second-order observation, variation in perspectives and reflexivity are helpful, as always, and, recalling and sharpening our discussions of re-politization, we argue that cultivation of reflexivity and observational capacity of governance and environment *disconnected from the strategy* is commendable. This might at first seem contradictory to other passages in this book, calling for more intense participation in transitional governance for transition, for re-politization more generally. However, and again echoing Machiavelli, we can understand such detached expertise, looking at strategy, its goal dependencies and reality effects without a stake in the strategy, as a new element of checks and balances which is in order. Strong citizens in a strong state; and if state and citizens collaborate towards a shared transition this does not void the need for checks and balances but demands some inventiveness towards additional checks.

Any strategy, and certainly an ambitious transition strategy, becomes part of a complex interplay between the elements of governance and between governance, community and environment. The intervention of strategy formation and the series of interventions coming with implementation land in a context which is never entirely understood by the strategist, while every intervention changes the context for the next step. What appears as transition, what is imagined as susceptible to strategy, what is labeled as strategy and as transition, comes out of the same evolving context, making it impossible to

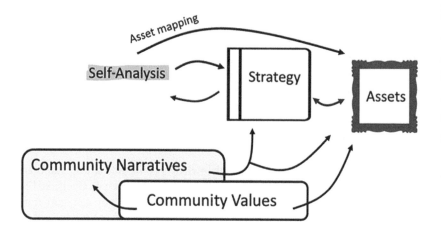

*Figure 14.2   Self-analysis and the coordination of community values,
                 narratives, assets and strategy²*

clearly distinguish between intentional or deliberate ones and unintentional
or unexpected ones. Which transformations are likely to emerge and to what
extent these can be attributed to strategy is impossible to say in advance, and is
a matter of observation in hindsight. This makes approaches that say otherwise
not only incorrect but highly problematic, as these misinform all involved,
and can become the reason for the failure of transitions already under way, for
erosion of trust in expertise, in governance, in strategy, hence for failure in the
next steering attempt. Those opposing change are often more realistic in their
assessment of affect, narrative, power relations and policy tools, and are better
strategists. What is needed, in the formulation of transition perspectives and in
concrete transition paths, is better analysis. Continuous analysis of changing
environments, and of governance itself, is of the essence, and such analysis
must include the ever-shifting relations between discursivity and institutions,
between tools of governance and the reality effects and goal dependencies they
trigger.

---

²   What is seen as valuable for a sustainable community future, as an asset, can
inspire strategy but can also be built through strategy. It never exists independently
from the values, identities, memories and other narratives marking the community.
Careful asset mapping therefore cannot exist without careful self-analysis.

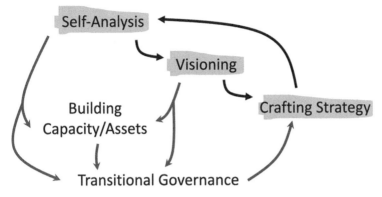

Figure 14.3   Crafting strategy for sustainable transitions[3]

CONNECTING DOTS

Strategy for transition needs a narrative and that narrative needs to be convincing on several grounds. If unpopular strategies are pushed through for the greater good, this greater good had better be accepted before the backlash hits. If the narrative turns pale and becomes unconvincing, coordination through the strategy will be hampered, as incentives evaporate, as trust and legitimacy dwindle, and as internal resistance increases. To avoid the rhetorical and then practical capture of transition discourse and strategy by sitting actors, their expertise, and their vested interests, values, narratives and ideologies, it can be useful to designate a new arena (see Chapter 10, on strategy) to advise or even govern the transition. Old and new actors can guard not only coordination, but also critical discussion of goals and process of transition. The distance between the new arena and the old ones can vary, and, as usual, no silver bullet can be provided. A neutral point of observation and intervention, for the redesign of arenas, does not exist, as everything in the community, every aspect of governance, will be subjected to the powers and the rules of governance. Furthermore, in social systems speaking of something, promoting the idea, is doing something, is changing the chances of implementation and creating a matrix for support and resistance.

---

[3]   Building a transition strategy is not always possible in a direct manner. In many communities, detours might be necessary, and these can include managing conflict, restoring or building assets, and building observational and institutional capacity. In some cases, it might be necessary to reform governance first towards a transitional form of governance, which is not the one implementing transition strategy, but a phase where capacity is being built so that strategy formation becomes possible.

Whether a new governance domain must be established, under the name of transition, depends on the pattern of differentiation. Is there a legitimate power to establish a new domain? Who is willing and able to articulate and impose a first-ordering principle? How does the transition narrative relate to other narratives in the community? Is there even support for the idea of transition and is this idea understood in a way that accommodates difference without collapsing? It is of the utmost importance, we believe, to guard against teleological and other normative assumptions of universality, superiority and eternity. Nature does not dictate a transition goal, nor does it reveal a logical path. Transitions can fail, several transitions can occur at the same time, and each transition will follow a unique path, navigating the transition dilemmas in its own way. The diversity of interpretive processes at play in a transition is staggering and the Peircean infinite semiosis, or relentless production of meaning, cannot be stopped because of a transition goal, however urgent and important this may seem. Imposing false certainties and moral superiorities on a community that might want to define and organize itself differently, is looking for trouble.

This brings us to identity. Identity for us has a double meaning. First as a narrative identity and second as the unicity and unity of an autopoietic process (Luhmann, 2008; Seidl, 2016). Narrative identities, of actors, communities, arenas, places, or governance itself, transform in governance as they transform governance. Ideological divisions and competing identity narratives might make strategy for transition seem impossible. Or new divisions might appear later, possibly engendered by the pain or shifting inclusions and exclusions caused by the transition process itself. Also, supportive factions, and new identity narratives giving transition a central place, can appear. We know that strategies can create their own support, through feedback loops stemming from reality effects. Alternatively, the need for transition and collective strategy can *suddenly* be perceived, when latent thresholds are crossed, when problems first ignored creep into the daily lives of more and more people. Discursive configurations which seemed to uphold old truths can suddenly crumble, affects of safety, pride and belonging can shift to their opposite in the blink of an eye.

Transitions often become the subject of identity politics which then polarizes communities, creates conflict within and outside governance, and makes coordination much more complicated. Changes, let alone transformative ones, become even less likely. Polarization does not benefit those interested in transition. It can benefit those attached to the status quo and the distribution of power, resources, the hierarchy of values it represents. And it can be attractive for those who see opportunities in instability, in polarization itself, or, for the more ambitious types, in a new order which might become possible through the process of change set in motion, or through an (engineered) backlash. All this makes strategy for transition a risky balancing act, walking on a razor's edge.

GOVERNABILITY

In this book we stretched up the strategy concept and modified it to fit the context of governance, based not on theoretical requirements, but on observation of strategy and governance, and on a very practical need to face Grand Challenges. If we accept that strategies come with goal dependencies in governance and reality effects outside governance, and that these goal dependencies and effects can diverge much from implementation, continuous self-observation in governance becomes as important as regular assessment of the effects of the transition strategy in the community (Van Assche et al., 2020, 2021). Both unexpected reality effects and unanticipated goal dependencies can be useful, however, and they can have a value in finding new paths in an old direction, or in modifying the strategy. Such occurrences can reveal more dependencies and their interplay and can provide insights useful for future tactics.

A general rule for optimizing the reality effects of strategy in the direction intended by transition proponents, and for aligning goal dependencies to this end, does not exist. Optimizing reality effects is a matter of collective wisdom, robust collective debate, and artful leadership by individuals and organizations. One can invoke Aristotelean *phronesis*, or Kantian practical judgment, but judgment it is. Good decisions never flow logically out of an abundance of information and clear reasoning, even in the presence of impeccable self-awareness. Neither do good decisions follow naturally out of identities and their values. Tension, contradiction, opacity and irresolvable uncertainty are always there (Antrop, 2006; Hillier, 2002; Pellizzoni, 2003). This might sound dramatic if we are hoping for a future artificial intelligence breakthrough, or an integrative decision support system, a perfect governance model, or any other prescriptive tool to save us from ourselves. It probably sounds different if we understand these limitations as enablers of freedom, creativity and adaptation and if we recognize that humans can judge and decide. The uncertainties faced by transition strategy do not only stem from the nature of deciding and organizing, and the co-evolutionary character of governance, but as we know by now, because transition strategy is per definition stretching the limits of governability.

Nothing in governance is ever stable, and everything is the product of co-evolution. This is not a problem for governance, as it has always operated in such an environment. It only becomes a problem when steering fictions dominate and big promises of certainty and change are taken too seriously. Many identities are less stable in governance than outside of it, because of the pressures exerted by collective decision-making, and the virtual allure of power. Objects and subjects, narratives of self, world, of past, present and future are under such pressure. Forms of knowledge and institutions can codify realities, and cán attempt to stop evolution, so governance can slow down change, yet, in governance, realities do not last long.

REFERENCES

Alvesson, M. & Kärreman, D. (2016). Intellectual failure and ideological success in organization studies: The case of transformational leadership. *Journal of Management Inquiry*, *25*(2), 139–152.

Antrop, M. (2006). Sustainable landscapes: Contradiction, fiction or utopia? *Landscape and Urban Planning*, *75*(3–4), 187–197.

Hillier, J. (2002). *Shadows of power: An allegory of prudence in land-use planning*. Routledge.

Luhmann, N. (2008). The autopoiesis of social systems. *Journal of Sociocybernetics*, *6*(2), 84–95.

Mansfield, H. (1979). *Machiavelli's new modes and orders*. Cornell University Press.

Mansfield, H. C. (1996). *Machiavelli's virtue*. University of Chicago Press.

Pel, B. (2021). Transition 'backlash': Towards explanation, governance and critical understanding. *Environmental Innovation and Societal Transitions*, *41*, 32–34. https://doi.org/10.1016/j.eist.2021.10.016

Pellizzoni, L. (2003). Knowledge, uncertainty and the transformation of the public sphere. *European Journal of Social Theory*, *6*(3), 327–355.

Rupnik, J. (2007). From democracy fatigue to populist backlash: Is East-Central Europe backsliding? *Journal of Democracy*, *18*(4), 17–25.

Seidl, D. (2016). *Organizational identity and self-transformation. An autopoietic perspective*. Routledge.

Turnheim, B. & Geels, F. W. (2012). Regime destabilisation as the flipside of energy transitions: Lessons from the history of the British coal industry (1913–1997). *Energy Policy*, *50*, 35–49. https://doi.org/10.1016/j.enpol.2012.04.060

Van Assche, K., Beunen, R. & Duineveld, M. (2016). Citizens, leaders and the common good in a world of necessity and scarcity: Machiavelli's lessons for community-based natural resource management. *Ethics, Policy & Environment*, *19*(1), 19–36.

Van Assche, K., Beunen, R., Gruezmacher, M. & Duineveld, M. (2020). Rethinking strategy in environmental governance. *Journal of Environmental Policy & Planning*, *22*(5), 695–708.

Van Assche, K., Verschraegen, G. & Gruezmacher, M. (2021). Strategy for collectives and common goods. Coordinating strategy, long term perspectives and policy domains in governance. *Futures*, *128*(5).

Vaughn, J. (1997). *Green backlash: The history and politics of the environmental opposition in the U.S.* Lynne Rienner Publishers.

Index

actor/institution (A/I) configurations 61–4, 72, 115–18, 124–5, 138
actors 6, 28–37, 99
   as arenas 55
   organizations as 139
adaptation 48, 152–3, 175, 212–15, 217
adaptive capacity 175, 212–13, 229, 233
adaptive governance 21, 213
adaptive strategy 101, 214–15, 217, 294
administration
   logic of 242
   politics relations 269–70
   relegation in 243
   role of 269–70
affect 94, 189–90, 192, 259
Alvesson, Mats 9, 97, 166, 168–9
arenas 30, 53–61, 127, 156, 173, 275, 297
Aristotle 34, 166, 279, 299
assets 235–8, 296
autopoiesis 63

backlash 12, 50, 253–66
Badiou, Alain 210
balance in governance/transition 152–84
belief/non-belief 256–9
big promises 1–16

Carson, Rachel, *Silent Spring* 133
centralization 234
certainty 100–101
change 74–5, 152–84
   fast response/slow response 233
   learning and 165–71, 174, 176
   performance of 161
   transition as 223
checks and balances 279–81
choices 102
civic republicanism 284
civil society models 282–3
clientelism 278

co-evolution 6, 44, 58, 61, 71
cognitive path dependencies 124–5, 127–9
communitarianism 283
community 19, 23, 87–107, 203–4, 210
   changing course 74–5
   environment relations 25
   futures reimagined/reconstructed 200–222
   power relations 23
community strategy 203–4
community trauma 194
community values 296
comparative learning 167–8, 169, 236
complex institutions 99–100, 118–19, 134–6, 204–5
complexity 30–31, 43, 45–6, 57, 96, 99–101
comprehensive governance 22
concepts in governance 17, 87–107
conflict 163–5, 172, 173, 258, 259, 260–61
   see also shocks
contingency 24–5, 46, 71, 101, 117, 138, 173, 271
corruption 254, 276, 277–9
counterstrategy 12, 109, 212, 253–66
cycles 75–7, 170–71
Czarniawska, Barbara 9, 162

dark learning 166–7, 258
De Saussure, F. 118
de-differentiation 233
de-politization 243, 257
dead institutions 50–52
decentralization 234
decision/institution distinction 43, 81
decision/policy/institutions disconnect 81
decision/site/arena coupling 53–5
deep forgetting 187–8
democracy 20, 43–4, 73, 98, 281–6